JUDICIAL REVIEW IN AN AGE OF MORAL PLURALISM

Americans cannot live with judicial review, but they cannot live without it. There used to be something characteristically American about turning the most divisive political questions – like freedom of religion, same-sex marriage, affirmative action, and abortion – into legal questions with the hope that courts can answer them. In *Judicial Review in an Age of Moral Pluralism*, Ronald C. Den Otter addresses how judicial review can be improved to strike the appropriate balance between legislative and judicial power under conditions of moral pluralism. His defense of judicial review is predicated on the imperative of ensuring that the reasons that the state offers on behalf of its most important laws are consistent with the freedom and equality of all persons. Den Otter ties this defense to a theory of constitutional adjudication based on John Rawls's idea of public reason and argues that a law that is not sufficiently publicly justified is unconstitutional. He thus addresses when courts should invalidate laws and when they should uphold them, even in the midst of reasonable disagreement about the correct outcome in the most challenging constitutional cases.

Ronald C. Den Otter is Assistant Professor of Political Science at California Polytechnic State University, San Luis Obispo. He received his J.D. from the University of Pennsylvania Law School and his Ph.D. in political science from UCLA. Professor Den Otter has also taught undergraduate courses in public law and political theory at California State University, Los Angeles; UCLA; and Pepperdine University.

Judicial Review in an Age of Moral Pluralism

Ronald C. Den Otter

California Polytechnic State University, San Luis Obispo

CAMBRIDGE
UNIVERSITY PRESS

CAMBRIDGE UNIVERSITY PRESS
Cambridge, New York, Melbourne, Madrid, Cape Town,
Singapore, São Paulo, Delhi, Tokyo, Mexico City

Cambridge University Press
The Edinburgh Building, Cambridge CB2 8RU, UK

Published in the United States of America by Cambridge University Press, New York

www.cambridge.org
Information on this title: www.cambridge.org/9781107404540

First published 2009
First paperback edition 2011

A catalogue record for this publication is available from the British Library

Library of Congress Cataloguing in Publication Data

Den Otter, Ronald C.
Judicial review in an age of moral pluralism / Ronald C. Den Otter.
   p.   cm.
Includes bibliographical references and index.
ISBN 978-0-521-76204-5 (hardback)
1. Political questions and judicial power – United States.   2. Cultural pluralism – United
States.   3. Public policy (Law) – United States.   I. Title.
KF5130.D46   2009
347.73′12 – dc22   2009011186

ISBN 978-0-521-76204-5 Hardback
ISBN 978-1-107-40454-0 Paperback

*This book is dedicated to my wife, Grace.
I could not have found a better person to spend the rest of
my life with.*

There is hardly a political question in the United States which does not sooner or later turn into a judicial one.
– Alexis de Tocqueville, *Democracy in America*

Contents

Acknowledgments	*page*	ix
Introduction		1
1 Public Justification and Constitutional Theory		22
2 Freedom and Equality in Constitutional History		52
3 The Challenge of Public Justification		81
4 Competing Conceptions of Public Reason		109
5 Constitutional Public Reason		139
6 The Limits of Public Justification		172
7 Standard Objections to Public Reason		200
8 Easier Cases		231
9 Harder Cases		262
10 The Case for Judicial Review		291
Conclusion		316
References		319
Index		337

Acknowledgments

This book began as a dissertation project when I was a graduate student at UCLA and has gone through numerous iterations since then. I would like to thank Barbara Herman, Brian Walker, Victor Wolfenstein, Mark Sawyer, Andrew Lister, Dan O'Neill, Michael Goodhart, Adam Winkler, and David Karol. In particular, I would like to express my gratitude to Andy Sabl, who was a wonderful mentor and could not have been more generous with his time when I was his graduate student.

At Cal Poly, Chris Den Hartog, Jean Williams, Alesha Doan, Craig Arceneaux, Anika Leithner, Beth Lowham, Mike Latner, Suzy Black, and Samantha Keller-Thomas have assisted me in various ways with this project. I have been blessed with wonderful colleagues. In particular, I would like to single out Matt Moore and thank him for all of the contributions that he has made to this book and all of the help that he has given me since we have been colleagues at Cal Poly.

Paul Frymer, Ann Davies, Scott Bowman, Mark Swofford, and Sam Ernst also helped me with different parts of this project. I would especially like to thank Pat Neal, Eileen Scallen, and Larry Solum, whose constructive criticism made this book much better than it otherwise would have been. I wish that I could repay the debt.

At Cambridge University Press, I would like to thank my editor, John Berger; my senior production controller, Paul Smolenski; my editorial assistant, Jason Przybylski; my senior project manager, Frank Scott; my copyeditor, Katherine Faydash; and Robert Swanson, who prepared the index. I also would like to thank the anonymous reviewers for their insightful comments on an earlier version of this manuscript.

One's personal life can never be entirely separated from one's professional life. With respect to the former, several people deserve special thanks: my brother, Doug Den Otter, and his wife, Debra Pettric. I could not have been given a better brother and a better sister-in-law. Above all, I would like to thank my wife, Grace. Without her, this book would not have been possible.

Over the course of my life, there are so many people to whom I owe the deepest gratitude for stimulating my intellectual development. I hope that I have not left out anyone who deserves to be mentioned, and if I have, then I apologize for the oversight.

A portion of the last chapter appears in the following article; "Democracy, Not Deference: An Egalitarian Theory of Judicial Review," 91 *Kentucky Law Journal* 615 (2002–2003).

Introduction

The purpose of this book is to explain how judicial review can be justified in a country like our own, which is committed to democratic self-rule but also to the freedom and equality of all of its members. A striking feature of the contemporary American political landscape is the prominence of the judiciary in making important constitutional choices that many other democratic countries leave to the people or to their elected representatives. There used to be something characteristically American about turning the most divisive political questions into legal questions with the hope that courts could answer them and thereby defuse political conflict. At the same time, the practice of judicial review has engendered understandable worries about the appropriate relationship between legislative and judicial power. Alexander Bickel once referred to judicial review as a "deviant institution" in a democracy.[1] A number of conservative critics of judicial activism have used what Bickel called the "counter-majoritarian difficulty" in trying to show that the judiciary is the most dangerous branch.[2] Robert Bork has written, "The progression of political judging, judging unrelated to law, . . . has greatly accelerated in the past few decades and now we see theorists of constitutional law urging judges on to still greater incursions into Americans' right of self-government."[3] According to Bork, America is "helpless before an antidemocratic, indeed a despotic, judiciary."[4] Lino Graglia has alleged

---

[1] Alexander Bickel, *The Least Dangerous Branch: The Supreme Court at the Bar of Politics*, 2nd ed. (New Haven, CT: Yale University Press, 1962), 18.

[2] See, e.g., Raoul Berger, *Government by Judiciary: The Transformation of the Fourteenth Amendment* (Cambridge, MA: Harvard University Press, 1977).

[3] Robert H. Bork, *The Tempting of America: The Political Seduction of the Law* (New York: Simon and Schuster, 1990), 351.

[4] Robert H. Bork, *Slouching towards Gomorrah: Modern Liberalism and American Decline* (New York: Regan Books, 1996), 119.

1

that "the Constitution has been made the means of depriving us of our most essential right, the right of self-government."[5]

These critiques do not only come from conservatives. Robert Dahl has maintained that alternatives to political decision making that take political power out of the hands of the people are unacceptably elitist.[6] Mark Tushnet and Larry Kramer have formulated theories of popular constitutionalism to undermine judicial supremacy.[7] Today, the ideological composition of the federal judiciary has led conservatives to be less concerned with the outcomes of important cases and thus less preoccupied with the purported abuse of judicial power than in the past. But surely, our worries about the legitimacy of judicial review should not ebb and flow with partisan change. What is at stake is nothing less than the best understanding of the constitutional limits on the coercive power of the state and the proper approach to judicial decision making to ensure that the state respects those limits. The U.S. Supreme Court usually has the final word on constitutional controversies, and the results that the Court reaches often divide Americans along partisan lines. In the June 2007 term, more than a third of the argued cases were decided by a single vote.[8]

In this book, I put forth a defense of judicial review that attempts to transcend partisanship by explaining how judges should decide the most difficult constitutional cases involving fundamental rights and equal protection.[9] I focus on the kinds of reasons that not only would render legislation constitutional, but also would legitimize judicial decisions.[10] That project may not matter to those who care only about results, but no principled defense of judicial review can succeed unless people can separate results from the reasons that judges use in their opinions as justification for those results. Even when people disagree on how a hard constitutional case ought to be decided, they still might recognize the adequacy of the reasons that support

[5] Lino A. Graglia, "Constitutional Law without the Constitution," in *A Country I Do Not Recognize: The Legal Assault on American Values*, ed. Robert H. Bork (Stanford, CA: Hoover Institution Press, 2005), 2.

[6] See Robert A. Dahl, *Democracy and Its Critics* (New Haven, CT: Yale University Press, 1989), 187–8.

[7] Mark Tushnet, *Taking the Constitution Away from the Courts* (Princeton, NJ: Princeton University Press, 1999); Larry D. Kramer, *The People Themselves: Popular Constitutionalism and Judicial Review* (New York: Oxford University Press, 2004).

[8] Anthony Lewis, "The Court: How 'So Few Have So Quickly Changed So Much,'" review of *The Nine: Inside the Secret World of the Supreme Court*, by Jeffrey Toobin, 54 *New York Review of Books*, December 20, 2007, 58.

[9] With respect to the former, I address only negative rights, that is, rights against state interference.

[10] Cf. Sonu Bedi, *Rejecting Rights: The Turn to Justification* (New York: Cambridge University Press, 2009). Bedi's provocative book argues for the conclusion that the acceptance of a principle of justification has a radical implication: the rejection of constitutional rights as the analytical framework for deciding constitutional cases that involve personal freedom and equal protection.

the result that they do not agree with.[11] One of the aims of this book is to convince readers that they must care more about the method than about the outcome.

I. CONSTITUTIONAL ADJUDICATION

At the outset, I posit that judges have to look outside the law for normative guidance.[12] They are not interpreting a novel or a poem but are expounding a constitution, and their interpretive errors, unlike those of literary critics, may have serious consequences. In hard cases, judges cannot simply discern constitutional meaning from the words of the text, from constitutional structure, from authorial intent, from the original linguistic context, from the case law, or from a combination of these factors.[13] On the contrary, judges must adjudicate; they do not simply gloss a text but assess the reasons that the state has offered on behalf of the law in question. At the point of application, they must bridge the gap between abstract constitutional clauses, such as due process and equal protection, and the particular facts of the case. In doing so, they also must offer their own reasons to support their decision to uphold or strike down the law whose constitutionality is being challenged.[14] It is difficult to imagine what else they could do when they have to decide, but the standard sources of law do not single out a clearly correct answer.[15] Nevertheless, conservative critics of judicial activism continue to accuse liberal judges of bridging those gaps illegitimately by basing their decisions on their own convictions of political morality.[16] Today, liberal critics also increasingly accuse conservative judges of inserting their own preferences into constitutional law.

[11] See Steven J. Burton, *Judging in Good Faith* (New York: Cambridge University Press, 1992), xii.

[12] See Laurence H. Tribe, *The Invisible Constitution* (New York: Oxford University Press, 2008), 7.

[13] See Stephen Macedo, *The New Right v. The Constitution* (Washington, D.C.: Cato Institute, 1987), 10.

[14] Ronald Dworkin insists that people can share an abstract concept, such as fairness, but disagree as to how that concept should be specified in particular instances. See Ronald Dworkin, *Law's Empire* (Cambridge, MA: Harvard University Press, Belknap Press, 1986), 70; Ronald Dworkin, *Justice in Robes* (Cambridge, MA: Harvard University Press, Belknap Press, 2006), 11–12. For his original account of the difference between a concept and a conception, see Ronald Dworkin, *Taking Rights Seriously* (Cambridge, MA: Harvard University Press, 1977), 134.

[15] See Dworkin, *Taking Rights Seriously*, 134.

[16] For example, Mark Levin alleges that activist judges "have abused their constitutional mandate by imposing their personal prejudices and beliefs on the rest of society." Mark R. Levin, *Men in Black: How the Supreme Court Is Destroying America* (New York: Regnery Publishing, 2005), 10.

Whatever one thinks about the truth of those accusations, it makes no sense to allege that judges have abused their power for failing to limit themselves to appropriate reasons unless there can be some rational manner of determining what kinds of reasons are appropriate in the first place.[17] In a constitutional democracy, a judicial decision cannot be legitimate if it is based on transparently nonlegal reasons. The commitment to rely upon the right kinds of reasons in the decision-making process is the essence of the judicial duty to uphold the law. No one in our legal culture thinks that a judge is authorized to rule against a litigant because she is Filipina or a woman. Similarly, a judge may not rely directly on "deep reasons," like those that are derived from their personal religious convictions, to strike down or uphold a particular law.[18] This widely shared principle can illuminate why some people were understandably disturbed when Justice Clarence Thomas once cast his opposition to affirmative action in Christian terms.[19] The trouble is not that Thomas has religious views or that those views shape his understanding of political morality when he assumes the role of citizen and votes in local, state, and national elections. Rather, the trouble lies in the fact that he might use those sorts of reasons as his primary reasons for striking down a particular affirmative action program, as if those reasons were appropriate in the context of constitutional adjudication.

A judge who upheld a law that banned sodomy on the ground that homosexuality is sinful or unnatural also would have relied on an inappropriate reason.[20] However, beyond this consensus, knowledgeable people disagree about exactly what kinds of reasons would qualify as legal reasons for purposes of constitutional adjudication. Not only do narrow and broad definitions of *legal* compete with one another, but also judges are divided over the force of such reasons in real cases. Some judges would promote economic efficiency or wealth maximization, others would further distributive justice, others would protect property rights, others would adhere to

---

[17] See Sotiros A. Barber and James E. Fleming, *Constitutional Interpretation: The Basic Questions* (New York: Oxford University Press, 2007), 19.

[18] As Lawrence Solum points out, if most judges were to rely on their deepest moral or religious beliefs, then moral and religious divisions in our society would "directly translate into legal divisions" and our courts would be divided along such lines. See Lawrence B. Solum, "Pluralism and Public Legal Reason," 15 *William and Mary Bill of Rights Journal* (2006), 12. One exception is Stephen Carter, who believes that "reliance by judges on religious convictions is as proper as reliance on their personal moral convictions of any other kind." Stephen L. Carter, "The Religiously Devout Judge," 64 *Notre Dame Law Review* (1989), 933.

[19] Armstrong Williams, "Two Wrongs Don't Make a Right for Thomas," *Charleston Post and Courier*, August 17, 1995, A-13.

[20] It is more common for the state to rely on such reasons. For instance, in *Bowers v. Hardwick*, the brief of the state "asserted that Georgia could reasonably believe that homosexuality ... 'epitomizes moral delinquency.'" See William N. Eskridge Jr., *Dishonorable Passions: Sodomy Laws in America 1861–2003* (New York: Viking Books, 2008), 240.

precedent or constitutional structure, others would look toward natural law, others would construct political compromises, others would defer to legislative majorities, others would foster civic virtues, and others would discover the original meaning of constitutional provisions.

Despite their differences, all of these diverse approaches to constitutional adjudication are predicated on the belief that judges who act in good faith must limit themselves to certain reasons in the decision-making process even when those reasons lead to a result that they dislike. A theory of constitutional adjudication must distinguish between relevant and irrelevant reasons, and it also must rank the relevant reasons according to their putative force. Otherwise, that theory would be incapable of providing the minimal guidance that a judge would need to decide a real case. On the assumption that most judges act in good faith most of the time, the real concern is not that runaway judges are inclined to abuse their power by legislating, but that they may be sincerely relying on the wrong kinds of reasons when they decide constitutional cases. Americans should care much less about the motives that lead to so-called judicial imperialism and much more about the reasons that underlie the most important constitutional decisions.[21] They should be troubled when a judge does not fulfill his or her judicial duty by upholding an unconstitutional law. Since the era of the Warren Court, liberals have had to defend their uses of judicial power as if there were an unwritten rule against such uses, while conservatives, who cloak themselves in the mantle of judicial restraint, have not had to justify their refusal to invalidate laws that should be invalidated.[22] Unfortunately, this defensive posture on the part of liberals allows conservatives to frame the debate over judicial review in a manner that not only serves conservative partisan ends by making it seem as if any decision that departs from the plain or original meaning of the constitutional text is illegitimate, but also obscures what should count as a good answer to a difficult constitutional question.

II. PUBLIC JUSTIFICATION

If law is not merely the extension of politics by other means, then there are better and worse answers to at least some constitutional questions, and the quality of those answers is contingent on the reasons that judges have offered in their opinions. A good theory of constitutional adjudication must

---

[21] If we take what they say in their opinions at face value, their reasons are transparent; the same cannot be said for their motives.

[22] As Stephen Macedo writes, "Judicial deference ... is not an avoidance of choice. Rather, it is a choice of majority power over individual liberty." Macedo, *The New Right v. The Constitution*, 27.

not only guide judges in making the best choice among the remaining plausible reasons after they have eliminated the bad ones but also must explain their plausibility. An even better theory of constitutional adjudication would include an independent normative standard to help the electorate decide which of those underlying reasons was most plausible and thus most likely to lead to the right answer in a particular constitutional controversy. Such a standard must distinguish a good constitutional argument from a bad one and a better one from a worse one when two or more of the arguments are not bad. The standard that I offer in this book is public justification. A legitimate decision is one that crosses the threshold of public justification, and the best decision is the one that is most publicly justified, that is, the one based on the strongest public reasons.

My concern with the public justification of public laws and judicial decisions is not only prudential in that a society whose laws are not sufficiently publicly justified is prone to constitutional crises. A decent society articulates the reasons that underlie its actions even when public officials would prefer to exercise their authority without attempts at justification. An even better society publicly justifies its most important laws to respect the freedom and equality of all of its members. The failure to do so not only would make some people's lives worse than they otherwise would be, but also would put into doubt the fairness of the American political system. When ordinary people have very little political influence, they are entitled to know the reasons that the state relies on when it exercises its coercive power over them. As I shall show, judges may legitimately invalidate laws that have clearly failed to meet the standard of public justification that I defend in this book. When the state puts forth reasons in a particular constitutional case that turn out to be insufficiently public, and a court rejects those reasons, that exercise of judicial review is warranted. After all, those reasons should not have been the basis of a statutory prohibition or classification in the first place.

I also explain how this standard of public justification limits the interpretive latitude that judges have when they decide real cases and thereby addresses the traditional concern that judicial discretion is too unconstrained to be consistent with the rule of law. Public justification is about the kinds of reasons that justify the uses of the coercive power of the state.[23] In hard constitutional cases, I do not sharply distinguish between legal and nonlegal reasons for two main reasons. First, when real judges have to decide

---

[23] Initially, John Rawls described the U.S. Supreme Court as "the exemplar of public reason." See John Rawls, *Political Liberalism* (New York: Columbia University Press, 1996), 231. Later, he wrote that public reason applies to the discourse of all judges in their decision making, and especially to those on the U.S. Supreme Court, and then added that public reason applies more strictly to judges than to citizens and their elected representatives. See John Rawls, "The Idea of Public Reason Revisited," in *The Law of Peoples* (Cambridge, MA: Harvard University Press, 1999), 133–4.

such cases and have already ruled out undeniably nonlegal reasons, they are frequently divided over which reasons are sufficiently legal and what force they ought to have. Judges must have the discretion to choose from a wide range of reasons and must be able to do so openly. Second, such cases present questions of public morality, and it is disingenuous for judges to pretend otherwise. Our understanding of the role that the judiciary should play in our politics will improve only when more people understand that constitutional adjudication is value laden, and a strict separation between legal and other kinds of reasons only conceals what judges do and must do in the most challenging constitutional cases.

Such a separation also makes it more difficult for them and us to evaluate the reasons that the state has offered on behalf of the law in question. Judges must accept only certain sorts of reasons as justification for statutes and must render a law unconstitutional when voters or legislators have failed to limit themselves to those reasons.[24] That is the defense of judicial review that lies at the center of this book. Judges serve as gatekeepers who ensure that the state does not act on the wrong kinds of reasons when it exercises or threatens to exercise its coercive power. The more significant the impact of the law, the more that law must be justified in the eyes of those who are burdened by it. That is not to say that the state can never clear this hurdle. For example, laws that prohibit murder, rape, assault and battery, theft, and fraud are unquestionably publicly justified. A reasonable person would understand why those actions are harmful and therefore criminal. A law that requires abortion, prevents interracial marriage, criminalizes premarital sex, or denies women access to education is clearly not publicly justified. There should be a strong presumption against laws that undermine freedom and equality that the state can overcome only if it can produce compelling reasons. The requirement of public justification, then, functions as a constraint on state action, and through the exercise of judicial review, judges determine when lawmakers have exceeded their authority.

It follows that judges should introduce only certain reasons to support their own constitutional conclusions. When they invalidate a law, judges must explain why the reasons that the state has offered on behalf of the law in question fall short of the standard of public justification. When they decline to invalidate a law, they must defend its constitutionality by showing that its underlying reasons are compelling. Reasons based on religious convictions and what Cass Sunstein calls "naked preferences" are not

---

[24] Although Rawls himself did not fully develop an ideal of legal or constitutional reason, "it is clear that a Rawlsian ideal of public reason has important implications for fundamental debates in legal theory." See Lawrence B. Solum, "Public Legal Reason," 92 *Virginia Law Review* (2006), 1474.

compelling.[25] Reasonable people could reject such reasons on the ground that they are too sectarian or are at variance with the public good. In addition, in the spirit of John Rawls, I contend that judges must not allow voters and legislators to appeal to the "truth" of their conceptions of the good life or their visions of a good society when they enact laws that undermine freedom and equality.

That contention is bound to be controversial and perhaps is counterintutive. In most settings, such appeals are not only commonplace but also perfectly acceptable. Normally, we do not censure people for relying on their deepest convictions in their public deliberations and voting behavior, and we may even admire them for remaining faithful to their consciences and being candid with us. As I see it, though, a higher standard of public justification would serve as a more meaningful constitutional limit on the coercive power of the state. In the realm of constitutional adjudication, reasons derived from deeper convictions are inappropriate because reasonable people are likely to be justified in not accepting such reasons. When judges are trying to decide a case on the basis of public reasons, they must write an opinion with a particular audience in mind, namely those who are likely to disagree with the decision, and try to convince them by giving them adequate reasons.[26] This task is especially important when judges decide to uphold a law that infringes upon personal freedom or treats some people unequally. In turn, dissenters should accept only reasons that are consistent with their freedom and equality.

Although my theory of constitutional adjudication as public justification is ideal, it is not far removed from constitutional history and practice. Consider the following examples. The strong presumption against the constitutionality of content-based restrictions and viewpoint discrimination in free speech law and the requirement that a statute have a secular purpose in establishment clause jurisprudence reflects the importance of the state's relying upon reasons that should be acceptable to everyone.[27] Justice Sandra Day O'Connor's endorsement test has a similar rationale; it is premised on the principle that the state may not send a message to "nonadherents that they are outsiders, not full members of the community."[28] The state may not enact a religious display, such as a nativity scene, that a reasonable observer would construe as the state's favoring one religion over others.[29] Similarly,

---

[25] Cass R. Sunstein, "Naked Preferences and the Constitution," 84 *Columbia Law Review* (1984), 1689–732.

[26] Cf. City of Cleburne v. Cleburne Learning Center, 473 U.S. 432, 455 (1985) (Stevens, J., concurring) ("I cannot believe that a rational member of this disadvantaged class could ever approve of the discriminatory application of the city's ordinance in this case" (which required a special permit for the establishment of homes for the mentally retarded).

[27] See Lemon v. Kurtzman, 403 U.S. 602 (1970).

[28] Lynch v. Donnelly, 465 U.S. 668 (1984).

[29] See, e.g., Allegheny County v. American Civil Liberties Union, 492 U.S. 573 (1989).

in equal protection clause jurisprudence, the state can neither classify certain people on the basis of certain immutable traits nor ground legislation in reasons that reasonable dissenters could never accept, such as stereotypes, contempt, or moral disapproval of lifestyle.[30] The importance of protecting a "discrete and insular minority" is based on the principle that people who lack political resources should not be at the mercy of legislative majorities.[31]

The preceding constitutional principles have this much in common: certain reasons, namely those that are too self-serving or sectarian, should not serve as the moral basis of certain laws. It is not always morally acceptable, in other words, for legislative majorities to take advantage of their superior position in the legislative process and give their views the force of law. The presence of nonpublic reasons often renders a particular law constitutionally suspect, and those reasons also explain why certain infamous constitutional cases, which are almost universally regarded as wrongly decided, were wrongly decided, at least in retrospect. In *Dred Scott*, the *Civil Rights Cases*, *Plessy v. Ferguson*, and *Korematsu*, neither the state nor the Court was able to come up with a sufficiently public argument, that is, an argument that the victims of such racial discrimination could have been expected to accept. Nor could a religious minority like the Jehovah's Witnesses have accepted the kinds of reasons that the Court offered in *Gobitis* to support the conclusion that their children could be required to salute the American flag in public schools.[32] The defendants in *Smith*, the infamous peyote case, could not have been expected to accept the majority's view that a court need not balance the state's interest in prohibition against the burden on the practice of their religion.[33]

The assumption that an unconstitutional law is not publicly justified can help to explain the outcome of some of the best-known, correctly decided fundamental rights and equal protection cases. That assumption also can illuminate the fundamentals of constitutional criminal procedure. No one wants to return to the days of coerced confessions, and a society that allows defendants who have been acquitted by a jury of their peers to be tried over and over again until the prosecution can obtain a conviction is not a society that most of us would want to live in. When people have been charged with a crime, they have a number of constitutional rights that ensure that they are able to defend themselves against those charges effectively in an adversarial system of justice. It would be unthinkable for the Court to allow a legislature to take away the rights to be informed of the charges against them, to

---

[30] See, e.g., U.S. Department of Agriculture v. Moreno, 413 U.S. 528 (1973); Romer v. Evans, 517 U.S. 620 (1996); Lawrence v. Texas, 539 U.S. 558 (2003).

[31] The phrase "discrete and insular minority" comes from Justice Harlan Stone's famous footnote 4 in United States v. Carolene Products, 304 U.S. 144 (1938).

[32] Minersville School District v. Gobitis, 310 U.S. 586 (1940).

[33] Employment Division v. Smith, 494 U.S. 872 (1990).

counsel, to discovery, to be given exculpatory evidence, to an impartial jury, to a speedy trial, and so forth. While most academics and legal professionals would describe these principles as rooted in procedural due process, another way to characterize the reasons that make a fair trial possible is that they are those that a reasonable person would consider essential to the fairness of the criminal justice system. Anyone who is charged with a crime would want and always does want to exercise the preceding rights. When people want to know whether the reasons offered in support of these rights are sufficiently public, they must ask themselves whether they, in the position of a criminal defendant, would insist on having those rights. If they would, then those reasons are likely to be sufficiently public. As always, the challenge is to answer the following question as honestly as possible: is that how I would like to be treated if I or someone I care about were in the same or similar circumstances?

III. REASONABLE DISSENTERS

The standard of public justification that I shall articulate and defend in this book is based on the unfairness of the state's reliance upon inappropriate reasons in some circumstances, and legitimate judicial decisions adequately explain whether the reasons that support the law in question are sufficiently public. Such decisions are not necessarily those that Americans actually accept at a given moment – surely, real people can be unreasonable – but those that an ideal reasonable dissenter would consider good enough.[34] There is a continuum, ranging from unarguably legitimate at one extreme to unarguably illegitimate at the other extreme. Whether a judicial decision is legitimate turns on the reasons that judges have mustered on its behalf. Although the content of those reasons will vary from case to case, judges who care about public justification should always address those who are likely to disagree with the result. Such an attempt is especially important

---

[34] I borrow the idea of reasonable rejectability from T. M. Scanlon, "Contractualism and Utilitarianism," in *Beyond Utilitarianism*, ed. Amartya Sen and Bernard Williams (New York: Cambridge University Press, 1984), 110. The difference between accepting a reason and not rejecting a reason is not only semantic. Instead, this difference goes to the heart of whether a particular law is publicly justified. To accept a reason is to see that reason as good enough for making one choice rather than another; that reason appears to be better than the other reasons, all things considered. To not reject a reason is to see that reason as not too bad to support the choice to be made, even if there are other reasons that the person making the judgment sees as stronger. This means that a person may believe that reason A is better than reason B and therefore, leads to a particular conclusion. At the same time, that person may also believe that reason B, which supports the opposite conclusion, should not be rejected because a reasonable person could believe that reason B is good enough. By "good enough," I mean that it does adequate justificatory work from an impersonal standpoint. For convenience, I use "would accept" and "could not reasonably reject" interchangeably.

in the most divisive constitutional cases, which the American people are more likely to care about.

Thus, judges must cast their constitutional arguments in ways that might appeal to reasonable dissenters, and this book defines an ideal reasonable dissenter as a person who is willing to be persuaded by the better argument, assumes that reasonable moral disagreement will characterize difficult constitutional cases, and will conclude that the legislation in question is publicly justified only when the state has produced sufficiently public reasons on its behalf. For such a hypothetical person, a good reason is one that is sufficiently public and a bad reason is one that is insufficiently public. In a perfect world, legislators would rely upon only sufficiently public reasons to justify public laws that infringe upon fundamental rights or make suspect or quasi-suspect classifications.[35] Unfortunately, real legislators often do not exercise such self-restraint, and that means that courts must distinguish sufficiently public from insufficiently public reasons. Reasons that are sufficiently public are those that honor the freedom and equality of all of the members of the political community.[36] Typically, they are as neutral as possible with respect to the wide range of reasonable conceptions of the good and normative political ideologies that currently exist in this country. They should be uncontroversial, which means that an ideal reasonable person could not reasonably reject them. Reasons that are insufficiently public are those that conflict with the freedom and equality of all of the members of the political community. Usually, they are based on perfectionist standards of human flourishing, on contested theories of political morality, or on controversial empirical claims. It would not be surprising that people would resent being coerced in the name of such a standard or theory that they probably never would adopt, with good reason, as their own. This kind of deeper disagreement about the best human life and the best political arrangements will always exist in a society such as our own that allows its members to make up their own minds about the comparative merits of different but reasonable ways of life.[37]

The existence of such deeper disagreement need not culminate in despair, but it should change the very way in which Americans think about the justification of public laws and judicial decisions. Judges must ensure that legislative majorities defer to what different individuals happen to believe to be most worthwhile in human life in the absence of compelling reasons to the contrary. No rational person would consent to a law that put his or her life plan in jeopardy. The standard of public justification defended in this

---

[35] Stephan Macedo argues that legislators must also present "public reasons for their actions." Stephen Macedo, *Liberal Virtues: Citizenship, Virtue, and Community in Liberal Constitutionalism* (New York: Oxford University Press, 1990), 186.

[36] I deliberately use the term *members* to include noncitizens as well.

[37] On this point, see Rawls, *Political Liberalism*, xviii.

book makes this sort of deference possible, thereby striking the right balance between legislative and judicial power. Above all, judges must not allow the state to rely upon the wrong kinds of reasons in depriving people of their choices about how to live or in denying them equal opportunity to achieve their ambitions. An argument that incorporates a premise that a particular way of life is sinful, unpopular, unnatural, unconventional, misguided, silly, or idiotic is exactly the kind of argument that the state must eschew. An argument that contains a premise that a particular way of life is superior to others or that certain people are by nature inferior is also insufficiently public.[38]

In imagining what it would be like to be a reasonable dissenter, judges must put themselves in the position of someone who would be adversely affected by a statute that infringed upon a fundamental or quasi-fundamental right or that made a suspect or quasi-suspect classification. They could not base their decision on theoretically ambitious arguments such as those that attempt to save competent adults from themselves; assess the merits of morally permissible ways of life; rely heavily upon controversial metaphysical, moral, religious, social, or economic theories; or deny that all persons are political and legal equals. There should be a constitutional requirement that certain sorts of legislation be publicly justified. No such explicit textual requirement exists, of course, but it is hard to make sense of some of the most cherished constitutional decisions in the areas of fundamental rights and equal protection without reference to an ideal of public justification. In the first half of the book, I hope to show that such an ideal is the most appropriate normative standard for constitutional adjudication in America. In deciding whether the law in question is publicly justified, judges first must examine the reasons that the legislators have offered to defend the law in question and assess the reasons that the state gives during the litigation. If judges cannot find sufficiently public reasons to save the statute in question, then they must strike it down. If judges are uncertain about the correct result, then they must try to figure out where the balance of public reasons lies, with a presumption in favor of personal freedom and equal treatment.

In such a situation, judges decide whether the reasons that the state has advanced would be adequate from the standpoint of an ideal reasonable dissenter who does not share the deeper beliefs of the majority but values his or her life plan and seeks to secure the resources that would enable him or her to realize it. Judges cannot concern themselves only with what strike them as the most cogent reasons in a particular case; they also concern themselves with the reasons that ought to appeal to others who have

---

[38] Cf. Bruce Ackerman, *Social Justice in the Liberal State* (New Haven, CT: Yale University Press, 1980), 10–11.

different, but reasonable, deeper convictions.[39] As Justice Benjamin Cardozo once put it, "The thing that counts is not what I believe to be right. It is what I may reasonably believe that some other man of normal intellect and conscience might reasonably look upon as right."[40] In this respect, the best reason would be a reason that every reasonable person would have to accept because of its undeniable relevance and force in that particular context. The existence of such a reason or its absence is what makes some constitutional cases easier than others. A law that is based on a racial or gender stereotype, for instance, would not be based on a reason that a reasonable person would accept. A reasonable person would reject that reason on the ground that it denies freedom and equality to some of the members of the political community. An imaginary reasonable dissenter should see at least one of the reasons put forth as good enough, which is not to say that he or she will fully agree with the outcome. A reason could be excellent from a personal standpoint but much worse from an impersonal standpoint. The fewer reasons that reasonable people have to reject the decision, the more publicly justified that decision is. That would help readers of the Court's decisions understand not only when such decisions are sufficiently publicly justified to be legitimate but also why one publicly justified decision may trump its rivals.

The purpose of my introducing public justification as a standard for the legitimacy of particular judicial decisions is not to pretend that constitutional controversies are easier than they really are or to claim that all reasonable people, after reflection, would reach the same conclusions. One should be suspicious of any theory of constitutional adjudication that spits out self-evident answers to the hardest of hard cases, like abortion and affirmative action, or even to comparatively less difficult cases, like medical marijuana, school vouchers, redistricting, and campaign finance reform. In such cases, reasonable people may disagree on whether a particular judicial opinion is sufficiently publicly justified even after they have acknowledged the value of public justification more abstractly. Nonetheless, the likelihood that it is almost impossible to determine where the balance of public reasons lies is not as troubling as it initially may appear to be. Public justification is about the reasons that judges ought to accept as justification for state coercion and is predicated on the possibility that reasonable persons may share some of the same "shallower" reasons on a case-by-case basis even in the midst of deeper moral disagreement. Reasonable people often will converge on the same answer in easy cases where constitutional law is more or less determinate, and they probably will share some of the same reasons.

---

[39] As Kent Greenawalt puts it, "A comprehensive view is 'reasonable' if it acknowledges the freedom and equality of citizens on which political liberalism rests." Kent Greenawalt, "On Public Reason," 69 *Chicago-Kent Law Review* (1994), 671.

[40] Benjamin N. Cardozo, *The Nature of the Judicial Process* (New Haven, CT: Yale University Press, 1949), 89.

In the most challenging constitutional cases, though, what matters are the kinds of reasons that produce those answers. Although people cannot wish away reasonable disagreement, recognition of what makes reasonable disagreement reasonable in the first place may lead dissenters to more willingly accept judicial decisions that they disagree with and give them less cause to engage in civil disobedience or to see those who disagree with them as acting in bad faith. As it turns out, moderate indeterminacy in hard cases is a blessing in disguise. People who exchange reasons with one another may acknowledge that a position is respectable even when they believe it to be morally mistaken.[41] A person could believe that the Court decided a case incorrectly but still believe the decision to be legitimate because the reasons that the Court offered to justify its decision were good enough, and that is the kind of legitimacy that is possible in a constitutional democracy like our own.

IV. THE CALIFORNIA SAME-SEX MARRIAGE CASES

An ideal of public justification, because of its abstractness, might seem to interest only those who study normative political or legal theory. The importance of this ideal transcends its academic setting, however, because everyone should care about whether the laws that they live under are sufficiently publicly justified. Otherwise, they do not care about their own freedom and equality or that of others. My impression is that they already do care, and our political and constitutional discourse presupposes that some arguments are more likely to be publicly justified than others. Recently, the California Supreme Court found that the failure to "designate the official relationship of same-sex couples as marriage" violates the California Constitution.[42] In writing the majority opinion, Chief Justice Ronald George advanced two main arguments. First, he insisted that there is a fundamental right to marriage under the California Constitution, and that its scope also covers same-sex couples. In doing so, he relied heavily on *Perez v. Sharp* – the case that established a constitutional right to interracial marriage in California – in showing that traditional understandings do not necessarily prevent the extension of constitutional rights.[43] Second, he claimed that the legislative classification in question, which denied gays and lesbians the right to marry, was based on a suspect trait, sexual orientation, which "does not constitute a legitimate basis upon which to deny or withhold legal rights."[44]

---

[41] Amy Gutmann and Dennis Thompson, *Democracy and Disagreement: Why Moral Conflict Cannot Be Avoided in Politics and What Should Be Done about It* (Cambridge, MA: Harvard University Press, Belknap Press, 1996), 2–3.

[42] In re Marriage Cases, 43 Cal. 4d 757, 780 (2008) (George, J., majority).

[43] Perez v. Sharp, 32 Cal. 2d 711 (1948).

[44] In re Marriage Cases, 43 Cal. 4d 757, 782 (2008) (George, J., majority).

The dissenters made two distinct but overlapping arguments. First, Justice Marvin Baxter insisted that the majority had overstepped its bounds by not permitting the meaning of marriage to change through ordinary democratic processes.[45] Second, Justice Carol Corrigan emphasized the extent to which statutory alternatives to marriage for same-sex couples, such as civil unions or domestic partnerships, satisfied equal protection requirements.[46]

Can this disagreement be rationally resolved? Or are we stuck in a world in which all that can be said, at the end of the day, is that some people like same-sex marriage and some people don't? If that is the case, then we might as well aggregate the preferences of the voters, as accurately as possible, to satisfy more people's preferences with respect to the issue and not concern ourselves with the quality of the competing arguments.[47] Nevertheless, it does not seem as if anyone's principled position on same-sex marriage can be reduced to a mere preference or that a utilitarian calculus based on those preferences would produce the right result. Those on both sides of the issue offer a wide variety of reasons that they take to be more than self-serving or sectarian to support their respective positions. In the California Supreme Court decision regarding same-sex marriage, those in the majority and those who dissented did not make some of the arguments that people normally make when they debate the issue. None of the justices argued that same-sex relationships are a positive good that our society should promote. Nor did any of the justices contend that such relationships thwart the will of God or are inconsistent with the teachings of the Roman Catholic Church. In constitutional discourse, certain arguments are out of bounds. Chief Justice George went out of his way to note that his view as an individual on the merits of same-sex marriage was irrelevant in determining the constitutional validity of the current legislative provisions.[48]

V. REASONABLE DISAGREEMENT

Here, the point is not to contend that any of the foregoing legal arguments are convincing but to see the relevance of public justification to constitutional adjudication. In subsequent chapters, I shall try to show that in such cases, the business of the judiciary is to determine whether the state has met its burden of providing sufficiently public reasons to justify the statute

---

[45] In re Marriage Cases, 43 Cal. 4d 757, 861 (2008) (Baxter, J., dissenting).

[46] In re Marriage Cases, 43 Cal. 4d 757, 878 (2008) (Corrigan, J., dissenting).

[47] This is what happened in California on November 4, 2008, when the voters approved Proposition 8, which overturned the California Supreme Court's decision and banned same-sex marriage by amending the California Constitution.

[48] In re Marriage Cases, 43 Cal. 4d 757, 780 (2008) (George, J., majority)

in question. That is not the only possible way to decide which constitutional argument carries the day, but my belief is that it is the fairest way to do so. As it turns out, knowing whether a case has been correctly decided according to the standard of public justification is more complicated than it may seem. One of the premises of this book is that the operation of human reason, even at its best, will never eliminate the reasonable disagreement that pervades our political life. Normative legal theory, just like its political theory counterpart, must confront what Rawls calls "the fact of reasonable moral pluralism," where disagreement about the nature of the human good in a free society not only is inevitable but also has political and constitutional implications. Reasonable people disagree about the nature of the human good and at times about justice as well, and it stands to reason that such disagreement will spill over into our most challenging constitutional controversies.[49]

If reasonable disagreement were not so pervasive, then public justification would not be so imperative. After adequate public deliberation and personal reflection, reasonable people would be able to identify the best argument in a particular political or constitutional controversy and act accordingly. In a homogeneous society with little or no deeper moral disagreement, there would be fewer dissenters, and those who dissent would be inappropriately motivated, poorly informed, dogmatic, or not very bright. Dissenters could be, as Jean-Jacques Rousseau would have said, forced to be free if they were to refuse to comply with the collective decision that the majority had made; their dissent would prove that they were wrong. If this were an accurate description of moral disagreement in the United States, constitutional issues such as abortion, affirmative action, capital punishment, gun control, the limits of free speech, the proper degree of separation between church and state, and the appropriate balance between civil liberties and national security would not be so intractable. One side would have the better argument, and the challenge would be to determine which political institution was best equipped to discern the strongest argument in the constitutional controversies that divide Americans.

However, these days, most scholars are not optimistic about the likelihood of more moral agreement. In fact, value pluralism and postmodernism seem to have shifted the burden of proof to those who still have faith in the force of the better argument to demonstrate that that moral argumentation in political life is not pointless. The very existence of moral disagreement, of course, does not prove that there is no right answer to a difficult moral question. Surely, disagreement over a particular moral or political issue could

---

[49] On reasonable, inevitable disagreement about the good, see Rawls, "The Idea of Public Reason Revisited," 131. On reasonable, inevitable disagreement about justice, see Jeremy Waldron, *Law and Disagreement* (Oxford, U.K.: Oxford University Press, 1999).

have a number of different sources. People may be obtuse or biased and therefore ignore any evidence that undermines their position. At the same time, the reasonable part of reasonable moral disagreement implies that it may be very difficult to know, or to justify to others, the right answer to a difficult question of political morality. Although the sincere attempts by both sides of a constitutional controversy to give each other their best public reasons does not guarantee anything like consensus, it increases the likelihood that the reasons that ultimately prevail are not unnecessarily controversial. When the Court exercises the power of judicial review, its objective must be to give sufficient reasons to reasonable dissenters who are likely to believe its decision to be mistaken, and satisfying this objective is extremely important when the state, through its laws, takes away individual freedom or treats people unequally. That is probably as close as any society can come to legitimizing its most important constitutional choices.

This book is about the sorts of reasons that would meet this minimal standard of public justification, not only in the abstract but in particular instances as well. My intention in these pages is to distinguish sufficiently public and insufficiently public reasons, to describe the kind of self-restraint that those who care about public justification must exercise, and to make the case that public laws and judicial decisions that are not publicly justified are not legitimate. The dilemma that such judges are likely to encounter is that, on the one hand, they cannot decide a hard case without making various sorts of judgments of political morality. On the other hand, those judgments are bound to be controversial because they cannot be proved correct in the midst of deeper moral disagreement. In such instances, it is futile to appeal only to abstract constitutional values such as freedom and equality as if such values alone could generate the correct outcome, no more than a mere appeal to racial equality could determine the constitutionality of a particular affirmative action plan.[50] All competent judges acknowledge the constitutional relevance of certain considerations, but that consensus often disappears when the meaning of an abstract constitutional provision must be specified. Agreement at an abstract level may only turn out to be agreement on easy cases. Although that is better than no agreement at all, it would be even better if there were less intense disagreement when the Court makes constitutional decisions that do not please everyone but are almost impossible to overturn.

---

[50] Even though a moral principle is justified, it does not necessarily follow that its application in a specific context is also justified. See Klaus Gunther, *The Sense of Appropriateness: Application Discourses in Morality and Law*, trans. John Farrell (Albany: State University of New York Press, 1993). H. L. A. Hart also distinguishes between the moral permissibility of a particular law and the criteria for its application to a particular case. H. L. A. Hart, *The Concept of Law*, 2nd ed. (New York: Oxford University Press, 1961), 160–7.

VI. THEORY AND PRACTICE

It might be thought that this book, like so many others before it, privileges constitutional theory over constitutional practice. That is true inasmuch as anyone who is trying to explain how constitutional choices should be made must offer not a piecemeal approach but a systematic theory about how judges are supposed to make them. A pragmatic approach to judicial decision making, like that of former Justice O'Connor, may be attractive because it seems to promote political compromise and encourage judges to take small steps under the banner of judicial modesty. At times, that strategy may produce better results and preserve judicial independence. However, despite its antitheoretical veneer, such an approach to judicial decision making also has a theoretical basis. Ultimately, all judges must take sides in complicated theoretical debates that involve even more complicated theoretical questions about freedom, equality, democracy, and constitutionalism. As Ronald Dworkin wrote, "[W]e have no choice but to ask [judges] to confront issues that, from time to time, are philosophical."[51] I will also explain why they should do so as openly as possible and how that openness would enable them to take responsibility for the constitutional choices that they make in our name. Judges who claim that their theory of constitutional adjudication has steered clear of such questions either are disingenuous or lack self-awareness. In a democratic society, a hidden or underdeveloped foundation for any such theory is problematic because it prevents people from evaluating it on its merits and seeing how that theory may have influenced the outcome of an important case.

At the same time, scholars should not neglect real cases, not only because those cases provide the data for constitutional theory but also because many Americans are not indifferent to their resolutions. Consequently, in the second half of the book, I move from the high ground of constitutional theory to the perspective of the judge who cares about holding the state to the standard of public justification in real constitutional controversies. Theories never apply themselves, and it behooves us to understand how judges should approach real cases to increase the likelihood that their decisions are publicly justified and thus legitimate. In rendering my theory of constitutional adjudication less abstract, I use some of the best-known constitutional decisions as examples of when the Court met or failed to meet the standard of public justification. In some instances, I explain why the concurring or dissenting opinion was more publicly justified. When none of the opinions is sufficiently publicly justified, I offer my own thoughts as to how such an opinion could have been written. The point is not to assert that these hypothetical opinions are necessarily correct but to illustrate the kinds of opinions that

---

[51] Dworkin, *Justice in Robes*, 73.

could be publicly justified. The claim that a particular argument has met this standard could be wrong, and it must be defended like any other claim.

Normally, those who defend judicial review deny or minimize its antidemocratic implications, and that approach is understandable in a society that is committed to constitutionalism and has a tradition of limiting what legislative majorities can do even when the underlying democratic procedure is fair. The most recent attempt to do so is found in Corey Brettschneider's thoughtful book *Democratic Rights*, in which he argues that democracy presupposes certain substantive values and that judges may invalidate laws that are at odds with such values.[52] As I shall show, though, the most honest rationale for the practice of judicial review is rooted in pessimism about the likelihood that ordinary citizens or their elected representatives could decide important constitutional cases competently.[53] In this sense, many of us are still reluctant democrats who accept a sharp distinction between democracy and constitutionalism and hope that nondemocratic means such as judicial review can serve democratic ends. In the end, judicial supremacy turns out to be the lesser of two evils: it is a safer bet in an imperfect world where the vast majority of citizens are either incapable of making informed, reflective decisions on basic questions of public morality or unwilling to make the effort to do so.

An ideal deliberative democracy in which the vast majority of citizens exchange reasons with one another in publicly justifying the most important political choices could probably do without the judicial part of judicial review.[54] There is no doubt that it would be better if more citizens were more informed, more tolerant, and more civic minded. In the complete absence of those civic virtues, it would not matter what courts did or did not try to do. When all is said and done, courts cannot save Americans from themselves, but they can help them to understand the importance of protecting the freedom and equality of everyone when certain constitutional questions arise. It would be a mistake to assume that ordinary people are worse than they really are and cannot be trusted to be minimally civic minded when they are supposed to be. It would be equally mistaken, though, to

---

[52] Corey Brettschneider, *Democratic Rights: The Substance of Self-Government* (Princeton, NJ: Princeton University Press, 2007).

[53] Contrast this view with that of Sanford Levinson. In speculating about what might happen at a new constitutional convention, Levinson writes: "[I] continue to have sufficient faith in the democratic ideal that I believe that most of the public, in a truly serious debate about the Constitution, could be persuaded to support the essential rights that are required for membership in a republican order." Sanford Levinson, *Our Undemocratic Constitution: Where the Constitution Goes Wrong (And How We the People Can Correct It)* (New York: Oxford University Press, 2006), 175.

[54] Cass Sunstein has written that the Constitution "was designed to create a deliberative democracy." Cass R. Sunstein, *The Partial Constitution* (Cambridge, MA: Harvard University Press, 1993), 19–20.

make unrealistic assumptions about their civic capacities and expect that our democratic politics would magically become more participatory and more deliberative if only our judiciary would stop making many of our most difficult political choices for us.

Among others who seek to limit the influence of the judiciary, Sunstein insists that "the real forum of high principle is politics, not the judiciary."[55] Certainly, that is not a descriptive statement, and there is very little reason to believe that our democratic life will become more deliberative or more principled anytime soon or that ordinary people will care more about politics or become better informed when they have few incentives to do so. Those are brute facts that should be regretted in a society that has democratic aspirations, but wishful thinking cannot substitute for realistic assumptions about what we can reasonably ask of citizens at this moment in our history. It is natural to want the best of both worlds, where democratic self-rule cohabitates with freedom and equality, yet far too often in the past, the democratic process has not protected individual rights from the will of legislative majorities or guaranteed equal treatment. Unless our political situation changes dramatically in the near future, Americans may have to settle for a less democratic liberalism to ensure that the state treats all people fairly. Different people reach different levels of cognitive development, and many of them have underdeveloped critical thinking skills.[56] Thus, some citizens will not be equipped to make informed and principled voting decisions. A person who does not realize that reasonable people can disagree on the most important constitutional questions is unlikely to be able to deliberate with the sort of minimal sophistication that the practice of public reasoning in political life requires. This fact may lead us to conclude that the level of civic competence that public deliberation and voting in a deliberative democracy demands is simply too high for most people.

It probably is unrealistic, then, to expect ordinary citizens to act as judges when they deliberate and vote on the most important constitutional questions. As a result, Americans are more justified in placing their bets on the judiciary as the branch that can more easily provide reasonable dissenters with the reasons that they are entitled to know when the state exercises its coercive power. At the heart of the debate over the scope of judicial review lie old normative questions about the proper relationship between individual rights and majoritarianism and what trade-offs are acceptable once it becomes evident that lawmakers cannot always be relied upon to respect the

[55] Cass R. Sunstein, *Legal Reasoning and Political Conflict* (New York: Oxford University Press, 1996), 7.

[56] See, generally, Patricia M. King and Karen Kitchener, *Developing Reflective Judgment: Understanding and Promoting Intellectual Growth and Critical Thinking in Adolescents and Adults* (San Francisco: Jossey-Bass Publishers, 1994); Deanna Kuhn, *The Skills of Argument* (New York: Cambridge University Press, 1991).

freedom and equality of everyone. Reliance on judicial review is less than ideal from any democratic standpoint, but it has the advantage of not radically departing from our political reality. An effective capacity to act from a sense of justice, as Rawls would say, makes a well-ordered society possible, and all of the judicial wisdom in the world cannot replace the importance of citizens taking responsibility for the political choices that others often make in their name. But that does not change the fact that judges are more likely to be able to identify sufficiently public reasons than citizens and their elected representatives are in the most important constitutional cases. That may not be music to democratic ears, but it has the merit of increasing the likelihood that the state will treat more people more fairly more often on the basis of reasons that most reasonable people can share.

ONE

Public Justification and Constitutional Theory

The purpose of this chapter is to spell out why an ideal of public justification is essential to both constitutional theory and practice. I begin with some thoughts on why Americans have mixed feelings about judicial review and how their ambivalence reflects understandable concerns about the abuse of judicial power in a democracy. After summarizing the shortcomings of textualism, I describe the appeal of originalist approaches to constitutional adjudication.[1] Some conservatives have used a crude form of originalism to mislead the public into thinking that judges who do not stick to the plain or original meaning of the text must be legislating from the bench. At present, perhaps because of what happened to Robert Bork in 1987, no one expects a nominee to out himself as an originalist. At the same time, a candidate's denial that judges make value judgments in important constitutional cases has become a code hinting at the nominee's originalist sympathies. In his recent confirmation hearing, John Roberts testified that judging is like calling balls and strikes.[2]

That metaphor suggests that a judge, who does his or her job properly, merely follows legal rules in deciding constitutional cases; a judge who makes a mistake either has made a factual error or has manipulated the law, like an umpire who has tampered with the strike zone. As I shall show, this characterization of judging is inaccurate. We should not only be concerned that originalists like Bork, Antonin Scalia, and Clarence Thomas would overturn some of the most cherished constitutional decisions. We

---

[1] By "originalist approaches," I mean the theory of constitutional interpretation where the meaning of a constitutional provision is determined by what it meant to most people at the time of its inception. In ascertaining its meaning, an interpreter examines historical sources and does not use moral reasoning in specifying its implications. The meaning of the Constitution is fixed by its public meaning in its original linguistic context, and subsequent interpreters are bound by that meaning.

[2] Christopher L. Eisgruber, *The Next Justice: Repairing the Supreme Court Appointments Process* (Princeton, NJ: Princeton University Press, 2007), 17.

should also wonder whether originalist judges can do what they claim to do in the decision-making process, that is, to "stick close to the text and the history."[3] A society that puts so much faith in its judiciary to decide some of its most important questions of political morality cannot afford judges who adhere to an approach to constitutional interpretation that makes it seem as if a judge could decide an important constitutional case simply by discovering how most people would have understood certain words at a particular moment in American history. The point is not only that originalism is more flawed than most nonoriginalist alternatives, but also that originalist judges are operating under a delusion that nonoriginalists are not operating under, namely that "original meaning made them do it."[4] Americans will always be divided over the outcomes of the most important constitutional cases and probably can live together despite these divisions as long as their judges do not conceal the value choices that underlie their decisions.

I. THE LEGITIMACY OF JUDICIAL REVIEW

A. Ambivalence

Although it is difficult to imagine America without judicial review, it is also difficult to see how Americans will ever be at ease with an institution that puts so much power into the hands of unelected judges who may be tempted to impose their visions of a good society upon the rest of us. As everyone knows, to ensure judicial independence, federal judges are not directly accountable to the electorate, and the decisions of the U.S. Supreme Court, even if poorly reasoned, are not easily overturned. Under such circumstances, it would be surprising if Americans did not question the wisdom of having the judiciary thwart the will of legislative majorities.[5] In terms of outcomes, judicial review is a double-edged sword. A person might be enamored of the activism of the Warren and early Burger courts but despise that of the Rehnquist and Roberts courts. Even if someone agrees with the result that the Court reached in *Roe v. Wade*, that person might be sympathetic to the view that it would have been better for the Court to have left the

---

[3] Robert H. Bork, "Neutral Principles and Some First Amendment Problems," 47 *Indiana Law Journal* (1971), 8.

[4] This expression is a slightly modified version of Tribe's "the Constitution made me do it." Laurence H. Tribe, *God Save This Honorable Court: How the Choice of Supreme Court Justices Shapes Our History* (New York: Random House, 1985), 57.

[5] This worry about excessive judicial power forms the basis of Sunstein's provocative idea of judicial minimalism as a response to the existence of reasonable moral disagreement in a democratic society. Cass R. Sunstein, *One Case at a Time: Judicial Minimalism on the Supreme Court* (Cambridge, MA: Harvard University Press, 1999).

decriminalization of American abortion laws to Congress or to the states.[6] At present, he or she not only has to worry that the Roberts Court will overturn *Roe* but also has to be concerned that the Court will read the Constitution in a way that advances other conservative causes, such as abolishing affirmative action, breaking down the wall between church and state, blocking campaign finance reform, and restricting the scope of gun control laws.[7] One could respond that there is the right kind of judicial activism and then there is the wrong kind of judicial activism, but a society that is used to the judicial resolution of political controversies will probably acquiesce to such activism in the pursuit of conservative ends as well.

If the relationship between Americans and judicial review is a less-than-happy marriage, then what makes divorce less attractive than it otherwise would be is the fear that without judicial oversight, America might be an even less democratic and less socially just country than it already is. Most Americans believe that the Court should conclusively adjudicate constitutional controversies.[8] Few constitutional law scholars have been willing to take a leap of faith by leaving the most important constitutional questions to the other branches of government or to the people themselves. Some of them even have urged the Court to interpret the equal protection clause to promote welfare rights.[9] That does not mean that they agree with all of the Court's decisions or find the reasoning that underlies them unproblematic. It is remarkable how uncontroversial judicial review remains in the midst of so much disagreement about what the justices should have done in the most contentious constitutional cases and so much suspicion about their motives in the wake of *Bush v. Gore*.[10] One explanation for that near consensus is that majority rule does not seem to be a fair procedure for settling conflicts concerning fundamental rights and equal protection. Americans trust legislative majorities most of the time but not all of the time. In the past, some of the most egregious mistakes of the Court have involved its failure to intervene and reinforce the principle that Americans are not at the mercy of such majorities.

Periodically, critics of particular judicial decisions indirectly attack judicial review itself. Edwin Meese once insisted that a Supreme Court decision is not legally binding because it does not establish the supreme law of the

---

[6] See, e.g., Ruth Bader Ginsburg, "Speaking in a Judicial Voice," 67 *New York University Law Review* (1992), 1208.

[7] See Jeffrey Toobin, *The Nine* (New York: Doubleday Books, 2007), 331.

[8] Larry D. Kramer, *The People Themselves: Popular Constitutionalism and Judicial Review* (New York: Oxford University Press, 2004), 228.

[9] See, e.g., Frank I. Michelman, "In Pursuit of Constitutional Welfare Rights: One View of Rawls' Theory of Justice," 121 *University of Pennsylvania Law Review* (1973), 962–1019.

[10] Richard Posner is more charitable, referring to the "rash of mistakes" that characterized the 2000 presidential election. Richard A. Posner, *Breaking the Deadlock: The 2000 Election, the Constitution, and the Courts* (Princeton, NJ: Princeton University Press, 2001), viii.

land.[11] Bork has proposed a constitutional amendment that would allow a simple majority vote in both houses of Congress to overturn any federal court decision.[12] From the opposite end of the political spectrum, Sanford Levinson has called for the creation of a new Constitution that would keep its most admirable parts but lose its most antidemocratic ones.[13] It is revealing that those who sincerely believe that judges misuse judicial review to achieve partisan results – whether they are to the right of the Warren Court or to the left of the Rehnquist or Roberts courts – cannot openly advocate its abolition. Even those who accept the claim that judges can abuse their power too easily are not likely to depart from more than two hundred years of constitutional practice. For better or for worse, divorce seems to be out of the question. There are many plausible historical explanations of what caused judicial oversight of democratic processes.[14] However, my concern is normative, that is, whether judicial review still has a place in a country like our own, and if it does, how its exercise can be improved so that judges are more likely to strike down laws that they should invalidate and uphold laws that they should not invalidate. That may sound simple enough, yet the difficulty of knowing when a judge has made the right decision lies at the core of many of the most contentious debates in normative constitutional theory.

There are at least a number of plausible approaches found in the literature, and all that anyone can do is defend a particular approach on the basis of its comparative strengths and weaknesses. Just as there is bound to be reasonable disagreement in normative political theory about correct outcomes, there is bound to be such disagreement in normative constitutional theory as well, and the harder the case, the more intractable this disagreement will be. When constitutional theorists have different but defensible ideas about the purposes of judicial review, they will not share the same ideas about how judges ought to discern constitutional meaning, and this disagreement will affect how they believe the Court should decide certain cases. Surely, Justice Scalia has a different vision of the role of courts in the American political system than, say, Justice John Paul Stevens or Justice Ruth Bader Ginsburg. The existence of this deeper disagreement may cause some of us

---

[11] Edwin Meese, "Law of the Constitution," 61 *Tulane Law Review* (1987), 983.

[12] Robert H. Bork, *Slouching towards Gomorrah: Modern Liberalism and American Decline* (New York: Regan Books, 1996), 117; Bork also writes, "[U]tterly disruptive behavior of left-liberal courts . . . doing away with judicial review altogether . . . would surely be better than our present situation." Robert H. Bork, "The Conservative Case for Amending the Constitution," *Weekly Standard*, March 3, 1977, 24.

[13] Sanford Levinson, *Our Undemocratic Constitution: Where the Constitution Goes Wrong (And How We the People Can Correct It)* (New York: Oxford University Press, 2006).

[14] There is excellent historical scholarship on this topic. See, e.g., Keith E. Whittington, *Political Foundations of Judicial Supremacy: The Presidency, the Supreme Court, and Constitutional Leadership in U.S. History* (Princeton, NJ: Princeton University Press, 2007).

to yield to skepticism, but I believe that its inevitability should not lead us to conclude that the development of a theory of constitutional adjudication is pointless or serves only to disguise partisanship. The objective is not to persuade everyone, but to provide normative guidance to judges and to those who read their opinions, and each theory has something to offer us, even if, in the end, we prefer one of its rivals. This is a challenge that theorists who have not abandoned judicial review cannot shrink from, and the theory of constitutional adjudication that they advance must explain what can be done to ensure that judges exercise the power of judicial review properly when they decide real cases.

It is reasonable to assume that there are better and worse defenses of particular theories of constitutional adjudication, and that despite reasonable disagreement about the quality of particular constitutional arguments, there are bad constitutional arguments that just about everyone would have to acknowledge as such. I doubt that anyone believes that the Constitution permits the state to abolish religious schools, to execute seven-year-olds for shoplifting, to stone to death those who are convicted of income-tax evasion, to sterilize Scientologists, to force women who fall below the poverty line to abort their fetuses to reduce future crime, to ban divorce, to take away children from their parents to prepare them for the Olympics, to criminalize adultery, or to deny driver's licenses to vegans.

Even for hypotheticals, these examples may seem to be far-fetched, but we should not overlook the consensus that would form around the easiest of easy constitutional cases. Consequently, we should be reluctant to accept claims, often advanced by political scientists, that the Constitution is an empty vessel that can be filled with whatever judges happen to put in it. Certain constitutional conclusions would make us puke, or at least feel nauseous, and that indicates that some constitutional arguments are likely to be unsound. Because I am concerned about the justification of public laws and judicial decisions and believe that it makes sense to see constitutional adjudication as a rational enterprise, I offer a normative, constructive account of American constitutional practice that is designed to cast light on some of the Court's most important constitutional decisions in the areas of fundamental rights and equal protection. Following Ronald Dworkin, I am working within what I see as best in the American constitutional tradition, and as much as possible, I am trying to avoid controversial claims about natural law like those of Michael Moore and others whose jurisprudence is metaphysically ambitious.[15] Although this tradition is diverse, my approach is recognizably liberal, antiperfectionist, and draws upon the most recent work of John Rawls and those who would have built upon his idea of public

---

[15] See, e.g., Michael Moore, "A Natural Law Theory of Interpretation," 58 *Southern California Law Review* (1985), 277–398.

reason. Whatever one thinks about liberalism, from the conservative right to the socialist left, its place in American political and constitutional history is beyond dispute.[16]

My commitment to the freedom and equality of all people aspires to be as uncontroversial as possible; it is not based upon a metaethical claim about the nature of moral reality, but rather reflects their undeniable importance in American history.[17] In the Declaration of Independence and the Gettysburg Address, Thomas Jefferson, and Abraham Lincoln appeal to freedom and equality, values that would have resonated with Americans. Since that time, at the national, state, and local levels, government has assumed a much more active role in the lives of its citizens, calling into question how limited government can be when most people expect it to perform numerous functions that would have been far from the minds of the founders. Today, there is a greater risk that the state will enact laws that infringe upon individual rights and discriminate against minorities. It may not be obvious whether the state has exceeded its constitutional authority in such instances when many Americans have grown accustomed to permitting the state to go forward with its legislative plans provided that it has sufficient popular support for them.

At the same time, the state is not supposed to force a particular conception of the good upon its citizens. As Justice Robert Jackson once eloquently put it, "If there is any fixed star in our constitutional constellation, it is that no official... can prescribe what shall be orthodox in politics, nationalism, religion, or other matters of opinion or force citizens to confess by word or act their faith therein."[18] For their theories to be taken seriously, constitutional law scholars must work within the tradition that they have inherited, but they can reconstruct that tradition in a number of plausible and interesting ways. No one who is knowledgeable about constitutional law could deny that freedom and equality have played a crucial role in the development of the meaning of the due process and equal protection clauses. It would be difficult to explain the outcomes of *Meyer v. Nebraska*, *Pierce v. Society of Sisters*, or *Lawrence v. Texas* unless one could refer to the principle that the state is not free to use whatever reasons it pleases as the basis of legislation.[19] It also would be difficult to be on the correct side

---

[16] On the diversity of the American political tradition, see Rogers Smith, *Civic Ideals: Conflicting Visions of Citizenship in U.S. History* (New Haven, CT: Yale University Press, 1997).

[17] Recently, in his value theory of democracy, Corey Brettschneider has tried to derive certain core values – political autonomy, equality of interests, and reciprocity – from the substantive or moral preconditions of self-government. See Corey Brettschneider, *Democratic Rights: The Substance of Self-Government* (Princeton, NJ: Princeton University Press, 2007).

[18] West Virginia State Board of Education v. Barnette, 319 U.S. 642 (1943).

[19] Meyer v. Nebraska, 262 U.S. 390 (1923); Pierce v. Society of Sisters, 268 U.S. 510 (1925); Lawrence v. Texas, 539 U.S. 558 (2003).

of certain cases that at present are almost universally regarded as rightly or wrongly decided – *Dred Scott*, the *Civil Rights Cases*, *Plessy*, *Lochner*, *Buck v. Bell*, *Korematsu*, and *Brown* – without reference to freedom and equality.[20]

That is not to say that at the time that they were decided, everyone was on the same side, yet it is remarkable how some decisions, which were not controversial at the time that the Court handed them down, would be considered outrageous according to current standards. In 2009 it is inconceivable that any morally literate person would advance an exclusive conception of citizenship that did not include nonwhite people and women or would insist that certain persons could be legally excluded from certain professions.[21] Almost everyone would reject the idea of separate but equal that the majority in *Plessy* relied upon in determining the meaning of equal protection of the laws in the context of racial segregation at the end of the nineteenth century. Someone who did not would unquestionably have the burden of proving that his or her underlying reasons were not racist or inegalitarian. Nor would it be easy for a defender of *Plessy* to deny the connection between state-sanctioned racial segregation and white supremacy. Similarly, the idea of freedom of contract found in the majority's opinion is *Lochner* is no longer widely accepted.[22] Some people would hesitate to see these changes in constitutional understanding as signs of moral progress, if only to avoid moral complacency in a society that still has a long way to go, but it seems that American history has settled certain constitutional questions for us.

Because certain past constitutional arguments no longer have any force, certain constitutional positions are no longer tenable. Although a few constitutional law scholars and judges might want to resurrect states' rights, undo incorporation, retract the New Deal, or restore the "lost" Constitution, certain constitutional understandings seem to be beyond reproach, and one should not be too eager to embrace an interpretive methodology that would turn contemporary constitutional practice on its head. Randy Barnett has called upon nonoriginalists to come clean by declaring whether

---

[20] William Rehnquist believed that *Dred Scott* and *Lochner* were wrongly decided as well, but he used these cases to illustrate the dangers of judicial overreach. See William H. Rehnquist, "The Notion of a Living Constitution," 54 *Texas Law Review* (1976), 700–4.

[21] As Judith Shklar writes, "The struggle for citizenship in America has . . . been overwhelmingly a demand for inclusion in the polity, an effort to break down existing barriers to recognition." Judith N. Shklar, *American Citizenship: The Quest for Inclusion* (Cambridge, MA: Harvard University Press, 1991), 3.

[22] That is not to say that there are no contemporary defenders of *Lochner*. See, e.g., Randy E. Barnett, *Restoring the Lost Constitution: The Presumption of Liberty* (Princeton, NJ: Princeton University Press, 2004), 211–18, 222–3; Richard A. Epstein, *Takings: Private Property and the Power of Eminent Domain* (Cambridge, MA: Harvard University Press, 1985), 128–9, 279–82.

they care at all about the meaning of the constitutional text.[23] In the interest of full disclosure, I will admit the following: I am sympathetic to Bruce Ackerman's view that the Constitution has been informally amended during special constitutional moments, to Laurence Tribe's idea of an invisible Constitution, and to Dworkin's notion of moral readings. Even if Barnett is correct about the initial importance of certain constitutional clauses that the Court has eviscerated over time, I do not see how we can return to a more libertarian understanding of constitutionalism in a nation that needs a strong government to provide so many essential social services.

As I see it, one of the strongest practical considerations against restoring the lost Constitution is that doing so would destabilize constitutional practice. That is not to say that just because a practice has existed that it should continue to exist, but it is to highlight the inherent difficulties of making the radical changes that fidelity to the "real" Constitution seems to call for. The text and precedent will continue to fail to constrain judicial decision making effectively, and thus a theory of constitutional interpretation must account for the likelihood that such formal constraints will never operate as intended. That fact may be regrettable, but it compels constitutional theorists to be more creative in looking for alternatives to the traditional ways of curbing judicial discretion. That is one of the reasons why I believe that an ideal of public justification should serve as the normative standard of constitutional adjudication in our country. The other reason is that any normative constitutional theory worthy of our consideration has to contain an account of how the state can be prevented from interfering with the most important personal decisions of its members without adequate justification for such interference. Obviously, there are a number of ways of specifying how this can be done, and in this book I will explain how judges can protect freedom and equality by holding lawmakers to an ideal of public justification.

That normative commitment to freedom and equality is not simply a product of my own imagination or some of the best scholarship in contemporary political theory; it also has been, and will continue to be, an important part of our constitutional tradition. In any important constitutional case, advocates do not want to concede that their position denies freedom to some people or is premised upon their inequality. It is far more difficult than it used to be for the law to treat certain people unequally on the basis of their race, ethnicity, gender, sexual orientation, immigration status, age, or mental or physical disability. After decisions like *Lawrence v. Texas*, it is no longer as easy to enact morals legislation that permits the state to criminalize behavior when it conflicts with traditional or conventional morality.[24]

---

[23] Barnett, *Restoring the Lost Constitution*, 356–7.
[24] Lawrence v. Texas, 539 U.S. 558 (2003).

The foregoing does not change the fact, though, that beyond widespread agreement on the importance of values like freedom and equality in the abstract, there is insufficient agreement on how judges ought to specify their meaning in real cases.[25] People who claim to adhere to the same principle may have very different ideas about its implications. Thus, disagreement seems to be an inescapable part of the dynamics of constitutional argumentation. The very need for constitutionalism itself is partly rooted in disagreement "about how common moral principles are to be applied correctly."[26] This disagreement in real constitutional cases is not only likely to be sincere but also likely to be reasonable in the sense that opposing sides will have good reasons that support their respective positions. Any theory of constitutional adjudication that does not take seriously the problem of reasonable disagreement will be of little use in the resolution of real constitutional controversies.

B. The Specter of Indeterminacy

The status of judicial review is arguably the most important issue in American constitutional theory and is linked to perennial worries about the objectivity or correctness of judicial decisions.[27] As Owen Fiss writes, "Objectivity implies that the interpretation can be judged by something other than one's own notions of correctness."[28] If there really is no way to identify a correct judicial decision, then it is not evident why a society like our own hands over so much power to unelected judges on the assumption that they are better equipped than the rest of us to make constitutional choices. The justification of judicial review, then, would seem to turn on two claims, either of which could be false: (1) there are more justified answers to constitutional questions, and (2) assuming that the former is true, judges are less likely to make mistakes than others are. All of this may sound unnecessarily esoteric, and most Americans are more familiar with these theoretical questions and care more about them when they manifest themselves in concrete constitutional controversies. Disagreement between liberals and conservatives over the proper scope of judicial review overlaps with disagreement about how judges should understand constitutional language. For conservative critics of liberal judicial activism, to misread or to ignore the plain meaning of a

---

[25] George Klosko writes that "abstract principles to which people subscribe actually contain numerous tacit qualifications, though people may not be aware of this until they face uncomfortable situations." George Klosko, *Democratic Procedures and Liberal Consensus* (New York: Oxford University Press, 2000), 57.

[26] Larry A. Alexander, "Constitutionalism," in *The Blackwell Guide to the Philosophy of Law and Legal Theory*, ed. Martin P. Golding and William A. Edmundson (Malden, MA: Blackwell Publishing, 2005), 248.

[27] On the latter point, see Robert W. Bennett, "Objectivity in Constitutional Law," 132 *University of Pennsylvania Law Review* (1984), 445.

[28] Owen W. Fiss, "Objectivity and Interpretation," 34 *Stanford Law Review* (1982), 744.

constitutional provision is to abuse judicial power. In almost everything that he has written since his defeat in 1987, Bork has accused liberal judges of not applying law but of imposing their own elitist values upon America.[29]

The problem with this line of criticism, despite its rhetorical appeal to many conservatives, is that it is not obvious what it means to ascertain the meaning of the constitutional text in hard cases. It also may not be clear, then, when a judge has deliberately ignored or simply misunderstood one of its provisions.[30] Although semantic constraints exist in easy cases, where constitutional law is more or less determinate, they disappear in more difficult cases when judges must specify the implications of abstract constitutional language. The less specific the constitutional language is, the more difficult the constitutional judgment is bound to be. As Richard Posner has written, "Legalism does exist, and so not *everything* is permitted. But its kingdom has shrunk and grayed to the point where today it is largely limited to routine cases, and so a great deal is permitted to judges."[31] In *The Concept of Law*, H. L. A. Hart traces the indeterminacy of legal rules to two sources: "our relative ignorance of fact," in that we cannot foresee all of the possible applications of a rule when we formulate it, and "our relative indeterminacy of aim," where unforeseen empirical features can change the aim of the applicable rule.[32] As one commentator explains, "Judicial discretion is inevitable, according to Hart, because it is impossible for social acts to pick out standards that resolve every conceivable question."[33]

Because legal rules have an open texture, fair-minded people will dispute their meaning in borderline cases, and judges will have to use their discretion to fill in the gaps between those rules and the empirical world to settle their meaning until the next borderline case comes along. The preceding observation also covers constitutional rules and principles. Even self-described textualists cannot answer every constitutional question only by consulting the words and then deducing a legal conclusion from a legal premise. For instance, the First Amendment refers to "abridging the freedom of speech," but it does not specify what speech consists of or what would constitute an abridgment of speech, and it does not include any examples. If Posner, Hart,

---

[29] See, e.g., Robert H. Bork, *Coercing Virtue: The Worldwide Rule of Judges* (Washington D.C.: AEI Press, 2003), 8–9.

[30] As Frederick Schauer observes, "For before we can argue intelligently about whether to go outside of the text, we ought to explore the meaning of the words *inside* the text. Only then will we know what counts as going 'outside.'" Frederick Schauer, "An Essay on Constitutional Language," 29 *UCLA Law Review* (1982), 797.

[31] Richard A. Posner, *How Judges Think* (Cambridge, MA: Harvard University Press, 2008), 1.

[32] H. L. A. Hart, *The Concept of Law*, 2nd ed. (New York: Oxford University Press, 1961), 125.

[33] Scott J. Shapiro, "The 'Hart-Dworkin' Debate: A Short Guide for the Perplexed," in *Ronald Dworkin*, ed. Arthur Ripstein (New York: Cambridge University Press, 2007), 30.

and many others are right about the necessity of judicial discretion, then the constitutional text and the case law that has supplemented its meaning over time are underdetermined with respect to the most important constitutional questions.[34] As Frederick Schauer puts it, "Constitutional language can tell us when we have gone too far without telling us anything else."[35] Nor can resorting to the case law solve the problem, as Schauer writes, because "it is clear that the relevance of an earlier precedent depends upon how we characterize the facts arising in the earlier case."[36] In hard cases, text and precedent will not yield unique, clearly correct answers even though they rule out many possible answers.[37]

At most, these formal constraints serve as a starting point, but they cannot do the intellectual work that must be done to answer a challenging constitutional question. Even if the Constitution is not wholly open ended, because words have core meanings, it may be so indeterminate so often that one might wonder whether most constitutional decisions can ever be legitimate. If the law does not constrain judges in hard cases, then there is no rule of law, and judges simply legislate and subject the population at best to their considered judgments and at worst to their whims. In addition, no method of constitutional interpretation can ensure good faith on the part of those who employ it.[38] At the point of application, judges must close the gap between abstract constitutional clauses, such as due process and equal protection, and the particular facts of the case, but they cannot look to the text or to the case law for assistance.[39] That is why the development of an explanation of what a judge is supposed to do in such circumstances is so imperative. That

---

[34] For a helpful distinction between the "indeterminacy" and "underdeterminacy" of the law, see Lawrence B. Solum, "Pluralism and Public Legal Reason," 15 *William and Mary Bill of Rights Journal* (2006), 19–20.

[35] Schauer, "An Essay on Constitutional Language," 828.

[36] Frederick Schauer, "Precedent," *Stanford Law Review* (February 1987), 577.

[37] See Steven J. Burton, *Judging in Good Faith* (New York: Cambridge University Press, 1992), xii; Kermit Roosevelt III, *The Myth of Judicial Activism: Making Sense of Supreme Court Decisions* (New Haven, CT: Yale University Press, 2006), 16, 19.

[38] Sotiros A. Barber and James E. Fleming, *Constitutional Interpretation: The Basic Questions* (New York: Oxford University Press, 2007), 115.

[39] Keith Whittington distinguishes between constitutional interpretation, which is "essentially legalistic" and where meaning is discovered, and constitutional construction, which is "essentially political" and where meaning is constructed because that part of the constitutional text has no discoverable meaning with respect to the constitutional question at hand. He also distinguishes both constitutional interpretation and constitutional construction from constitutional creation, where new constitutional meaning is invented. Such creation amends the constitutional text through creating a new authoritative meaning even when the Constitution has not been formally amended. Constitutional constructions or creations should only become part of the Constitution, he writes, when they have been "ratified by the sovereign people and formally embedded in the supreme law." Keith E. Whittington, *Constitutional Interpretation: Textual Meaning, Original Intent, and Judicial Review* (Lawrence: University Press of Kansas, 1999), 7–12.

discretion does not mean that judges can use whichever reasons they happen to prefer. Despite their deep differences, both originalists and nonoriginalists believe that judges who act in good faith must limit themselves to certain reasons in the decision-making process even when those reasons lead to a result that they dislike. What should concern us is not that most judges have the wrong motives but that they may be sincerely incorporating the wrong kinds of reasons into their constitutional decisions.

Nevertheless, some conservative critics of liberal judicial activism continue to accuse so-called activist judges of acting in bad faith. In response to Justice William Brennan's famous remark that originalism is "little more than arrogance cloaked in humility," Steven Calabresi writes that "[i]t would . . . be arrogant to discard [the constitutional] text in the name of instead following the teachings of *Future Shock* or *The Greening of America*."[40]

That caricature is a classic example of the false choice that some conservatives use when trying to establish that those who adhere to nonoriginalist theories of constitutional adjudication must be legislating from the bench: either judges are legitimately drawing an inference from the constitutional text or they are relying upon illegitimate reasons, namely their own partisan convictions, in deciding a case. Not only does this characterization oversimplify judging, but it also misleads the public into believing that if judges are not reading the Constitution narrowly, then they must be improvising. The debate over judicial restraint and judicial activism is much more complicated than interpreting the Constitution or ignoring it to reach a preferred outcome on nonlegal grounds. As one scholar remarks, "The debate should thus not be over activism versus nonactivism but rather over what kind of activism . . . is acceptable."[41] When the implications of a particular constitutional provision are not self-evident, one should not necessarily conclude that a judicial opinion that recognizes a right that is not explicitly spelled out in the constitutional text is obviously poorly reasoned or disingenuous. Many of the most important constitutional rights are unenumerated, and it is at least arguable that abstract constitutional language and precedent imply them.

II. A FEW WORDS ON ORIGINALISM

A. Overview

Sophisticated constitutional theorists reject the foregoing oversimplification between interpreting and legislating and recognize the inadequacies of a

---

[40] Steven G. Calabresi, "Introduction: A Critical Introduction to the Originalism Debate," in *Originalism: A Quarter-Century of Debate*, ed. Steven G. Calabresi (Washington D.C.: Regnery Publishing, 2007), 10.

[41] Jeffrie G. Murphy and Jules L. Coleman, *Philosophy of Law: An Introduction to Jurisprudence*, rev. ed. (New York: Westview Press, 1990), 36.

literalist or strict constructionist interpretive methodology. Even though such a method would be more viable if the Constitution were more detailed and contained concrete examples of correct applications, borderline or hard cases will still arise. The real issue, then, is what counts as a legitimate constitutional construction.[42] As Barnett writes, "There is nothing illicit about construing [sic] the Constitution. Given the limits of interpretation, construction is inevitable and the Constitution would not long survive without it."[43] When judges must supplement the constitutional text when its terms are vague or ambiguous, there are at least a number of plausible ways of filling the gaps, and originalism is one well-known way of doing so.

Everyone agrees that the Constitution ought to be thought of as a set of instructions that provides guidance for interpreters in specifying the limits of the power of the state. For instance, whether a punishment is cruel and unusual for constitutional purposes would require the judge to decide whether the punishment in question, such as executing juveniles or the mentally retarded, falls into the category of "cruel and unusual."[44] Originalists and nonoriginalists disagree, though, over the best way of following these instructions, and originalists will want to prevent the interpreter from basing the decision on his or her own convictions of political morality and not on those that are embodied either in the constitutional text as it was originally understood or in traditional morality.[45]

Like most other originalists, Bork seeks to restrict the scope of judicial review to minimize the likelihood that judges will usurp the power of lawmaking bodies.[46] In his scholarly writings, one of his aims is to demonstrate that original understanding is the only possible means through which judicial review, which is an antimajoritarian practice, can be squared with democratic self-rule. Judges who invent constitutional meaning and then strike down a statute on the basis of that invention illegitimately make a political decision that ought to be left to the people or their elected representatives. The inferences that the judge draws in reaching constitutional conclusions, Bork believes, must come from premises that are clearly spelled out in the constitutional text or are rooted in the specific intentions of the framers when constitutional provisions must be supplemented.[47]

---

[42] On the difference between interpretation and construction, see Barnett, *Restoring Our Lost Constitution*, esp. 118–30.

[43] Ibid., 128.

[44] Roper v. Simmons, 543 U.S. 551 (2005); Atkins v. Virginia, 536 U.S. 304 (2002).

[45] James B. Staab, *The Political Thought of Justice Antonin Scalia: A Hamiltonian on the Supreme Court* (Lanham, MD: Rowman and Littlefield Publishers, 2006), xx.

[46] Bork, "Neutral Principles and Some First Amendment Problems," 35.

[47] Ibid., 13, 17.

Justice Scalia has a similar approach to constitutional adjudication. As one commentator observes, his "original meaning" approach to constitutional interpretation is best described in terms of text and tradition.[48] The judge must apply the textual meaning of the constitutional language when that language is clear, and thus must pay close attention to the plain meaning of the words.[49] For instance, the Eighth Amendment prohibits "cruel and unusual punishments," not "cruel or unusual punishments" or "cruel and unusual wars." Here, Scalia is on the firm ground of linguistic practice. Surely, when those words were written, their authors had something in mind, and when others ratified those words, they meant something to the ratifiers as well. When constitutional language is not sufficiently clear, the judge must apply "the specific legal tradition flowing from that text" and ask how the society that adopted those words would have understood them.[50] For Scalia, that the constitutional prohibition on cruel and unusual punishment would not have covered capital punishment in the late eighteenth century is a definitive reason for not reading that clause to bar the death penalty today.

In such instances, judges should try to discover the original meaning of the words in question by recovering their original linguistic context. As such, their role is that of a linguistic historian. As one scholar has explained, that is not the same as trying to discern the original authorial intent.[51] As Scalia remarked during his confirmation hearing in 1986, "What I look for in the Constitution is precisely what I look for in a statute: the original meaning of the text, not what the original draftsmen intended."[52] Those who ratified the Constitution endorsed its public meaning, not the intentions of its authors. The subjective intentions of individual framers are no more legally relevant than the subjective intention of a person who enters into a contract but has an idiosyncratic understanding of its terms. Those who live under the Constitution are bound by the meaning of what was written, not by what some or even all of the framers intended those words to mean when they put them down on paper. Their mental states are relevant only insofar as they might clarify the meaning of words or phrases that were vague or ambiguous at the time of their adoption. The objective is not to eliminate judicial discretion but to reduce the likelihood that judges will be able to substitute their own political convictions for those of the people who lived at the time of the enactment of the constitutional provision in question.[53]

---

[48] Ralph A. Rossum, *Antonin Scalia's Jurisprudence: Text and Tradition* (Lawrence: University Press of Kansas, 2006).

[49] Ibid., 2.

[50] Ibid.

[51] Ibid., 21–2.

[52] Ibid.

[53] Antonin Scalia, "Originalism: The Lesser Evil," 57 *Cincinnati Law Review* (1989), 864.

B. Critique

In a number of well-known cases, Scalia has encountered the inherent diffi-culty of comparing and contrasting the past and the present.[54] The trouble is not necessarily that so much time has passed that it is impossible to discover the original meaning of a particular constitutional provision. On the contrary, excellent scholarship over the past twenty years has illumi-nated the original meaning of some of the most important parts of the Constitution.[55] Rather, it is not clear how an originalist judge is supposed to translate past constitutional meanings into the present without relying upon his or her own convictions of political morality. Because a consti-tutional question cannot frame itself, even originalist judges must develop their own understanding of the constitutional relevance of the particulars of the cases that they must decide.[56] Judges can describe a fact pattern in at least a number of plausible ways, and past constitutional understandings do not force them to emphasize some features of the case over others when those understandings themselves are open to interpretation. For example, they must determine whether burning a flag or a cross counts as speech or whether a policy that has a disproportionate impact upon a racial minority triggers equal protection clause analysis.

In a common law system, if there is an earlier case that is sufficiently similar to the case at hand and one set of reasons had outweighed the other set in that earlier case, then a person can argue that consistency dictates the same result in the present case. Still, that person would have to show that the two cases compared have sufficiently similar material facts to be analogous. The harder the case, the more likely there will be at least one plausible counterargument that supports the conclusion that the two cases in question are not sufficiently similar. We ought to expect new cases to differ in some respects from previous cases and for the strength of reasons to vary according to their context and the extent to which they are stronger or weaker in combination with other reasons. Although fairness requires that judges treat like cases alike, the unique details of new cases almost always put into some doubt whether an earlier case is sufficiently similar to the case at hand. The trick is to determine when two cases are close enough in the relevant respects to warrant the same kind of treatment. Judges have a great deal of work to do, then, in figuring out whether two cases are truly analogous.

---

[54] Texas v. Johnson, 491 U.S. 397 (1989); R.A.V. v. City of St. Paul, 505 U.S. 377 (1992); Virginia v. Black, 538 U.S. 343 (2003); see, e.g., his dissent in Grutter v. Bollinger, 539 U. S. 306 (2003).

[55] See, e.g., Barnett, *Restoring Our Lost Constitution*, esp. 153–334.

[56] As H. L. A. Hart once wrote, "Particular fact-situations do not await us already marked off from each other, and labeled as instances of a general rule, the application of which is in question; nor can the rule itself step forward to claim its own instances." Hart, *The Concept of Law*, 123.

When judges or lawyers appeal to precedent, they claim that the previous rationale for treating A in one manner is a good-enough reason for treating a subsequent case B in the same manner. The relevance of an earlier precedent depends on how the judge characterizes the material facts of the earlier case. No two appellate cases are factually identical down to the last detail, but they may be sufficiently similar in the relevant legal respects for a judge to decide that the holding of a previous case also controls the new case. Although more carefully drafted rules will make applications easier, few people think that the solution to the problem is for judges to try to address every contingency in their opinions. In some respects, the holding of each case is tied to the particular facts of the case, and in the future, other judges will have to determine how fact-specific that particular holding is, especially in borderline cases. As Immanuel Kant pointed out long ago, a rule cannot contain additional rules for its application in all of the circumstances in which it is possibly applicable.[57] At some point, rules run out, and at times, they also must be qualified, and that requires judgment on the part of the person who is trying to apply that rule in particular circumstances. The need for judgment arises in the first place because of doubt about how rules should be applied.[58]

It may not be obvious, but originalists also engage in a type of analogical reasoning when they attempt to translate the past into the present. Upon closer examination, this kind of reasoning is crucial to the soundness of any originalist argument. Surely, the original meaning of any constitutional provision would have included at least some exemplary cases. At the time of ratification of the Constitution, most people would have understood certain constitutional words to cover some cases and not others. Without such exemplary cases, their agreement on constitutional meaning would have been a mere consensus on words. The execution of someone by the electric chair may not be the contemporary equivalent of burning that person at the stake, but an originalist has considerable discretion in determining the relevant similarities and differences between the exemplary punishments on the original list and the punishment in question. Even if the founders had wanted that list to be exhaustive, until the Constitution was amended, and even if they had wanted future interpreters to apply the clause banning cruel and unusual punishments as narrowly as possible, an originalist judge still has to analogize the punishment at issue to those on the list, decide whether it would fall within the original meaning, and be able to defend that comparison effectively. Unless exactly the same punishment in question

---

[57] Immanuel Kant, "Theory and Practice," in *Kant's Political Writings*, ed. Hans Reiss, trans. H.B. Nisbet (New York: Cambridge University Press, 1994), 61.
[58] Richard B. Miller, *Casuistry and Modern Ethics: A Poetry of Practical Reasoning* (Chicago: University of Chicago Press, 1996), 18.

is on the original list, he or she will have to figure out whether it is close enough to anything else on the list.

Thus, one might not be convinced that originalists, who claim that they are merely applying past understandings to a contemporary constitutional problem, are really doing so, even if they are competent linguistic historians. When judges must determine the constitutionality of an affirmative action plan, they must determine whether that plan denies certain people equal protection of the laws. In formulating an answer, originalists could look for analogues, the mid-nineteenth century functional equivalents of affirmative action plans. Originalists are hesitant to admit that they must make the same sorts of normative choices as nonoriginalists, because such an admission would call into question the most significant ostensible advantage of originalism as a theory of constitutional interpretation: it does a superior job of limiting the discretion of judges when they decide constitutional cases, and thus of preventing the abuse of judicial power.

Justices who have no view of the purposes of judicial review are like nominees who have no view of *Roe v. Wade*: either they are not qualified to serve on the Court or they are not being honest with us. Justice Scalia adheres to a particular normative political theory that underwrites his originalism.[59] With respect to civil rights, he is preoccupied with preventing "backsliding" where the other branches of the federal government or state governments take away constitutional rights.[60] There is nothing politically neutral about Scalia's approach to constitutional interpretation. Over and over again, he makes deliberate choices based on his own best understanding of the political values that are exemplified in the American political tradition, and like Bork, he believes that the state usually has the authority to do whatever it wants to do. This trend would not be problematic for nonoriginalist judges who are candid about their convictions of political morality. But as one scholar notes, "[If] Scalia's jurisprudence is guided by Hamiltonian political principles, [t]hen Scalia is not the neutral robot that he sometimes portrays himself as."[61] Scalia's originalism makes it far more difficult for judges to recognize or create new rights.[62] Undeniably, this is a value choice, and he cannot be faulted for that, but he can be criticized for not being sufficiently self-aware about how his deeper convictions have affected and will continue to affect his constitutional decision making.

A constitutional question involving racial discrimination that arose under the equal protection clause in the late nineteenth century may raise a comparable moral concern today, but it is not the same constitutional question when the material facts differ. It is peculiar to think that a constitutional

---

[59] Staab, *Political Thought of Justice Antonin Scalia*.

[60] Rossum, *Antonin Scalia's Jurisprudence*, 137.

[61] Staab, *The Political Thought of Justice Antonin Scalia*, xxx.

[62] Ibid., xix–xx.

question involving such discrimination that arose more than one hundred years ago is the same question that arises today or in the future. At most, such a question is similar inasmuch as it falls under the general principle that discriminating against people on the basis of a morally irrelevant characteristic such as race is wrong. But surely, the kind of racism that existed in America after the Civil War differs in kind from the sort of racism that exists today. Scalia has a point that we have at least some ability to figure out what people in 1791 or in 1868 thought about the meaning of particular constitutional provisions, but that ability is much less helpful than it initially appears to be. The real question for originalists involves the similarity of the present case to those of the past, and they should not beg the question by assuming that a contemporary constitutional question is close enough to a past constitutional question for original meaning to provide an answer.

Since the founding of the country, there have been momentous political, economic, and social changes in the United States. For nonoriginalists, this state of affairs is not problematic because they are comfortable with the idea that constitutional meaning must evolve over time in adapting to new circumstances. By contrast, originalists are bound by the fixed meaning of the Constitution, and in discerning its present-day implications, they must decide what is relevantly similar and relevantly different between the past and the present. They have to figure out what the constitutional provision in question, which is frozen in time, originally meant. That means that they must investigate what sorts of cases most people of that time would have thought those words covered. For example, the meaning of cruel and unusual punishment probably would have covered medieval torture techniques. One way to understand how original meaning is fixed is to assume that almost everyone of that time would have seen the clause as banning certain punishments even if there were borderline cases that would not have commanded consensus. The original meaning, then, is near unanimity on exemplary cases. With reference to those cases, someone who searches for original meaning can try to determine whether the punishment in question would have fallen under "cruel and unusual."

For historians of early American history, perhaps the most serious intellectual challenge is to understand the world of the founders as they understood it without projecting contemporary meaning on it. Because of the passage of so much time, I believe that the burden of proof is on the originalist to demonstrate that the practice in question is the equivalent of a past practice for constitutional purposes. Thus, originalists must also must compare and contrast the case in front of them to the cases that were on the original list of cruel and unusual punishments. A judge cannot simply conclude that "because it's not on the original list, it's not banned," because that would beg the question; it may not be evident whether that punishment really is on the list. An originalist may be right that hanging someone today is close enough to hanging someone more than two hundred years ago but that person still has to formulate an analogical argument that supports that conclusion.[63]

Nonetheless, originalists like Bork and Scalia implicitly assume that most important contemporary constitutional questions are the same or at least sufficiently similar so that an appeal to original understanding can answer them. No originalists would deny that the world has changed, but they will deny that the meaning of the Constitution has changed. That would not be so troubling if they were historians whose only task was to discern the original meaning of a particular constitutional provision, but as judges, they must specify its implications in a very different context. Although Scalia admits that the "greatest defect" of originalism is "the difficulty of applying it correctly," he characterizes this difficulty as a matter of understanding an ancient text, as if interpreters did not have to apply its parts in contemporary circumstances.[64] In his mind, an originalist judge faces the same methodological difficulties that a historian would face. However, this is false. A judge is not a historian; a judge must apply constitutional provisions to particular circumstances, and as a result, the difficulties that the judge encounters will be those of casuistry.

It does not make a lot of sense to insist that a judge could engage in a thought experiment in which he or she would travel back in time and speculate about what the founders intended a particular constitutional provision to mean. As Barnett has pointed out, originalists have shifted from original intention to original meaning.[65] They no longer concern themselves with what the framers intended the language of the Constitution to mean when they put those words down on paper. Instead, they focus on what those words would have meant to most people in that particular linguistic context. According to Barnett, this shift has rendered originalism less vulnerable to some of the "most telling practical objections to originalism."[66] For the sake of argument, let us imagine that new historical evidence emerges that proves beyond a shadow of a doubt that all people of that period would have understood the implications of each abstract constitutional provision in exactly the same way.[67] Would this discovery be the Holy Grail for originalists? Would there be anything left to be said on behalf of any nonoriginalist approach?

[63] Analogical reasoning is more complicated than it may seem to be. See Hilary Putnam, *The Many Faces of Realism* (LaSalle, IL: Open Court Publishing, 1987), 73.

[64] Scalia, "Originalism: The Lesser Evil," 856.

[65] Barnett, *Restoring the Lost Constitution*, 92. See also Antonin Scalia, *A Matter of Interpretation* (Princeton, NJ: Princeton University Press, 1997), 16–18, 37–8.

[66] Barnett, *Restoring the Lost Constitution*, 93.

[67] This is what Dworkin refers to as "expectations originalism." See Dworkin, "Comment," in Scalia, *A Matter of Interpretation*, 116.

Such a discovery would not end the debate between originalists and nonoriginalists, nor would it be nearly as significant as it might appear to be. In effect, historical approaches to constitutional adjudication ask the judge to imagine how people in a particular time and place would have decided a particular contemporary case. Historical investigations into past understandings of constitutional meaning may be of some use, but they cannot take the place of the judgment that a judge must exercise in trying to solve a contemporary constitutional problem. Originalists turn to history to limit themselves to the reasons that the founders or their generation would have shared to curb their own discretion and to minimize the abuse of judicial power. As Bork once wrote in an opinion, "[It] is the task of the judge in this generation to discern how the framers' values, defined in the context of the world that they knew, apply to the world we know."[68]

The trouble is that Bork does not specify what this act of judgment consists of, and this claim is crucial to his version of originalism and originalism more generally. Even if history can illuminate how narrow that constitutional principle in question is supposed to be, the judge still has to apply that principle to circumstances that the founders did not foresee. Suppose that the equal protection clause encapsulated a narrow antidiscrimination principle that was limited to African American men and an originalist judge were asked to apply it today. It is true that, compared with a broader principle like "the state shall not discriminate against anyone on the basis of race or any other morally irrelevant characteristic," it seems that the former principle would be easier to apply, but that would turn on the particulars of the case. If the judge has to determine the constitutionality of a particular affirmative action plan, he or she still has to make a both a factual and moral judgment about the nature of discrimination at issue and determine whether it falls under equal protection of the laws. Is preferential treatment of African American men by the Freedmen's Bureau during Reconstruction the constitutional equivalent of using race as a plus factor in medical school admissions?[69] Those kinds of questions will be more complicated in some cases than in others, but even a relatively narrow principle still will have plenty of borderline applications.

The trouble with originalism does not end here. Even if an originalist establishes the implications of the original meaning of the particular constitutional provision in question with sufficient historical evidence, he or she still has to be worried about the results that such a method would produce in certain cases. It is extremely hard to ignore how someone could use a semiautomatic weapon in a mass killing today in a way that a person in

---

[68] Ollman v. Evans, 750 F.2d 970, 995 (D.C. Cir. 1984).
[69] On the history of this period, see Eric Foner, *Reconstruction: America's Unfinished Revolution 1863–1877* (New York: Harper Collins Publishers, 1988), esp. 124–75.

the late eighteenth century could never have used a musket.[70] Whatever a person thinks of the rationale of the Court's recent decision in *District of Columbia v. Heller*, which established a constitutional right to individual ownership of handguns, that person has to question the wisdom of a decision that will probably make it much more difficult for the states to reduce crime and handgun-related violence, especially in the most dangerous neighborhoods.[71] It would be difficult to take someone seriously who insists that the equal protection clause of the Fourteenth Amendment still permits racially restrictive covenants, racially segregated public schools, bans on interracial marriage, or the barring of women from the practice of law simply due to the fact that its authors and ratifiers or most people in 1868 thought that equal protection of the laws did not cover such cases. That might explain why originalists go to such great lengths to show how *Brown v. Board of Education* can be defended on originalist grounds.[72]

An originalist judge not only travels back in time but also returns to the present and is supposed to apply the values of a specific historical period to contemporary constitutional problems.[73] But it is not evident how a judge is supposed to conduct this thought experiment. Is the judge supposed to imagine how a representative person of that period would have applied those past values to the present? If so, does that person know how our world has changed since that time? Can judges be confident that their interpretations of the past do not reflect how they would like to see it? These questions are important because originalists cannot concede that judges must look beyond how most people would have understood the words in question in their original linguistic context and still maintain their fidelity to an interpretive approach that purports to be independent of the judge's convictions of political morality.

---

[70] As Cass Sunstein puts it, with respect to the right to bear arms, "it is extremely hard to think our way back into a world in which standing armies seem a major threat to liberty and in which state militias are an indispensable safeguard." Cass R. Sunstein, "The Most Mysterious Right," review of *Why the Constitution Can't End the Battle over Guns*, by Mark Tushnet, *New Republic*, November 19, 2007, 46. Richard Posner makes a similar point: "The Framers of the Bill of Rights could not have been thinking of the crime problem in the large crime-ridden metropolises of twenty-first century America." Richard A, Posner, "In Defense of Looseness: The Supreme Court and Gun Control," *New Republic*, August 27, 2008, 33.

[71] District of Columbia v. Heller, 554 U.S. __, 128 S. Ct. 2783, 171 L. Ed. 2d 637 (2008).

[72] See, e.g., Robert H. Bork, *The Tempting of America: The Political Seduction of the Law* (New York: Simon and Schuster, 1990), 82; Michael McConnell, "Originalism and the Desegregation Decisions," 81 *Virginia Law Review* (1995), 947. For Ronald Dworkin's criticism of Bork's attempt to ground *Brown* in originalism, see Ronald Dworkin, "The Bork Nomination," *New York Review of Books*, August 13, 1987, 3, 6, 8, 10.

[73] Michael McConnell explicitly recognizes the need for judgment and therefore believes that the originalist judge must adopt the mind-set of the framers. See, e.g., Michael W. McConnell, "On Reading the Constitution," 73 *Cornell Law Review* (1988), 359.

Much more often than not, the principles that the founders left us will provide little or no guidance. That is so because the context of constitutional questions inevitably changes over time. As Barnett concedes, in practice, it may be very difficult to sharply distinguish between "construction" and "interpretation."[74] Even if a person is unsympathetic to the idea of a living constitution, he or she has to concede that judges cannot ignore what we now know about our world when they frame and answer constitutional questions. If we were to learn that lethal injection causes the person to be executed to suffer intolerable pain, and that that pain is much worse than anything that the framers or their generation had ever contemplated, then that fact would be undeniably relevant in determining the constitutionality of that mode of execution. Originalists cannot be content with knowing which particular punishments most people in 1791 would have considered covered by those words when they must decide whether the method of execution, such as the electric chair, the gas chamber, hanging, firing squad, or lethal injection, are cruel and unusual today. The point is not only that some of those methods did not exist at the founding of the country but also that, at best, hanging someone in 1791 is a remote cousin of hanging someone in 2008. The physical act is the same, but its moral meaning could be, and probably is, different. Scalia concedes this point when he confesses that he may be a "faint-hearted" originalist for being unwilling to uphold a fictional law that imposes the punishment of flogging.[75]

For originalists, a dead American Constitution is supposed to fix constitutional meaning, but even Scalia has been forced to acknowledge the weakness of this view in certain constitutional cases. In *Kyllo v. United States*, the Court had to decide whether a federal agent's use of a thermal-imaging device at 3:20 A.M. from across the street to measure the heat emanating from inside a home to detect the use of halide lights to grow marijuana indoors was a "search" under the Fourth Amendment.[76] Although the device detected only heat radiating from the surface of the home and lasted only a few minutes, Scalia concluded that the use of such a device was a search because the homeowners' reasonable expectation of privacy had been violated. As he wrote, "This assures preservation of that degree of privacy against government that existed when the Fourth Amendment was adopted."[77]

It would have been pointless to investigate whether the original meaning of search included thermal imaging because that kind of technology did not

---

[74] Barnett, *Restoring Our Lost Constitution*, 128.

[75] What bothers him is that most people in 1789 would not have considered flogging cruel and unusual punishment, and thus, even today, an originalist who is not faint-hearted must allow the state to impose such a punishment if it wishes to do so. Scalia, "Originalism: The Lesser Evil," 864.

[76] Kyllo v. United States, 533 U.S. 27 (2001).

[77] Ibid., 34.

exist in 1789. This example indicates that even Scalia must exercise his own judgment in closing the gap between the century of the founders and our own and ask how the framers would have seen this kind of physical intrusion by the government into the interior of a private residence. What else could he have done but engage in this sort of thought experiment? This problem is not limited to the preceding case but cuts to the heart of what is wrong with originalism more generally. Here, whether he realizes it or not, Scalia has yielded a crucial point to his critics; namely, judges are not bound by the original list that specified the particular kinds of searches that required a warrant when the Fourth Amendment was conceived. This is not simply an instance in which the original meaning could not be divined. The more serious problem is that this is true of other constitutional questions as well because all of them are new in important respects when their context changes.

The original meaning of the Constitution is not its contemporary meaning, even though the two meanings may overlap, and the fact that judges must apply its provisions drives home this point. The Constitution is not simply a political text to be interpreted, like Thomas Hobbes's *Leviathan* or Edmund Burke's *Reflections on the Revolution in France*. When someone teaches an introductory course in political theory, he or she may ask students what John Locke would have thought about a particular contemporary political issue, such as accommodating religious differences. Usually, the purpose of such a question is to stimulate a critical response on the part of the students by having them draw inferences from Locke's *First Letter Concerning Toleration* in helping them to formulate their own interpretations of the text and to recognize its contemporary significance. When a professor poses such a question, however, he or she is not really asking whether it is possible to find a modern-day multiculturalist inside of a seventeenth-century political thinker like Locke. Some of Locke's arguments for tolerance may be as relevant today as they were in the past, but Locke simply did not have a view about whether Amish parents have a right not to send their children to public school past the eighth grade.[78]

My point is not that the meaning of political ideas can never transcend their historical context. Political and constitutional theorists can use the ideas of the past as a resource in addressing the problems of the present, but it would be arrogant of them to assert that they were speaking for Locke or could have read his mind. At best, they can speculate about what Locke would have thought, which is one way of thinking about the implications of Lockean arguments for toleration in a world that is far removed from that of Locke. What they would be doing is giving their best interpretation

---

[78] Wisconsin v. Yoder, 406 U.S. 205 (1972). However, according to Martha Nussbaum, Locke was not in favor of accommodating or making exceptions for religious minorities. See Martha C. Nussbaum, *Liberty of Conscience: In Defense of America's Tradition of Religious Equality* (New York: Basic Books, 2008), 122.

of Locke's or Lockean ideas and applying them to circumstances that Locke would not have anticipated or fully understood. There is nothing wrong with their doing so, provided that they are sufficiently aware of and candid about their own intellectual contribution in the presentation of those ideas that are, in the end, their own.

At present, for a variety of reasons, the vast majority of constitutional law scholars and judges are not convinced that historical understandings can limit judicial discretion in the manner that most originalists claim that they can. That is not to say that respectable defenses of originalism do not exist, like those of Barnett and Keith Whittington, or that people do not have other normative reasons for adopting an approach to constitutional adjudication that tries to "lock in" constitutional meaning.[79] Whittington admits that originalism is unlikely to provide the kind of constraints that originalists desire because originalist judges are likely to face the "same difficulties and temptations" as nonoriginalist judges.[80] As I have tried to show here, though, the problem is not that judges often act in bad faith. Instead, the responsibility of choosing wisely is on their shoulders. Thus, a judge should not make the discovery of original meaning more significant than it really is, not because words have no core meaning or because historical understandings are always elusive, but because the primary task of the interpreter is to apply a narrow or broad constitutional principle to new circumstances. The most interesting, important, and divisive constitutional cases will call for what Barnett and Whittington refer to as "construction" or "creation" – when the judge must extend or decline to extend the scope of a given constitutional provision in a new factual context – and the more time that passes, the more different that context will be.[81]

Originalism is like a vampire that cannot be killed, no matter how many stakes its critics drive through its heart. It may be a mistake to read too much into the Senate's rejection of Robert Bork, whose "nomination was a crucial test of originalism as an approach to constitutional interpretation,"[82] and it is unlikely that nonspecialists understand its content. A return to such an approach is problematic because constitutional judgment requires a substantial conceptual contribution from the judge. I do not expect anything that I have just said to convince any committed originalist of the error of his or her ways, but I hope to have demonstrated that applying the original meaning

---

[79] See, e.g., Keith E. Whittington, "The New Originalism," 2 *Georgetown Journal of Law and Public Policy* (2004), 601; Whittington, *Constitutional Interpretation*; Barnett, *Restoring Our Lost Constitution*.

[80] Whittington, *Constitutional Interpretation*, 4.

[81] On the difficulty of distinguishing between interpretation and construction, see Barber and Fleming, *Constitutional Interpretation*, 96–7.

[82] Johnathan O'Neill, *Originalism in American Law and Politics: A Constitutional History* (Baltimore: Johns Hopkins University Press, 2005), 161.

of any part of the Constitution to a unique set of facts is more complicated than most originalists have acknowledged, and that even if judges could discover original meaning, such meaning would be out of touch with our political reality. As Thomas Grey pointed out years ago, strict adherence to an originalist, or what he called an interpretivist approach to constitutional adjudication, would result in an "extraordinary radical purge of established constitutional doctrine."[83] A return to originalism would not only destabilize constitutional practice but also produce morally unacceptable results in too many areas of constitutional law.[84]

In response to recent nonoriginalist critiques, Whittington has tried to differentiate the old originalism of Bork, Scalia, and others from the new version, which is supposed to be an improvement. According to him, the old originalism was "a reactive theory motivated by substantive disagreements with the recent and then-current actions of the Warren and Burger [c]ourts."[85] The new originalism is supposed to be less partisan and no longer so closely linked to judicial restraint or to the fear that judicial review is a weapon in the hands of unprincipled liberal judges.[86] It may be true that such semioriginalism is less susceptible to the criticisms that I articulated herein, but I still maintain that what a particular constitutional provision meant in the past tells us little about what it means today when a judge must extend or decline to extend its scope.[87] As Barnett has acknowledged, "[U]ncertain applications will arise outside of" the core meaning of constitutional provisions.[88] As such, originalists must produce a plausible account of how original judges can cope with such applications within what Hart called the "penumbra of uncertainty" while remaining faithful to original meaning. Without a principled way of distinguishing between two or more constructions on originalist grounds, the strict restraint that originalist judges are supposed to be operating under is suspect.

III. PHILOSOPHICAL APPROACHES TO CONSTITUTIONAL ADJUDICATION

In the end, all theories of constitutional adjudication have their liabilities, but some of those liabilities are much more serious than others. Apart from

---

[83] Thomas Grey, "Do We Have an Unwritten Constitution?" *Stanford Law Review* (February 1975), 713.

[84] See Paul Brest, "The Misconceived Quest for the Original Understanding," 60 *Boston University Law Review* (1980), 223.

[85] Whittington, "New Originalism," 601.

[86] Ibid., 604.

[87] For a criticism of the claim that the so-called new originalism is new or better able to address nonoriginalist critiques of it, see Barber and Fleming, *Constitutional Interpretation*, 92, esp. n.32.

[88] Barnett, *Restoring Our Lost Constitution*, 120.

the foregoing philosophical concern about the inherent difficulty of applying any principle to an unforeseen set of facts and the undesirable results that even semioriginalism would produce, the prospects of real judges' living up to its requirements are bleak. It is revealing that almost all contemporary judges, who have to decide real cases, would not attach the originalist label to themselves. An ideal of public justification is a more realistic normative standard of constitutional adjudication than any originalist alternative, and it would be easier to determine whether a judge, in his or her written opinion, had met that standard, which would not require extensive historical analysis. More important, the use of such a standard would protect the freedom and equality of all of the members of the political community, and the overarching importance of that objective is what justifies judicial review in the first place.

My desire is not only to preach to the converted; even if I have not won the heart and mind of any originalist, I hope that those who have originalist sympathies or would like to see constitutional decision making become more rule-like do not deny the possibility that judicial discretion in hard cases must be structured by something other than the original meaning of the constitutional provision at issue. That leaves us with a wide range of nonoriginalist options, and I shall not summarize them here. Instead, I shall conclude this chapter by saying a bit about Ronald Dworkin's provocative idea that constitutional adjudication requires a fusion of constitutional law and moral philosophy. Dworkin has become famous for insisting that judges, when they specify the meaning of abstract constitutional clauses, must do quite a bit more than textual exegesis and historical research.[89] Over the years, he has incurred the wrath of originalists who seek to make constitutional decision making more rule-like and of conservatives who dislike the liberal results that his method generates. Others, who have little in common with Bork and Scalia, have claimed that Dworkin is an "infidel" of the law.[90] With the exception of Justice William Brennan, Dworkin is the figure who is most responsible for developing and defending the notion of a living or organic Constitution that was under siege during the Reagan revolution.

Any complicated constitutional theory, including Dworkin's, is subject to both deliberate and innocent misrepresentation. I hope that the reader is not predisposed to believe that, for Dworkin, it is acceptable for judges to rewrite the Constitution in the name of social justice. As an interpretive strategy, "constitutional integrity" constrains moral reading; judges are not free to decide a case exclusively on the basis of their deepest personal convictions but instead must "fit" their moral judgment(s) with "the structural

---

[89] Ronald Dworkin, *Taking Rights Seriously* (Cambridge, MA: Harvard University Press, 1977), 149.
[90] Lawrence Lessig, "Fidelity in Translation," 71 *Texas Law Review* (1993), 1260.

design of the Constitution as a whole, and also with the dominant lines of past constitutional interpretation by other judges.[91] While this distinction between reliance on one's own deepest moral convictions and reliance on them within the constraints of constitutional integrity is bound to be clearer in theory than in practice, which Dworkin acknowledges, judges who act in good faith are much more constrained than they may initially appear to be when they take seriously the requirement that new constitutional decisions cohere with old ones and with the normative political theories that have occupied the American political landscape. Judges are not free to indulge in moral philosophy and turn any moral argument that they happen to like into a constitutional argument. As Dworkin has written, judges should think of themselves as involved in the collective enterprise of writing a chain novel, where in writing the next chapter, they are limited by what happened in the preceding chapters.[92] According to Dworkin, judges are both authors and critics.[93]

This does not mean that lines of past cases in a complex legal system are actually consistent. As one commentator writes, "The law is considerably harder to interpret as a whole than a poem or novel."[94] That is not only because multiple texts constitute American law and render it far more complex than any literary work, but also because law is often a product of the clash of interests and political compromises. As a result, law in any nonideal human society will always be tainted by injustice, and one would expect a lack of unity in certain areas of constitutional law when different judges with different judicial philosophies have been on the bench. The task of the ideal judge is to render the case law as coherent as possible and to place lines of cases under concrete principles. That implies that there will be inconsistencies in the case law and that the judge will have to exercise discretion in determining which cases are consistent with the overarching principle that covers them.[95] Not surprisingly, there will be mistakes, not only because of the fallibility of human judgment but also because all real judges are subject to various sorts of institutional demands. An ideal judge must identify and correct mistakes by limiting or ignoring their gravitational force. There are two basic kinds of mistakes: a past decision that makes an arbitrary distinction and thus is out of place in a particular series of cases and a past decision that is based on an unappealing moral principle.[96] For

---

[91] Ronald Dworkin, *Freedom's Law: The Moral Reading of the American Constitution* (Cambridge, MA: Harvard University Press, 1996), 10.

[92] Ronald Dworkin, *Law's Empire* (Cambridge, MA: Harvard University Press, Belknap Press, 1986), 229–38.

[93] Ibid., 229.

[94] Arthur Ripstein, "Introduction: Anti-Archimedeanism," in *Ronald Dworkin*, ed. Arthur Ripstein (New York: Cambridge University Press, 2007), 15.

[95] Dworkin, *Taking Rights Seriously*, 119.

[96] Ibid.

Dworkin, an "unappealing" principle is an unjust one.[97] When the rationale of a case falls under such a principle, the gravitational force of a precedent, even if it is consistent with a series of other decisions, is overridden.[98]

The preceding raises a difficult question, which I cannot even begin to address here, about what kinds of moral considerations, according to Dworkin's view, are extralegal and thus inappropriate. As Dworkin points out, a judge who had deep socialist convictions could not simply interpret the equal protection clause to mandate equality of wealth or to abolish the private ownership of the means of production.[99] Some principles are simply not to be found in the constitutional theory, practice, language, or history of the United States. In constitutional cases, judges must rely on their own best understanding of the moral principle(s) that render the American constitutional tradition as coherent and as just as possible.

This description of what a judge is supposed to do in a hard case leads to the following problem. If coherence is the requirement, then there is no independent moral standard. But if there is such a standard, then an ideal judge does not maximize coherence. It is possible, of course, that a commitment to coherence and a commitment to do what justice requires may conflict.[100] The more unjust the society, the more likely the judge is to encounter this dilemma. In such a situation, even an ideal judge may have to choose between coherence and justice or try to strike a balance between them. As I see it, that a judge would have to make such a choice is not an objection to Dworkin's theory of law but reflects the tension between trying to remain faithful to the values of the past and simultaneously adopting a critical attitude toward them. As Gerald Postema emphasizes, integrity is a second-rate virtue; it would not be necessary, as a substitute for justice, in an ideal society where there was not "serious disagreement about what justices requires."[101]

None of what I have just written about Dworkin does justice to his voluminous writings on jurisprudence or deals with objections to his theory of law, but my purpose has only been to establish that he sees his theory of law as rooted in a constructive interpretation of our legal tradition. This can be said of any philosophic approach to constitutional adjudication that requires judges to exercise their own best moral judgment in certain situations. Judges, like the rest of us, have inherited a constitutional history,

---

[97] Ibid., 122.

[98] Ibid., 123.

[99] Dworkin, *Freedom's Law*, 11.

[100] Dworkin is committed to an overarching principle of justice that requires that government treat all of its citizens with equal concern and respect. Dworkin, *Taking Rights Seriously*, 272–3.

[101] Gerald J. Postema, "Integrity: Justice in Workclothes," in *Dworkin and His Critics*, ed. Justine Burley (Oxford, UK: Blackwell Publishing, 2004), 300–1.

and our disagreements about constitutional meaning reflect our sincere differences over the best normative interpretation of that history.[102] From the standpoint of public justification, the trouble is not with the results that Dworkin's theory of law as integrity would produce but with the reasons offered on their behalf. My approach is designed to minimize the controversy that Dworkin's essentially open-ended moral readings would invite under conditions of moral pluralism and the burdens of judgment. A reasonable person is more likely to be justified in not seeing a judicial decision as publicly justified when the truth of one or more of the premises in the constitutional argument can be reasonably disputed. Reasonable people, who disagree at a deeper level, should be able to see these reasons as good enough, even when they do not fully agree.

I believe that the existence of reasonable disagreement in constitutional controversies must change the very way in which we must think about constitutional adjudication. Judges who exercise judicial review cannot simply aim to capture reasons that Americans actually share, not only because judges are poorly equipped to do survey research but also because Americans, with respect to certain constitutional questions, may not be reasonable. In the absence of radical changes, the judiciary will continue to have the institutional responsibility of ensuring that the uses of the coercive power of the state are as justified as they possibly can be. My aim in this chapter has been to establish that moral judgment on the part of judges is inevitable in hard cases where interpretation ends and construction begins and to suggest that a standard of public justification can constrain judicial discretion at least as well as any of the alternatives. I have also tried to disclose the intuitive appeal of such a standard: judges should not appeal to reasons that they believe to be right, but to reasons that they sincerely believe that other reasonable people would and should accept as justification. Adherence to this standard would do a much better job of legitimizing public laws and judicial decisions under current conditions. I am less concerned that the decisions that judges reach in the most important constitutional cases are morally correct according to an independent standard of moral truth and more concerned that they are sufficiently publicly justified in the eyes of those who are reasonable and must live under them. In a perfect world, they would coincide, and in our world, they should at least overlap.

My approach, then, has much in common with those of Rawls and Stephen Macedo, who insist that sincere efforts at public justification on the part of citizens is the most appropriate response to the existence of reasonable arguments on both sides of many divisive constitutional questions.

---

[102] That may help to explain why utilitarianism, as a theory of right action, has such a prominent place in the history of ethics but such an undistinguished place in American constitutional theory.

An ideal of public justification enables judges to make the kinds of moral judgments that they have to make in hard cases without forgetting an essential point: the best constitutional argument is not necessarily the best moral argument when reasonable people are likely to have good reasons for disagreeing about the soundness of such arguments. In addition, my theory avoids the excessive caution on the part of the judiciary that Cass Sunstein now advocates from the standpoint of Burkean minimalism. Politically, for those on the left, it makes sense to urge restraint on the part of a judiciary that is increasingly unsympathetic to liberal causes. But a Court that does not take chances and proceeds incrementally will not be able to constrain legislative majorities appropriately, and that means that it will be too easy for the state to put the freedom and equality of at least some of its citizens in jeopardy without adequate justification.

TWO

Freedom and Equality in Constitutional History

In the previous chapter, I described the limitations of formalist approaches to constitutional adjudication to explain why judges often must look outside the law for normative guidance. That is why an ideal of public justification is indispensable to constitutional adjudication. In this chapter, I begin to articulate what public justification is, why it is important, what it can accomplish, and how it could guide judges when they delineate the constitutional limits on the coercive power of the state. In particular, I will explain how such a normative standard would facilitate the evaluation of the quality of constitutional arguments, thus making it possible to know when a public law or judicial decision is sufficiently publicly justified and therefore legitimate. That does not mean that a standard of public justification would dictate a single result in a hard constitutional case or that all reasonable people would always agree that the judicial opinion in question meets or fails to meet that standard. After all, legal reasoning never has been, and never will be, deductive. At the same time, when discretion is inescapable, I will show how such a standard would not only generate the right answers in easy cases but also help judges to identify the relevant reasons and weigh them appropriately even in the hardest of hard cases. The use of such a standard would clarify what counts as a good or bad reason in constitutional decision making and address the skeptical worry that there is no right or better answer to the most important constitutional questions.

My other aim is to render the concept of public justification less abstract by rooting it in a commitment to freedom and equality. In doing so, I shall show how public justification is implicit in a number of the best-known Court decisions that establish the fundamental right of all people to formulate and pursue their life plans and to prevent the state from discriminating against people on the basis of certain traits. In the eyes of the law, all of us are equals, and the state may not interfere with any reasonable life plan without compelling reasons for such discrimination. That principle of noninterference should help us to understand the kind of self-restraint that lawmakers should exercise; they must eschew reasons that an ideal reasonable dissenter would reject. In assessing the reasons that the state has offered on behalf of the legislation in question, judges must decide whether those reasons are compelling enough to save the law in question. The state has the burden of proof of producing such reasons. If the judge is not convinced that the state has satisfied it, then he or she should invalidate the law, thereby giving the benefit of the doubt to the reasonable dissenter who is burdened by the law and denies that the law in question is sufficiently publicly justified.[1] If the judge decides to uphold the law, then he or she has to explain why an ideal reasonable person would not reject the reasons that the state has offered as justification.

I. STANDARDS OF REVIEW

When judges decide to uphold a law, it is imperative that they defend the outcome with reasons that would justify the coercion that the state may threaten or exercise to enforce that law. The more serious the impact of this coercion on the lives of some persons, the stronger this justification should be, because people who have no opportunity to consent to a law that they are subject to should not be forced to comply with it without an adequate explanation of why it binds them. This requirement is particularly important in instances where the state enacts a law that infringes upon freedom of choice. As the Court put it in *Planned Parenthood v. Casey*, "Matters... involving the most intimate and personal choices a person may make in a lifetime, choices central to a person's dignity and autonomy, are central to the liberty protected by the Fourteenth Amendment."[2] If that seems too abstract, then just ask yourself how you would feel if the state used its coercive power to prevent you from doing something that you believe to be essential to the quality of your life and furthermore refused or failed to give you reasons that you could accept. In both instances, the law would be a substantial obstacle in your path, but the former would be worse because

---

[1] The presumption in favor of individual freedom is found in many places in the liberal tradition. See, e.g., the very beginning of *Anarchy, State, and Utopia*, where Nozick writes, "Individuals have rights," and then asks, "How much room do individual rights leave for the state?" Robert Nozick, *Anarchy, State, and Utopia* (New York: Basic Books, 1974), ix. See also Stephen Macedo, *The New Right v. the Constitution* (Washington, D.C.: Cato Institute, 1987), 60–1. Contrast this approach with that of James Bradley Thayer, where a court should invalidate a law only if it is contrary to any reasonable understanding of the constitutional text. James B. Thayer, "The Origin and Scope of the American Doctrine of Constitutional Law," 7 *Harvard Law Review* (1893), 138–52.

[2] Planned Parenthood v. Casey, 505 U.S. 851 (1992).

the state would not have even bothered to treat you as a person who has who an equal right to live as you please. As political equals, we are entitled to a sincere attempt at public justification, and it would be even better if the state could provide such reasons that meet this standard more often than not.

In our society, law-making bodies often do an awful job of providing such reasons, and therefore, it is incumbent upon judges to make sure that the state is not acting upon the wrong reasons. In other words, reasons must do the justificatory work.[3] To defend the law in question, of course, is not necessarily to succeed, but a judicial opinion that adequately defends the reasons that underlie the purpose and foreseeable effects of the legislation in question is superior to one that does not make such an attempt or does so poorly. That does not mean that reasonable people will always agree on whether a particular argument is publicly justified. In the end, nothing can take the place of fair-mindedness and thoughtful deliberation, but that would be true in any situation in which someone is trying to give reasons to another person with the hope that that person will come to see them as good reasons as well. Through appeals to freedom and equality, the Court honors the standard of public justification. At least some cases that almost all people today believe to be incorrectly decided exemplify the situation that concerns me where the state has failed to produce sufficiently public reasons but the Court mistakenly permits the state to use such reasons as the basis of its legislation.

In this section, I plan to use a few well-known constitutional cases to illustrate how public justification has operated in constitutional practice, but before I venture into that territory, I want to sketch the relationship between public justification and standards of review. The idea that certain laws must be clearly publicly justified to be laws at all captures the rationale of heightened standards of review.[4] To say that a statute is unconstitutional is to say that the state did not provide adequate reasons to save the legislation whose constitutionality is being challenged. The case for judicial review would seem to hinge on whether the judiciary can perform this function better than any other political institution. The Court assesses the reasons that

---

[3] For a detailed exposition of this point, see Sonu Bedi, *Rejecting Rights: The Turn to Justification* (New York: Cambridge University Press, 2009).

[4] Heightened standards of review are based on a presumption of unconstitutionality. For strict scrutiny, the state can rebut this presumption only if it can show that it has a compelling interest and that the legislative means that it chose to use are narrowly tailored to achieve that interest. For intermediate scrutiny, the state can rebut this presumption only if it can show that it has an important (something less than "compelling" but something much stronger than "legitimate") interest and that the legislative means that it chose to use are substantially related (something less than the tight means-ends fit required by narrow tailoring but something more than a mere rational relationship between the means and the end) to achieve that interest.

the state has offered on behalf of the law in question and, in some instances, calls into question the motives of those who enacted the legislation.[5] In constitutional cases, heightened standards of review, like strict and intermediate scrutiny, compel the state to produce very good reasons in support of the legislation in question on the assumption that such reasons probably do not exist. That is a significant constitutional limit on the legislative power of the state.

As everyone now knows, most of the time, the state does not have good-enough reasons for basing its legislative classifications on race or gender. Over time, the Court has extended this rationale to other groups that are likely to be at the mercy of legislative majorities. For instance, the Court has invalidated laws that discriminated against the children of illegal aliens, those who were born out of wedlock, and the mentally retarded.[6] The state cannot classify certain people on the basis of certain immutable traits or ground legislation in reasons that reasonable dissenters could never accept, such as stereotypes, contempt, or moral disapproval of lifestyle.[7] Unfortunately, it is not always evident what makes a state's interest sufficiently compelling or sufficiently important to pass the first part of a heightened standard of review, which is another way of saying that judges may not know a good reason when they see one or may disagree over its weight even when they acknowledge its relevance.

In applying a heightened standard of review, the words *compelling* and *important* do not mechanically determine the kinds of reasons that the state may rely upon, especially when in the past different judges have decided different cases differently because they have different ideas about how the three standards of review should be applied. For example, Justice William Brennan and Chief Justice William Rehnquist were at odds over the kinds of state interests that would be sufficiently legitimate to pass the first part of rational basis standard of review. Their disagreement could be explained as a product of partisan politics, but it also could be explained in more principled terms; namely, that they sincerely disagreed about what kinds of reasons would justify certain kinds of statutory classifications. Unlike Rehnquist, Brennan was not as willing to defer to legislative judgments even when the state had made a nonsuspect classification on the basis of plausible reasons. Instead, he turned a more critical eye to the real reasons that the state may have relied upon, because he was not convinced that the legislatures could be trusted to limit themselves to the right kinds of

---

[5] See, e.g., Romer v. Evans, 517 U.S. 620 (1996); Wallace v. Jaffree, 472 U.S. 38 (1985); New York City Transit Authority v. Beazer, 440 U.S. 568 (1970) (White, J., dissenting).

[6] Plyer v. Doe, 457 U.S. 202 (1982); Clark v. Jeter, 486 U.S. 456 (1988); City of Cleburne v. Cleburne Living Center, 473 U.S. 432 (1985).

[7] See, e.g., U.S. Department of Agriculture v. Moreno, 413 U.S. 528 (1973); Romer v. Evans, 517 U.S. 620 (1996); Lawrence v. Texas 539 U.S. 558 (2003).

reasons in their treatment of unpopular groups.[8] That is not to say that *compelling* or *important* are meaningless terms. Words have core meanings, and the case law makes it quite clear that certain state interests either are or are not compelling or important. One way of understanding what makes a compelling state interest compelling is that the interest is based on a reason that is unquestionably public; an ideal reasonable person could not reject it because of its undeniable importance in that context. The burden is on the state to demonstrate the force of this reason, and its force is bound to vary with the circumstances.

This is also true in other areas of constitutional law. In free speech jurisprudence, if someone is merely offended by what a political speaker says or by how he or she says it, the state may not ban the political speech.[9] The distinction that the Court draws between advocacy and incitement in *Brandenburg* is predicated on the thought that it cannot be too easy for the state to claim that speech, which is critical of the government, will cause others to break the law and therefore may be censored.[10] Nor can the state simply insist that it has content-neutral reasons to suppress the political speech in question. As Frederick Schauer writes, "[A]n ordinance prohibiting marches by Communists but permitting marches by certain other political parties can obviously not be one that is designed to prevent obstruction of traffic, or prevent noise."[11] By contrast, the state has compelling reasons, such as preventing the abuse of children, for banning the distribution of child pornography and even the private possession of it.[12] Even if a person is sympathetic to *Stanley v. Georgia*, which protects the possession of obscene material in the home, he or she still can appreciate why the state ought to be allowed to treat child pornography differently.[13]

The point of these examples is to show that an ideal of public justification is not divorced from constitutional doctrine that just about everyone would accept. Beyond easy cases, the justices have considerable discretion and may reach different results, and there may be no obvious way of proving that one result is more justified than its alternative. Consider these more difficult cases. There are public reasons on both sides of the debate over the constitutionally required standard of fault in defamation cases. A person can appreciate the risk of self-censorship when the state is permitted to use a standard of fault, like strict liability or negligence, but also see why there are public reasons that support the adoption of a lower standard that would

---

[8] See, e.g., U.S. Department of Agriculture v. Moreno, 413 U.S. 528 (1973).

[9] See, e.g., Cohen v. California, 403 U.S. 15 (1971).

[10] Brandenburg v. Ohio, 395 U.S. 444 (1969).

[11] Frederick Schauer, *Free Speech: A Philosophical Inquiry* (New York: Cambridge University Press, 1982), 204.

[12] New York v. Ferber, 458 U.S. 747 (1982); Osborne v. Ohio, 495 U.S. 103 (1990).

[13] Stanley v. Georgia, 394 U.S. 557 (1969).

better protect the reputation of public figures and perhaps encourage the media to be more responsible in its reporting. If that person believes that *New York Times v. Sullivan* was correctly decided, like most of us do, he or she probably believes that Justice Brennan was right in thinking that the public reasons that favored an actual malice standard outweighed those that supported a lower standard of fault.[14]

Some scholars defend the *Miranda* warning as a plausible solution to the problem of coerced confessions because it clarifies what the police are allowed to do when they question suspects.[15] As such, it can be defended on public policy grounds that are no longer as controversial as they used to be. What this defense of *Miranda* leaves out, however, is an equally important moral concern: the unfairness of taking advantage of the suspect's ignorance of his or her constitutional rights and the likelihood that the environment in which the interrogation takes place will cause the suspect to give a false confession. The suspect's freedom is at stake, not to mention how a criminal conviction would affect those close to him or her and any future employment prospects. *Miranda* was about the practical difficulties of enforcing the privilege against self-incrimination and about enhancing the fairness of how the state treats those who have been arrested, and people who are morally thoughtful do not care only about the conviction rate.

A person who believes that *Miranda* was correctly decided will worry that the police are tempted to use morally questionable interrogation techniques in extracting confessions or incriminating information from suspects whom they believe to be guilty.[16] One has only to imagine what it would be like to be in the position of a suspect or criminal defendant to see why such a rule might be justified. Some reasonable people support the *Miranda* rule because they recognize the various considerations that would lead a reasonable person to be concerned about the integrity of the criminal justice system. At the same time, another reasonable person could come up with his or her own public reasons, like the importance of not depriving jurors of "reliable, highly probative evidence" in criminal cases.[17] A reasonable person who believes that *Miranda* was incorrectly decided will emphasize the extent to which that decision and its progeny make it more difficult for the police and prosecutors to do their jobs: to convict the guilty and to exonerate the innocent.

---

[14] New York Times Co. v. Sullivan, 376 U.S. 254 (1964).

[15] See, e.g., Kermit Roosevelt, *The Myth of Judicial Activism* (New Haven, CT: Yale University Press, 2007), 73–4.

[16] Miranda v. Arizona, 384 U.S. 436 (1966). We should recall that Earl Warren was once a district attorney. Bernard Schwartz, *Super Chief: Earl Warren and His Supreme Court – A Judicial Biography* (New York: New York University Press, 1983), 12–14.

[17] See, e.g., Akhil Reed Amar, *The Constitution and Criminal Procedure: First Principles* (New Haven, CT: Yale University Press, 1997), 88.

II. FREEDOM

Anyone who cares about constitutional law probably has a number of constitutional decisions that he or she puts into one of two categories: obviously rightly decided or obviously wrongly decided. When that person defends judicial review, he or she uses the obviously-rightly-decided case to show what the Court, at its best, can accomplish, and when disparaging judicial review, he or she will draw on the obviously wrongly decided case to demonstrate how much damage a misguided Court can do. It is important to keep in mind the fact that the judiciary does not introduce legislation. At most, through its exercise of judicial review, it can veto the legislation in question. In this section, I want to use examples that I take to be more or less uncontroversial to transcend the partisanship and preoccupation with results that pervade our contemporary constitutional disagreement. As I shall show, what certain well-known, no-longer-controversial Court decisions have in common is that the laws in question either were or were not clearly sufficiently public justified. In the obviously wrongly decided cases, the Court let the state rely upon insufficiently public reasons to justify legislation but those reasons were inconsistent with a commitment to the freedom and equality of all people.

Buck v. Bell is a notorious decision, not only because of its outdated eugenics rationale, encapsulated in Justice Oliver Wendell Holmes's notorious remark that "[t]hree generations of imbeciles are enough."[18] The commonwealth of Virginia had justified the law in question, which authorized forced sterilization for "mental defectives," on two grounds: "the health of the patient" and "the welfare of society."[19] The state believed that a "mental defective" who could not procreate was more likely "to become self-supporting with benefit to themselves and society."[20] Although Holmes did not elaborate on this point, a "mental defective," especially a woman, who could not reproduce would not have children that she was incapable of caring for. The state also maintained that mental retardation was hereditary and that by sterilizing "mental defectives," it was reducing the number of such defectives "to prevent," as Holmes remarked, "our being swamped with incompetence."[21] In his majority opinion, Holmes spends half of his time confirming the adequacy of the procedural safeguards put in place to protect "the patients from possible abuse" in showing that the statute met the minimal requirements of due process of law.[22]

[18] Buck v. Bell, 274 U.S. 200 (1927).
[19] Ibid., 205.
[20] Ibid., 206.
[21] Ibid., 207.
[22] Ibid., 206–7.

Today, it is easy to attack the eugenics rationale for the statute in question and Holmes's opinion on the ground that each relies upon bad science, but I believe that this case reveals something else: in constitutional law, when a fundamental right to procreate is at stake, most people are no longer likely to look favorably upon the underlying utilitarian rationale for the sterilization statute. Unlike Holmes, a contemporary judge would be more likely to give much less weight to the welfare of society and much more weight to the right of any person not to be involuntarily sterilized. Holmes undervalued the importance of this right, comparing the sterilization in question to compulsory vaccination and citing a precedent to that effect.[23]

Holmes is not morally sensitive to what it would have been like for a person to be subject to such a statute, regardless of its procedural safeguards, and this observation tells us something about why the law in question is not publicly justified. Today, most people would see procreation as a human right, and the state could have explored other, less draconian options that may have served its legislative end equally well. The point is not that this case would have turned out differently if the Court had opted for analysis under the equal protection clause but that its deferential attitude toward the reasons that the state put forth to defend its sterilization law is deeply troubling. The Court handed down *Skinner v. Oklahoma* only fifteen years later but exhibited more sensitivity toward the impact that involuntary sterilization could have on a human life.[24] The statute in question, Oklahoma's Habitual Criminal Sterilization Act, permitted the state to sterilize a person who had been convicted of three or more "felonies involving moral turpitude" as long as the procedure would not result in "detriment to his general health."[25] The Court did not explicitly overturn *Buck v. Bell* and instead predicated its decision on equal protection grounds.[26] As Justice William Douglas pointed out, the statute treated certain kinds of felonies differently than others. One could be convicted of the felony of embezzlement numerous times and still not be subject to the punishment of sterilization, whereas a thief who was convicted of the felony of stealing chickens three or more times would be subject to sterilization.[27]

Within the framework of the equal protection clause, Douglas ostensibly based his decision on the irrationality or inherent unfairness of punishing some repeat offenders more harshly than others who had committed comparable crimes, but in reading in between the lines, Douglas has a different moral concern. Even if Oklahoma had subjected all repeat offenders similarly situated to the same punishment, namely sterilization, it is unlikely that

---

[23] Ibid., 207.
[24] Skinner v. Oklahoma, 316 U.S. 535 (1942).
[25] Ibid., 536–7.
[26] Ibid., 538–9.
[27] Ibid.

he would have reached a different result. That is not an observation about the material facts of the holding but a way of understanding why Douglas did not believe that the sterilization statute was publicly justified. As he wrote, "We are dealing here with legislation which involves one of the basic civil rights of man. Marriage and procreation are fundamental to the very existence and survival of the race."[28] As Justice Brennan put it many years later, "If the right to privacy means anything, it is the right of the individual, married or single, to be free from unwarranted government intrusion into matters so fundamentally affecting a person as the decision whether to bear or beget a child."[29] Certainly, Douglas was not concerned that the human race would go extinct as a result of such laws, but he was legitimately concerned with the abuse of the procedure by the state, its irreversibility, and its gravity. The nature of the punishment probably encouraged Douglas to examine the law more critically and to conclude that it was unconstitutional because its underlying reasons were not strong enough to publicly justify it.

Conservatives have ridiculed Douglas's reasoning in *Griswold v. Connecticut* for its lack of connection to the constitutional text and to precedent and for his reliance upon the astronomical metaphor of penumbra. Robert Bork has written that "[n]one of the amendments cited, and none of their buffer or penumbral zones, covered the case before the court."[30] Conservatives like Bork would have us believe that Douglas created a constitutional right of privacy out of thin air and then had the audacity to pretend that such a right was an implication of abstract constitutional language. But as I explained in the previous chapter, once we reject formalist approaches to constitutional adjudication, it is not evident that Douglas is as idiotic or unprincipled as his conservative critics make him out to be. In his opinion, he begins by going out of his way to explain that the law in question "operates on an intimate relation between husband and wife and their physician's role in one aspect of the relationship."[31] Bork believes that this concern is irrelevant to the correct resolution of the case.[32] As Douglas points out, though, a law that forbids the use of contraceptives "seeks to achieve its goals by means having a destructive impact upon that relationship."[33] Douglas raises the specter that the police might "search the sacred precincts of marital bedrooms for telltale signs of the use of contraceptives" for its rhetorical effect.[34] As I see it, his real concern involves the extent to which

---

[28] Ibid., 541.

[29] Eisenstadt v. Baird, 405 U.S. 453 (1972) (Brennan, J., writing for the majority).

[30] Robert H. Bork, *The Tempting of America: The Political Seduction of the Law* (New York: Simon and Schuster, 1990), 98.

[31] Griswold v. Connecticut, 381 U.S. 479 (1965).

[32] Bork, *Tempting of America*, 97.

[33] Griswold v. Connecticut, 381 U.S. 485 (1965).

[34] Ibid.

such a law impermissibly interferes with the right of a married couple to make the most important decisions about the nature of their relationship.

That may sound sentimental, but most people would not see the decision as to whether to have children as trivial or a matter that they would want to delegate to others, nor would they believe it was reasonable to ask a married couple to abstain from sex unless their intention was to procreate. That is not to say that in 1965 and even today there are not people who maintain that birth control is immoral, but Douglas was getting at an essential constitutional principle: the state cannot impose laws that significantly infringe upon a person's pursuit of his or her conception of the good without articulating reasons that an ideal reasonable person would not reject. This was not just "an uncommonly silly law," as Justice Potter Stewart put it in his dissent,[35] but a law that forced sexually active couples, including those who are married, to risk an unwanted pregnancy without a compelling justification. Does anyone really want to live in a society where it is so easy for the state, on the basis of bad reasons, to be able to put any sexually active couple in such a dilemma?

This point transcends the context of birth control. From the facts that everyone wants to live a good life, and that most people want to have as much control over it as possible, it follows that they are reluctant to allow the state to make personal decisions for them. Most Americans believe in the value of "moral freedom," by which individuals are supposed to figure out for themselves what a good life consists of.[36] The trouble is that too frequently people fail to see how this principle extends beyond their parochial concerns. They are appalled at how easy it is for the state to take private homes for public use through the power of eminent domain in *Kelo* because, as homeowners, they can imagine what it would be like for the state to take away their own homes with such a weak justification.[37] That is not a mere observation about the meaning of the takings clause or the value of property rights, but it implicates a legitimate concern about the extent to which the state can enact laws that demand significant and perhaps ultimately unjustified sacrifices from some people. At the same time, because they cannot put themselves in the shoes of others, they have difficulty in understanding why others seek rights that they are not inclined to exercise. For many people, to recognize an abstract right, like the right to make the most important personal choices about how to live, is one thing, but to recognize a particular manifestation of that abstract right is something else.

Public justification is not limited to the context of procreation. A reasonable person also would reject an argument that a particular way of life

---

[35] Ibid., 527 (Stewart, J., dissenting).

[36] Alan Wolfe, *Moral Freedom: The Impossible Idea That Defines the Way We Live Now* (New York: W. W. Norton, 2001), 195.

[37] Kelo v. City of New London, 545 U.S. 469 (2005).

is sinful, unconventional, unnatural, or foolish. In *Bowers v. Hardwick*, Michael Hardwick challenged a Georgia statute that prohibited consensual sodomy on the ground that he had a fundamental constitutional right to engage in such conduct.[38] In a 5–4 decision, the Court upheld the Georgia statute and the majority concluded that, unlike the rights of married people or unmarried heterosexuals to sexual autonomy, the Constitution does not protect such rights for gay people.[39] In the majority opinion, Justice Byron White characterized the legal issue as "whether the Federal Constitution confers a fundamental right upon homosexuals to engage in sodomy and hence invalidates the laws of the many States that still make such conduct illegal and have done so for a very long time."[40] He then differentiated the case from past privacy cases dealing with family, marriage, and procreation and announced that the Court would not establish a new constitutional right that would protect sodomy between consenting adults.[41] Last, he distinguished *Bowers* from *Stanley v. Georgia*, which protects the right to possess obscene material in the privacy of one's own home, insisting that the latter decision was rooted in the First Amendment.[42]

Today, there are not too many academics that would be eager to embrace either the result or the reasoning in *Bowers v. Hardwick*.[43] What is striking about White's opinion is the narrow way in which he frames the constitutional issue. His description of the case does not come close to capturing all of the morally relevant considerations. In particular, he fails to acknowledge how the law in question discriminates against gay people who are sexually active and infringes upon their freedom to engage in consensual sexual activity. This failure is not simply a manifestation of the well-known levels of generality problem, where the putative constitutional right is defined either narrowly, such as the right to same-sex sexual intercourse, or more broadly, such as the right to sexual intimacy for all adults. Like the dissenting opinion, one could argue that this case is really about "the right to be left alone."[44]

---

[38] Bowers v. Hardwick, 478 U.S. 186 (1986).

[39] After his retirement, Lewis Powell remarked, "I probably made a mistake in that one [*Bowers*]." He also told a reporter, "I do think that it was inconsistent in a general way with *Roe*. When I had the opportunity to reread the opinion a few months later, I thought the dissent had the better of the arguments." John C. Jeffries Jr., *Justice Lewis F. Powell: A Biography* (New York: Fordham University Press, 2001), 530.

[40] Bowers v. Hardwick, 478 U.S. 190 (1986).

[41] Ibid., 190–1.

[42] Stanley v. Georgia, 394 U.S. 557 (1969); Bowers v. Hardwick, 478 U.S. 194 (1986).

[43] One prominent exception is John Finnis. Interestingly, although Finnis believes that the law should discourage same-sex sex acts, he does not support a legal prohibition on such conduct. See John Finnis, "Is Natural Law Theory Compatible with Limited Government?" in *Natural Law, Liberalism, and Morality: Contemporary Essays*, ed. Robert P. George (Oxford, U.K.: Clarendon Press, 1996), 17.

[44] Bowers v. Hardwick, 478 U.S. 199–200 (Blackmun, J., dissenting).

One of the problems is that the majority opinion focuses only on the physical aspect of the conduct in question. By upholding the statute against constitutional challenge, the Court permits states to criminalize the sexual dimension of nonheterosexual romantic relationships even among those who have a long-term loving relationship.[45] In other words, White failed to appreciate that two men could be as committed to each other as a man and a woman could. Until *Lawrence v. Texas*, this decision allowed a state to prosecute gay people who are not celibate and to imprison them, including those who would marry if that option were available to them.[46] White's position denies how sexuality helps to form one's identity, apart from the cruelty of prosecuting and punishing someone for such a "crime," even when such prosecutions were uncommon. For White, there is no such constitutional right; as such, the state is not prevented from acting upon the kinds of reasons that it offers to defend the statute. But this conclusion is problematic because the Court does not seem to recognize the importance of the right or liberty interest in question.

The majority opinion never explains, or even addresses, why a same-sex relationship is a less morally meaningful encounter than a heterosexual relationship. The majority seems to believe that appeals to conventional or traditional Judeo-Christian morality are good enough, constitutionally speaking, even though the public was and still is divided over the morality of same-sex relationships. On the basis of stereotypes, one cannot assume that gays and lesbians are less likely to reach out to each other in a loving relationship than straight people are. Nor did the majority opinion explain why gay and lesbian couples could accept the reasons that were offered on behalf of the decision. In fact, the Court makes no pretense of even trying to do so. The majority opinion should have addressed what was also at stake in *Bowers v. Hardwick*: the right of a loving couple to enjoy sexual intimacy as a part of their love for each other. That opinion also should have articulated why the state's reasons ought to trump the reasons that would have supported the opposite conclusion. Even Harry Blackmun's dissent overlooks this point because he defines the right at stake as one of sexual privacy, whereas the reach of the Georgia statute extended far beyond casual sexual encounters.

That being gay or lesbian is immoral or misguided is simply not a proposition that a gay or lesbian person, who is burdened by the law in question, could accept. Not only is it predicated on a claim about the value, or of lack thereof, of a particular way of life, but it also reflects a moral judgment about identity. Nor could he or she accept the claim that because someone

---

[45] See Stephen Macedo, "Sexuality and Liberty: Making Room for Nature and Tradition?" in *Sex, Preference, and the Family: Essays on Law and Nature*, ed. David M. Estlund and Martha C. Nussbaum (New York: Oxford University Press, 1997), 92.

[46] Lawrence v. Texas, 539 U.S. 558 (2003).

is gay or lesbian or has same-sex sexual relationships, he or she must remain celibate and not enjoy the protection of the law the way that heterosexual couples do. The more likely the premises of an argument can be reasonably rejected, the more likely the argument is insufficiently publicly justified. That many people of a particular group share a view about how they would like to be treated would be best evidence of how an imaginary reasonable person would respond to the reasons that the state had offered on behalf of the law in question. That would not require uncritical acceptance of the reasons that actual dissenters prefer but would compel one who cares about public justification to take them more seriously. Ideally, a public justification that is good enough would also convince most actual reasonable dissenters, but that would depend on a number of external factors outside of the Court's control.

In the famous *Cruzan* right-to-die case, the Court ruled that a competent person has a constitutional right to refuse lifesaving hydration and nutrition and decided that the comatose person would have to have expressed his or her wish to die in such circumstances by "clear and convincing evidence."[47] A law that prohibited someone from refusing such treatment in all circumstances would be insufficiently publicly justified. A reasonable person would conclude that the comatose patient should be able to choose whether to remain on life support, which is consistent with *Cruzan*. The Court's ruling with respect to the evidentiary standard is predicated on the belief that the state may see a false positive, where a person who would not want his or her life support terminated but has such support terminated, as a more serious error than a false negative, where a person who would want his or her life support terminated but does not have such support terminated. As such, the state may protect the choice of comatose patients who would not want to have their life support withdrawn at the expense of not protecting the choice of those who would want to die under those circumstances. Otherwise, a lower evidentiary standard, like preponderance of the evidence, would have been more appropriate. Whether one believes that the Court decided *Cruzan* correctly, it is clear that the kinds of reasons that the state used as the basis for its legislation were public in principle: respect for the wishes of the comatose person. The challenge would be to determine whether the state had given too much weight to minimizing the possibility that someone who would not want to die would have his or her life support terminated, as opposed to forcing someone who would have wanted to die to remain on life support because the evidentiary standard was too difficult to meet.

In terms of public reasons, it is much more difficult to defend the result that the Court handed down in *Washington v. Glucksberg*, the famous

---

[47] Cruzan v. Missouri Department of Health, 497 U.S. 261 (1990).

physician-assisted suicide case.[48] Writing for the majority, Chief Justice Rehnquist refused to extend the right to die recognized in *Cruzan* to physician-assisted suicide. In that case, Rehnquist did not try to squeeze an answer to this constitutional question out of the text or precedent. Instead, he emphasized the fact that our history and constitutional tradition have never protected the right to assistance in committing suicide and distinguished this practice from the constitutional right to refuse unwanted medical treatment, based on a philosophical distinction between acts and omissions.[49]

Here, what is at stake is the freedom of a person to decide whether he or she wants the option of professional aid in ending her life. For a person who wants to die, the distinction between being assisted in suicide and terminating life support is not morally significant.[50] The question, then, is whether the state has an adequate justification for the law in question, which would prevent that person from legally exercising such an option in all circumstances. One who takes a public reasons approach to deciding the constitutionality of a statute that prohibits physician-assisted suicide would concentrate on the reasons that the state has offered in defending the ban on physician-assisted suicide. According to Rehnquist, the state has three primary interests: the preservation of human life; protecting the integrity and ethics of the medical profession; and protecting vulnerable groups from abuse, neglect, and mistakes.[51] First, Rehnquist worries that those who suffer from depression and other mental disorders might not opt for physician-assisted suicide if their medical condition were diagnosed and treated.[52] Second, he mentions that the trust, which is essential to the physician-patient relationship, might be undermined if physicians were allowed to end their patients' lives. Third, he is concerned with the "real risk of subtle coercion and undue influence in end-of-life situations."[53] To clarify this point, Rehnquist explains that families, who could not afford the "substantial financial burdens of end-of-life health-care costs," might pressure the patient to end his life prematurely.[54] Rehnquist also feared that there might be a slippery slope from voluntary euthanasia to involuntary euthanasia.[55]

Because Rehnquist believes that there is no constitutional right to physician-assisted suicide, the state had to demonstrate only a rational basis for its prohibition of physician-assisted suicide.[56] As far as he is concerned,

---

[48] Washington v. Glucksberg, 521 U.S. 702 (1997).

[49] Ibid., 710–19.

[50] Ronald Dworkin et al., "Assisted Suicide: The Philosophers' Brief," 44 *New York Review of Books*, March 27, 1997, http://www.nybooks.com/articles/1237, p. 8.

[51] Washington v. Glucksberg, 521 U.S. 728–33 (1997).

[52] Ibid., 730.

[53] Ibid., 732

[54] Ibid.

[55] Ibid., 732–3.

[56] Ibid., 728.

the foregoing interests are "unquestionably important and legitimate," and thus the Court "need not weigh exactingly the relative strengths of these various interests."[57] However, Rehnquist puts the cart before the horse. From the standpoint of public justification, where there would be a strong presumption against the constitutionality of such a law because of its potential impact on a person who is terminally ill, his analysis is flawed. All of the reasons that Rehnquist lists are potentially public reasons in the following way: if they are accurate, then an ideal reasonable person would accept one or a combination of them and might conclude that the statute in question is publicly justified. Surely, those reasons support the claim that the state may carefully regulate such suicides. Nevertheless, Rehnquist does not make much effort to defend these reasons or to offer more convincing empirical evidence. Instead, he gives the state the benefit of the doubt by assuming that its reasons, at least taken together, are good enough. This conclusion might have been justified if Rehnquist had explained why the reasons override a person's right to determine whether and how to end his or her life in certain circumstances.

Some fully rational people who are terminally ill will seek to end their lives to avoid intolerable pain or an undignified death, and their deciding to do so is at least intelligible, if not justified. Many of Rehnquist's concerns most likely could be addressed through the careful regulation of physician-assisted suicide, as opposed to a more sweeping ban that he permits the state to enact. The obvious criticism of Rehnquist's position is that he seriously undervalues the importance of allowing a person to control "the manner of her death, professional medical assistance, and the avoidance of unnecessary and severe physical suffering."[58] Rehnquist should have explained why the state had sufficient reason to prolong the life of a terminally ill patient against her will. Perhaps no one could really know in the abstract what she would want to do in such a situation, yet that does not absolve Rehnquist from defending his decision to uphold the law in question to a reasonable dissenter who doubts that the state's reasons meet the standard of public justification. Even when he was terminally ill with thyroid cancer, Rehnquist refused to retire from the bench and sought medical treatment.[59] That remark is not an ad hominem attack on him or a judgment about the correctness of his personal decision but is intended to show that it was important to him – as it would be to all of us – to decide how we would cope with a terminal illness. No law forced him to refrain from seeking chemotherapy, and no law prevented him from seeking such treatment. Rehnquist's failure to ensure that Washington's prohibition of physician-assisted suicide was

[57] Ibid., 735.

[58] Ibid., 790 (Breyer, J., concurring).

[59] Jan Crawford Greenberg, *Supreme Conflict: The Inside Story of the Struggle for Control of the United States Supreme Court* (New York: Penguin Books, 2008), 18–19.

publicly justified does not mean that someone could not have put together a better defense of the statute than Rehnquist did. But to appeal to tradition or to the will of legislative majorities is not to explain adequately why the law in question is publicly justified.

III. EQUALITY

As an approach to judicial decision making, public justification is present in many areas of constitutional law even though judges do not use the term *public justification* or the phrase *public reasons*. As everyone familiar with constitutional law knows, there is a very strong presumption against the constitutionality of legislation that infringes upon a fundamental right or makes a suspect classification on the basis of race or ethnicity or, in some instances, immigration status. A similar presumption exists in the context of gender discrimination, where the state is expected to produce very good reasons on behalf of its legislative classification to ensure its survival. In *United States v. Virginia*, where the Court invalidated the all-male admissions policy at the Virginia Military Institute (VMI), Justice Ruth Bader Ginsburg held that gender classifications cannot be based on stereotypes about what men and women are naturally suited for, and the state cannot use those stereotypes to deny all women equal opportunity.[60] Today, it would be unthinkable for the Court to uphold a law barring factory work by women for more than ten hours a day on the ground that "as healthy mothers are essential to vigorous offspring, the physical well-being of a woman becomes an interest of public interest and care,"[61] or to prevent women from being put in the jury pool because a "woman is still regarded as the center of home and family life."[62] A reasonable person simply could not be committed to the equality of all people, including women, and at the same time accept such archaic justifications.

The idea of "exceeding persuasive justification," which Justice Ginsburg advances in *United States v. Virginia* as the new standard of review for gender classifications, expresses a commitment to giving adequate reasons to those who are burdened by the legislation in question, such as being denied equal opportunity.[63] A woman who was qualified to attend an all-male military academy such as VMI but was denied the opportunity solely because of her gender could not be expected to accept the reasons that VMI offered in defense of its admissions policy: to save its unique, traditional adversative system of military education for its cadets or to enhance diversity

---

[60] United States v. Virginia, 518 U.S. 515 (1996).
[61] Muller v. Oregon, 208 U.S. 412 (1908).
[62] Hoyt v. Florida, 368 U.S. 57 (1961).
[63] United States v. Virginia, 518 U.S. 515 (1996).

of educational choice in Virginia by enabling both genders to attend single-gender institutions of higher learning. The Court doubted that these reasons were the real reasons for the single-gender admissions policy. Most likely, the real reasons were based on stereotypes about what men and women are naturally suited for, including ones about the inability of women to succeed in combat or leadership roles. But even if one took VMI's ostensible reasons at face value, a woman who was denied admission on their basis still could reject them as not good enough to deny every single woman the opportunity to receive a state-subsidized military education when that opportunity was available to all men, even to those who were indifferent to or ill suited for military service.

Although the Court did not explicitly announce a new standard of review for sexual orientation in *Romer v. Evans*, the majority made it clear that animus toward unpopular groups could not underlie a legislative classification.[64] In that case, the Court ruled that the state lacked legitimate reasons for preventing cities and towns from protecting gays and lesbians from private discrimination in public accommodations. As in the case of gender discrimination, one approach to determining the constitutionality of the legislative classification in question is to ask whether those who are being put at a legal disadvantage could accept the state's reasons as good enough. Could someone who voted for Amendment 2 to the Colorado Constitution, which would have prevented Colorado cities from protecting gays and lesbians from discrimination, expect someone who was gay or lesbian to accept at least one of the following reasons: legal protection against such discrimination constitutes special treatment, or the people of Colorado are permitted to express their moral disapproval of homosexuality by discriminating against gays and lesbians for no other reason but such disapproval. It is obvious, I think, that someone who was gay or lesbian could not be expected to accept either reason in favor of Amendment 2, which operated as an anti-antidiscrimination measure, by preventing cities from legally protecting gays and lesbians from private discrimination in public accommodations. The presumptions against these sorts of legislative classifications capture the essence of public reason: it is unfair to deprive someone of his or her freedom or to treat someone unequally unless the state can produce reasons that an ideal reasonable person would accept without reservation as sufficient justification.

One could object that I have selected an example that is too easy to agree with and that other, more controversial examples exist where reasonable people are bound to disagree about what fairness would require. That is true, but we should begin with easy cases, which is the right place to start. In addition, there are other counterexamples that would weaken the claim

[64] Romer v. Evans, 517 U.S. 620 (1996).

that members of the legal culture never see eye-to-eye on the easiest of easy cases, like the right to competent legal representation for the indigent in felony cases. A lawyer who was intoxicated, slept through parts of the trial, or had inadequate legal training or courtroom experience would not be someone who had done his or her minimal duty as an advocate in an adversarial system of justice. It would be hard to know what more to say to someone who insisted that a defendant in a capital case is not entitled to effective assistance of counsel. How compelling could that person's reasons be? He or she might sincerely believe that God would not let an innocent person be convicted or that a person who is charged with a crime must be guilty, but surely these are not reasons that a reasonable person would accept. We would expect that the right to effective assistance of counsel in a capital case would be almost intuitive to those who live in a decent society and want to minimize the risk that an innocent person will be mistakenly executed. Most people would see the force of the reasons that underlie this right with little or no reflection, and I doubt that a person who denies their force could be persuaded by another reason that explains their force.

The point is not simply based on a factual observation that reasonable people would agree that a defendant should not be incarcerated or put to death when he or she has a right to, but has not received, adequate legal advice. Rather, reasonable people no longer seriously dispute such matters of criminal procedure, however controversial they may have been at their inceptions, and that agreement cannot be explained in terms of mere shifts in public opinion over time. Any person who is a defendant in a capital or felony case and who cares about his or her future would not find the kind of legal representation described earlier acceptable. While some conservatives deride the excesses of the Warren Court, most of them have come to accept most of the impact that the Court has had on constitutional criminal procedure. Historically, one can describe the liberal attempt to create a more just society as the cause of the evolution of constitutional meaning that occurred during this time. But the real issue, today, is whether these changes have been ratified in the sense that they can be defended in terms of public reasons. One does not have to believe that all history is progress to believe that people may come to recognize that a reasonable person could not possibly hold a particular position any longer because of its patent unfairness and that those who held that position in the past were unreasonable with respect to that issue.

Over time, certain constitutional positions have transcended partisan disagreement and have been transformed into almost self-evident constitutional truths. Other positions, even those that were widely held in the past, have died slow, painful deaths. As Lincoln would have put it, this nation did have a "new birth of freedom." One of the great challenges of American history has been to specify the political and legal implications of freedom and equality in the midst of deep conflict over their meaning.[65] There have been winners and there have been losers, and that helps to explain why certain constitutional arguments are no longer plausible, whatever basis or lack thereof, they have in the constitutional text or in its original meaning.[66] No one any longer believes that race, gender, or property ownership should exclude a person from political participation or from pursuing a particular profession. American history could have turned out very differently than it did, and all of us can imagine political events that would have led to a more or less egalitarian political life. Those who have the responsibility of making constitutional choices must work within the constitutional tradition that they have inherited, and that necessitates understanding what a commitment to freedom and equality implies in real cases. Otherwise, one could make no sense of the case law that has fixed the core meaning of the equal protection and due clauses over time.

The commitment to a nation "conceived in liberty and dedicated to the proposition that all men are created equal" is found in some of the literature on public opinion as well. At present, most Americans support democratic procedures.[67] That suggests that Americans are also committed to fairness in collective decision making in the abstract, which is not to say that they always agree on what fairness requires in particular instances. It would be hard to understand such a commitment without the underlying belief that the law should not disadvantage anyone unless that law can be sufficiently justified to that person inasmuch as he or she is rational and seeks to maximize the chances of realizing his or her conception of the good. To be committed to democratic norms is to be committed to a deeper value – that people deserve to be treated in a way that takes into account their equal interest in living a good life – even when people cannot always live up to this commitment or agree on its implications. It makes sense to construe the deeper meaning of American constitutionalism as a commitment to the overarching principles that all people deserve an equal share of freedom and are entitled to an adequate explanation when the state uses its power to cut into this share. That is not the only possible interpretation, but at least such an interpretation is consistent with the widespread rejection of a notorious constitutional doctrine like separate but equal.

Still, there are Americans who still hold inegalitarian beliefs of different kinds concerning race, gender, and sexual orientation or who do not believe that individual freedom is the paramount value. In the United States, there

---

[65] This is one of the themes of Judith N. Shklar's *American Citizenship: The Quest for Inclusion* (Cambridge, MA: Harvard University Press, 1991).

[66] In other words, just like Great Britain, the United States also has an unwritten constitution. See Gordon S. Wood, "The Fundamentalists and the Constitution," *New York Review of Books*, February 18, 1988, 37–40.

[67] Klosko, *Democratic Procedures and Liberal Consensus*, 116.

will never be unanimous agreement on which value is the most important or on how those values should be ranked in cases of conflict. That is one of the reasons why legal theorists must look elsewhere for normative help. Postmodernists and value pluralists attach great significance to the brute existence of moral disagreement in human societies and to the inherent difficulties of achieving anything like consensus on the most controversial matters of political morality. This disagreement exists and will continue to exist in a free society, but that does not mean that, constitutionally speaking, no one ever knows a good or bad argument when he or she sees it.

To argue for certain constitutional conclusions is to ignore not only precedent but also settled constitutional meaning on some of the most obvious implications of freedom and equality. It would be hard to take seriously a person who contends the state may force women to cover their heads in public, deny transsexuals the privilege of driving, or forbid lesbians from teaching in public schools. The values of freedom and equality that explain why certain constitutional arguments no longer write have become part of the constitutional vocabulary of reasonable people who care about treating others fairly and are not indifferent to the quality of their lives. No one wants to be treated as a second-class citizen or to have the state enact laws that make it less likely that he or she will live a good life for no better reason than that a legislative majority had an external preference that it turned into a law. That is something that all of us have that in common. It is simply a failure of moral imagination not to be able to step outside of one's own partial point of view to see why others have life plans of their own that are equally important.

Not everyone, of course, would accept this analysis. In *Romer v. Evans*, Justice Scalia wrote that people are "*entitled* to be hostile to homosexual conduct."[68] Whether he is right turns on how this hostility may be expressed. On the one hand, Americans may exhibit their moral disapproval of same-sex relationships by forming organizations that treat homosexuality as a sickness and offer therapy to those who want to be "cured." In a free society, all people have a fundamental right to criticize the lives of others. They even have the right to express their belief that homosexuality is immoral in a public forum near the funeral of a gay person who is the victim of a hate crime. On the other hand, they are no more entitled to express such hostility through law than they are to express such hostility toward any group of people on the basis of moral disapproval. Scalia's claim that the majority has taken sides in a "culture war," and by implication the wrong side, and his insistence that the decision to strike down Amendment 2 to the Colorado Constitution is "an act, not of judicial judgment, but political

---

[68] Romer v. Evans, 517 U.S. 620 (1996) (Scalia, J., dissenting).

will,"[69] may have rhetorical bite in a society that worries about the abuse of judicial power, but his position and the reasons that underlie it could not be accepted by an ideal reasonable person.

Indeed, by permitting the state to act upon such reasons, Scalia is also taking sides. In the language of public justification, he fails to give sufficiently public reasons to reasonable dissenters and makes no effort to do so, as if the quality of their lives were beside the point. He seems to think that the very fact that large numbers of people believe homosexuality to be wrong makes it so, at least for constitutional purposes, and that the majority in *Romer* is simply substituting its own preferences for those of the voters of Colorado. This is simply the wrong way to characterize the issue in this case. By passing Amendment 2, the voters of Colorado permitted private people to discriminate against gays and lesbians and nullified existing ordinances that forbade such discrimination. An employer who was "hostile toward homosexual conduct"[70] was entitled to fire an employee because of his or her sexual orientation, and a landlord who disliked gays and lesbians could refuse to rent an apartment to them. Scalia downplays both the real and symbolic effects of such a law, because he wants to characterize Amendment 2 as a legitimate expression of the popular will. As he sees it, that will is ultimately morally correct, has the proper democratic pedigree, or both. Neither of these lines of reasoning would come close to meeting the standard of public justification, but Scalia does not seem to care that the reasons that he offers could never be accepted by someone who is gay or lesbian or who is concerned that all people should not be discriminated against in the absence of a compelling justification.

Consider a final example. In "Toward Neutral Principles of Constitutional Law," Herbert Wechsler criticized *Brown v. Board of Education* on the ground that its justification was not "neutral."[71] Wechsler believed that the legal issue could be reduced to two types of associational preferences: the preferences of African Americans to attend integrated public schools and the preferences of whites to attend segregated public schools. According to him, the Court had not advanced a neutral principle to justify the decision to favor the preferences of African Americans, and therefore the decision itself was constitutionally suspect. This criticism rests on the assumption that the associational preferences of each racial group are comparable, which overlooks not only the historical context of racial discrimination but also its unjust social, political, and economic ramifications. But in *Brown*, the Court was not just taking sides in a partisan debate or culture war over the wisdom of racial integration in public schools. Rather, the Court did

---

[69] Romer v. Evans, 517 U.S. 620, 653 (1996) (Scalia, J., dissenting).

[70] Ibid., 644.

[71] Brown v. Board of Education, 347 U.S. 483 (1954); Herbert Wechsler, "Toward Neutral Principles of Constitutional Law," 23 *Harvard Law Review* (1959), 1.

not treat the conflicting preferences as moral equivalents because what was at stake was whether the state would be required to treat all Americans, regardless of their race, with equal respect. It takes little vision to appreciate how government-sanctioned segregation of public facilities, the enforcement of racially restrictive covenants, and exclusionary residential zoning creates a racial caste system. Wechsler's challenge to the legitimacy of *Brown* fails because he did not see what was obvious to many other people even at that time: that state-supported racially segregated public education is predicated on white supremacy; thus, a preference for such segregation is not morally on par with a preference for integration.

No one believes any longer that *Brown* was wrongly decided.[72] A theory of constitutional interpretation that gets *Brown* wrong is like a moral theory that cannot explain why child molestation or genocide is wrong. Although everyone knows that *Brown* prohibits the state from racially segregating its primary and secondary public schools, *Brown* also stands for the principle that racial segregation of public facilities by law, apart from the specific concerns about children and their education, reinforces the subordination of African Americans. As Chief Justice Warren wrote, "To separate them [school children] from others of similar age and qualifications solely because of their race generates a feeling of inferiority as to their status in the community that may affect their hearts and minds in a way unlikely ever to be undone."[73] This sentence should be interpreted as a moral claim about equality of all people in the eyes of the law. Even Justice Stanley Reed, who was sympathetic to the separate but equal doctrine, convinced himself that his initial view that the racial segregation of public schools was constitutional was not premised on the inferiority of African Americans.[74] To make the holding of *Brown* contingent upon methodologically suspect social psychology research is to miss the underlying moral message: racial segregation is unconstitutional because it is designed to subordinate African Americans.

The same could be said of racial segregation outside of the context of public education as well. The racial segregation of public facilities like pools, golf courses, hotels, theaters, and restaurants denies the fundamental right to be treated as an equal to those who are not permitted to interact with or occupy the same physical space as their "betters." Years before *Brown* and the modern civil rights movement, in his dissent in *Plessy v. Ferguson*, Justice Harlan exposed the real reason behind the Louisiana statute that

---

[72] Jack M. Balkin, "*Brown* as Icon," in *What* Brown v. Board of Education *Should Have Said: The Nation's Top Legal Experts Rewrite America's Landmark Civil Rights Decision*, ed. Jack M. Balkin (New York: New York University Press, 2001), 4.

[73] Brown v. Board of Education, 347 U.S. 483 (1954).

[74] Bernard Schwartz, *A History of the Supreme Court* (New York: Oxford University Press, 1993), 293.

mandated racial segregation of passenger cars: "But everyone knows that [the Louisiana statute at issue] had its origin in the purpose, not so much to exclude white persons from railroad cars occupied by blacks, as to exclude colored people from coaches occupied or assigned to white persons." He closed with the following thought: "[B]ut in view of the constitution, in the eye of the law, there is in this country no superior, dominant, ruling class of citizens. There is no caste here. Our constitution is color-blind."[75] Similarly, in *Loving v. Virginia*, the Court found an antimiscegenation statute to be unconstitutional and rejected state interests such as preserving "the racial integrity of its citizens" and preventing "the corruption of blood" and "the obliteration of racial pride."[76]

IV. DEFERENCE TO LEGISLATIVE MAJORITIES

The harder the case, the harder it will be to decide where the balance of public reason lies, but a judge who is committed to holding the state to the standard of public justification will make the best decision that he or she can. In the preceding examples, I have tried to illustrate the kinds of reasons that would clearly not be publicly justified. In very hard cases, many arguably public justifications will have premises whose truth can be reasonably disputed, apart from whether they support the inference that the person who puts forth the argument wants others to make. Whether a particular argument meets, comes close to meeting, or fails to meet the standard of public justification requires good faith and good judgment on the part of not only those who put forth the argument but also those who are supposed to assess that argument.

In the name of judicial restraint, some law professors, and not only those on the right, insist that judges should avoid making value choices whenever possible. For example, Kermit Roosevelt believes that most value choices should be left to the legislature.[77] As he sees it, the Court's recognition of a right to same-sex marriage would be legitimate provided that the Court was merely recognizing a more or less national consensus.[78] In essence, this is what the Court did in *Lawrence v. Texas* when it struck down a Texas law that prohibited consensual, same-sex sex between adults. At that time, only thirteen states had such laws on the books, and those laws were rarely, if ever, enforced. However, this approach takes the bite out of judicial review and makes it too easy for the state to coerce people of the basis of controversial reasons. My point is not that legislative decisions are never

---

[75] Plessy v. Ferguson, 163 U.S. 537 (1896).
[76] Loving v. Virginia, 388 U.S. 1 (1967).
[77] Roosevelt, *Myth of Judicial Activism*, 101.
[78] Ibid., 108.

entitled to deference, but rather that what matters, above all, is the kind of reasons that the legislature offers on their behalf.

In fundamental rights and equal protection cases, the burden of proof is on the state to explain why the arguments that it has put forth are sufficiently public to restrict personal freedom or to treat certain people unequally. If the state cannot clearly meet its burden, then the argument is insufficiently public and the law in question is unconstitutional. In exercising the power of judicial review, the judiciary decides whether the reasons that a law-making body has offered in defense of the law in question have met or have come close enough to meeting the standard of public justification. As I will spell out later in the book, compared with citizens and their elected representatives, judges are under a much stricter duty of self-restraint when they write their opinions. That does not mean, however, that legislators should see themselves as free to legislate on any basis whatsoever, because they, too, have a duty to uphold the Constitution. Thus, they should avoid imposing conceptions of the good on any of their constituents, particularly on those that are likely to be underrepresented in the legislative process.[79] Above all, members of law-making bodies must sincerely believe that the legislation in question could be justified to reasonable dissenters and be able to defend their position when asked to do so. As much as possible, they should avoid controversial grounds so that the judiciary does not have to do more work than it really needs to do in delineating the constitutional limits of the coercive power of the state.

Today, in our country, that is a tall order. As Jeremy Waldron notes, "It is no surprise that much of the jurisprudential antipathy toward legislation is heard in the United States, where standards of drafting are low."[80] That is true, but unfortunately, in the past, the other branches of government have put the Court in an unenviable position by asking its justices to adjudicate political controversies that cannot be easily settled through ordinary political procedures.[81] As a result, over time, most Americans have come to expect the Court to settle the most controversial of political controversies. It is not so much that judges try to save the people from themselves but that they have saved legislators from having to make difficult and controversial choices that carry political risk. Judges usually defer to legislative judgments with respect to nonfundamental rights and nonsuspect classifications by

---

[79] See Justice Stone's famous footnote 4 from *United States v. Carolene Products Co.*, 304 U.S. 144 (1938).

[80] Jeremy J. Waldron, "Legislation," in *The Blackwell Guide to the Philosophy of Law and Legal Theory*, ed. Martin P. Golding and William A. Edmundson (Malden, MA: Blackwell Publishing, 2005), 237.

[81] This is not limited to the past one hundred years. See, e.g., Bernard Schwartz's account of the *Dred Scott* case. Bernard Schwartz, *A History of the Supreme Court* (New York: Oxford University Press, 1993), 105–25.

employing the rational basis standard of review. The standard rationale for such deference is that legislatures are better than courts are in assessing the empirical evidence, weighing the costs and benefits of legislative proposals, and predicting their likely consequences.

Roosevelt claims that such deference is not warranted only when there is good reason to believe that a legislature will not act in good faith or competently.[82] For example, a court is more likely to turn a skeptical eye toward racial classifications because historically, racial majorities have discriminated against racial minorities and denied them equal opportunity. Descriptively, Roosevelt is right, but normatively his position overemphasizes the importance of judicial oversight to ensure the procedural fairness of the legislative process. I believe that courts should take a less passive approach in ensuring that legislators rely upon sufficiently public reasons as the moral basis of public laws until they do a better job of publicly justifying the laws that all of their constituents must live under. No thoughtful person believes that the state is entitled to use the law to discriminate against those who lack political influence and to make their lives worse. The traditional criteria for treating a group as a suspect or quasi-suspect class – a history of discrimination, an immutable characteristic, and political powerlessness – are still useful. Still, there is also something to be said for protecting other groups against other kinds of unjustified discrimination, particularly those who are especially vulnerable, like the elderly, the mentally retarded, the disabled, and noncitizens, even when they do not meet the traditional criteria as well as a racial or ethnic minority would. Like many others, Roosevelt has faith that democratically accountable legislatures usually will act fairly in distributing the benefits and burdens of social cooperation. For him, courts should give legislators the benefit of the doubt unless they have good reason to doubt their motives.

This view is conventional and understandable but less justified than it may initially appear to be. Excessive judicial deference to legislative judgments and the presumption of constitutionality that underlies it is not the virtue that so many commentators believe it to be. At present, there is substantial agreement between liberals and conservatives on this point about judicial deference, because conservatives do not want to see the liberal activism of the Warren Court return and because liberals believe that an increasingly conservative judiciary is likely to use its power to further its own partisan ends. For different reasons, then, both conservatives and liberals are likely to advocate restraint on the part of the judiciary as a modus vivendi. Politically, that is unsurprising, but in this book I have been trying to establish a more principled, ideologically neutral understanding of the constitutional limits on the coercive power of the state. In many instances, legislators simply do

---

[82] Roosevelt, *Myth of Judicial Activism*, 183.

not give much thought to whether the legislation that they enact could be justified to those who are adversely affected by it.[83] Legislatures often fail in publicly justifying public laws because they have little or no incentive to do so. For this reason, an approach to judicial review in which courts defer to legislative judgments in the absence of a clear mistake is not appropriate most of the time. A strong presumption in favor of the laws that majoritarian politics produces makes sense only when those laws are publicly justified.

That is not to say that there are never other grounds for such deference on a case-by-case basis: lack of institutional expertise, high decision costs, unacceptable risk of error, and so forth. But it is to say that judges must make it more difficult for legislatures to rely on reasons that reasonable dissenters justifiably reject to protect individual rights and to ensure equal treatment. One cannot simply assert that a theory of constitutional adjudication should not take sides in a debate over the proper ends of judicial review. It is not as if other theories of constitutional adjudication are silent on the purpose of judicial review, its relationship to democratic decision making, and the amount of deference that legislative decisions deserve. A judicial opinion must explain the outcome of a case, and there are an almost infinite number of ways in which a judge can offer such an explanation. Any theory of justification must rule out certain reasons on the ground that they are bad reasons; otherwise, justification would be impossible. In the context of constitutional adjudication, public justification is predicated on an ideal of reciprocity, that is, on the possibility that reasonable persons, who are committed to freedom and equality, can share certain reasons as being good reasons, which is to be expected in easy cases, and can recognize certain reasons as not being bad reasons, which is to be hoped for in more difficult cases.

In a democracy, legislative majorities are supposed to rule. At the same time, no one in our constitutional culture believes that democratic majorities should be permitted to turn their will into law in all circumstances. On reflection, few Americans would be willing to allow the state to restrict their personal freedom on the mere basis of the procedural fairness of the legislative process or of the aggregated preferences of the majority. No one would want to concede to the state the authority to enact laws on such bases and risk putting the success of his or her life plan in jeopardy. That is one way of understanding the implications of a commitment to freedom

---

[83] There is a voluminous literature in political science on congressional voting behavior that establishes that such voting is predominantly a function of constituent preferences, personal policy preferences, and partisan pressures. See David Mayhew, *Congress: The Electoral Connection* (New Haven, CT: Yale University Press, 1974); Richard F. Fenno, *Homestyle: House Members on Their Districts* (Glenview, IL: Scott Foresman, 1978); Keith T. Poole and Howard Rosenthal, *Congress: A Political-Economic History of Roll Call Voting* (New York: Oxford University Press, 1997).

and equality. In terms of public justification, the challenge is to achieve more agreement on their implications or at least to explain why reasonable disagreement is reasonable when consensus is out of reach. In short, judges should not defer to legislative judgments unless those legislators can publicly justify that law to those who will be adversely affected by it. Respect for reasonable dissenters as political equals with important life plans of their own requires nothing less.

A standard of public justification does not dictate results in hard cases but provides a vocabulary and common mode of reasoning that makes an exchange of reasons possible, thereby increasing the likelihood that the decision rendered will be legitimate even in the absence of consensus. Perhaps the main reason, when all is said and done, that everyone supports constitutional limits on the coercive power of the state is that it is hard to imagine that anyone would risk his or her happiness by putting an unpopular or unconventional life plan into the hands of those who may be hostile to that so-called lifestyle. Ideally, the life plans of others should matter no more than what we think of their haircuts or fashion sense. In real human societies, though, people are often tempted to impose their deepest convictions on others because they are "right" and others are "wrong." That social phenomenon, or what John Stuart Mill referred to as the "logic of persecutors," is not going to disappear anytime soon. Perhaps, in a more tolerant society, that would not happen as much as it does, and in such a society, there would be less need for the exercise of judicial review than there is today.

One could object that I have made it far too easy for judges to ignore the will of democratic majorities and to abuse their power by doing what they think is best and not what is constitutionally mandated. One could also object that I have overestimated the ability of real judges to render publicly justified decisions even under the best of conditions. Both those objections may be valid, but those same concerns are equally applicable to legislators and to other political actors. As it currently stands, it is far too easy for legislators to enact laws that are not publicly justified, especially when those who are discriminated against cannot retaliate against them. The presumption in favor of deference to legislative judgments should not be considered self-evident, and those who are preoccupied with the purported abuse of judicial power or with judicial incompetence must look more closely at the past and present flaws of the law-making process. They cannot simply claim that elected representatives are directly accountable to their constituents and insist that democracy is working well because the preferences of legislative majorities have been aggregated accurately. A decent society treats all persons as equals in the sense that all reasonable life plans are equally important, which means that reasonable dissenters would not reject the reasons that have been offered in support of laws that restrict those life plans.

To not care about whether other reasonable people would accept them not only is to be indifferent to the lives of others but also reflects a failure to appreciate that it is not only our society but theirs as well.

The more important the case in terms of its impact on people's lives, the more the Court should subject the reasons of the legislature to careful scrutiny to ensure that those reasons are good enough. But does that mean that a legislature could not act on the basis of a controversial political or social theory? In other words, does a legislature have to exercise the same kind of self-restraint that judges are supposed to exercise? For example, would it be unconstitutional for Congress to redistribute wealth on the basis of the Marxist maxim "from each according to his ability, to each according to his need"? The short answer is that it probably would be if that distributive principle could not be publicly justified, but legislators could try to make the case that it would be justified in the language of public reasons. In terms of the division of labor, legislators should see themselves as having the freedom to experiment with reasons that are arguably public and then see how judges and the electorate respond to them, say, in the pursuit of greater economic equality. The self-restraint demanded of them, then, should not be as strict as that of the judiciary.

By contrast, judges are under a stricter duty because they often have the final word on the constitutional controversies that they adjudicate and they are not directly accountable to the electorate. For instance, a judge could appropriately uphold the law that the Court invalidated in *Lochner* because that law was publicly justified.[84] That is not intended to be an argument that maximum-hour or minimum-wage laws are necessarily fair. The point is that for a law such as that one to be found to be constitutional, the Court must try to determine whether the reasons that the state has put forth on behalf of such legislation are sufficiently public. That a reasonable person would see such reasons as improving health and safety in the workplace and leveling the playing field between labor and management with respect to negotiating the terms of employment would count in favor of the public justification of the law.[85] In deciding whether to uphold or strike down the law in question, judges must not rely on the alleged correctness of controversial normative political theories. In his dissent in *Lochner*, Justice Oliver Wendell Holmes makes a similar point when he refers to the inappropriateness of the majority's reliance on "Mr. Spencer's *Social Statics*."[86] Today, a judge could not use John Rawls's difference principle to strike down legislation that gave a tax break to the wealthy to stimulate investment but that did not

[84] Lochner v. New York, 198 U.S. 45 (1905).

[85] See Lawrence H. Tribe, *The Invisible Constitution* (New York: Oxford University Press, 2008), 131.

[86] Lochner v. New York, 198 U.S. 75 (1905) (Holmes, J., dissenting).

help the least advantaged group.[87] Rawls himself no longer believes that the difference principle is a constitutional essential.[88]

Just about everyone expects certain things from constitutional adjudication: consensus, legitimacy, predictability, transparency, and fairness. The primary normative question, as I have characterized it, is whether any theory can meet these expectations under conditions of moral pluralism, in which people may not be able to live together on the basis of mutual respect because of their deeper differences. It is possible to ask too much of a theory of constitutional adjudication, but it also possible to ask too little from such a theory. Judges can mitigate the inevitable divisiveness that characterizes a morally pluralistic society such as our own, and they are uniquely situated, because of their relative independence from the other branches of government and public opinion, to ensure that the state relies on reasons that reasonable dissenters should not reject. This function is particularly important in a society that provides little space for political participation on the part of ordinary people and has few forums in which people exchange reasons with one another, thus increasing the risk that the most important laws are not sufficiently publicly justified. Because most persons have very little influence in the legislative process, they are likely to feel not only that law is coercive but that it is unjustified coercion as well.

The point is not that all persons will necessarily agree with the reasons that the Court puts forth to defend the constitutional right to abortion or to invalidate a particular affirmative action plan. Rather, people who are subject to the coercive power of the state are entitled to such explanations, and law-making bodies often fail to put together an adequate justification. Indeed, too frequently, they do not even make any effort to do so. Although that is not the only purpose of the judiciary, people who care about living in a society that makes a conscientious effort to promote the quality of the lives of all of its members cannot be indifferent to the fact that our political institutions often do not come close to producing reasons that could serve as the moral basis of the exercise of coercion by the state.

---

[87] The difference principle requires that "social and economic inequalities are to be arranged so that they are to the greatest expected benefit of the least advantaged." John Rawls, *A Theory of Justice: Revised Edition* (Cambridge, MA: Harvard University Press, Belknap Press, 1999), 72.

[88] John Rawls, *Political Liberalism* (New York: Columbia University Press, 1996), 228–9. However, Rawls also believes that a social minimum would be a constitutional essential.

THREE

The Challenge of Public Justification

In this chapter, I go into more detail what public justification is, why it is important, and how reasonable people could offer reasons that they sincerely believe other reasonable people would accept. I then explain what makes hard constitutional cases hard by drawing on accounts of the nature of reasonable disagreement found in contemporary political theory literature. In doing so, I hope to show that this kind of disagreement, as intractable as it may be at times, need not lead to skepticism about the possibility of the rational resolution of constitutional controversies. Although most of us these days doubt the ability of formalist or deductive methods to provide correct answers, at least in hard cases, it does not follow that any constitutional argument is as good as any other constitutional argument. One can appreciate why reasonable judges might reach different results in such cases and not conclude that the process of giving reasons is futile. The kinds of reasons that a judicial opinion incorporates will determine whether that opinion is legitimate. There is a world of difference between an opinion that meets or comes close to meeting the standard of public justification that I defend in this book and an opinion that clearly falls short of that. I then conclude with some thoughts on the weaknesses of skeptical challenges to the objectivity of legal reasoning.

I. THE CONCEPT OF PUBLIC JUSTIFICATION

A. Public Justification in Political Theory Literature

Recently, a number of prominent political theorists have emphasized the centrality of public justification to liberalism as a political theory.[1] They often

---

[1] See, e.g., Ronald Dworkin, "Liberalism," in *A Matter of Principle* (Cambridge, MA: Harvard University Press, 1985), 181–204; Gerald F. Gaus, *Value and Justification: The Foundations of Liberal Theory* (Cambridge: Cambridge University Press, 1990); Stephen Macedo, *Liberal Virtues: Citizenship, Virtue, and Community in Liberal Constitutionalism* (Oxford,

link such justification to the principle of liberal neutrality, which requires state action to be neutral toward different conceptions of the good.[2] For them, just as the state is not supposed to establish a religion, it is not supposed to favor one conception of the good over others. Thus, liberal neutrality constrains state action and helps to determine its legitimacy. The more coercive the state action, the more likely a more convincing justification for what the state has decided to do is called for. Other theorists who would describe themselves as deliberative democrats insist that public justification plays an indispensable role in the practice of democratic citizenship.[3] According to them, everyone is entitled to an explanation of the use of political power and a state that either refuses to offer such an explanation or fails to produce a satisfactory one has not treated its citizens with the respect that they deserve. Such a failure may mean that the law in question is not sufficiently publicly justified to bind everyone who is subject to it. People who care about the freedom and equality of others seek adequate justification before they coerce others. It follows that they must produce reasons in defense of the law in question that they sincerely believe others would and should accept.[4] If they do not believe that those reasons exist, then they should not impose that law on others.

An ideal of public justification will never be fully realized in practice, but a decent society should aspire to rational consensus when collective decisions have the force of law and when those who refuse to comply may be fined, incarcerated, or even executed. In the words of Stephen Macedo, "Only public reasons that all ought to be able to accept can count as good reasons

U.K.: Clarendon Press, 1991); Jeremy Waldron, "Theoretical Foundations of Liberalism," in *Liberal Rights: Collected Papers: 1981–91* (Cambridge: Cambridge University Press, 1993), 36–7; Thomas Nagel, *Equality and Partiality* (New York: Oxford University Press, 1991), 3; Thomas Nagel, "Moral Conflict and Political Legitimacy," 16 *Philosophy and Public Affairs* (1987), 215–40.

[2] There is substantial disagreement in the literature over exactly how the concept of neutrality should be understood. However, there are two basic ways of understanding liberal neutrality: neutrality of justification and neutrality of effect. The former requires the state to have an uncontroversial justification for its decision to promote a particular conception of the good. This has been the "dominant formulation of the neutrality principle." The latter requires the state to not do anything that has the effect of promoting a particular conception of the good, which would be impossible. See Steven Wall and George Klosko, "Introduction," in *Perfectionism and Neutrality: Essays in Liberal Theory*, ed. Steven Wall and George Klosko (Lanham, MD: Rowman and Littlefield, 2003), 8.

[3] See, e.g., Seyla Benhabib, *Situating the Self: Gender, Community and Postmodernism in Contemporary Ethics* (Cambridge, U.K.: Polity Press, 1992), 24; Joshua Cohen, "The Economic Basis of Deliberative Democracy," 6 *Social Philosophy and Policy* (1989), 30.

[4] Jonathan Quong refers to this as the "sincerity requirement." See Jonathan Quong, "Three Disputes about Public Justification: Commentary on Gaus and Vallier," 3, unpublished paper, http://publicreason.net/2008/09/26/ppps-the-roles-of-religious-convictions-in-a-publicly-justified-polity/.

for lawmaking."[5] The basic idea is that "I can be rationally convinced of the worthiness of a norm only if I suppose that others are rationally convinced, which in turn depends on their supposing that I am rationally convinced."[6] In the end, some people will not be persuaded that public justification is as important as other objectives, like socioeconomic justice, economic efficiency, or self-government. At the same time, we live in a society where all of us are vulnerable to all sorts of coercion without our consent.[7] A society that is committed to public justification would increase the likelihood that the people who are subject to its laws understand and accept their justifications.

The trouble is that to demand that the state's explanation for its actions be understandable and acceptable to the least competent or most unreasonable persons is unrealistic. Thus, theorists who are sympathetic to public justification usually qualify this ideal by maintaining that only reasonable persons have to receive such an explanation.[8] But to avoid charges that they are excluding too many people, they define *reasonable* as broadly as possible. According to John Rawls, an unreasonable person is "unwilling to honor, or even propose, except as a necessary public pretense, any general principles or standards for specifying fair terms of cooperation.[9] On its face, that definition would cover just about everyone; a reasonable person only has to be minimally morally motivated to exchange reasons with others and to share the benefits and burdens of membership in that society. Without a distinction between reasonable and unreasonable persons, it would be impossible for the state to meet any standard of public justification. An irrational or unreasonable dissenter would be able to veto every proposed state action and thereby maintain the status quo.[10]

Beyond these basics, what public justification entails both in theory and in practice is contested. Some, but not all, liberals take the following route toward justification. For a morally pluralistic society like our own, conceptions of the good or what Rawls calls "comprehensive doctrines" in *Political Liberalism*[11] are likely to be too controversial to serve as the basis

[5] Macedo, *Liberal Virtues*, 195.

[6] I borrow this characterization from William Rehg, who is interpreting the principle of reciprocity that is implicit in Habermasian discourse ethics. William Rehg, "Discourse and the Moral Point of View: Deriving a Dialogical Principle of Universalization," 34 *Inquiry* (1990), 44–5.

[7] Even the minimal state of Robert Nozick would have a police force and legal system, and therefore would coerce its citizens. See Jonathan Wolff, *Robert Nozick: Property, Justice, and the Minimal State* (Stanford, CA: Stanford University Press, 1991), 36.

[8] On this point, see Steven Wall, *Liberalism, Perfectionism and Restraint* (Cambridge: Cambridge University Press, 1998), 110–11.

[9] John Rawls, *Political Liberalism* (New York: Columbia University Press, 1993), 50.

[10] See David Estlund, "The Democracy/Contractualism Analogy," 31 *Philosophy and Public Affairs* (2003), 397–400.

[11] John Rawls, *Political Liberalism* (New York: Columbia University Press, 1996).

of the political morality that regulates our political life. That claim does not merely reflect the sociological fact of the existence of moral disagreement over issues like abortion, capital punishment, and affirmative action but rather cuts much deeper. It is unlikely that reason, even under the best of epistemic circumstances, would compel all reasonable persons to acknowledge the superiority of a single conception of the good. Therefore, those who care about public justification avoid appeals to the truth of their respective religious or secular conceptions of the good. Such appeals to truth may be counterproductive inasmuch as they make political discourse less civil and more chaotic than it otherwise would be. Even if one is convinced that a particular claim is true, its purported truth is not, by itself, a sufficient reason to use that claim as the basis of coercion; that claim must also resonate with other reasonable people.

This insight is especially important when citizens and public officials are tempted to appeal to their truth of their respective conceptions of the good and, by implication, assert that those of others are false. As Bruce Ackerman explains, "Somehow or other, citizens of a liberal state must learn to talk to one another in a way that enables each of them to avoid condemning their own personal morality as evil or false."[12] Thus, other reasonable people must also see the reason(s) offered as adequate justification for the law in question, or else they will be forced to accept laws that they not only reject but also may have good reasons for rejecting. A reasonable person not only gives certain kinds of reasons but also accepts certain kinds of reasons. It may be difficult, though, to characterize an ideal of public justification in a manner that is acceptable to everyone; thus, what might count as an impartial or sufficiently public reason in a particular instance may not be evident.

In individual constitutional cases, in the eyes of many reasonable people, there may be good reasons that support contradictory conclusions, and this state of affairs cannot be reduced to the ignorance, dogmatism, self-interest, or psychological pathologies of the participants. As such, we cannot always expect reason to lead us to the same conclusion, and it would be wrong to impose laws on those who are not unreasonable. As one commentator explains, if a person is rational, and he or she rejects a particular justificatory reason, then rejection alone indicates that the reason in question is prima facie not sufficiently justified.[13] Unless one can locate a flaw in his or her reasoning, that person would seem to be warranted in not accepting the argument that others have put forward as justification. It is true that "sometimes we can be extremely confident that the basic standards [of rationality]

---

[12] Bruce Ackerman, "Why Dialogue?" 86 *Journal of Philosophy* (1989), 12.

[13] Gerald F. Gaus, "Liberal Neutrality: A Compelling and Radical Principle," in *Perfection and Neutrality: Essays in Liberal Theory*, ed. Steven Wall and George Klosko (Lanham, MD: Rowman and Littlefield , 2003), 144.

have been flouted."[14] Although a person may begin with a premise that is patently false or rely on a non sequitur, the validity or soundness of his or her argument normally will not be so easy to assess. This concern about the difficulty of meeting the standard of public justification has an interesting implication: a conception of the good or comprehensive doctrine could turn out to be true but still fail to qualify as a public reason.[15] That is the case because conceptions of the good are inherently controversial; they are premised on reasons that reasonable people can and do reject.

This book has a similar normative concern but focuses on the public justification of the laws that the Court scrutinizes when it exercises the power of judicial review. In the midst of scholarly preoccupation with the legitimacy of regimes and the acceptability of abstract principles of justice, it is also worthwhile to understand what the public justification of a judicial decision and a public law might consist of when real judges have to decide real cases that will affect real people. Most Americans do not understand the dynamics of the judicial process very well.[16] But when they are expected to accept the legitimacy of these decisions, they will ask for and are owed an explanation of whether there are constitutional rights to abortion, same-sex marriage, or physician-assisted suicide; why affirmative action policies may violate the equal protection clause; or why the right to keep and bear arms is either an individual or a group right. Even when there is consensus among Americans about abstract principles of justice, that consensus tends to break down the moment that they try to apply those principles to challenging cases.[17] While most Americans agree on the form of such principles, they disagree about their content. What public justification requires in individual constitutional cases, then, merits scholarly attention as well. The importance of public justification is not limited to those who are committed to some form of liberalism or deliberative democracy but includes anyone who cares about the procedural and substantive fairness of collective decision-making in politics and seeks to secure the consent of others through an exchange of reasons. Today, any political theory worthy of our allegiance will have to include an explanation of how moral conflict is to be resolved under conditions of moral pluralism. Otherwise, we risk leaving the reasonable life plans of many persons at the mercy of the coercive power of the state.

In a normatively perfect world, the public justification of every collective decision would be rooted in reasons that everyone would accept as the best

[14] Ibid., 152.

[15] Ibid., 154.

[16] See David M. O'Brien, "Preface," in *Judges on Judging: Views from the Bench*, 2nd ed., ed. David M. O'Brien (Washington, D.C.: Congressional Quarterly Press, 2004), vii.

[17] Amy Gutmann and Dennis Thompson, *Democracy and Disagreement: Why Moral Conflict Cannot Be Avoided in Politics and What Should Be Done about It* (Cambridge, MA: Harvard University Press, Belknap Press, 1996), 35.

reasons with full knowledge that they were indeed the best reasons. There would be no worries about spurious consent, false consciousness, or demagoguery. In such a world, the exercise of political authority by the state through its public laws would not be morally problematic because each person would have had the opportunity to nullify each proposed collective decision. People could not later complain that they had been unjustifiably coerced when they refused to comply with a law that they had not only agreed to and that was publicly justified beyond a shadow of a doubt. Something like this political arrangement is what Jean-Jacques Rousseau had in mind when he imagined in *The Social Contract* how each individual will could be in harmony with the general will. That everyone would acknowledge the soundness of the same argument in a normatively perfect world would be even more demanding than the anarchist requirement of unanimity, in which a decision is collectively binding only when everyone in the community has actually consented to the proposal in question, regardless of whether they share any of the same reasons.[18]

Ideally, for a public law to be legitimate, all persons would actually consent or would have consented if they were properly informed, appropriately motivated, and minimally rational. The purpose of the public justification of the most important public laws is to produce reasons that dissenters could not reasonably reject, thereby legitimizing such laws.[19] Compared with other kinds of influence, the threat of coercion that underlies such laws is more serious because a person who fails to comply, even as a matter of conscience, may be forced to do what he or she believes to be wrong when the personal costs of noncompliance are too high. As much as possible, such laws should be rooted in rational consensus. The practice of public reasoning in a deliberative democracy by citizens themselves or by their elected representatives aspires to such consensus even though actual consensus is out of the question in a country as large and diverse as our own. A commitment to an ideal of public justification illustrates that justification is not simply a matter of formulating a sound argument in an attempt to adjudicate the most important political conflicts; it also involves a self-imposed duty to reason from a common point of view by relying on premises that others either already accept or could be expected to accept as good enough.[20] That "leads us," as T. M. Scanlon writes, "into taking other people's interests into account in deciding what principles to follow."[21]

[18] Robert Paul Wolff, *In Defense of Anarchism* (Berkeley: University of California Press, 1970).

[19] T. M. Scanlon, "Contractualism and Utilitarianism," in *Utilitarianism and Beyond*, ed. Amartya Sen and Bernard Williams (New York: Cambridge University Press, 1984), 110.

[20] John Rawls, *Collected Papers* (Cambridge, MA: Harvard University Press, 1999), 394.

[21] T. M. Scanlon, *What We Owe to Each Other* (Cambridge, MA: Harvard University Press, Belknap Press, 1998), 202.

The practice of public reasoning over time would exhibit the mutual respect that citizens owe one another as members of the same political community and reduce the need for civil disobedience by making the relationship between political authority and individual conscience less morally troubling.[22] Dissenters would have far less reason to become civil disobedients if the reasons that the state offers as the justification for the most important public laws are undeniably fair. The importance of public justification cannot be separated from moral concerns about the legitimacy of the state forcing its inhabitants, through its criminal and civil laws, to alter their morally permissible behavior. It is basic to the liberal tradition that morality places limits on the content of legislative decisions.[23] That implies that certain reasons do not count as good-enough for certain kinds of statutory prohibitions and classifications. The creation and enforcement of some laws are more trivial than those of others because of how they affect people's chances of pursuing and achieving their ends. But when a law forbids conduct that it should permit or when the absence of a law fails to prevent others from doing what they should not be allowed to do, some people's lives will be worse than they otherwise would be.

In addition to Rawls, other well-known political theorists have used the existence of deep moral disagreement as the point of departure for their theories of political legitimacy.[24] Bruce Ackerman's idea of "conversational constraints" is designed to take questions about the nature of the good life off the political agenda of the liberal state.[25] Charles Larmore maintains that when two people disagree about a problem, "each should prescind from the beliefs that the other rejects" to increase the likelihood of reaching consensus on the disputed issue.[26] As Thomas Nagel remarks, "When can I regard

---

[22] This kind of public justification is also an essential part of normative theories of deliberative democracy. For Amy Gutmann and Dennis Thompson, when citizens or their elected officials disagree morally, they "should continue to reason together to reach mutually acceptable decisions." Gutmann and Thompson, *Democracy and Disagreement*, 1. According to James Bohman, deliberative democracy is "any one of a family of views according to which public deliberation of free and equal citizens is the core of legitimate political decisionmaking and self-government." James Bohman, "The Coming of Age of Deliberative Democracy," 6 *Journal of Political Philosophy* (1998), 401.

[23] Joel Feinberg, *Harm to Others: The Moral Limits of the Criminal Law* (New York: Oxford University Press, 1984), 4.

[24] See, e.g., Jeremy Waldron, *Law and Disagreement* (Oxford, UK: Oxford University Press, 1999); Gutmann and Thompson, *Democracy and Disagreement*; William A. Galston, *Liberal Purposes: Goods, Virtues, and Diversity in the Liberal State* (New York: Cambridge University Press, 1991); William A. Galston, *Liberal Pluralism: The Implications of Value Pluralism for Political Theory and Practice* (New York: Cambridge University Press, 2002); Bruce Ackerman, "Why Dialogue?" 86 *Journal of Philosophy* (1989), 5–22; Thomas Nagel, "Moral Conflict and Political Legitimacy," 16 *Philosophy and Public Affairs* (1987), 215–40; Charles Larmore, "Political Liberalism," 18 *Political Theory* (1990), 339–60.

[25] Ackerman, "Why Dialogue?" 16.

[26] Larmore, *Patterns of Moral Complexity*, 53.

the grounds for a belief as objective in a way that permits me to appeal to it in political argument, and to rely on it in political argument, and to rely on it even though others do not in fact accept it and even though they may not be unreasonable not to accept it? What kinds of grounds must those be, if I am not to be guilty of appealing simply to my belief, rather than to a common ground of justification?"[27] A reason that is good from one's own standpoint in a particular context may not be nearly as good from that of another person, and his or her rejection of that reason may be justified. In such circumstances, it would be wrong to use that reason to impose a law on another person unless others who are reasonable also would accept that reason as justification. The acceptability of that reason takes the place of consent. Thus, deliberators must eschew some reasons as inappropriate when they seek to convince other reasonable people. As much as possible, the reasons that they use as justification should be acceptable from an impersonal standpoint; those reasons cannot be contingent on deeper convictions that other reasonable people have good reasons for rejecting.

In a liberal society like our own, there is no established church or official conception of the good, and the state is not supposed to judge different ways of life on their merits or coerce citizens in the name of their "higher" or "better" selves.[28] Not only is the state unlikely to be able to do so fairly, but under conditions of moral pluralism, it also lacks a metric for making such qualitative judgments. Although legislative purposes may be neutral, the effects of laws can never be neutral toward all conceptions of the good.[29] There will be winners and losers, and a decent society must be concerned that some laws leave some people too badly off, in the sense that they cannot meaningfully form, revise, and pursue their respective conceptions of the good. A piece of legislation that had that foreseeable effect would not be justifiable to a reasonable person who wants to increase the likelihood that he or she will flourish. Such legislation would not be a legitimate use of the coercive power of the state unless it had a compelling justification. The problem of political legitimacy reflects the worry that there may be no shared basis of public justification under permanent conditions of moral pluralism. Citizens with different conceptions of the good may also disagree

---

[27] Nagel, "Moral Conflict and Political Legitimacy," 232.

[28] There are perfectionist liberals who advance autonomy as the conception of the good that should underlie political morality. See, e.g., Wall, *Liberalism, Perfectionism and Restraint*. However, in the beginning of his book, Wall explains that such an ideal of human flourishing is not necessarily elitist, hostile to pluralism, or universal. Nor would adherence to it necessarily require the state to use its power to advance it in all circumstances. This soft perfectionism may not seem to differ substantively from the antiperfectionist liberalism of Kant and Rawls, but as Wall points out in the last chapter, his version of liberalism, in which the state may promote autonomy, has different public policy implications (205–33).

[29] On this point, see Galston, *Liberal Purposes*, 4–9; Macedo, *Diversity and Distrust*, 188–211.

on matters of public morality because moral disagreement about the good may lead to disagreement about the fundamentals of justice as well.[30] In the absence of such justification, dissenters can rightfully challenge legislation on the ground that a reasonable person could reject its underlying reasons.

The reasons that are supposed to justify public laws ought to legitimize, in other words, what otherwise would be unjustified coercion, which is essential in a society like our own where ordinary persons have so little political influence. The reasons offered as justification must be fair to everyone in the sense of recognizing the right of each person to have an equal chance to formulate and achieve his or her own morally permissible ends. The state must treat each life plan as fairly as possible, and that means that some reasons cannot serve as the basis of legislation. Even when sincere deliberators cannot reach consensus about the fairness of particular public laws, a vote that takes place after such deliberation is more likely to be legitimate in the eyes of deliberators who have been exposed to all of the relevant arguments and who have had a chance to convert others to their point of view. The process of exchanging reasons in good faith to make widely acceptable collective decisions also may generate public opinion that is more informed and public deliberation that is more sophisticated.[31] A commitment to public justification is based on a more cooperative, less antagonistic style of collective decision making that eschews the kind of politics in which individuals or groups merely attempt to advance their respective interests or parochial ideals without proper consideration of the freedom and equality of others.

B. Two Basic Approaches to Public Justification

As I have explained, those who care about public justification under conditions of moral pluralism maintain that deliberators who attempt to publicly justify their political conclusions must exercise self-restraint by steering clear of reasons that are too controversial to serve as the moral basis of state coercion. For them, there is an important difference between the personal and the public justification of collective decisions.[32] In the latter case, it is not productive for a person who is sincerely trying to convince others to rely on premises that he or she already knows they would reject, particularly when they do not have bad reasons for such rejection. If a person were trying to convince an atheist that abortion is wrong, he or she would not appeal to ensoulment, divine commands, theology, or natural law but rather would look for other reasons that someone who was not religious still might accept.

---

[30] See, e.g., Waldron, *Law and Disagreement*.

[31] See, e.g., James S. Fishkin, *The Voice of the People: Public Opinion and Democracy* (New Haven, CT: Yale University Press, 1995).

[32] See, e.g., Gerald Gaus, *Justificatory Liberalism* (New York: Oxford University Press, 1996), 11.

The strength of different reasons would vary with the particulars of the case, but a person who wants to do more than preach to the choir will have to exercise some degree of self-restraint. Judges also care about convincing others, and no judge wants to be perceived by other legal professionals as someone who writes poorly reasoned opinions.[33] That person is not free, then, to rely on any reasons that he or she pleases or to assume that all of the relevant legal reasons are equally forceful. In such instances, the person's discretion involves identifying all of the relevant legal reasons, and the most justified decision is the one that balances the relevant reasons on the basis of their comparative weight most appropriately.

There are two basic ways of trying to publicly justify a public law or judicial decision. A judge could adopt a populist approach by trying to determine whether most Americans believe, say, capital punishment to be constitutional, or the judge could look outside the borders of the United States to see how other countries have answered the same question.[34] That empirical approach would have the advantage of the Court's not getting too far ahead of public opinion or not being too out of sync with the law of other nations. It is not evident, though, compared with other political actors that are directly accountable to the electorate, why courts would be better equipped to make such assessments. Nor is it clear why public opinion in the most important constitutional cases should be decisive. After all, some Americans might change their minds about the moral permissibility of capital punishment if they were better informed about its flaws.[35] The trouble with such a populist approach to public justification is that in trying to secure the approval of real people, the reasons put forth might not be morally acceptable. One can easily imagine a judge writing an opinion that relies on reasons that many people in a particular society would share but at the same time are based on falsehoods or prejudices. When the Court handed down these decisions, many white Americans would have accepted the white supremacist rationale of *Plessy v. Ferguson* or the national security rationale of *Korematsu*, but I doubt that many of us today would want to use those cases as examples of a publicly justified decision.

Alternatively, a judge could try to identify the reasons that reasonable people should identify and weigh properly in the most contentious constitutional cases, on the basis of their best understanding of the implications of

---

[33] This concern would fall under what Judge Kozinski refers to as "self-respect" and respect from colleagues. See Alex Kozinski, "What I Ate for Breakfast and Other Mysteries of Judicial Decision Making," in *Judges on Judging: Views from the Bench*, 2nd ed., ed. David M. O'Brien (Washington, D.C.: Congressional Quarterly Press, 2004), 77.

[34] Gerald Gaus refers to a conception of public reason that aims at actual acceptance by the members of that community as populist. See Gaus, *Justificatory Liberalism*.

[35] See, e.g., Hugo Adam Bedau, "A Reply to Van Den Haag," in *The Death Penalty in America: Current Controversies* (New York: Oxford University Press, 1997), 457–69.

political ideals like freedom and equality. For example, federal laws such as the 1964 Civil Rights Act and judicial decisions such as *Brown v. Board of Education*, which are predicated on the principle that racial discrimination is wrong, are publicly justified. Such laws and judicial decisions are publicly justified in two slightly different senses. First, they are publicly justified because they rest on principles that most Americans share at an abstract level but do not depend on any particular person's views. Second, and more important, they are publicly justified because they reflect principles that anyone living in a constitutional democracy ought to accept, even if not everyone accepts them. A fair system of social cooperation can be maintained over time only if its laws respect the freedom and equality of all persons who are a part of that system. A commitment to the equal importance of the lives of all persons, and not just those of those who are wealthy or powerful, is implicit in an ideal of public justification. It follows that everyone must enjoy access to the same benefits and opportunities without suffering discrimination, unless that discrimination serves a compelling state interest. A rational person would not consent to a law that undermines his or her ability to live a good life unless that person is convinced that such a law is absolutely necessary. No society that aspires to treat everyone fairly can use the law to force only some of its members to sacrifice the quality of their lives simply on the basis of the aggregated preferences of a legislative majority.

From the standpoint of public justification, legitimate judicial decisions are not those that Americans actually accept at a given moment – surely, real people can be unreasonable – but those that an ideal reasonable dissenter would see as good enough. That is bound to be challenging because, as Laurence Tribe writes, "Those who always look at charges of unequal treatment from the viewpoint of the people on the top rather than through the eyes of those at the bottom . . . predictably tend to miss the point."[36] The person who offers the public justification in question ought to be convinced that an ideal reasonable person would not reject the reasons that he or she has offered. Likewise, the person who must evaluate the justification in question also must believe that his or her acceptance or rejection of the reasons that he or she has been given is justifiable. If most actual dissenters accept the reasons in question as adequate, then the person who offers the justification usually can be even more confident that the decision is close enough to being publicly justified.

The tension between what people ought to accept when they are reasonable and what real people at a particular moment in time do accept will always exist in imperfect human communities. The more unjust a society is, the more serious this tension will be. That means that, in a society like

---

[36] Laurence H. Tribe, *God Save This Honorable Court: How the Choice of Supreme Court Justices Shapes Our History* (New York: Random House, 1985), 148.

our own, a reason could be sufficiently publicly justified but not politically efficacious in the sense that most actual reasonable persons would accept it. Likewise, a reason could be politically efficacious but not sufficiently publicly justified. In terms of public justification, it would be preferable if the reason in question satisfies both criteria; that reason not only would be acceptable from a common point of view but also almost all reasonable people would see it as such. In a society with too many unreasonable people, judges will often have to choose between publicly justified and politically efficacious reasons. That would be one way of characterizing a country like our own that tolerated the institution of slavery for so many years and had such difficulty in implementing civil rights legislation. A decent society hopes that these two kinds of reasons overlap more often than not, and it designs its political institutions to increase the likelihood that a publicly justified reason also is politically efficacious.

A publicly justified law reflects the principle that, in the eyes of the law, no reasonable life plan is any better or any worse than any other reasonable life plan. A life plan is reasonable when its pursuit does not infringe on the equally important right of others to pursue their respective conceptions of good. A law that significantly interferes with a person's right to form, revise, and pursue his or her conception of the good is not likely to be publicly justified. Similarly, a law that makes this equal right less equal for some of the members of that society is also not likely to be publicly justified. There is a presumption that laws that infringe on personal freedom or treat some persons unequally are not sufficiently publicly justified. A publicly justified judicial decision is legitimate, and there is a continuum, ranging from unarguably legitimate at one extreme to unarguably illegitimate at the other extreme. Where a judicial decision falls turns on the reasons that judges have mustered on its behalf, and reasons that are not derived from the principle that all lives are equally important are suspect.

In the previous chapter, I elucidated how an ideal of public justification captures the rationale of heightened standards of review and would explain the more or less uncontroversial outcomes of certain well-known cases. I also made it clear that some kinds of coercion, such as those that are designed to protect people from serious harm, are unquestionably publicly justified. A criminal does not have the right to assault or murder people at will or to steal their personal property. But a standard of public justification must illuminate more difficult cases as well, and it is evident that judges often do not see eye to eye in such cases. For instance, in *Lawrence v. Texas*, it is clear that Justices Rehnquist, Scalia, and Thomas did not believe that the Texas law, which prohibited consensual, same-sex sex between adults, ought to trigger a heightened standard of review.[37] Nor were they, nine years

[37] Lawrence v. Texas, 539 U.S. 558 (2003).

earlier, eager to subject a legislative classification based sexual orientation to something more than the traditional rational-basis standard of review.[38] In these two cases, it is clear that they believe that the state may act on the basis of reasons that real dissenters would reject.

That belief follows from their understanding of when a heightened standard of review should be triggered, and it would not surprise any first-year law student that conservative and liberal judges have different methods of determining when a right is fundamental or when the state has made a suspect or quasi-suspect legislative classification. The problem of a lack of agreement over the character and application of standards of review is compounded by the fact that so much of legal reasoning in a common law system is ad hoc.[39] Although judges are supposed to use analogical reasoning as a tool to produce uniformity and increase predictability, it is often not clear what a good analogy consists in.[40] That would help to explain why two competent judges might sincerely disagree about which material fact(s) in a particular case makes that case sufficiently similar to or sufficiently different from other cases that might serve as precedent. In an adversarial system of justice, attorneys make fine distinctions in a manner that advances their clients' interests, but that does not make it any easier for the judge to determine rationally the relative weight of the relevant reasons in particular cases. Lawyers and judges can cite particular cases to show that particular state interests have been found to be compelling or important, but one can always respond that the context of the case at hand somehow differs from those of past cases. In the recent Seattle and Louisville affirmative action cases, for instance, Chief Justice John Roberts distinguished the importance of racial diversity in higher education, which the Court found to be a compelling state interest in *Grutter v. Bollinger*, from that of such diversity in primary and secondary education, and he also maintained that school districts were using race as more than a mere "plus factor."[41]

An ad hoc approach is hardly the equivalent of having a systematic theory that can lay out the kinds of reasons that tend to be compelling or important more generally and account for what makes them compelling or important. If a judge does not understand the underlying theoretical rationale for a series of cases, then the judge is in no position to discern whether the case at hand really is sufficiently similar to be added to that series. The judge must be somewhat familiar with the abstract principle before he or she can recognize

---

[38] Romer v. Evans, 517 U.S. 620 (1996).

[39] The basic pattern of legal reasoning is reasoning from case to case. See Edward H. Levi, *An Introduction to Legal Reasoning* (Chicago: University of Chicago Press, 1949), 1.

[40] Analogical reasoning is more complicated than it may seem to be. See Hilary Putnam, *The Many Faces of Realism* (LaSalle, IL: Open Court Publishing, 1987), 73.

[41] Parents Involved in Community Schools v. Seattle School District No. 1, 551 U.S. 701 (2007) (Roberts, J., majority).

particular instances of it. Without such deeper understanding, the judge is more prone to latch onto superficial similarities or differences and miss more relevant similarities and differences. One is hard pressed, for instance, to see purposeful discrimination against African Americans throughout American history as the constitutional equivalent of reverse discrimination against white persons in affirmative action programs, even when one still believes that such programs are unconstitutional on other grounds. Whereas a Jim Crow law undeniably conveys a message of racial inferiority to African Americans, an affirmative action program that is designed to compensate certain ethnic and racial minorities for past racial injustices and to offset current racial discrimination is not as obviously morally repugnant.

A shared standard of constitutional adjudication like public justification may be theoretically ambitious, but attempts to comply with it would encourage judges to view themselves as engaged in the same enterprise and to have similar ideas about what that enterprise entails even in hard cases. In theory, adherence to such a standard would improve the quality of constitutional argumentation by making it more deliberative. At first glance, that aim might appear to be unnecessary. After all, compared with what usually takes place in electoral and legislative politics, most judges already seem to do a much better job of exchanging reasons with one another. But the point is not to improve, comparatively speaking, but to legitimize judicial decisions that are so difficult to overturn. After reading the majority, concurring, and dissenting opinions in many important constitutional cases, one often doubts that the author of the opinion was sincerely trying to convince those who were likely to disagree. Far too many opinions read less like exercises in persuasion and more like personal reflections on why the author of that opinion reached the conclusion that he or she did, as if judges were more concerned with preaching to the converted or removing any lingering doubts in their own minds than with convincing others that they have the better argument. Descriptively, that may be attributed to the fact that majority opinions are sometimes cobbled together to secure the support of other judges who are inclined to dissent or who are undecided. Otherwise, that opinion might not turn out to be a majority opinion at all. Or that may result from a judge's being more concerned with being right than with securing the support or praise of his or her colleagues.[42]

Nevertheless, in their opinions, judges should not be afraid to acknowledge the strength of the reasons that support the opposite conclusion. Clarity, or trying to make a decision more rule-like, should not be purchased at the price of pretending that a legal argument is stronger than it really

---

[42] Cf. Antonin Scalia, "The Dissenting Opinion," *Journal of Supreme Court History* (1994), 33–44 (where Scalia refers to having the luxury of not having to accommodate the views of his colleagues as an "unparalleled pleasure").

is. In particular, judges must avoid understating the strength of the reasons that the other side offers in an understandable but misguided effort to remove doubt. To pretend that constitutional controversies are easier than they really are is to mislead those who read judicial decisions. There may be more to be said on behalf of oversimplification in the name of clarity in other areas of law. As long as the Court decides the most important constitutional cases, however, it must not hide their complexity. If a judicial opinion is not intellectually honest, then people will not be able to assess its quality. A good opinion is not one-sided, and an even better opinion not only would be as explicit as possible about the reasons that lead to the result but also would explain why those reasons, and not others, are better, all things considered.

Usually, there is nothing wrong with openly sharing with the rest of the world the reasons that one takes to be strongest when a personal or collective decision has to be made. In the context of constitutional adjudication, though, this is not what a judge should be doing. Although a judicial opinion in a constitutional case is supposed to elaborate on what the Constitution requires, that does not necessarily mean that a judge simply exercises his or her own best judgment in applying an abstract constitutional provision to the particular facts of the case to be decided in the name of, say, distributive justice or wealth maximization. This mistake on the part of most judges is more serious than initially it may appear to be because it undermines the very legitimacy of judicial review under conditions of moral pluralism and puts into doubt the obligation of elected officials and citizens to comply with such decisions. A theory of constitutional adjudication must both point to the right answer in a hard case and contain a standard that would elucidate why that answer is better than all of the other plausible answers. Such a theory can do so only when judges write their opinions in a manner that engages the best arguments of likely dissenters and explains why their arguments should not prevail.

Above all, judges must not see doubt as an enemy to be vanquished at all costs. Such thinking leads not only to poor reasoning but also to poor decisions, which is not something that a society that relies so heavily on judicial review can afford. While I do not want to argue this point here, the more judges care about results, the more likely they are to write one-sided opinions. That happens both on the Left and on the Right, and that should not happen as much as it does, especially when judges are exposed to a wide variety of constitutional arguments during the appellate process. One of the functions of dissents in judicial opinions is to force the majority to deal with "the hardest questions urged by the losing side."[43] That does not guarantee, though, that the author of a majority opinion will deal with the hardest questions adequately. The deeper psychological problem may be

---

[43] William J. Brennan Jr., "In Defense of Dissents," 50 *Hastings Law Journal* (1999), 674.

that most of us have too much confidence in our own beliefs and thus make too little effort to understand the positions of those with whom we disagree, even when we take ourselves to be open minded. As Cass Sunstein has recently shown, most people tend to self-segregate into like-minded groups in which they are not exposed to different points of view.[44] By not addressing the merits of ideas that they reject, people will not risk undermining their confidence in the truth of their deepest convictions. At times, unfortunately, the same can be said of judges. Thus, many majority opinions do not do what they are supposed to do: provide good-enough reasons to those who are likely to disagree with the decision so that they are obligated to comply with it.

D. The Consequences

Sunstein is famous for advancing the view that judicial opinions ought to be minimal in that they attempt "to provide rulings that can attract support from people with diverse theoretical commitments."[45] His idea of judicial minimalism is attractive inasmuch as he takes the problem of public justification in the midst of moral pluralism seriously and offers a solution that is arguably more democratic than that of Rawls. In a morally pluralistic society such as our own, it will be challenging to find reasons that the vast majority of reasonable people can and should share in resolving constitutional controversies. There also may be something to be said for leaving some fundamental issues undecided so that the people and their elected representatives can respond to them.[46] A minimalist U.S. Supreme Court is less likely to render decisions prematurely, and thus less likely to get too far ahead of public opinion and generate unnecessary controversy. There would be fewer backlashes and less shrill rhetoric about judges' overstepping their bounds and so on. Sunstein has the alleged overreaching of the Warren Court in mind.[47] Courts make mistakes, but even when they are right, the perceived legitimacy of their decisions may still be disputed.[48]

By saying no more than necessary to justify a particular outcome, Sunstein is convinced that democratic deliberation will be stimulated.[49] This "decisional minimalism" has a consequentialist rationale; it is designed to promote reason giving among citizens and their elected representatives.[50] Such decisions also are supposed to encourage ordinary people to accept more

---

[44] See, e.g., Cass R. Sunstein, *Republic.com* (Princeton, NJ: Princeton University Press, 2001).
[45] Cass R. Sunstein, *One Case at a Time: Judicial Minimalism on the Supreme Court* (Cambridge, MA: Harvard University Press, 1999), x.
[46] Ibid.
[47] Ibid., xiii.
[48] Ibid., 5.
[49] Ibid., 4.
[50] Ibid., 5.

civic responsibility for the political choices that public officials make in their name. A relatively modest rationale on behalf of the outcome of a particular case, Sunstein hopes, places the responsibility of clarifying the implications of constitutional values on the shoulders of the people themselves. With respect to same-sex marriage, a judge committed to judicial minimalism would proceed cautiously into the thicket, believing that the function of the judiciary is to leave the most important questions to be decided democratically. As such, the judge's opinion would prompt the electorate to contemplate certain questions, such as whether alternatives to marriage, such as civil unions or domestic partnerships, are inherently demeaning.[51] An incompletely theorized judicial opinion could raise the question of what equal treatment entails without providing an answer by judicial fiat.

It is not hard to appreciate what Sunstein is trying to do in a democratic society where self-rule is supposed to be more than a mere slogan. On the one hand, he is sensitive to the traditional concern that it is difficult to control unelected federal judges who cannot be easily removed from office.[52] On the other hand, unlike the most extreme advocates of popular constitutionalism, he makes room for the judicial decision making that most of us have come accept as one of the defining characteristics of American constitutionalism. For Sunstein, minimalists "pay close attention to the particulars of individual cases."[53] By contrast, maximalists are "those who seek to decide cases in a way that sets broad rules for the future and that also gives ambitious theoretical justifications for outcomes."[54] Sunstein hopes that abortion rights will be protected where the people and their elected representatives, through democratic processes, would find widely acceptable "creative solutions."[55] The other branches "might appropriately understand the antidiscrimination right [against gays and lesbians] more broadly than the Court does."[56] He also claims that judicial minimalism is not easily characterized as liberal or conservative.[57] He tells us that Justices

---

[51] As Jeffrey Rosen puts it, "The central question is whether it's possible to create a separate-but-equal category of civil unions for gays and lesbians without demeaning them." Jeffrey Rosen, "Justice Delayed: The Case against California's Gay Marriage Decision," *New Republic*, June 11, 2008, 9. As Andrew Lister points out, "[I]t is not obvious that same-sex marriage is preferable to the abolition of civil marriage, or its replacement with universal civil unions, or the creation of a menu of different but equal, officially recognized relationships." Andrew Lister, "How to Defend (Same-Sex) Marriage," review, oo *Polity* (2005), 1.

[52] In American history, only nine federal judges have ever been impeached, and only four of those were convicted. David M. O'Brien, "Judicial Review and American Politics: Historical and Political Perspectives," in *Judges on Judging: Views from the Bench*, 2nd ed., ed. David M. O'Brien (Washington D.C.: Congressional Quarterly Press, 2004), 2–3.

[53] Sunstein, *One Case at a Time*, 9.

[54] Ibid., 9–10.

[55] Sunstein, *Legal Reasoning and Political Conflict*, 180–1.

[56] Ibid., 181.

[57] Sunstein, *One Case at a Time*, x.

Scalia and Thomas are maximalists and that both the Marshall and Warren courts issued many maximalist opinions.[58] An opinion can be maximalist in terms of its width (its scope or sweep) and minimalist in terms of its depth (its theoretical justification), or vice versa. *Roe v. Wade* was wide in the sense of settling a range of issues concerning abortion but not deep in the sense of giving a sophisticated theoretical account of the foundations of the right to abortion.[59]

If by "theoretically ambitious" Sunstein means the kind of insufficiently public reasons that I have in mind as candidates for exclusion, our positions are not so far apart after all. However, as I have tried to explain, courts have the primary institutional responsibility of ensuring that legislation is based on sufficiently public reasons when legislatures have failed to limit themselves to such reasons. If we had confidence that the other branches of government or the people themselves could perform this function as well as or better than judges could, we would not be a society that turns so many political questions into constitutional questions in the first place. As I see it, it is not at all clear why a minimalist judicial decision would generate public deliberation any more than a maximalist decision would. A controversial maximalist decision may have exactly the same effect, depending on what was said, how it was said, and the political circumstances. Even Sunstein admits that minimalism is "an appropriate course only in certain contexts."[60] It is not as if the Court automatically preempts public deliberation simply by handing down a decision that sweeps widely and has a theoretically ambitious rationale. In fact, the more controversial the result, the more likely people are to respond to it, regardless of what the Court actually said in the majority opinion. A theoretically ambitious judicial opinion may generate considerable controversy and provoke a response from those who disagree, thereby catalyzing public deliberation. In addition, it is not evident why not saying too much matters more than the reasons that lead to a particular judicial decision. In a judicial opinion, it is possible to say too much, just as it is possible to say too little, but in terms of public justification, the point is not to say too much or too little but to produce an opinion that a reasonable dissenter could accept under the circumstances. As such, what matters is the content of that opinion and how well the judge has articulated his or her position in the language of public reasons.

Ultimately, we would hope that Americans would pay closer attention to what the Court has said and not uncritically accept the rationales that it offers for its most important decisions. Personally, I am not optimistic that most Americans will care about most Supreme Court opinions, read

[58] Ibid., 11.
[59] Ibid., 18.
[60] Ibid., 54.

them carefully, understand them fully, and then form their own considered judgments about them. For better or for worse, we seem to be stuck with judicial supremacy.[61] That does not mean that Americans and their elected representatives should play such a passive role, but it does suggest that a theory of constitutional adjudication should not be based so much on a controversial empirical claim that minimalist judicial decisions will stimulate constitutional discourse in the public sphere in the name of a civic republican ideal that is probably outdated.

I hope that the reader also accepts without argument the claim that judicial opinions that purport to justify certain constitutional outcomes often fall far short of convincing reasonable dissenters. A judge might claim that he or she does not care about publicly justifying decisions to others, but it is hard to believe that any judge would be indifferent to how others perceive the reasoning that underlies them. The judge is more likely to dispute what public justification consists in and to disagree with critics about whether he or she has met that standard in a particular case. That is not to say that judges should turn a blind eye to the likely consequences of their decisions. It is well known that by not specifying an immediate remedy for de jure racial segregation in *Brown*, Chief Justice Warren was trying to avoid antagonizing segregationists.[62] The same might be said for courts' not getting too far ahead of the views of most Americans on plural marriage and even on same-sex marriage.[63] Perhaps the circumstances of *Brown* are rare, if only because the meaning of racial equality in America is more settled now than it was in the past. Most of the time, judicial opinions need not be crafted according to speculative judgments about how the other branches of government and the people themselves will respond to them. As it turns out, *Brown* may have "stymie[d] progressive racial change and bolster[ed] the political standing of racial extremists" in the South.[64] When the Court is supposed to explain the meaning of freedom and equality in the most difficult constitutional cases, it must do so without excessive concern for public opinion. At times, that will require the Court to have the courage to make unpopular decisions when the balance of public reasons compels them, and the other branches of the federal government, the states, and the American people will react to what the Court has done.

[61] Larry D. Kramer, *The People Themselves: Popular Constitutionalism and Judicial Review* (New York: Oxford University Press, 2004), 232.
[62] See Jack M. Balkin, *What* Brown v. Board of Education *Should Have Said: The Nation's Top Legal Experts Rewrite America's Landmark Civil Rights Decision* (New York: New York University Press, 2001), 37.
[63] Recently, Jeffrey Rosen has worried that the California Supreme Court's recent decision to overturn the statewide ban on same-sex marriage may lead to a backlash not only in California but in the entire United States. Rosen, "Justice Delayed," 9.
[64] Michael J. Klarman, Brown v. Board of Education *and the Civil Rights Movement* (New York: Oxford University Press, 2007), x.

For purposes of public justification, then, it is not imperative that real dissenters see the reasons that the Court has put forth as good enough, even though that would be desirable. The constitutionally required desegregation of public schools in the name of racial equality is not a reason that someone like George Wallace would have accepted. It is too convenient for judges to exaggerate the severity of the expected public reaction to a controversial decision and use such severity as an excuse for not making the most appropriate decision. The Constitution is not a suicide pact, but nor is it an invitation to follow the election returns or to engage in survey research. Recent scholarship has shown that the effects of the Court's decisions are not likely to be as significant as scholars used to believe.[65] Furthermore, the people and their elected representatives can respond to an extremely unpopular decision by amending the Constitution itself or by limiting the appellate jurisdiction of the federal courts. Consequences matter, but it may be virtually impossible, especially for judges, to predict the consequences in constitutional cases with enough accuracy to justify a utilitarian or pragmatic theory of judging.[66] In the past few years, some scholars have argued that *Dred Scott* did not further destabilize, and may have temporarily preserved, the antebellum political regime.[67]

Even if it were better institutionally situated to do so, the Court is not just another policy-making body, and constitutional cases are not personal injury or contracts cases. As Ronald Dworkin has written, "[Q]uestions about law are always questions about the moral justification of political power."[68] In the end, judges must make a sincere effort to put forward sufficiently public reasons in trying to reach reasonable dissenters, not out of strategic considerations but out of a principled concern for limiting the coercive power of the state to protect the dignity of all persons. After all, who else is likely to do so? That does not mean that judges must assign the kind of weight to the deepest convictions of dissenters that those dissenters would prefer. Ideally, most real dissenters will be reasonable enough to accept reasons that are good enough even though real people are not always reasonable and what may count as a good reason in one case may not

---

[65] See Gerald N. Rosenberg, *The Hollow Hope: Can Courts Bring About Social Change?* (Chicago: University of Chicago Press, 1991).

[66] Even if judges had more foresight, a utilitarian normative theory of judging would require a more elaborate theoretical and moral defense than Judge Richard Posner has put forth. In his most recent book, for example, Posner quickly dismisses Dworkin's principles as mere preferences and seems to assume the some theory of consequentialism should guide judicial decision making. See Richard A. Posner, *How Judges Think* (Cambridge, MA: Harvard University Press, 2008), 175.

[67] Mark Graber, Dred Scott *and the Problem of Constitutional Evil* (New York: Cambridge University Press, 2007), 39.

[68] Arthur Ripstein, "Introduction: Anti-Archimedeanism," in *Ronald Dworkin*, ed. Arthur Ripstein (New York: Cambridge University Press, 2007), 4.

necessarily be a good reason in another case when the material facts differ. In terms of improving judicial review, the concern is not that judges act in bad faith but that many of them go about deciding constitutional cases in the wrong way.

E. The Exchange of Reasons

Public justification is a normative ideal that reflects the liberal conviction that it is wrong to use the coercive power of the state to establish a particular conception of the good or to disadvantage those who adhere to different conceptions without sufficient justification. Like all normative ideals, it is far from perfectly realized in any human society. At the same time, it is not too much to ask of judges to address the concerns of likely dissenters when they write judicial opinions to settle the most important constitutional questions. By "justification," I mean a normative speech act whose purpose is to explain what ought to be done by producing reasons on behalf of a proposed action.[69] These reasons are not any reasons whatsoever but are assumed by the person who advances them to be good reasons from an impersonal standpoint as well.[70] In other words, those who are or who might be affected by the decision could also accept them.[71] The idea is that, whatever the discursive context, others are more likely to share some reasons because of their inherent fairness. The aim of a person who seeks to justify a choice is to find these reasons and to convince those who are owed such justification that the reasons offered meet this standard of fairness by taking into account the equal importance of the lives of others. A reason that is truly fair is not fair simply because others believe it to be so, but it is likely to be believed to be fair because it is fair under the circumstances; it is a consideration that does not favor the ends of some over others.

The person who is trying to justify a choice must act in good faith by resisting the temptation to manipulate his or her audience with rhetoric or misinformation, the way in which a trial lawyer might do to win a case, a candidate running for public office might do to win an election, or a marketer might do to sell a product or service. That person cares not only about what decision is reached but also about how that decision is reached, because the discursive quality of the deliberation is what legitimizes the outcome. That person accepts the fact that others can be justified in not accepting his or her deepest convictions and avoids the temptation to present the choice to be made in terms that exaggerate the strengths of her position and understate its weaknesses. The trouble is not so much that ordinary people consciously try

---

[69] Most generally, "reasons" are "considerations that count in favor of" something. See Scanlon, *What We Owe Each Other*, 17.

[70] See Nagel, *Equality and Partiality*, 10.

[71] Jürgen Habermas, *Moral Consciousness and Communicative Action*, trans. Christian Lenhardt and Sherry Weber Nicholsen (Cambridge, MA: MIT Press, 1990), 63.

to mislead others, but that they often falsely believe that they have presented their case as fairly as possible and, in doing so, have addressed the concerns of those who disagree with them.

There is nothing mysterious about the process of sincerely trying to give good reasons to others in an effort to persuade them that they also have reasons for doing what we would like them to do. Indeed, we expect them to do likewise. This give-and-take process is an inescapable part of everyday communication that is designed to culminate in rational agreement. Each participant treats others, as Immanuel Kant would have said, as "ends-in themselves," that is, as beings whose rational abilities entitle them to reasons. Respect for their autonomy requires nothing less, and to be sufficiently impartial is to see the situation from a common standpoint. At worst, *mutual understanding* means understanding the real issues that divide you from those who disagree with you. At best, it means coming to an understanding that everyone freely accepts. In the real world, deliberators may fail for a variety of reasons. They may not be used to trying to convince others through an exchange of reasons. Instead, they may be in the habit of manipulating, deceiving, or threatening others to get what they want or of relying on rhetoric, weak circumstantial evidence, or bad arguments. If they do not know their fellow deliberators well enough to know what sorts of reasons they are more likely to accept, then they are much less likely to persuade them or even understand their concerns.

The objective of persuasion requires self-restraint on the part of all of the participants in the sense that they limit themselves to appealing to reasons that others are likely to share. One of the main differences between an attempt to manipulate and a genuine attempt to persuade is not only the attitude of the person who is trying to persuade but also his or her approach. People do not simply offer to others the reasons that they personally believe to be most compelling, nor do they necessarily offer the reasons that their target audience is most likely to accept. Alternatively, people try to find the reasons that they sincerely take to be optimal, in the sense that everyone should be able to acknowledge them after due reflection, and assume that most people are reasonable enough to be able to do so. The best reasons are not necessarily those that others actually accept but those that a reasonable person should accept. At times, even the most reasonable persons may not actually accept the reasons that they should accept. Their resistance to the force of the better argument could result from a number of different causes, but those who try to meet the standard of public justification make every conceivable effort to find the subset of reasons that not only would be accepted but also should be accepted because of their fairness. In a particular discursive context, when a collective choice has to be made, there is no way of knowing whether these reasons exist until deliberators have made a careful effort to find them.

II. THE LIMITS OF HUMAN REASON

A. Inevitable Reasonable Disagreement

The problem of public justification is not a problem that would disappear if our political institutions and practices were more deliberative or if ordinary people were brighter, better informed, or more open-minded. Rather, the view that principles of political morality and their applications can be rationally justified has met stiff opposition from theorists who are suspicious of all claims of moral truth.[72] These skeptics allege that the Enlightenment project is misconceived and that further attempts to give its values a more rational basis are doomed to failure and may even be counterproductive. John Gray insists that the effort of Enlightenment thinkers to give political morality a foundation in reason has not been successful and never will be.[73] Michel Foucault maintains that such attempts lead to new forms of domination.[74] Alasdair MacIntyre contends that rationality is a culturally conditioned concept, and that it alone cannot provide a foundation for morality in the modern world.[75]

Today, these kinds of skeptical attacks on reason, truth, and morality are no longer so fashionable, but anyone who teaches undergraduate courses knows how difficult it is to induce students to look more critically at the moral relativism that many of them take for granted – you have your opinion and I have my opinion and that's the end of the matter. Even those who have not succumbed to skepticism about the possibility of reaching agreement through moral argumentation in political life are far less certain than they used to be about the ability of human reason to ground political morality.[76] Jeremy Waldron writes, "[M]oral realists will insist stubbornly that there really is, still, a fact of the matter out there. And maybe they are right. But is it surprising how little help this purely existential confidence

---

[72] According to Charles Taylor, for Foucault, "There are only different orders imposed by men on primal chaos, following their will to power." Charles Taylor, "Foucault on Freedom and Truth," 12 *Political Theory* (1984), 175. Friedrich Nietzsche also is famous for his genealogical attempts to unmask the authority of reason. Claims to truth, he believed, were really expressions of a more basic psychological drive, the will to power.

[73] John Gray, *Enlightenment's Wake: Politics and Culture at the Close of the Modern Age* (London: Routledge, 1995), 66.

[74] See, e.g., Michel Foucault, *Discipline and Punish: The Birth of the Prison*, 2nd ed., trans. Alan Sheridan (New York: Vintage Books, 1979).

[75] MacIntyre believes that for rational moral argumentation to take place, a community of shared value is a precondition. However, the liberal commitment to individualism and value pluralism precludes the existence of such a community. Alasdair MacIntyre, *After Virtue*, 2nd ed. (Notre Dame, IN: Notre Dame University Press, 1981).

[76] This kind of skepticism, which is prevalent in the humanities, particularly in literature departments, attacks certainty and justification while leaving belief, commitment, and practice intact. See Martha Nussbaum, "Skepticism about Practical Reason in Literature and in the Law," 107 *Harvard Law Review* (1994), 716–17.

is in dealing with our decision-problems."[77] The epistemic concern is that the existence of moral pluralism may prevent citizens from convincing the other members of their political community that their political arguments are sound.[78] That does not mean that people are so far apart that they cannot even agree on what counts as a reason. Normally, people can still agree on the relevance of a reason even when they disagree on its force. In a situation of choice, to exercise bad judgment is to overlook certain reasons or to miss their significance. The content of those reasons varies with the particulars of the circumstances.

The task of rational justification or of defending the significance of certain reasons is considerably more complicated under current conditions of moral pluralism because standard liberal solutions, modeled on freedom of conscience and tolerance, may turn out to be inadequate.[79] People may reasonably contest what counts as a good argument or even what counts as a good reason even though such justification is supposed to produce reasons that dissenters could not reasonably reject. The deeper the moral conflict and the more complicated the facts, the less likely it is that consensus will result from public deliberation. As one commentator observes, "[W]e must . . . wonder whether the scope of what is 'reasonable for all to accept' turns out to be so small as to be irrelevant for most political disagreements."[80] It may not be evident that the rejection of the reasons offered by one side or the other is rationally warranted. This worry about meeting the minimal requirements of justification is not radically skeptical in the sense of assuming that the truth conditions of moral propositions are unknowable or that such conditions are only relative to a particular time and place. Rather, this worry is premised on the inherent difficulty of putting together a sound argument about political principles or their specifications that would persuade all reasonable persons who already are divided over the nature of the human good and probably are divided over the fundamentals of justice, as well. Reasonable people who are certain that they are right about, say, the immorality of abortion or capital punishment, are likely to encounter other reasonable people who are equally certain that these practices are morally permissible, and a reasonable person, in the face of reasonable disagreement, is then less

---

[77] Jeremy Waldron, "Deliberation, Disagreement, and Voting," in *Deliberative Democracy and Human Rights*, ed. Harold Hongju Koh and Ronald C. Slye (New Haven, CT: Yale University Press, 1999), 222.

[78] Erin Kelly and Lionel McPherson, "On Tolerating the Unreasonable," 9 *Journal of Political Philosophy* (2001), 38.

[79] Fred D'Agostino refers to Rawls's idea of moral pluralism as a "weak" or epistemological doctrine, by which he means that the burdens of judgment (the inherent limits of human reason) will produce reasonable disagreement in at least some cases of public morality. Fred D'Agostino, *Free Public Reason: Making It Up As We Go* (New York: Oxford University Press, 1996), 7.

[80] James Bohman, "Public Reason and Cultural Pluralism," 23 *Political Theory* (1995), 255.

likely to be confident in the correctness of her views. Unless such a person can identify a clear mistake in the reasoning of someone who disagrees with him or her, how can that person know that his or her judgment is superior?

As Waldron remarks, "[E]ven among those who accept the proposition that some views about justice are true and others false, disagreement will persist as to which is which."[81] This epistemic situation exists because there is no infallible decision procedure for determining what or who is right in a hard case. Contemporary neo-Kantians acknowledge that moral judgment cannot be reduced to a practical algorithm.[82] At its best, political argumentation is still not formal argumentation in which conclusions are deduced from premises. Nor is there a widely accepted scientific method that would lead those who initially disagree to converge on an answer based on shared methodological assumptions or on the balance of empirical evidence.[83] In other words, unlike an empirical claim, a normative claim cannot simply be tested "against the world." In hard cases, citizens who deliberate with one another in good faith will often adduce evidence and reasons that can be reasonably disputed and will rarely, if ever, settle a political controversy to the satisfaction of everyone. From this moderately skeptical perspective, that a proposition is really true or false, that is, whether it corresponds to moral facts or coheres with other moral beliefs, is much less significant than the inherent difficulty of justifying that proposition to others who not only disagree but also seem to have good grounds for disagreeing.

It may not be evident, then, which side has the better argument, but that is not the equivalent of the skeptical claim that no argument is better than any other argument or that truth is a point of view. Instead, even when there is consensus about the form that a good argument should have, where the premises purport to make the conclusion more likely, there often seems to be no decisive reason for choosing one good argument over another good argument after the deliberators have eliminated the bad arguments. This phenomenon becomes a political and legal concern when the failure of reasonable persons to identify the best argument leads to opposite conclusions, each of which appears to be equally rationally justified. How could one be certain enough to know what counts as a sound argument in a particular context when it is not clear whether the premises are true, especially normative ones, or whether those premises, even if they are true, support the conclusion? How could one still have confidence that he or she has identified the best argument? If people are not really sure that they are right and

[81] Waldron, *Law and Disagreement*, 3.

[82] Onora O'Neill, *Constructions of Reason: Explorations of Kant's Practical Philosophy* (Cambridge: Cambridge University Press, 1989), x; Barbara Herman, "The Practice of Moral Judgment," in *The Practice of Moral Judgment* (Cambridge, MA: Harvard University Press, 1993), 73–93.

[83] Waldron, *Law and Disagreement*, 178.

that those who disagree with them are wrong, how could such people be so willing to use the coercive power of the state to subject those who may reasonably disagree with them to their will? Isn't it likely that in a hard case each answer is equally justified? The right answer, then, is not relative to a particular perspective, which would mean that there could be a number of right answers, but is so elusive that it might as well not exist.

In Rawlsian terminology, the burdens of judgment dramatically increase the likelihood of reasonable disagreement in politics.[84] As Rawls notes, the empirical evidence may be conflicting and complex, words and concepts can be vague, deliberators may disagree about the weight of the relevant considerations, and their life experiences may differ and affect their judgment.[85] Moreover, for any political decision, when there is a plurality of criteria and no impartial means of ordering them, the criteria may be indeterminate in their application.[86] This may mean that even those who agree on the relevant values may rank them differently, producing different outcomes, each of which appears to be rationally justified.[87] The epistemic difficulty lies in demonstrating to all reasonable persons that a particular answer to a particular question of political morality, like abortion or capital punishment, is the best answer. Rawls himself did not cast the burdens of judgment in skeptical terms because he feared that such an approach would jeopardize the overlapping consensus of reasonable comprehensive doctrines that he hoped would form around his political conception of justice.[88] Rather, these burdens reflect the circumstances that make actual agreement about fundamental political questions "far more difficult."[89] By contrast, Brian Barry makes it clear that skepticism about knowledge of the human good changes the way in which reasonable people must think about justice.[90] If a person does not know that his or her position is correct, then that person is not justified in imposing it on others.[91] In the end, whatever its metaphysical source, the public justification of political principles and the cases that might fall under them is bound to be challenging for a society that is committed

---

[84] Initially, Rawls called the "burdens of judgment" the "burdens of reason." See John Rawls, *Collected Papers*, ed. Samuel Freeman (Cambridge, MA: Harvard University Press, 2001), 475–8. The former, I believe, is a better description, because *judgment* captures the difficulties of applying a rule, principle, standard, or norm to real situations of choice.

[85] For Rawls's account of the burdens of judgment, see John Rawls, *Political Liberalism* (New York: Columbia University Press, 1996), 54–8. See also John Rawls, *Justice as Fairness: A Restatement*, ed. Erin Kelly (Cambridge, MA: Harvard University Press, Belknap Press), 35–7.

[86] See Gerald F. Gaus, *Contemporary Theories of Liberalism: Public Reason as a Post-Enlightenment Project* (Thousand Oaks, CA: Sage Publications, 2003), 12.

[87] Ibid.

[88] Rawls, *Political Liberalism*, 62–3.

[89] Ibid.

[90] Brian Barry, *Justice as Impartiality* (Oxford, U.K.: Clarendon Press, 1995), esp. part 2.

[91] Ibid., 142.

to finding a moral basis for its laws that almost everyone can share but that may lack that very basis.

The foregoing concerns put into some doubt the possibility of the public justification of principles of justice or political morality under the best of epistemic conditions. Furthermore, today, fewer people would share Kant's optimism that the public use of reason would enlighten people.[92] Even if more people were more enlightened, many political theorists doubt the likelihood of resolving our most intractable moral disagreements through an exchange of reasons.[93] As Gerald Gaus puts it, "The task of Post-Enlightenment liberalism is to show that our reason does not *always* lead us to disagree."[94] The failure to settle their political disagreements through public deliberation might mean that those who have not been convinced by the arguments that the state has offered in defense of its public laws might be justified in not complying with them. The refusal of dissenters to acknowledge their authority might be warranted when these laws are not supported by reasons that most people either actually share or would share if they were more skilled at selecting the best argument among the remaining good arguments.

B. Skepticism about Legal Reasoning

These kinds of worries about the possibility of justification are not unique to political theory; they also appear in skeptical challenges to the rationality of legal reasoning in general and to constitutional reasoning in particular. When judges write an opinion and are sincere, they believe that the reasons that they advance to defend their conclusion are stronger than other reasons that either support the same conclusion or lead to the opposite conclusion. Unless judges are unprincipled and only desire to reach a particular result, then the reasons in their opinions are the reasons that they believe that others should find compelling as well. If most lawyers, judges, and law professors thought that those reasons either were excellent or terrible, then at least within the legal community, there would be near consensus on the quality of the particular constitutional argument being evaluated, and that intersubjective agreement might constitute, or be best evidence of, the soundness of that argument.

But to achieve such agreement is easier said than done. It has been said, "The trouble with constitutional law is that no one knows what counts as an argument."[95] In fact, the trouble seems to be that no one knows

---

[92] Onora O'Neill, "The Public Use of Reason," in *Constructions of Reason: Explorations of Kant's Practical Philosophy* (Cambridge: Cambridge University Press, 1989), 28–50.

[93] See, e.g., Macedo, *Liberal Virtues*, 6–7.

[94] Gaus, *Contemporary Theories of Liberalism*, 19.

[95] Michael J. Gerhardt et al., *Constitutional Theory: Arguments and Perspectives*, 2nd ed. (Newark, NJ: LexisNexis Publishing, 2000), 1.

what counts as a *good* argument, which is another way of saying that even well-informed, appropriately motivated people will never converge on the same standard, see eye to eye on how that standard should be applied in particular cases, or agree on whether the reasons that support the decision in question are acceptable. However, a normative ideal of constitutional adjudication must presuppose the possibility that there are good and bad and better and worse reasons. That is not to say that we always know which is which, but just because disagreement is sincere does not necessarily mean that it is reasonable or intractable. Nor does such disagreement imply that reasonable persons, who disagree about the correct result in a hard case, cannot acknowledge that an argument that supports the opposite conclusion is not bad. They may be able to see that the other side has put forth reasons that are good enough under the circumstances even when they prefer other reasons and hope to change the minds of those who disagree with them in the future. In that way, a judicial decision still can be legitimate on the basis of the quality of its underlying reasons, even in the midst of sincere and reasonable disagreement over the correctness of its outcome.

More often than not, those who engage in constitutional argumentation seem to know at least a plausible constitutional argument when they see it. Typically, practitioners know what kinds of arguments judges will listen to, which is not to say that judges will ultimately accept them. By itself, that does not prove that there are better and worse constitutional arguments, but it does indicate that most deliberators in real constitutional controversies proceed as if they have the better argument and that those who disagree with them not only are wrong but also can be convinced, after an exchange of reasons, that they are wrong. We can and should explain why this is possible, and one of the goals of this book is to formulate a defensible distinction between good and bad and better and worse reasons in the context of constitutional adjudication. A standard of public justification is also designed to encourage judges to use the same vocabulary and mode of reasoning when they write their opinions. That not only would render constitutional discourse more coherent and more transparent but also would narrow the range of permissible constitutional arguments and enable others to assess their quality. In some instances, that may produce less constitutional disagreement; in others, it may illuminate the nature of intractable reasonable disagreement. Ideally, judges would meet or come close to meeting this standard in the most important constitutional cases, thereby justifying the use of judicial review. A society that shares a standard of public justification is a society that tries to avoid imposing laws on reasonable dissenters without proper justification, whatever other defects it may have.

FOUR

Competing Conceptions of Public Reason

In the previous chapter, I tried to show how a concern about public justification emerges when the state legislates on the basis of reasons that reasonable people may be justified in rejecting. In exercising the power of judicial review, the judge assesses the quality of the reasons that the state has offered on behalf of the law in question. The less controversial the underlying reasons, the more publicly justified, and thus legitimate, that law is likely to be. After taking into account a presumption of freedom and equality, if the judge concludes that a reasonable person would accept those reasons, then the law is constitutional. If a reasonable person would reject the reasons, then the law is unconstitutional. An ideal of public justification serves a normative standard for the use of public reason.[1] However, those who adhere to this ideal are divided over how to draw the line between public and nonpublic reasons and whether deliberators may rely on nonpublic reasons in certain situations. As a consequence, there are "competing conceptions of public reason."[2] In this chapter, my aim is to sketch the debate about public reason, to spell out the similarities and differences of the three basic paths to public justification, and to identify some of the main questions about how such justification can be accomplished.

I. THE THREE CONCEPTIONS

According to Lawrence Solum, there are three basic principles of public reason: "laissez-faire," "exclusion," and "inclusion."[3] Laissez-faire means

---

[1] Lawrence B. Solum, "Constructing an Ideal of Public Reason," 30 *San Diego Law Review* (1993), 730.

[2] Lawrence B. Solum, "Inclusive Public Reason," 75 *Pacific Philosophical Quarterly* (1994), 217.

[3] Lawrence B. Solum, "Pluralism and Public Legal Reason," Symposium: Religion, Division, and the Constitution, 15 *William and Mary Bill of Rights Journal* (2006), 11; See also Lawrence B. Solum, "Public Legal Reason," 92 *Virginia Law Review* (2006), 1466; Solum, "Constructing an Ideal of Public Reason," 741–53.

that all reasons are potentially public reasons and that deliberators should offer their best reasons, whatever their content or origin, as justification. Exclusion means that deliberators should rule out many reasons in advance as nonpublic, especially those derived from their respective conceptions of the good, even when they personally believe that a deeper reason is correct and therefore justifies the law in question. The more exclusive the principle of public reason, the narrower the set of sufficiently public reasons will be. Inclusion means that "at least some public reasons [may] be included in at least some contexts" where a deliberator "offer[s] a sincerely held public reason for each position advanced."[4] An inclusive principle permits the use of nonpublic reasons, but a person who introduces such reasons still must explain how they are consistent with the principle of reciprocity that is implicit in the practice of public justification.

Although he does not employ the term *laissez-faire*, Jürgen Habermas's discourse ethics are based on such a principle of public reason. Deliberators engage in an essentially unrestricted exchange of reasons in an ideal speech situation, which "provides [them] with a rational basis for testing the truth or legitimacy of [their] claims."[5] The participants should feel free to present all of their best reasons, including those based on their respective conceptions of the good, in the search for intersubjective agreement. For Habermas, the requirement that citizens deliberate about what is good for all does not mean that they must eschew appeals to controversial religious and philosophical convictions. For example, with respect to the question of same-sex marriage, a deliberator may put together a deep argument about the value of such marriage or the quality of the lives of those who are not straight and invite other deliberators to assess the merits of such claims. As such, the set of potentially sufficiently public reasons is about as wide as it possibly could be.

Alternatively, Gerald Gaus subscribes to an exclusive principle of public reason, believing that when the state acts, no reasonable person should reject the reasons that underlie that action.[6] If a reasonable person could reject the justification that the state has advanced for the legislation in question, and the state enacts that law anyway, then that law is illegitimate. Gaus's position is predicated on a very strong presumption in favor of individual freedom and against state action that infringes on such freedom. Thus, for him, the set of sufficiently public reasons that the state could legitimately rely on to justify

---

[4] Solum, "Pluralism and Public Legal Reason," 11; See also Solum, "Constructing an Ideal of Public Reason," 741–2.

[5] Stephen K. White, *The Recent Work of Jürgen Habermas: Reason, Justice and Modernity* (Cambridge: Cambridge University Press, 1988), 1.

[6] Gerald F. Gaus, "Liberal Neutrality: A Compelling and Radical Principle," in *Perfectionism and Neutrality: Essays in Liberal Theory*, ed. Stephen Wall and George Klosko (New York: Rowman and Littlefield, 2003), 138.

its laws is narrow, and the state bears the burden of demonstrating that it has met the standard of public justification that would legitimize the legislation at issue. Depending on which principle of public reason a person adheres to, he or she will have either a broader, like Habermas, or narrower, like Gaus, pool of possibly sufficiently public reasons to draw from. In between these two extremes lie a number of intermediate or inclusive positions, such as that of John Rawls, in which deliberators may introduce nonpublic reasons in some circumstances, provided that those reasons strengthen the ideal of public reason or at least do not weaken it.

II. LAISSEZ-FAIRE PUBLIC REASON

A. Hobbes and Kant

Historically, Immanuel Kant is the primary source of the idea of public justification, at least as most contemporary liberals and deliberative democrats have understood the idea.[7] Nonetheless, it is worth pointing out that there is a Hobbesian alternative that does not demand the exchange of moral reasons. For Thomas Hobbes, public reason is the reason of the sovereign.[8] The sovereign is supposed to resolve the political conflicts that arise in the midst of pluralism and destabilize politics. By contrast, for Kant, and neo-Kantians like Rawls and Habermas, public reason is more democratic; its authority is not located in one person, the sovereign, but in the free exercise of the reason of the people.[9] Although Hobbesian public reason also tries to solve the problem of pluralism, the Rawlsian and Habermasian public uses of reason are not instrumental in the way that Hobbes or a neo-Hobbesian like David Gauthier imagine them to be. In *Morals by Agreement*, Gauthier develops a Hobbesian instrumental approach to public justification that is best described in terms of bargaining or strategic interaction.[10] Such an approach is supposed to be based on a more realistic picture of human psychology and the incentives that are more likely to motivate real people, thereby increasing the likelihood of compliance. As one commentator remarks, "In Gauthier's picture the parties are involved in a process of economic negotiation with one another, each seeking to drive the best bargain they can get."[11]

Although Rawls and Habermas are not indifferent to political stability, both of them also seek to make their respective societies more just and more

---

[7] The basic idea of public reason can be found in the political writings of Hobbes and Rousseau as well. See Solum, "Constructing an Ideal of Public Reason," 754–6.

[8] David Gauthier, "Public Reason," 12 *Social Philosophy and Policy* (1995), 30.

[9] Solum, "Constructing an Ideal of Public Reason," 759.

[10] David Gauthier, *Morals by Agreement* (Oxford, U.K.: Clarendon Press, 1986), 221.

[11] Chandran Kukathas and Philip Pettit, *Rawls: A Theory of Justice and Its Critics* (Cambridge, UK: Polity Press, 1990), 33.

democratic through the use of reason in the public sphere. Despite their differences, the Rawlsian and Habermasian projects attempt to ground the minimal moral requirements of political life in the practice of public reasoning by free and equal persons. Thus, it is imperative not only that all people participate in the discursive formulation of the collective will but also that, in doing so, they exchange reasons with one another as freely as possible without interference from external sources of authority. As Onora O'Neill puts it, "Reason . . . has no transcendent foundation . . . . What makes agreement of a certain sort authoritative is that it is agreement based on principles that meet their own criticism."[12] As Kant himself writes, "For reason has no dictatorial authority: its verdict is always simply the agreement of free citizens, of whom each one must be permitted to express, without let or hindrance, his objections or even his veto."[13] His criterion of reciprocity rules out force, coercion, and deception because such actions make it "impossible for their victims to consent."[14] For Kant, to give a reason to another person is to respect his or her rational abilities by treating that person as a being who can evaluate, accept, and reject reasons. As O'Neill writes, "Restrictions of the public use of reason not only will harm those who seek to reason publicly, but will undermine the authority of reason itself."[15]

B. Habermas

Habermas is famous for trying to give Kantian ethics a less metaphysically ambitious foundation by advancing a dialogical reconstruction of Kant's idea of practical reason in which "the justification of norms and commands requires that a real discourse be carried out and thus cannot occur in a strictly logical form, i.e., in the form of a hypothetical process of argumentation occurring in the individual mind."[16] The universality of a maxim, then, can be determined only through the discursive testing that would occur in an ideal speech situation, and the aim of his discourse ethics is to secure intersubjective agreement among those who are appropriately motivated. As Thomas McCarthy writes, "The emphasis shifts from what *each* can will without contradiction to what *all* can agree to in rational discourse.[17] Thus,

---

[12] Onora O'Neill, "The Public Use of Reason," in *Constructions of Reason: Explorations of Kant's Practical Philosophy* (Cambridge: Cambridge University Press, 1989), 38.

[13] Immanuel Kant, *Critique of Pure Reason*, trans. Norman Kemp Smith (New York: St. Martin's Press, 1965), 593 (A737–38/B767–68).

[14] Christine M. Korsgaard, "The Reasons We Share," in *Creating the Kingdom of Ends* (Cambridge: Cambridge University Press, 1996), 295.

[15] O'Neill, "The Public Use of Reason," 37.

[16] Jürgen Habermas, *Moral Consciousness and Communicative Action*, trans. Christian Lenhardt and Shierry Weber Nicolsen (Cambridge, UK: Polity Press, 1990), 68.

[17] Thomas McCarthy, "Kantian Constructivism and Reconstructivism: Rawls and Habermas in Dialogue," 105 *Ethics* (1994), 45.

a person could not test the validity of any truth claim only in his or her own mind or against an independent standard woven into the fabric of the universe. Habermas replaces Kant's "monological" categorical imperative with a discursive procedure aimed to ensure that each participant may affirm or deny the reasons that others have offered. According to Habermas, "[T]here must be complete freedom on both sides to express whatever beliefs or feelings or attitudes arguably have a bearing on the matter at issue."[18]

The openness and procedural fairness of a Habermasian ideal speech situation is intended to generate the only kind of universality or objectivity that is possible in a world where morality no longer can have a transcendent foundation. Habermas is also suspicious of those who believe that political philosophy should be ambitious. As he sees it, philosophy ought to confine itself "to the clarification of the moral point of view and the procedure of democratic legitimation. . . . It leaves substantial questions that must be answered here and now to the more or less enlightened engagement of the participants."[19] This is the basis of his claim that Rawls's neo-Kantian approach is insufficiently dialogical because of its reliance on devices such as the original position and reflective equilibrium. According to Habermas, in Rawls's thought, philosophy does too much heavy lifting in the following way. Rawls makes a number of crucial, substantive assumptions about the conditions that characterize modern societies; the value of human beings; their moral psychology; the place of cooperation in a human society; and the nature of a fair initial situation of choice in explaining how one could arrive, in a thought experiment, at the two principles of justice that are supposed to regulate the basic structure of a well-ordered society. Rawls believes that everyone should be able to accept these assumptions; either they have a prominent place in the history of political or moral philosophy or they are empirically uncontroversial.

Alternatively, Habermas believes that such assumptions rule out too much at the outset. They take the place of or at least devalue the public deliberation that must do most of the justificatory work in a democracy. Habermas's point is not that these presuppositions are too strong, indefensible, or morally mistaken. Indeed, I think that even Rawls's most vociferous critics would have to concede that he is working at an abstract level with ideas that are prominent in Western societies and their political traditions. Rather, from Habermas's point of view, the trouble is that the presuppositions are not subject to discursive validation in an ideal speech situation. For example, the Rawlsian model of a hypothetical agreement that occurs in the original position is normatively inadequate because "it fails to provide

---

[18] Frederick A. Olafson, "Habermas as Philosopher," 100 *Ethics* (1990), 645.
[19] Jürgen Habermas, "Reconciliation through the Public Use of Reason: Remarks on John Rawls's Political Liberalism," 92 *Journal of Philosophy* (1995), 131.

the scope for the reflexivity that is essential to the idea of morality."[20] For Habermas, in numerous places, the Rawlsian framework places unnecessary restrictions on deliberators, and thereby reduces the likelihood that they will feel the "force of the better argument." Habermas has in mind "the more open procedure of an argumentative practice that proceeds under the demanding presuppositions of the 'public use of reason' and does not bracket the pluralism of convictions from the outset."[21] The public use of reason is not the equivalent of the use of public reason, because no one can specify what kinds of reasons count as sufficiently public reasons prior to real discourse in an ideal speech situation.

Solum refers to the kind of position exemplified by Habermas as the "principle of laissez-faire" because deliberators do not have to distinguish at the outset between public and nonpublic reasons.[22] They introduce what they take to be the best reasons, whatever their content or sources, expect their fellow deliberators to do the same, and wait to see how others will respond to their reasons. A deliberator need not exercise any self-restraint when he or she tries to meet the criterion of reciprocity implicit in an ideal of public justification. As long as everyone is permitted to participate, deliberators may bring their deeper beliefs to bear on the most important political questions. As such, the range of reasons that people may draw from is as wide as it possibly could be. An atheist may oppose prayer in public school on the ground that religion is harmful superstition, and a religious person may support such prayer on the ground that it will lead to the salvation of the soul. One could come out against capital punishment for those who are convicted of raping children on the ground that those who commit such crimes will be condemned to eternal hellfire. One could argue for the opposite conclusion on the ground that people who commit such heinous crimes have forfeited their right to life. That is not to say that any of these reasons, without further elaboration, would be good reasons, but it is to say that in a laissez-faire regime, all of these arguments may meet the criterion of reciprocity; they have to be tested in real discourse before they can be rejected.

There are limits, of course, with respect to what practical reasoning can accomplish. A person might not care at all about sharing reasons with others when he or she believes that he or she has no duty to do so. A person might listen to what they have to say but only to amuse him- or herself, like Thrasymachus in Plato's *Republic*. Indeed, a person might not have any moral qualms about persecuting others because they are wrong or imposing his or her will on those who disagree because he or she has the power to do so.

---

[20] J. Donald Moon, "Practical Discourse and Communicative Ethics," in *The Cambridge Companion to Habermas*, ed. Stephen K. White (New York: Cambridge University Press, 1995), 148.

[21] Habermas, "Reconciliation through the Public Use of Reason," 118–19.

[22] Solum, "Inclusive Public Reason," 219.

This kind of person is unlikely to bother trying to justify actions to others or to secure their consent when he or she does something that will affect them. Such people will simply do as they please, and when they restrain themselves, they will do so out of prudence. Fortunately, few Americans fall into this category, which is not to say that they are as reasonable or as tolerant as they could be.[23] In many situations, most people care about securing the consent of others and try to do so through the exchange of reasons. Thus, to accept the laissez-faire principle or any neo-Kantian principle of public justification is to care about the moral basis of the uses of the coercive power of the state and to reject the view that the reasons that support such uses are irrelevant; can never be shared; or are nothing more than tastes, preferences, or self-serving rationalizations.

American constitutionalism means that the power of legislative majorities to enact their will into public laws must be limited and that judges have the primary responsibility, when they exercise the power of judicial review, of delineating these limits. To claim that judges must restrain themselves and others, however, is not to claim that citizens are under the same or even a comparable duty. In terms of public justification, the argument against any sort of self-restraint on the part of citizens is straightforward. This position may appear to be self-evident to those who believe that everyone deserves an equal right to express their deepest political views and to have those views influence the formation of public policy. Unlike elected officials who have taken an oath to uphold the Constitution, have official duties, must avoid conflicts of interest, and are supposed to be accountable to their parties and constituents, it is not obvious why ordinary citizens should have a civic duty to limit themselves to certain reasons when they enter the public realm and advocate certain political positions. In a democracy, shouldn't citizens view themselves and their fellow citizens as free to rely on whatever reasons they see fit? Or at least shouldn't they view themselves as free to express their deepest convictions in political life, provided that others also have the same right to do likewise?

There is constitutional doctrine in a number of different areas that supports this view. In *Brandenburg v. Ohio*, the Court made it nearly impossible for speech to count as constitutionally unprotected incitement unless the government can show that the speaker unequivocally intended his or her speech to cause people to break the law and that that speech was likely to have that effect almost immediately.[24] In the absence of an emergency in which there is no time for good speech to counteract bad speech, what the person said or

---

[23] For the view that most Americans have accepted the basic principles of liberal democracy, see Alan Wolfe, *One Nation, After All: What Middle-Class Americans Really Think about God, Country, Family, Racism, Welfare, Immigration, Homosexuality, Work, the Right, the Left, and Each Other* (New York: Viking Books, 1998).

[24] Brandenburg v. Ohio, 395 U.S. 444 (1969).

wrote is likely to be constitutionally protected advocacy. In almost all cases, a court will let the value of the self-expression or the possible value of the content of the speaker's message override the state's interest in preventing breaches of the peace; permitting speech that may cause others to break the law is a justifiable risk. The judicial rejection of the "heckler's veto" reflects the same assumption that unpopular speech is likely to have at least some value.[25] Nor do citizens have to use appropriate language when they express their political beliefs.[26] In fact, unconventional forms of expression deserve considerable constitutional protection because of the importance of the rhetorical effect on their audience in an age when it is not easy to capture and keep listeners' attention.[27] The courts have also made it perfectly clear that content-based restrictions are presumptively unconstitutional, including those designed to protect unwilling listeners from hate speech.[28] That means that bigots and fools have the same free-speech rights as those who are more likely to put those rights, morally speaking, to better use. Apart from the value of whatever such persons might contribute to the free marketplace of ideas, people have a fundamental right to express themselves, especially with respect to matters of public concern, and equal treatment entails their having a fair opportunity to share their deepest beliefs with the rest of the world.

Thus, there would seem to be not only a strong presumption against state censorship of speech on the basis of its content but a similar presumption against asking citizens to restrict themselves to certain kinds of reasons in political discourse as well.[29] One might respond that even though the state should never have the authority to force citizens to limit themselves to certain reasons, but to ask them to do so out of a concern for civic respect or tolerance is another matter. Citizens should have a self-imposed civic duty to restrain themselves, provided that others reciprocate. This is Rawls's basic position in *Political Liberalism*. Nonetheless, it still may seem counterintuitive to ask or expect people to bracket what they see to be the most promising reasons for settling a particular political or legal conflict. How can someone, for example, who sincerely believes that Catholic teachings condemn capital punishment, birth control, abortion, or same-sex relationships be expected to bracket these convictions in political or constitutional discourse? People usually expect others to give them their strongest reasons

[25] Feiner v. New York, 340 U.S. 315 (1951) (Black, J., dissenting) ("But if, in the name of preserving order, [the police] ever can interfere with a lawful public speaker, they must first make all reasonable efforts to protect him").

[26] Cohen v. California, 403 U.S. 15 (1971).

[27] Ibid.

[28] Virginia v. Black, 538 U.S. 343 (2003); R.A.V. v. City of St. Paul, 505 U.S. 377 (1992); Collin v. Smith 578 F.2d 1197 (7th Cir. 1978).

[29] See, e.g., Kent Greenawalt, *Private Consciences and Public Reasons* (New York: Oxford University Press, 1995), 52.

so that if they care about what is true or right, they will reflect more deeply, possibly change their minds, or have more confidence in their initial position.

There are a number of well-known defenses of the right of people to express their deepest convictions without undue interference from others or from the state. First, knowledge has both intrinsic and instrumental value. The alternative is ignorance, with which people will have a poorer under-standing of themselves, others, and their world but still have to act or refrain from acting. Today, in the United States, even outside of political science departments, many writers are alarmed by widespread ignorance "of the basic facts involving the most important [political] issues that we face."[30] No thoughtful person wants to return to a world in which those who challenge the teachings of the Catholic Church are branded heretics and, if they refuse to recant, are imprisoned or burned at the stake. One of the dangers of keeping one's best reasons to oneself is that others, including those who have not yet been born, might be deprived of information that might help them to make better decisions in the future. In some instances, it is even wrong to withhold information that others may be entitled to on the ground that such information would help that person make a better-informed or more autonomous choice. Second, freedom from state intervention is a nec-essary but not a sufficient condition of the successful operation of the free marketplace of ideas. People must still be willing to offer their best ideas to see whether they survive the competition. Their truth would depend on whether they can prevail in a fair fight, and it stands to reason that an idea that defeats its rivals over and over again is more likely to be rationally justified. As most people know, Alexander Meiklejohn ties the justification of free speech to democratic theory. In a democracy, people have a right to speak their minds and others have a duty to listen to what each person has to say in the name of democratic self-rule.[31] Third, apart from its effects on the search for truth and democracy, one might believe that self-expression is either intrinsically or instrumentally valuable in that it allows people to be creative and experiment, and therefore to live more authentic lives.

Although the appeal of the laissez-faire approach is intuitive, there are two basic problems with such an approach. First, under conditions of moral pluralism and the burdens of judgment, this approach would make it almost impossible for deliberators to find common ground.[32] Habermas insists on an open-ended discourse, which includes all voices and perspectives, but it is not clear how such communication, even under ideal circumstances, could produce anything like consensus, especially when deliberators are

---

[30] See, e.g., Rick Shenkman, *Just How Stupid Are We? Facing the Truth about the American Voter* (New York: Basic Books, 2008), 3.

[31] Alexander Meiklejohn, *Free Speech and Its Relation to Self-Government* (New York: Harper and Brothers, 1948), 22.

[32] See, e.g., Solum, "Public Legal Reason," 1476–7.

permitted to appeal to their respective secular and religious conceptions of the good. A person who favors the laissez-faire principle cannot, ahead of time, rule out appeals to unreasonable comprehensive beliefs. He or she cannot know that such a belief is unreasonable until it has been tested discursively and has failed to meet the approval of other deliberators. That means that people are free to appeal to whatever they feel like appealing to and hope that it sticks. I suspect that such unconstrained communication will not come close to generating the kind of consensus that many liberals and deliberative democrats hope for. An unrestricted ideal of deliberation opens the floodgates to all sorts of reasons that stand no chance of being widely acceptable. In all of that commotion, deliberators probably will not identify the reasons that reasonable people are more likely to share. The truth is that pluralism in our country is as wide and as deep as it possibly could be, and there is an unfortunate tendency among academics to romanticize difference and to underestimate the extent to which such pluralism poses a serious, and perhaps insurmountable, barrier to public justification.

At the same time, people who are critical of more restrictive ideals of public reason have a legitimate concern: such prior restraints may discriminate against the perspectives of the marginalized and the unconventional, and thus preclude the mutual understanding and respect that is possible even in a society that will always be divided over the nature of the human good. Seyla Benhabib goes even further than Habermas, maintaining that not only conceptions of justice but also conceptions of good should be on the public agenda.[33] It is not clear why consensus on a conception of good needs to be achieved, though, and such a proposal would not be so problematic if the discourse in question were not supposed to culminate in a shared understanding of what would be acceptable to everyone. Normally, people can agree to disagree, but that slogan is not helpful when a society must make collective decisions that will have the force of law. If Americans do not want to fail in this enterprise of publicly justifying the most important public laws, then they have to be able to see the world through the eyes of others. The trouble is that an anything-goes, laissez-faire principle is likely to encourage people to think that their deeper beliefs have much more appeal to others than they really do and to reproduce, and perhaps exacerbate, the reasonable disagreement that already exists in our politics.

A society whose members could always keep their deeper differences private, whose deeper convictions had no political implications, and who were not tempted to extend their sectarian convictions to the public realm would not need a principle of public reason in the first place. But that would not

---

[33] Seyla Benhabib, *Situating the Self: Gender, Community and Postmodernism in Contemporary Ethics* (New York: Routledge, 1992), 169.

accurately describe contemporary America or any other pluralistic society. Those who try to publicly justify their political positions must know the sorts of reasons that others might find acceptable without relying on their own deeper convictions. Those convictions are likely to be too controversial to serve as the moral basis of the exercise of coercive state power under conditions of moral pluralism. A theory of public justification must offer an account of the sorts of general reasons that deliberators could introduce in public deliberation so that most reasonable people could recognize more or less the same reasons as good enough reasons in justifying the most important public laws. Ideally, most reasonable people would accept sufficiently public reasons. As such, they would be politically efficacious as well.

In many instances, we take the existence of such reasons for granted and often do not notice them. A person who proposes the decriminalization of homicide, rape, child molestation, theft, or assault and battery would not be taken seriously. That would not be the case because that person could not produce any reasons at all for such a proposal. Indeed, such people could have their own self-serving reasons or reasons that they believe others would share, but it is obvious why a reasonable person would not accept them. In more difficult cases, such consensus is not likely to be secured when citizens offer any reasons or arguments that they please, as if they were concerned only with justifying their position to themselves or to like-minded others. There is an important difference between a political or constitutional argument that is sound from a personal or private point of view but not publicly justified and a constitutional argument that is sufficiently publicly justified and thus good enough to legitimize the law in question. A nation that cannot distinguish between them may not be deeply unjust or undemocratic, but it will probably do a worse job than it could do of respecting the freedom and equality of all of its members.

Although most discourses aimed to produce consensus or at least minimize disagreement are more constrained than people often realize, this point is often not fully appreciated. Depending on the context, people usually limit themselves to certain kinds of reasons when they are trying to convince others. Academic discourse is often severely constrained, which is one of the reasons why it is so difficult to do interdisciplinary work. In everyday matters, not all reasons will be relevant to the task at hand. For instance, during a hiring decision, faculty members will make judgments about how well candidates in question fit the job description, whether they can teach certain courses, whether they will be competent in the classroom, whether their research agenda is promising, and whether they appear to be collegial. There may be other reasons that faculty members have for supporting or opposing particular candidates that they may not share with their colleagues, but most people have intuitive notions about the relevance of certain considerations. I might like one candidate better than another because of her partisan politics, socioeconomic background, knowledge of mixed martial arts, or her willingness to play infield on the department's softball team. But surely, those are reasons that I will not raise during the department meeting involving the hiring decision and ought not to rely on when I cast my vote. The danger of the kind of unrestricted deliberation that Habermas and other deliberative democrats typically favor is that the more open and unrestrained the deliberation, the less likely we are to reach agreement or at least understand why we disagree.

II. EXCLUSIVE PUBLIC REASON

A. Overview

The opposite of the laissez-faire principle of public reason is exclusive public reason, which would exclude at least some sorts of nonpublic reasons in some situations. As Solum puts it, "An ideal of public reason that excluded all nonpublic reasons would employ a simple principle of exclusion."[34] The thought is that deliberators should exercise the strictest self-restraint possible by presuming that the reason that they plan to offer as justification could probably be rejected by a reasonable person. As Solum points out, there are a number of possible principles of exclusion.[35] One might define public reasons as those that everyone already accepts.[36] The trouble with this version is that such a principle of exclusion would "constrict public reason to the vanishing point."[37] There will always be at least one person who denies the truth of at least one of the premises in a political argument or who rejects an inference as unwarranted. There will always be sincere disagreement, and if one takes the facts of reasonable moral pluralism and the burdens of judgment to heart, that disagreement is likely to be reasonable as well. One who adheres to a viable principle of exclusion, then, will have to incorporate some notion of reasonableness into her standard of public justification. There are different ways of defining what is reasonable or unreasonable, but at the outset, the participants must avoid certain kinds of reasons. According to Solum, "A more plausible and less stringent exclusionary principle might exclude all reliance of the subset of contested beliefs that concern morality."[38] Another exclusionary principle might exclude all religious beliefs or exclude all deeper beliefs.[39]

---

[34] Solum, "Inclusive Public Reason," 219.
[35] Ibid., 220.
[36] Ibid.
[37] Ibid., 221.
[38] Ibid.
[39] Ibid., 222.

A. Gerald Gaus's Semilibertarianism

Recently, a number of well-known antiperfectionist liberals have stressed the importance of limited self-restraint on the part of citizens and public officials in public deliberation and collective decision making. Robert Audi maintains that citizens should not deprive others of their personal freedom unless they can produce adequate secular reasons for such a deprivation.[40] Thomas Nagel distinguishes "between what justifies individual belief and what justifies appealing to that belief in support of the exercise of political power."[41] Charles Larmore believes that the state must try to remain as neutral as possible with respect to "disputed and controversial ideals of the good life."[42] Bruce Ackerman contends that political decisions should not rest on claims that one conception of the good is superior to its rivals.[43] Gerald Gaus is one of the few liberals who recognizes that a theory of public justification may have libertarian implications; it may lead to a state of affairs in which state inaction is the rule and not the exception. In the words of one commentator, he constructs a "theory of reasonable and justified belief and uses this to demonstrate that very little in the way of social and political principle can, in fact, be justified to all."[44] For Gaus, "The aim of public justification is to provide everyone with good reasons for embracing principles and policies; it does not require that everyone actually accepts them."[45] Although he rules out popular acceptance as the criterion of public justification, he insists that there is a vast difference between personal and public justification, and that this difference is the defining feature of reasonable pluralism.[46] One could have very good reasons for opposing abortion or supporting affirmative action, but those reasons, judged from an impersonal standpoint, may not meet the higher standard of public justification in the sense of being adequate in the eyes of others who are equally reasonable.

That claim is not particularly controversial among antiperfectionist liberals like Rawls and Nagel, but Gaus draws a number of subtle but important distinctions among different kinds of justifications in demonstrating how inherently difficult it is to be confident that the public justification that one

---

[40] Robert Audi, "The Separation of Church and State and the Obligations of Citizenship," 18 *Philosophy and Public Affairs* (1989), 278.

[41] Thomas Nagel, "Moral Conflict and Political Legitimacy," 16 *Philosophy and Public Affairs* (1987), 229.

[42] Charles Larmore, *Patterns of Moral Complexity* (New York: Cambridge University Press, 1987), x.

[43] Bruce Ackerman, *Social Justice in the Liberal State* (New Haven, CT: Yale University Press, 1980), 10–11.

[44] Christopher Bertram, "Theories of Public Reason," 2 *Imprints* (1997), 76.

[45] Gerald F. Gaus, "Public Justification and Democratic Adjudication," 2 *Constitutional Political Economy* (1991), 257.

[46] Gerald F. Gaus, *Justificatory Liberalism: An Essay on Epistemology and Political Theory* (New York: Oxford University Press, 1996), 11.

has offered cannot be reasonably rejected. A justification is "inconclusive" when it is based on good but not fully convincing reason(s) and a justification is "indeterminate" when the reasons for opposite conclusions cancel out each other.[47] A justification is "victorious" when its challengers have been given ample opportunity to propose counterarguments to defeat it but have failed and the person who offers such a justification must be convinced, beyond a reasonable doubt, that the justification in question is warranted to override the "epistemic authority" of those who reasonably disagree.[48] In boxing terms, the champion must have beaten all of the top contenders and must have won each bout, if not by knockout or technical knockout, then by a lopsided unanimous decision. Because victorious justifications are rare, the area of reasonable disagreement is extremely broad.[49] This is not a post-modernist point about the impotence of reason or the impossibility of truth, but it reflects the epistemic challenge of being able to justify public laws to others who are reasonable but disagree with us. As Gaus writes, "We must be extremely cautious in claiming that others are in error about what they ought to believe."[50] Reasons that appear to be sufficiently impartial or publicly justified may not, on reflection, warrant coercion on the part of the state. Gaus sets the bar high; reasonable disagreement over reasons derived from deeper convictions could also extend to reasonable disagreement over regulatory principles of justice and their specifications. In theory, a reason derived from a conception of the good could clear the bar, but almost all reasonable people would have to agree that it does. Gaus also insists that a controversial ranking of reasons does not meet the standard of public justification.[51]

The kind of arguably radical liberal neutrality that Gaus advances "severely limits what policies a state can pursue" but "it is not a libertarian principle as that is normally understood."[52] It may not be libertarian in the sense that the state has the authority only to prevent force, threat of force, theft, and fraud, and to adjudicate civil law disputes.[53] But it has semilibertarian overtones and, as Gaus admits, his principle of radical liberal neutrality "precludes most contemporary legislation."[54] That is so because this principle incorporates such a high standard of public justification. This standard does not necessarily lead to complete state inaction, but unquestionably it makes it very difficult for the state to overcome the strong

---

[47] Ibid., 151–8.
[48] Ibid., 147–51.
[49] Ibid., 13.
[50] Gaus, "Liberal Neutrality," 154.
[51] Ibid., 157.
[52] Ibid., 159.
[53] See Robert Nozick, *Anarchy, State, and Utopia* (New York: Basic Books, 1974), ix.
[54] Gaus, "Liberal Neutrality," 160.

presumption of individual liberty under which people may do whatever they want to do most of the time. It is possible to set the bar too high, just as it is possible to set it too low, but the consequence of Gaus's position is that most public laws, including those that are enacted to further distributive justice, are not sufficiently publicly justified.

B. Strict Self-Restraint

The idea of strict self-restraint as the most important civic duty is an implication of the liberal principle of neutrality on the part of the state and tolerance on the part of individual citizens. Scholars are divided over exactly how strict that restraint should be with respect to which political matters and which political actors. Nevertheless, for those who believe in some form of self-restraint, each citizen must play a particular role, namely one in which he or she does not simply permit the coercive power of the state to establish a particular religion or conception of the good or to deprive others of their personal freedom on the ground that a particular way of life is sinful or foolish. The stricter the self-restraint, however, the more difficult it will be for ordinary persons to live up to this civic ideal. As Bernard Williams observes, to be genuinely tolerant, people must respect the freedom of conscience or autonomy of their fellow citizens more than they value their own deepest moral convictions in cases of conflict.[55]

For psychological and institutional reasons that I shall spell out later, I believe not only that it is desirable but also that it is more feasible to demand strict self-restraint from judges than from citizens or their elected representatives. This belief is an important part of my defense of judicial review in the last chapter of the book. When they take office, judges waive the right to act on reasons that conflict with performance of their legal duties, and that includes all legally irrelevant reasons. Just as judges can reach the right result for the right reasons, they can reach the right result for the wrong reasons. That would describe the thinking of most of those who agree with the outcome of *Roe v. Wade* but are displeased with the reasoning behind it. The law admits some reasons and excludes others, and an essential part of good judging involves knowing how to make such fine distinctions even in difficult cases. But when law and morality are not easily separated in American constitutional discourse and decision making, and many Americans have come to expect the Court to decide the most important questions of political morality, legally relevant reasons cannot be defined too narrowly. Not every moral reason is a legal reason as well, but judges often do and should incorporate such reasons into their decisions, provided that those reasons are not unduly controversial. At the same time, judges

---

[55] Bernard Williams, "Toleration: An Impossible Virtue?" in *Toleration: An Elusive Virtue*, ed. David Heyd (Princeton, NJ: Princeton University Press, 1996), 18–27.

wield quite a bit of power, and it is sensible to insist that they articulate, as clearly as possible, the grounds for their decisions in the most controversial constitutional cases. That the law guides judicial decision making and that judges must decide which reasons are legally relevant does not mean that they have the authority to redefine the meaning of legally relevant to include moral reasons that are derived from their respective conceptions of the good or from other controversial sources.

Just about everyone is sympathetic to Kent Greenawalt's view that "judicial opinions should be cast in terms that are broadly public."[56] The alternative would be to permit judges to rely on controversial values and disputed empirical claims that would eventually damage the reputation of the judiciary. A judicial opinion should be acceptable from as many moral perspectives as possible to avoid constitutional crises. Just as important, it would seem to be grossly unfair to base laws on controversial reasons, particularly when reasonable persons have good reasons not to accept them, and then to use those laws to restrict the individual freedom of those who lack the numbers or resources to defend their interests in the democratic arena. Arguably, that is an abuse of legislative power. It is not obvious, though, what "broadly public" means in a morally pluralistic society such as our own, and those who believe that public justification is important are divided over the most appropriate way of honoring this ideal.

At minimum, a person who exercises the strict self-restraint that Gaus envisions is a person who not only is sincerely trying to convince others and, in turn, is willing to be convinced by them but also is morally committed to acknowledging that the life plans of others probably have at least some value. Thus, that person searches for certain kinds of reasons to justify coercive laws, namely reasons that should be acceptable to others, provided that others reciprocate. Those reasons would be constitutionally legitimate. That does not necessarily mean that there is a single common standpoint that everyone occupies when they are reasonable. Indeed, there may be multiple ways of meeting the minimal requirements of reasonableness in a particular situation, and thus public reasons may conflict as well.[57] Further deliberation may not produce consensus when deliberators try to abstract from the particularities of the case at hand. Deliberators may have to accept that not everyone can share the same reasons because of the inherent difficulties of comparing the strength of the remaining public reasons and of being confident enough to know where the balance lies.

That does not mean, however, that all standpoints are equally reasonable or that all reasons are sufficiently public. That sort of subjectivism or

---

[56] Greenawalt, *Private Consciences and Public Reasons*, 7.
[57] See James Bohman, "Public Reason and Cultural Pluralism," 23 *Political Theory* (1995), 259.

relativism has to be avoided. A person is not relying on sufficiently public reasons when his or her decision would have been different but for deeper convictions. That person's position against same-sex marriage could not be based exclusively on Scripture when he or she would have reached the opposite conclusion without reliance on this source of moral authority. In the absence of religious prohibitions, for example, it would be hard to understand what is so morally problematic about same-sex relationships, whereas even if religious texts had nothing to say about murder, slavery, or theft, it would still be obvious why such conduct is wrong. Nor could another person's opposition to prayer in public schools be based entirely on the ground that religion is poison or that faith stunts intellectual development. Such strict self-restraint requires nothing less than a stronger moral commitment to eschew reasons that others cannot be reasonably expected to accept so that these people are not coerced without proper justification. The very idea of self-restraint that underlies an exclusive principle of public reason is intuitive: if one cares about respecting the choices that others make about how they would like to live, then those choices can be restricted only by reasons that it would not be unreasonable to expect that person to accept. Thus, as Gaus makes clear, one must assume that a reasonable person probably has good reasons for holding the views that he or she does even when their strength is not immediately apparent. That is a much stronger constraint than many advocates of public justification are comfortable with, but it reflects the liberal presumption that personal freedom cannot be restricted in the absence of compelling reasons for such a restriction, and that each person is entitled to an equal share of freedom. After all, most people would not want to live in a society where others could take away their freedoms or treat them unequally with insufficient justification.

Most of us limit ourselves to particular reasons in particular discursive settings when we care about treating others as equals and want to continue to reap the benefits of social cooperation. If most of us did not already have intuitions about the distinction between public and nonpublic reasons, then we would often be at cross-purposes and talk past one another. We would simply not know which reasons might count as plausible reasons in a certain discursive setting and have no rational way to proceed when a decision has to be made. That is perhaps the best explanation of why communication between two people from different cultures breaks down more easily; they simply have different preconceptions about what would constitute a good reason for acting in a situation of choice. Although some multiculturalists tend to exaggerate cultural differences, as if others were from a different planet, cultural norms sometimes diverge. A person who was raised in an Asian culture is likely to have different ideas of what it means to be a good parent, spouse, or child than is someone who grew up in the United States, and those who are first generation are often torn between the cultural expectations of their families and those of the majority in this country.

That said, even people with dissimilar upbringings and belief systems are likely to identify some of the same reasons as good reasons in some contexts. If that were not the case, then people would never be able to assimilate into other cultures or be able identify with the ups and downs of the lives of others. What we have in common as human beings does not guarantee anything like consensus, but it narrows the range of reasons that might turn out to be sufficiently public, thereby making at least reasonable disagreement possible. This commonality would seem to be a presupposition of communication aimed at persuasion. Two reasonable persons could still disagree when they take the views of others seriously but conclude that the balance of reasons cuts against the position that the others are advocating. In the real world, what is most challenging is to ask people to exercise strict self-restraint when they have to make very important collective decisions, when they do not personally know the others that they are supposed to give sufficiently public reasons to, when they are convinced that those who disagree with them are wrong, and when they have trouble understanding how a reasonable person could possibly disagree with them.[58] At times, it may be very easy to find reasons that others can be reasonably expected to share, depending on the details of the case. In our society, there is near consensus on the wrongness of racial and gender discrimination. At other times, it may be next to impossible to find such reasons. But that would become apparent only after the deliberators have made a sincere attempt to find common ground and have failed to do so.

At minimum, to be convinced by a public reason is to be convinced by a reason that others can share in spite of disagreement at a deeper level. A reasonable person would be able to say to another reasonable person, "I believe that your deeper beliefs are false but understand that you have the same belief about my convictions. I also understand that as a reasonable person, you believe that your reasons are better than mine, whereas I believe that mine are better than yours. Normally, we could agree to disagree, but when we have to make a collective decision that will have the force of law, we are committed to finding reasons that are mutually acceptable, which is not to say that we will always find them. But our objective need not be consensus, even though that would be preferable. Rather, because both of us cannot have our way and a perfect compromise may not exist, what we should aspire to is finding reasons that the dissenter, whoever it turns out to be, would accept as sufficient justification for that position. Whoever seeks

---

[58] As Deanna Kuhn has shown, people often have difficulty formulating objections to their own positions, and even when they do so, they have difficulty in rebutting them. See Deanna Kuhn, *The Skills of Argument* (Cambridge: Cambridge University Press, 1991), 139–46.

to enact his or her view into law has the burden of providing the other with sufficiently public reasons."

The preceding means that a reasonable person must imagine whether that reason would be a sufficient reason from the standpoint of another reasonable person who is also appropriately motivated to find a mutually acceptable conclusion but does not, and cannot ever reasonably be expected to, share his or her deeper beliefs. Above all, public reasoning requires people to see their common social world through the eyes of others before they make political choices that deprive them of their freedom and equality. That does not imply that it will be easy to adopt this impartial point of view anymore than it implies that the adoption of such a view would mean that all reasonable persons would always reach the same conclusion. Deeper convictions are bound to affect how people identify and weigh the public reasons that are relevant in determining the outcome. In filling in the details, even citizens who seek to fulfill their duty of civility to others by honoring public reason will have to exercise their own best judgment with the knowledge that their judgment is fallible.

Still, that does not mean that there is no point to trying to be fair-minded when a person cares about giving reasons to others that they may share. Nor does it mean that people who try to give reasons to others must defer to their subjective preferences or to their idiosyncratic beliefs, whatever they may be. That someone intensely desires a particular outcome does not necessarily mean that that person is entitled to that outcome. Nor does the very fact that a person believes a particular reason to be a good reason make it so. Rather, the point is that each deliberator must try to put forth reasons in good faith that others could consider sufficient in that particular context; deliberators should view themselves as having the burden of proving to that person that the reasons that they have offered are adequate. Above all, they have to eschew bad reasons. For someone like Gaus, this burden will not be impossible, but it will be very difficult, to meet. That will require the person advancing the public justification to explain how the law in question is consistent with respect for the freedom and equality of everyone, and the chances are that it will fall short. In rare instances, one may be able to show that legitimate concerns, such as public health and safety, override the presumption in favor of letting people do what they would like to do. One would have to make this determination on a case-by-case basis and would not define the police power of the state so broadly that it would eviscerate the foregoing presumption.

At times, even deliberators who limit themselves to widely acceptable reasons are likely to reasonably disagree about whether a particular reason is genuinely public. Here, the person who has introduced the reason in question would have to explain to others who are skeptical why, indeed, that reason is sufficiently public. The litigant in a child-custody dispute that has a serious substance-abuse problem or is prone to violence may not consider those reasons as sufficient to award custody to the other parent or to put a child in foster care, but those are reasons that a reasonable person should accept with awareness of the likely consequences of such personal problems to the fulfillment of parental responsibilities. A father may not want to pay child support, but by itself, that desire would not justify his failure to fulfill his moral and legal obligation to his child. The trick is to avoid subjectivism where what counts as a reason is solely determined by whether the likely dissenter actually accepts or rejects that reason while at the same time not ignoring what real people believe and not imposing reasons on them that a reasonable person could reasonably reject. That would involve paying closer attention to why that person rejects the reason offered, which may provide insight into why the reason in question is not as public as it may initially appear to be.

There are two basic problems with an exclusive principle of public reason. First, it may make it too difficult for the state to enact legislation. As I noted earlier, using Gaus's position, such a principle has semilibertarian implications in the sense that it would favor state inaction over action. As Andrew Lister puts it, "Requiring that state actions be reasonably non-rejectable would give a veto over state action to anyone with a reasonable difference of factual beliefs or ranking of accepted values."[59] Second, such a principle would be very hard to implement because it may be hard to know which reasons are the real reasons that underlie a particular political position. Elizabeth Wolgast has expressed the concern that a deliberator who casts arguments in terms of public reason may be speaking disingenuously.[60] She worries that compliance with such a principle requires people to misrepresent their real reasons in the name of political decorum. Deliberators will reach a conclusion on the basis of deeper, nonpublic reasons and then use sufficiently public reasons as an after-the-fact justification. That is a legitimate concern, but it should not be exaggerated. The use of public reason requires good faith that a person who sincerely tries to comply with its norms has not made up his or her mind already. A person who is trying to public justify a position on a fundamental political question must be introspective about whether he or she has sufficiently public reasons for reaching the same conclusion that he or she would have reached on nonpublic grounds. Nothing can save that person from a lack of goodwill toward others, self-awareness, or competence. Someone could believe that there are public reasons for the constitutional right to abortion, such as the value of gender equality and reproductive choice, and believe that a human fetus becomes a person

---

[59] Andrew Lister, "Public Justification and the Limits of State Action," *Politics, Philosophy, and Economics,* forthcoming 2010.

[60] Elizabeth A. Wolgast, "The Demands of Public Reason," 94 *Columbia Law Review* (1994), 1943–4.

with a right not to be killed only when it is viable. Alternatively, one could believe that the practice of abortion undermines respect for the sanctity of all life, which is arguably a public reason, and believe that a fetus achieves personhood at conception and thus has a right not to be killed.

In principle, a person could have both nonpublic and public reasons that support the same conclusion, and this is usually the case. The danger that Wolgast identifies is that one might be tempted to reach a conclusion on the basis of nonpublic reasons and then offer public reasons to others that he or she does not really endorse to conceal the real reasons. Psychologically, this temptation would be understandable, especially when one cares deeply about the outcome of a particular constitutional case. At the same time, people who care about public justification have to make the best effort to determine whether they really have sufficient public reasons that support the conclusion that they would reach on the basis of their deepest convictions. After reflection, if they do not have such public reasons, then they should not offer them in the name of public justification – and if they do so, then they have not lived up to their civic duty.

III. INCLUSIVE PUBLIC REASON

A. Overview

In between the extremes of laissez-faire and exclusive public reason lie a number of intermediate positions, or inclusive principles. By definition, "[a]n inclusive ideal of public reason is one that requires citizens to advance public reasons in public debate on political questions, but that does not require them to exclude supporting nonpublic reasons."[61] According to Solum, there are several principles of inclusion.[62] For example, Kent Greenawalt favors a conception of self-restraint that permits citizens, particularly those who are religious, to "speak to the implications of their comprehensive views" under certain circumstances.[63] The only constraint on their use of nonpublic reasons is that they must not be incompatible with the public reasons that they also put forward as justification.

Bruce Ackerman's "neutral dialogue" approach to public justification aims at convergence on a mutually acceptable conclusion from different starting points.[64] This approach is premised on the possibility that delib-erators can show those who disagree with them, and vice versa, that the

---

[61] Solum, "Inclusive Public Reason," 218–19.

[62] Ibid., 223.

[63] Greenawalt, *Private Consciences and Public Reasons*, 152.

[64] Ackerman writes, "Liberalism does not depend on the truth of any single metaphysical or epistemological system. Instead, liberalism's ultimate justification is to be found in its strategic location in a web of talk that converges upon it from every direction." Ackerman, *Social Justice in the Liberal State*, 361.

reasons that they have for rejecting the political position in question "are not as persuasive as [they] might have thought: *that even within* [their] *own view of the world*, [they] should find ultimately unpersuasive the reasons [they] can give for [their] initial disquiet."[65] One might be able to show a Christian who opposes same-sex marriage that his or her opposition is incompatible with the Christian principle that one should hate the sin and love the sinner. The trouble with this solution is that it assumes that many people are confused; they are simply unaware of the implications of their deeper beliefs, and if others could enlighten them, they would see that they are mistaken. This may be an accurate description of some people, but under conditions of moral pluralism and the burdens of judgment, it often will be hard to explain to someone why you have a better understanding of his or her own deeper beliefs and their implications than that person does. As a result, Ackerman's other idea of coping with the phenomenon of moral pluralism is more promising. The adoption of "conversational restraint," in which participants "put the moral ideals that divide [them] off the conversational agenda of the liberal state," increases the likelihood that reasonable people will not be at odds with one another.[66] Ackerman explicitly contrasts his approach with that of Habermas because the "argumentative aim is not to discover the ultimate moral truth...[but to] provide each citizen with...a way of reasonably responding to their continuing moral disagreement."[67]

Ackerman believes that citizens are "free to proclaim the goodness of their good" but also that no citizen should assert that his or her conception of the good is superior to those of others.[68] This is an important constraint, and without it, it is hard to imagine that deliberators would not talk past one another because of their diverse deeper beliefs. At the same time, it is not evident how "proclaiming the goodness of their good" is compatible with not asserting its superiority. As Peter De Marneffe has pointed out, Ackerman has not adequately distinguished between "reasons that come from a conception of the good and reasons that come from a conception of the right."[69] It is not clear, then, what reasons are "allowed into neutral dialogue."[70] This is problematic because, although Rawls deliberately does not fix the content of public reason, deliberators must have some rough idea of what kinds of reasons are likely to be sufficiently public.

[65] Ibid., 357.
[66] Bruce Ackerman, "Why Dialogue?" 86 *Journal of Philosophy* (1989), 16.
[67] Ibid., 19.
[68] Ackerman, *Social Justice in the Liberal State*, 375, 369.
[69] Peter De Marneffe, "Rawls's Idea of Public Reason," 75 *Pacific Philosophical Quarterly* (1994), 250n17.
[70] Ibid.

C. Rawlsian Public Idea

I want to finish this chapter by sketching Rawls's conception of public reason and how that understanding evolved over time into an inclusive principle.[71] Although Rawls did not use the term *public reason* in *A Theory of Justice*, "the concept itself has always been at the heart of his philosophy," as one commentator writes, "playing an indispensable part in the theory of justice as fairness."[72] Rawls frames the problem of public justification in the language of intractable moral pluralism, that is, reasonable, good-faith disagreement about the nature of a good human life. The existence of such pluralism means that "[t]he aim of political liberalism is to uncover the conditions of the possibility of a reasonable public basis of justification on fundamental political questions."[73] Rawlsian public reason addresses the worry that principles of justice and the public laws that follow from them cannot be sufficiently publicly justified, and thus popularly supported for the right reasons, in the absence of greater moral or religious homogeneity.[74] Initially, Rawls did not envision such an ambitious role for public reason in his well-ordered society.[75] The parties in the original position were supposed to agree only to norms of such reason as guidelines for applying the principles of justice in the midst of reasonable disagreement about what they would require.[76] In *Political Liberalism*, the purpose of public reason is to outline the kinds of reasons and arguments that would meet the minimal requirements of public justification when political choices have the force of law.

The scope of public reason refers to the kinds of questions that the ideal of public reason covers. A narrow scope means that public reason applies to only constitutional essentials and matters of basic justice. A broad scope means that public reason applies to "all political decisions where citizens exercise coercive power over one another."[77] Rawls never claims that all political debate in all forums over all political matters should take place within the parameters of public reason. He explicitly limits the scope of public reason to the most important political questions, what he calls "constitutional essentials" and "matters of basic justice."[78] Most of

---

[71] Rawls, *Political Liberalism*, 247; See also Solum, "Inclusive Public Reason," 218.

[72] Charles Larmore, "Public Reason," in *The Cambridge Companion to Rawls*, ed. Samuel Freeman (New York: Cambridge University Press, 2003), 368.

[73] Rawls, *Political Liberalism*, xxi.

[74] For Rawls's original theory of public reason, see Rawls, *Political Liberalism*, 212–54. For his more recent views on public reason, see Rawls, *Justice as Fairness*, 89–94; John Rawls, "The Idea of Public Reason Revisited," in *The Law of Peoples* (Cambridge, MA: Harvard University Press, 1999), 131–80.

[75] Samuel Freeman, *Rawls* (New York: Routledge, 2007), 372.

[76] Rawls, *Political Liberalism*, 226–7.

[77] See Jonathan Quong, "The Scope of Public Reason," 52 *Political Studies* (2004), 234.

[78] Rawls, *Political Liberalism*, 213–14, 219.

the time, deliberators may invoke their deepest convictions and are not under a self-imposed civic duty to offer public reasons.[79] Still, it would be preferable to offer such reasons, especially when it may not be easy to strictly separate the most important political questions from less important ones.[80]

Nonetheless, a number of commentators have misunderstood how limited the scope of public reason is.[81] Such reason applies only in certain circumstances, and Rawls believes that reasonable persons think differently about the reasons that they can reasonably expect others to accept when the position that they advocate will be backed by the coercive power of the state. In a society such as our own, "epistemic abstinence" on the part of citizens and their elected representatives is the most appropriate response to the existence of reasonable disagreement in political life. As Joseph Raz writes, "Rawls's *epistemic abstinence* lies in the fact that he refrains from claiming that his doctrine of justice is true. The reason is that truth, if it is true, must derive from deep, and possibly nonautonomous, foundations, from some sound comprehensive moral doctrine. Asserting the truth of the doctrine, or rather claiming that its truth is the reason for accepting it, would negate the very spirit of Rawls's enterprise."[82] This characterization is slightly misleading because citizens may believe that one of the political conceptions of justice is true. It is up to them to figure out the connection between their deeper beliefs and the political conception of justice that they prefer. This latitude forms the basis of the overlapping consensus of reasonable comprehensive doctrines that Rawls hopes will develop over time in a well-ordered society. But Raz is correct to point out that, in many circumstances, Rawlsian citizens should refrain from introducing and relying on nonpublic reasons even when they believe that those reasons are true or right.[83]

According to Rawls, such abstinence is predicated not on skepticism about moral knowledge – a person who offers a public reason to another can also believe that that reason is true according to her belief system – but on the overarching civic importance of giving reasons to others that they can reasonably be expected to accept as justification for coercion on the part of

---

[79] As examples of questions that usually do not involve constitutional essentials and matters of basic justice, Rawls lists tax legislation and laws regulating property, the environment, pollution, wildlife conservation, and funding of the arts. Rawls, *Political Liberalism*, 214.

[80] On this point about, see Kent Greenawalt, "On Public Reason," 69 *Chicago-Kent Law Review* (1994), 685–9.

[81] See, e.g., Michael J. Sandel, "Political Liberalism," review, 107 *Harvard Law Review* (1994), 1789.

[82] Joseph Raz, "Facing Diversity: The Case for Epistemic Abstinence," 19 *Philosophy and Public Affairs* (1990), 9.

[83] Rawls refers to this as the "apparent paradox of public reason." Rawls, *Political Liberalism*, 218.

the state. The legitimate grounds of such coercion cannot be based on sectarian convictions, especially those that are unquestionably controversial, because reasonable people have good reasons to dispute their truth. That means not only that public officials must limit themselves to widely acceptable reasons when they legislate about constitutional essentials and matters of basic justice but also that citizens must do the same when they deliberate in the public realm about such fundamentals and vote for candidates for public office. Although voting is necessary when further deliberation and reflection will not produce consensus and a collective decision must be made, voting is not a private act insofar as it constitutes an indirect exercise of coercive political power. Thus, voting requires self-restraint on the part of citizens and of their elected representatives, who must guard against relying on reasons that are too partial to win the assent of others. Each should base a vote on his or her own best understanding of what public reason requires. A citizen who does not vote according to norms of public reason fails to live up to the "duty of civility" by displaying a willingness to restrict the freedom of fellow citizens on the basis of inappropriate reasons.[84] To appeal to nonpublic reasons is to place oneself in an unequal relation to those who are properly considered political equals.[85]

Rawls believes that more agreement on political fundamentals is desirable so that society is not only stable but also stable for the right reasons. By that, he means that, most of the time, most people support the regulatory principles of justice that constitute his political conception of justice out of a principled concern for the quality of the lives of everyone. For Rawls, rejecting public reason has serious consequences. As one commentator writes: "To reject the claims of public reason at this level is to opt out of rational dialogue, it is to take a position outside the language game of rational discussion. One must be willing to say to others: 'I cannot give you a reason you accept, and I am not willing to attempt to give you a reason or to offer my reasons for your perusal. I shall simply do as I wish, given my point of view.' That is an extreme position."[86]

The unwillingness of citizens to justify their vote to fellow citizens through reasons that might be acceptable to them also puts into doubt the legitimacy of public laws. It is not evident why a dissenter would be bound morally to obey a law that is not predicated on fair reasons or at least on a sincere attempt to provide them in the name of reciprocity. The practice of public reasoning addresses this concern; it makes public justification, and thus minimal political legitimacy, possible because public reasons are limited to reasons that are sufficiently independent of deeper sectarian convictions and the controversy that surrounds them.

---

[84] As Rawls makes clear, this is not a legal duty. Ibid., 217.

[85] I owe this phrasing to Pat Neal.

[86] Bruce W. Brower, "The Limits of Public Reason," 91 *Journal of Philosophy* (1994), 26.

As Rawls sees it, understanding the ideal of public reason is vital to conducting oneself as a democratic citizen who treats others as political equals.[87] Reasonable citizens do not vote their narrow interests, tastes, or preferences – nor do they appeal to what they believe to be right or true according to their own comprehensive doctrines.[88] When one assumes the role of citizen, the balance of public reasons must resolve the most important political questions. That also means that citizens are supposed to vote for candidates who honor the limits of public reason, thereby ensuring that public officials will observe them as well. The existence of intractable moral pluralism compels deliberators to appeal to authorities that are acceptable to those with whom they disagree to meet the minimal requirements of political legitimacy and thereby avoid unjustified coercion. Thus, public justification must be addressed to others and must begin with what is, or can be, held in common.[89] In treating their fellow citizens as political equals, deliberators cast their arguments in ways that are likely to appeal to reasonable persons who, like themselves, have important life plans of their own. A premise that cannot be known or justified apart from its deeper theoretical sources fails to satisfy the requirement of reciprocity built into public reason because it could not support a mutually acceptable conclusion. Citizens who reason from premises that they already know others, who are equally reasonable, will not accept fail to respect their right not to be coerced on the basis of reasons that they could not be reasonably expected to share.

In the introduction to *Political Liberalism*, Rawls refers to the "inclusive view" as the "wide view" of public reason.[90] The inclusive view is much less restrictive than the original exclusive view, whereas the wide view of public reason is somewhat more restrictive than the inclusive view.[91] Rawls's wide view allows citizens and public officials to appeal to nonpublic reasons, provided that they are also able to produce public reasons to support their positions on the political fundamental in question. Initially, Rawls's inclusive view of public reason required everyone to defend their positions on fundamental political questions in terms of public reasons, but under certain nonideal conditions, he permitted deliberators and voters to give one another nonpublic reasons as well. The wide view still requires them to give priority to public reasons over nonpublic ones in cases of conflict. A person, then, could not vote in good faith on a constitutional essential according to nonpublic reasons unless he or she also had at least one nontrivial public reason that supported the same position.

[87] Rawls, *Political Liberalism*, 218.
[88] Ibid.
[89] Ibid., 100.
[90] Ibid., lii.
[91] Ibid., 247–52.

Rawls was initially inclined to the exclusive view but switched to the inclusive view because the exclusive view was "too restrictive."[92] The inclusive view permits deliberators, under certain circumstances, to present their deeper convictions, as long as they do so in a manner that strengthens the idea of public reason itself.[93] As Patrick Neal observes, according to the inclusive view, public reasons act as a "theoretical chaperone" to nonpublic reasons.[94] In "The Idea of Public Reason Revisited," Rawls introduces "the proviso," and moves even farther away from the exclusive view to what he calls the wide view of public reason, in which the use of deeper convictions no longer has to be accompanied by their chaperone but in which public reasons must be offered in "due course."[95] These qualifications lead to a much less exclusive principle of public reason.[96]

Normally, those who object to a broadly Rawlsian approach to public justification are taking issue not with the very idea of public justification – indeed, even Hobbes had such a conception, as I mentioned earlier – but with the route that Rawls believes is most likely to lead to such justification. Those who want to live in a society that makes a sincere effort to publicly justify its constitutional choices must be able to produce reasons that their fellow citizens could accept as adequate. The more difficult the case, the more challenging this task is going to be. Because they may not be able to find mutually acceptable reasons despite their best efforts, consensus is best thought of as a counterfactual regulative ideal that increases the likelihood that collective decisions are legitimate in the eyes of most of the people who must live under them.

Rawls himself acknowledges that on some questions, the "best that we can do" is to sincerely believe that the balance of public reasons supports one conclusion in a particular case and that "those who oppose it can nevertheless understand how reasonable persons can affirm it."[97] The failure to reach unanimous collective decisions in real public deliberation, though, would mean that some reasonable dissenters still may be coerced on the basis of reasons that do not persuade them and perhaps should not have persuaded them. That unanimity is out of the question in the real world is regrettable, but that possibility should not lead to the anarchist conclusion that political authority is necessarily incompatible with the autonomy or freedom of each citizen.[98] The objective is not to replicate the kind of consensus that might

[92] Ibid., 247.

[93] Ibid.

[94] Patrick Neal, "Is Public Reason Innocuous?" 11 *Critical Review of International Social and Political Philosophy* (2008), 133.

[95] Rawls, "The Idea of Public Revisited," 145.

[96] On this point, see Neal, "Is Public Reason Innocuous?" 133–4.

[97] Rawls, *Political Liberalism*, 253.

[98] See, e.g., Robert Paul Wolff, *In Defense of Anarchism* (Berkeley: University of California Press, 1970).

have existed in Rousseau's small imaginary republic of civic-minded persons but to avoid, as much as possible, unfairly imposing public laws on dissenters who have good reasons to dissent. There is an important moral difference between a reason that is minimally acceptable and a reason that falls short of public justification and calls into question the obligation of reasonable dissenters to obey the law.

Like Rawls, those who are committed to some principle of public reason believe that it is either imprudent or fundamentally unfair for groups of persons who enjoy numerical advantages to impose their sectarian convictions on others without proper justification. As one commentator puts it, "When you limit yourself to reasons accessible to others, disagreement amounts to divergent exercises in common reason, rather than sectarian ideological war where your opponent's reasons seem to be weapons from an alien arsenal"[99] Thus, persons who live in liberal societies must have a certain sort of attitude, namely one that is tolerant in the sense that people have a right "to live as they choose and to influence others," and that right "is not conditional on their agreement with me about what the right way to live is."[100] When a person assumes the role of liberal citizen, he or she cannot conceive of political decisions, which are not self-regarding, as analogues to personal decisions. That others could not reasonably be expected to share a reason that such a person believes to be a good reason is a decisive reason for not relying on that reason when a decision that will have the force of law has to be made. This is so because people ought to think of others as political equals who deserve fair treatment even when they reject the value of their life plans or fear that their participation in political life will push their society in the wrong direction. Others are entitled to the same right to pursue their reasonable conceptions of the good because it is their community too.

A principle of public reason defines the contours of public deliberation and voting on fundamental political questions; it does not take the place of public deliberation and judgment in individual constitutional cases. Such reason does not decide hard cases in advance and cannot tell deliberators how to classify fundamental political questions, how to draw causal inferences, how to deal with conflicting empirical evidence, how to predict consequences, how to rebut presumptions, how to weigh competing normative considerations, or how to break ties. That is the responsibility of individual citizens, their elected representatives, and judges, who must provide reasonable dissenters with adequate, context-sensitive reasons to justify the imposition of coercive laws. But the more exclusive or inclusive the principle is, the more or less likely certain fundamental political questions will

---

[99] Robert Westmoreland, "The Truth about Public Reason," 18 *Law and Philosophy* (1999), 283.

[100] T. M. Scanlon, "The Difficulty of Tolerance," in *Toleration: An Elusive Virtue*, ed. David Heyd (Princeton, NJ: Princeton University Press, 1996), 232.

be resolved in certain ways. There is a lot to be said on behalf of some kind of inclusive principle of public reason, especially when ordinary citizens are supposed to comply with it. Rawls himself mentions the importance of forming a sociological basis that would "encourage citizens to honor the ideal of public reason."[101] Solum maintains that the advantage of employing an inclusive principle is that it provides room for nonpublic reasons, thereby reducing the likelihood that real people will be torn between their deepest beliefs and their civic duty to provide others with sufficiently public reasons. In particular, having nonpublic reasons play a supporting role "would foster civility and the civic virtue of tolerance."[102]

This is a prediction based on an empirical claim, and it may be accurate. I am not prepared to say that Solum is wrong, but my intuition is that the more that ordinary people introduce reasons based on their conceptions of the good, the more divided they will be, at least with respect to the most divisive questions of political morality. After all, learning from others' deeper beliefs can always take place in the background culture in many different forums when constitutional essentials and matters of basic justice are not at stake. No reasonable person will be opposed to fostering civility and tolerance, but in a society that is not well ordered in some ways, most people have to learn how to be reasonable in the sense of developing the skill of giving reasons to others that those people could not reasonably reject. Today, most people are probably in the habit of using nonpublic reasons even though they think that those reasons are sufficiently public. It is common in American politics, for example, for people to insist that their deeper beliefs provide all the justification that is necessary for their political positions. If I did not believe that others did not have the same reasons to share my deeper beliefs, then I probably would not be as wedded to the deepest beliefs that I have developed over the course of my life.

That belief is natural, but in a society like our own, all people need to become more aware of the kinds of reasons that they would look for when they are sincerely trying to publicly justify their position to those who disagree with them. That is the kind of justification that public laws and constitutional decisions can have under conditions of moral pluralism and the burdens of judgment. Their correctness stems from the quality of the arguments for or against a particular conclusion, and their quality is a function of whether an ideal reasonable person would be justified in rejecting their premises or their inferences. The challenge for deliberators is to put together arguments in particular constitutional cases that would win the allegiance of an ideal reasonable person, and different theorists have different ideas about what this process entails. At their best, reasonable people

[101] Rawls, *Political Liberalism*, 249.
[102] Solum, "Inclusive Public Reason," 223–5.

can be motivated to give reasons that others may share and probably can do so reasonably well most of the time. The very practice of everyday communication suggests that an exchange of reasons is just that: a series of sincere, reciprocal attempts at rational persuasion. A society whose members make sincere attempts at public justification may come closer to legitimizing its most important constitutional choices than a society whose members do not even try to exercise such self-restraint. That is why reasonable people also must agree, more or less, on which principle of public reason best exemplifies a commitment to the freedom and equality of all persons.

FIVE

Constitutional Public Reason

In the previous chapter, I reviewed the three basic principles of public reason – laissez-faire, exclusion, and inclusion – and described their strengths and weaknesses. In this chapter, I defend an exclusive principle of public reason as the best interpretation of an ideal of public justification. Such a principle, where the set of public reasons is narrow, is more likely to lead to publicly justified laws and judicial decisions under conditions of moral pluralism. This defense is partially based on the claim that an exclusive principle of public reason better squares with the requirements of judging.[1] An exclusive principle would require "exceedingly persuasive justification" for the law in question, which would be more difficult for the state to satisfy than the alternative principles of public reason in fundamental rights and equal protection cases. When legislation involves constitutional essentials, the state must produce reasons that an ideal reasonable dissenter could not reject, or else the law in question is unconstitutional. The constitutional requirement that the most important laws be unquestionably publicly justified would foster the same basic equal legal rights for all of the members of the political community.[2]

The use of an exclusive principle also would help those who read judicial opinions to know when the Court has decided a case incorrectly. That is more important than it may seem. A morally pluralistic society like our own always has been, and always will be, trying to temper the moral disagreement that causes political conflict. Although, recently, political philosophers have given a lot of attention to the idea of public justification, law professors have not done so. As a result, not much has been written about the relationship of public justification to constitutional adjudication and its implications for

---

[1] Rawls himself believes that "the idea of public reason applies more strictly to judges than to others." John Rawls, "The Idea of Public Reason Revisited," in *The Law of Peoples* (Cambridge, MA: Harvard University Press, 1999), 134.

[2] Rawls refers to this first principle of justice as "equal basic liberties." John Rawls, *Political Liberalism* (New York: Columbia University Press, 1996), 5.

judicial review and real constitutional controversies. This oversight is surprising because those who reject formalist and originalist approaches are often nudged toward a more "philosophic" approach to constitutional decision making.[3] One exception to this lack of scholarly attention is Lawrence Solum, who has developed what he refers to as an ideal of "legal public reason," which is a "subset of the ideal of public reason" that serves as "a normative standard for the practice of justification by lawyers, judges, and other officials."[4] Solum's ideal is more ambitious than my own in the following way: he seeks to clarify the complex relationship between an ideal of public reason and normative legal theory and practice. Alternatively, my exclusive principle of public reason is a subset of legal public reason because it has a more limited purpose: to structure constitutional argumentation in fundamental rights and equal protection cases and to explain what counts as an adequate constitutional argument.

Solum also believes that a more exclusive principle of public reason, one that is narrower than Rawls's own view, is more appropriate for judges.[5] It would be odd for anyone, in a society that is saturated with rhetoric about the abuse of judicial power, to invite judges to include moral reasons in their opinions.[6] Early in his academic career, even Ronald Dworkin went out of his way to ensure his readers that his idea of a moral reading did not permit judges to do whatever they pleased.[7] That judges should use only certain reasons in their opinions, then, is not controversial, but judges also must ensure that others do not rely on the wrong kinds of reasons in the legislative process. Thus, judges must hold lawmakers accountable to the standard of public justification as well, and that means that when the state has failed to meet this standard, a judge would be justified in invalidating the law in question. This basic idea is already implicit in certain areas of constitutional practice, and therefore would not require an overhaul of contemporary constitutional law.

I. EXCLUSIVE PUBLIC REASON

A. Overview

In terms of public justification, reasons can be insufficiently public in three different ways: (1) they are based on unverifiable or controversial empirical

---

[3] I borrow this term from Sotirios A. Barber and James E. Fleming, *Constitutional Interpretation: The Basic Questions* (New York: Oxford University Press, 2007), xiii.

[4] Lawrence B. Solum, "Public Legal Reason," 92 *Virginia Law Review* (2006), 1453.

[5] Ibid., 1473.

[6] Ronald Dworkin, *Freedom's Law: The Moral Reading of the Constitution* (Cambridge, MA: Harvard University Press, 1996), 3.

[7] See, e.g., Ronald Dworkin, *Taking Rights Seriously* (Cambridge, MA: Harvard University Press, 1977), 128–9.

claims (that are at least as likely to be false as they are to be true), (2) they are too closely tied to the content of a conception of good or a comprehensive view, or (3) they are deeply rooted in a political ideology. From the standpoint of either the person who offers or who is asked to accept or reject a particular public justification on behalf of a constitutional conclusion, there are three kinds of public justifications: (1) one that a reasonable person should accept because the argument clearly relies on sufficiently public reasons, (2) one that a reasonable person should reject because the argument clearly contains insufficiently public reasons, and (3) one that a reasonable person may (or may not) accept as good enough because, on balance, the reasons offered are arguably sufficiently public (a close call). Those lines will not be bright in hard cases, but that is how people who care about public justification should approach assessing not only the justifications that others have advanced for their consideration but their own as well.

As I have mentioned, it is more or less obvious why judges should eschew nonpublic reasons in their opinions. The position of the Catholic Church on same-sex marriage is not a reason that Chief Justice Roberts or Justices Scalia, Kennedy, Thomas, or Alito could legitimately rely on in deciding whether there is a constitutional right to such marriage. In *Romer v. Evans*, Scalia defends the view that the state may make legislative classifications based sexual orientation on the ground that legislative majorities may enact their will into law even when their will is based on moral disapproval.[8] As he saw it, unlike those in the majority, he was not "taking a side in a culture war" but respecting an outcome of a procedurally fair democratic process in which the majority of those who voted had expressed their preferences or convictions. What Scalia said in his dissenting opinion is as revealing as what he did not say; it would have been unthinkable for him to have claimed that those who engage in "unnatural" sexual acts not done for the purpose of procreation are acting immorally and that the state may discriminate against them on that basis alone. One could read in between the lines and attribute something like the foregoing position to Scalia, but it would be more charitable to take what Scalia wrote at face value. Some scholars have contended that in *Romer* the Court applied more than rational-basis standard of review in rendering unconstitutional Amendment 2 to the Colorado Constitution.[9] In the language of public reason, the Court looked at the reasons that the state had offered for the discrimination in question more skeptically and concluded that they were not consistent with the freedom and equality of gay and lesbian persons. Scalia's position in

---

[8] Romer v. Evans, 517 U.S. 620 (1996) (Scalia, J., dissenting).
[9] See, e.g., Evan Gerstmann, *Same-Sex Marriage and the Constitution* (New York: Cambridge University Press, 2004), 18.

Romer is revealing on this point; it indicates that Scalia also knows that certain reasons cannot form the basis of a legitimate law. That is why he devoted time in his dissenting opinion to explain that prejudice against gays and lesbians was not what motivated Colorado voters to approve Amendment 2.

As I would like to show in this chapter, meeting the standard of public justification requires adherence to and application of an exclusive principle of public reason. Thus, judges should employ only "shallow" arguments in their opinions, and that rules out direct reliance on all comprehensive religious and moral views.[10] More important, and more controversially, they must hold the state to such a principle as well. If you care about convincing another reasonable person, then you appeal to premises that that person already accepts or is likely to accept on reflection, and that limits the kinds of reasons that you can offer others as justification ahead of time. The challenge, then, is to be aware of the kinds of reasons not only that others would find persuasive but also that they would be justified in accepting as good enough on a case-by-case basis.

Initially, for Rawls, to comply with the principle of public reason was to avoid going any deeper than necessary. Such shallow arguments are more likely to persuade because "there is more agreement on the shallow than on the deep" and it is "easier to move someone to a new conclusion from something she agrees with than from anything else."[11] The appeal of this idea is intuitive, I believe, and even those who reject Rawlsian liberalism probably understand why this idea seems to have so much appeal in a society characterized by moral disagreement. We could begin with what we believe to be true, as those who favor a laissez-faire principle of public reason advocate, but that strategy is likely to work only when the audience more or less already shares our deepest convictions. The aim is not simply to secure the agreement of others but to find reasons that secure this agreement because of their fairness. Also, shallow arguments, which typically involve counterexample, thought experiment, simple observation, and uncontroversial empirical theory, are more likely to be accessible and, therefore, easier to evaluate.[12] That is not to say that everyone shares this aversion to the use of nonpublic reasons, but current political discourse suggests that deeper arguments are not likely to do what they are supposed to do under conditions of moral pluralism: convince reasonable people who are already divided over the nature of the human good that the reasons in question are sufficient to do the required justificatory work.

---

[10] The term *shallow* appears in S. A. Lloyd, "Relativizing Rawls," 69 *Chicago-Kent Law Review* (1994), 719.

[11] Ibid., 721n27.

[12] Ibid., 720.

B. Empirical Claims

A reasonable person should accept a constitutional argument that relies primarily on factual premises that are very likely to be true and to support the legislation in question. Such a person should not rely on empirical claims that are likely to be false, cannot be verified, or are unduly controversial. For example, the advocacy of abstinence is not an effective way of educating teenagers about birth control.[13] That driving under the influence of alcohol increases the risk of accidents and fatalities on the highways is beyond dispute. That the production of child pornography exploits and harms children is also uncontested.[14] By contrast, some empirical claims are false and therefore cannot serve as a sufficiently public reason, like the claim that homosexuality is a choice or that it causes earthquakes.[15] Other empirical claims cannot be verified and, as such, are also insufficiently public. Catharine MacKinnon once claimed that consumption of hardcore pornography leads to rape.[16] From the standpoint of public justification, the trouble with this claim is that it is not clear or at least clear enough that exposure to such pornography causes men to commit violence against women.[17] Even if there were a correlation between seeing violent sexual images and committing certain crimes, it would be hard to prove that one causes the other. After all, men who enjoy hardcore pornography may already be predisposed to such violence. In the language of statistics, the challenge would be to disaggregate the independent variables. If MacKinnon's claim were true and uncontroversial, then it could serve as a public reason, and no doubt, it would be a very strong one. An argument that is designed to support the conclusion that the production and consumption of pornography is the primary cause of or contributes to gender inequality also would count as an attempt at public justification, which is not to say that it would meet the standard of public justification.[18] A claim that virtual child pornography "whets the appetites of pedophiles and encourages them to engage in illegal conduct" is also too empirically contestable to count as a sufficiently public reason.[19] The same could be said about the claim that gay men should not be allowed to teach in

---

[13] See Alesha E. Doan and Jean Calterone Williams, *The Politics of Virginity: Abstinence in Sex Education* (Westport, CT: Praeger Publishing, 2008).

[14] Although exploitation and harm are moral concepts, they have factual dimensions as well because certain facts are morally relevant in determining whether someone has been exploited or harmed.

[15] I owe the latter example to Pat Neal from personal correspondence.

[16] Catharine A. MacKinnon, *Only Words* (Cambridge, MA: Harvard University Press, 1993), 16.

[17] There is no consensus on this question in the academic literature.

[18] See, e.g., Catharine A. MacKinnon, "Francis Biddle's Sister: Pornography, Civil Rights, and Speech," in *Feminism Unmodified: Discourses on Life and Law* (Cambridge, MA: Harvard University Press, 1987), 163–97.

[19] The government made this argument in Ashcroft v. Free Speech Coalition, 535 U.S. 234 (2002).

public schools because they are more likely to molest students than straight men are. The point is not only that causal inference can be problematic; it should not be too easy, furthermore, for the state to put forth a controversial causal claim in which the independent variable (possible cause) is merely correlated with the dependent variable (effect) or with a prediction about likely consequences that is too speculative for others to share.

Cass Sunstein has emphasized the importance of judges' having "a better sense of [the] underlying facts" when they decide cases.[20] It is true that legal disputes often have empirical dimensions and that it would be useful to know, for instance, whether the use of a negligence standard in cases where public figures sue for defamation would really have the chilling effects that those who support the *New York Times* actual malice standard fear. But it is not obvious that a better understanding of the facts would make it less imperative for judges to offer theoretical defenses of their conclusions in constitutional cases when they also must take sides in debates in normative constitutional theory. Hard constitutional cases are hard precisely because they often involve disputed issues of public morality, and constitutional arguments that incorporate moral premises, some of which may not be obviously true or false, will be difficult to assess. For the purpose of public justification, the moral premises that are more likely to be "true" or widely acceptable appeal to a "thin theory of the good," that is, to the idea that everyone has an interest in securing the resources that make a good life possible.[21] In practice, this means that deliberators who are trying to meet the standard of public justification will appeal to the freedom and equality of all persons on the assumption that no reasonable life plan is any better or any worse than any other reasonable life plan. By implication, premises that are based on denials of the freedom and equality of some persons will be suspect in the eyes of those who are supposed to decide whether the argument in question has met the standard of public justification.

In most of the most important cases, I doubt that whether the state has met the standard of public justification frequently will turn on disagreement over the truth of empirical claims about what causes what effects and so on. At the same time, it is true that such claims are often wrapped up in the most contentious political matters. For instance, if it turns out that affirmative action programs really do exacerbate racial tensions or that capital punishment really does deter murder, then the position of those who oppose the former and support the latter would be more likely to be publicly justified. The use of a controversial empirical reason as a justification for a public law may not seem to be as obviously problematic as the use of a deep

---

[20] Cass R. Sunstein, *One Case at a Time: Judicial Minimalism on the Supreme Court* (Cambridge, MA: Harvard University Press, 1999), 254.

[21] On the thin theory of the good, see John Rawls, *A Theory of Justice*, rev. ed. (Cambridge, MA: Harvard University Press, Belknap Press, 2003), 347–50.

sectarian reason. On the one hand, it is true that to coerce people on the basis of a controversial empirical claim is to coerce them on the basis of a reason that they could reasonably reject. On the other hand, a law-making body is usually better positioned to evaluate the quality of an empirical claim than a court, and in some circumstances, it would be advisable to allow a legislature either to experiment in the face of empirical uncertainty or to assume that a particular behavior, such as smoking in public places, is a serious public health concern, even if the jury is still out.

As I see it, the trouble is that the state too often has used, and will continue to use, empirical justifications to mask what are really controversial moral judgments that negatively affect the lives of some of its citizens. It should not be too easy to conceal the moral beliefs that underlie a particular partisan position. For instance, those who oppose same-sex marriage often claim that the recognition of such a right will undermine opposite-sex marriage, but they do not specify the nature of the cause-and-effect relationship between them. Thus, the Court has to be wary of the abuse of empirical claims. The principle of exclusive public reason is not deontological in the sense that the consequences do not matter. Indeed, judges must have a keen eye for how a law may undermine freedom and equality. The point is that it should not be too easy for the state to circumvent the constitutional requirement that laws involving constitutional essentials be publicly justified by insisting that judges ought to defer to the fact-finding of legislative bodies.

II. HOW TO DISTINGUISH BETTER FROM WORSE PUBLIC ARGUMENTS

A. Public versus Nonpublic Reasons

Judges must do more than simply guard against using nonpublic reasons in their own opinions. They should also ensure that law-making bodies limit themselves to sufficiently public reasons when they enact legislation that involves constitutional essentials. That claim is bound to be more controversial because it would make it more difficult for the state to enact certain kinds of legislation. Judicial review would have more bite and courts would not have to be so respectful of legislative judgments that compromised freedom and equality. Some state actions are more coercive than others are.[22] The more coercive the law, the more publicly justified that law should be. At the same time, that does not mean that an ideal of public justification, premised on an exclusive principle of public reason, would return us to the infamous *Lochner* era, in which the Court used the doctrine of substantive due process to prevent the federal government from regulating all sorts of economic

[22] See Gerald F. Gaus, "Liberal Neutrality: A Compelling and Radical Principle," in *Perfection and Neutrality: Essays in Liberal Theory*, ed. Steven Wall and George Klosko (Lanham, MD: Rowman and Littlefield, 2003), 147.

activities. Today, almost all of us take the constitutionality of such regulation for granted, and I believe that most economic classifications still ought
to be subject to the rational basis standard of review.

As Stephen Macedo has pointed out, though, it is not clear why the
Constitution sanctions a double standard in which personal liberties, unlike
economic ones, are subject to a heightened standard of review.[23] As he
argues, "[E]conomic liberty is bound up with ... personal liberty and self-
definition."[24] His idea of "principled activism" is designed to accommodate what he views as equally important economic liberties and property
rights.[25] Even Macedo makes clear that his position is not that "we must
leap boldly back to the *Lochner* era."[26] Unfortunately, he does not go into
much detail about the implications of a more libertarian style of judicial
review. The refusal to resurrect *Lochner* suggests that he is not prepared
to go as far as some libertarians are prepared to go. That refusal can be
explained in a number of different ways, but it seems to me that the strongest
reason for accepting the double standard that Macedo condemns is that regulation of the economy is not morally or constitutionally on par with legal
restrictions on people's personal lives. The state must be permitted to enact
laws that are designed to improve the quality of the lives of those who are
disadvantaged and to enhance fair equality of opportunity. By contrast, the
state should not be allowed to use its power to deny anyone an equal share
of freedom. It should be easier, then, for the state to meet the standard of
public justification in the context of economic regulation than in that of
fundamental rights and equal protection involving suspect or quasi-suspect
legislative classifications. In addition, the burden of proof to show that the
state has failed to produce sufficiently public reasons falls on the person who
is challenging the economic classification in question. That position, which
is not controversial, is found in contemporary constitutional doctrine, but
it does not imply that every economic classification should be upheld.

I am reluctant to embrace Macedo's view that "[e]conomic liberty is a
constitutional value, and property rights have a place in and deserve some
weight."[27] The challenge here for him would be to specify exactly what
he means by "deserve some weight." In cases of economic regulation, the
critical standard of reasonableness that Macedo puts forth, I fear, would
not serve the end of creating equal shares of freedom.[28] My view is not that
the state is constitutionally required to advance this end but, in a society

---

[23] Stephen Macedo, *The New Right v. the Constitution* (Washington, D.C.: Cato Institute,
    1987), 54.
[24] Ibid., 83.
[25] Ibid., 59.
[26] Ibid., 84.
[27] Ibid., 67.
[28] Ibid., 66.

that is still inegalitarian in multiple ways and does not provide fair equality of opportunity for all of its members, that state legislatures and Congress should be able to experiment with laws that are designed to ensure that more freedom for some does not entail so much less freedom for others. Social programs that are developed to guarantee that all persons have access to basic goods and services are publicly justified. That is the case because, from the standpoint of public justification, the state may act to enhance the freedom and equality of the most disadvantaged, such as those who fall below the poverty line; their condition should be a legislative priority.

Rawls himself no longer believes that the difference principle is a constitutional essential, whereas fair equal opportunity and a social minimum still are.[29] He explains that one of his concerns is that it would be difficult to determine whether this principle has been satisfied.[30] Frank Michelman adds, "Rawls may be taken to suggest that we probably would not want an independent judiciary dictating, in the constitution's name, all of the decisions involved in carrying out its mandate."[31] There is no doubt that Rawls has some practical concerns in mind, yet I also take him to be saying that the constitutionalization of the difference principle would not be publicly justified. Surely, there could be reasonable disagreement about its meaning and its implications. This interpretation would be consistent with his attempt in *Political Liberalism* to make his political conception of justice acceptable for the right reasons from as many standpoints as possible.

Gerald Gaus envisages only a limited form of judicial review.[32] But under current conditions, less passivity on the part of the judiciary would be essential to protecting the freedom and equality of everyone. In matters of constitutional essentials, with respect to the reasonable rejectability of a reason, the bar should not be set too low. When a constitutional essential is at stake and state action compromises it, the state has the burden of meeting the standard of public justification. That means that judges must be able to distinguish between public and nonpublic reasons not only in principle but also in real cases. They also must be able to explain why one argument based on public reasons is better than another argument that also is cast in such terms. An exclusive principle of public reason must provide guidance for anyone who seeks to publicly justify a constitutional choice to others or who wants to know whether he or she should accept such a justification. In a constitutional case, for a meaningful exchange of reasons to occur, the

---

[29] Rawls, *Political Liberalism*, 228–9.

[30] Ibid.

[31] Frank I. Michelman, "Rawls on Constitutionalism and Constitutional Law," in *The Cambridge Companion to Rawls*, ed. Samuel Freeman (New York: Cambridge University Press, 2003), 404.

[32] Gerald F. Gaus, *Justificatory Liberalism: An Essay on Epistemology and Political Theory* (New York: Oxford University Press, 1996), 279.

deliberators must proceed as if there were a set of reasons superior to all of the others. When deliberators sincerely remain open minded and try to convince others, they take for granted that some reasons are bound to be stronger reasons than others, and their strength or weakness is not wholly dependent on the subjective beliefs of those who are participating in the deliberative process.

The consensus that exists on the fundamentals of American constitutional law can be explained in terms of the acceptability of the reasons that underlie settled or nearly settled positions. The reasons that the state used to justify the internment of Japanese Americans in *Korematsu* were bad reasons; they were bad reasons not because many people later came to see them to be so but because they were not rooted in fact and would not have been acceptable to Japanese Americans who were victimized by President Roosevelt's executive order. Not only were the legislative means not narrowly tailored to the legislative end of preventing espionage and sabotage; it is now evident that the state was acting on the basis of racist reasons. There is no other way to interpret the assumption that Japanese Americans were more likely to be disloyal.

In constitutional cases, lawyers, judges, public officials, and the rest of us cannot ignore what the Court has said in particular cases. Comparatively, moral and political argumentation is less constrained than its constitutional counterpart because the deliberators can make just about whatever arguments they please without reference to constitutional language, history, structure, or precedent. A lot turns on the details of the case, but the basic idea is this: the person who offers the reasons in support of the legal conclusion to uphold a particular law is convinced that others who are reasonable do not have good reasons to reject them.[33] If people have reasonable doubts, then they should assume that the reasons that they want to use are insufficiently public. They then have two choices: they can start over by trying to find other reasons that are sufficiently public, or they can conclude that the law in question is not publicly justified and thus unconstitutional.

Because most of us are likely to give ourselves the benefit of the doubt by seeing our own best reasons as undeniably public when they may not be so, reasonable people can resist this tendency by assuming that they bear the burden of proof in showing that their reasons meet the standard of public justification when they seek to coerce others. This requires self-reflection on their part and a willingness to entertain the possibility that the reasons that they favor are not as compelling as they initially appear to be. That will be challenging but not impossible. After all, we already ask judges to do something like that when they decide constitutional cases. That

---

[33] Cf. Jeffrey Reiman, *Justice and Modern Moral Philosophy* (New Haven, CT: Yale University Press, 1990), 1 ("We must be able to show that the other person is mistaken . . . . For that, we must be able to show that the principle invoked is somehow true or valid beyond a reasonable doubt").

another reasonable person rejects a reason does not necessarily mean that the reason in question is not public; that would depend on the reason(s) for such rejection. Are his or her reasons for rejection merely self-serving or sectarian, or are they reasons that other reasonable people might accept? Are they reasons that do not favor the freedom and equality of some over others? At minimum, the existence of such disagreement should cause a reasonable person to respond to the objections to his or her position that others have raised and to reconsider that position. Reasonable persons are not concerned just with whether they are right according to some independent epistemic standard but also with whether they are confident enough in their judgment to coerce those who refuse to comply with it.

The standard of public justification that underlies my theory of constitutional adjudication is not meant to predetermine results serving liberal or secular ends. Consider Justice Brennan's well-known dissent in *Gregg v. Georgia*, where he wrote that capital punishment was cruel and unusual punishment because it contradicts the "intrinsic worth" of the person put to death and is "degrading to human dignity."[34] This kind of argument is insufficiently public because it is premised on disputed claims about what gives human beings value. By contrast, an argument against capital punishment that relies on the mental torture of the condemned, the unacceptable risk that an innocent person may be put to death, the likelihood that racial bias may have led to a capital sentence, the possibility that the method of execution might cause excruciating pain, or the fact that low-income defendants often fail to receive effective assistance of counsel would have the form of a sufficiently public argument. If they are true, those facts and their moral significance constitute reasons that an ideal reasonable person would not reject. That does not mean, though, that any of these sufficiently public reasons would necessarily defeat other sufficiently public reasons that would support the constitutionality of capital punishment, such as its deterrent effect and its appropriateness as a punishment for the most heinous crimes. Either conclusion would require additional argumentation within the parameters of public reason.

Just as liberal arguments do not always pass the test of public justification, conservative ones do not always fail them. When Justice Scalia writes in his dissent in *Lee v. Weisman* that "maintaining respect for the religious observances of others is a fundamental civic virtue that government can and should cultivate,"[35] he was trying to draw on reasons that everyone could share. A reasonable person would recognize the value of the development of a tolerant attitude on the part of future citizens. That is why reasons based on the minimal requirements of civic education and the public or

---

[34] Gregg v. Georgia, 428 U.S. 153, 229 (1976) (Brennan, J., dissenting).
[35] Lee v. Weisman, 505 U.S. 628 (1992) (Scalia, J., dissenting).

common good are usually so compelling. All of us would prefer an option in which everyone benefits and no one is burdened too severely. That is not to say that Scalia was correct in asserting that prayers at middle school and high school graduation ceremonies foster good citizenship, particularly when such prayers may coerce nonbelievers and thus be counterproductive. The point is not that Scalia was necessarily right but that he was attempting to make an argument that may have been good enough to convince a reasonable dissenter. His argument has the right form, and that is the beginning of a sincere attempt at public justification. Recently, when Justice Kennedy defended the constitutionality of the Partial-Birth Abortion Ban Act in part on the paternalistic ground that a woman who has had an abortion might suffer from "severe depression and a loss of self-esteem," he probably was not relying on reasons that a woman, who is in a better position to predict whether she will have any regrets, could accept.[36] She might be willing to accept the risk of such regret or she might even proceed with the procedure even though she knows that she will have regrets because of the personal costs of pregnancy and an unwanted child. As a result, this particular argument was insufficiently publicly justified, but this failure would not preclude Kennedy and others like him from trying to argue for the same conclusion on other sufficiently public grounds. Nor would this mean that paternalistic arguments are ruled out in all contexts, but their soundness is contingent on whether the state clearly has reasons that would override the right of the person to make her own life choices. In terms of public justification, it would probably be much easier to defend, on paternalistic grounds, less intrusive laws like those involving Social Security and the mandatory wearing of seat belts. No rational person would want to be impoverished in old age or to die or be seriously injured in an auto accident.[37]

Rawls tells us that people meet the standard of public justification when they frame their political arguments in "the values expressed by the principles and guidelines that would be agreed on in the original position."[38] For him, public justification requires people to imagine whether their reasons would be acceptable to everyone, including those who would be most negatively affected by the law in question. In their role as citizens, people have a right to have the state respect their freedom and equality by not passing laws based on reasons that they could reasonably reject. They also have a corresponding duty to their fellow citizens to treat them like they would like to be treated. People should not coerce others or allow them to be coerced without adequate justification. In this manner, an ideal of reciprocity is built into the very notion of Rawlsian citizenship.

[36] Gonzales v. Carhart, 550 U.S. __ 124, 159 (2007) (Kennedy, J., majority.).
[37] Neither of these examples, of course, involves a constitutional essential.
[38] Rawls, *Political Liberalism*, 227.

Jeremy Waldron objects that this conception of public reason would be far too controversial to serve as the basic framework in which both the principles and details of reasonable disagreements about justice would be worked out.[39] If the purpose of public reasoning is to make reasonable agreement on principles of justice and their applications more likely, then it would be counterproductive to use a civic language or mode of civic reasoning that would employ a method that itself cannot escape the reasonable moral disagreement that it tries to distance itself from. If Waldron has characterized Rawls's conception of public reason accurately, then there is not much to be said on its behalf as a solution to the problem of public justification under conditions of moral pluralism. A principle of public reason cannot perform its function if it is too controversial in the eyes of the reasonable members of the political community.

The reciprocity implicit in a standard of public justification requires deliberators to appeal to reasons that their fellow deliberators share or could come to see as good enough.[40] In defending an exclusive principle of public reason, I rely less on a distinction between so-called political and nonpolitical values and more on a distinction between perfectionist and nonperfectionist reasons and arguments. This distinction captures not only the spirit of the Rawlsian project and the proper place of freedom and equality in our political life but also that of certain theories of egalitarian liberalism, and deliberative democracy more generally, that try to avoid conflating two questions: that of the most acceptable justification for the uses of the coercive power of the state and that of the correctness of different conceptions of human flourishing. Arguments that are based on theories of what is most valuable in human life, that criticize the personal decisions of others on the merits, or that attempt to restrict the behavior of others in the name of their higher selves are classic examples of perfectionism. This is one of the reasons why appeals to the principle that competent adults should make their own choices about how they ought to live and to the principle that discrimination is not justified on the basis of morally irrelevant characteristics are so powerful in a society like our own. All reasonable people understand why such reasons are likely to be decisive, and thus they are likely to tell us when the state has acted inappropriately. I am not suggesting that it would always be easy to identify which arguments based on freedom and equality were better than the others in real constitutional controversies or that perfectionist arguments cannot have both perfectionist and nonperfectionist premises. But I am saying that defining the criterion of reciprocity in nonperfectionist terms can help judges

[39] Jeremy Waldron, *Law and Disagreement* (New York: Oxford University Press, 1999), 153–4.
[40] Amy Gutmann and Dennis Thompson, *Democracy and Disagreement* (Cambridge, MA: Harvard University Press, Belknap Press, 1996), 14.

and the rest of us to know what to look for not only in the arguments of others but in our own arguments as well.

Let us assume that Waldron has misunderstood the relationship that Rawls envisages between the original position and public justification. What Rawls has in mind is not that all reasonable persons would accept and be guided by the two principles of justice, especially given how controversial the second principle of justice has turned out to be, in their public deliberations and voting behavior. Rather, by "values," Rawls has in mind the importance of ensuring that the state treats each person as if his or her life plan is equally important. Just as the original position is designed to construct principles of justice acceptable to everyone who must live under them, including the worst off, a person who aims at public justification seeks to distribute the benefits and burdens of social cooperation as fairly as possible.

The natural question, then, is what kind of argument is more likely to be acceptable to a hypothetical reasonable person who also seeks an outcome that others can live with because of its fairness. We already know that certain arguments will be ruled out from the start. I doubt that a reasonable person would believe that the state may infringe on the fundamental right to procreate because some people are likely to be bad parents or base the right to vote on one's SAT score. But that leaves a lot of space between clearly insufficiently public and clearly sufficiently public justifications. Recall that public reason is public with respect to a particular audience, namely those who do not and never will share the same conception of the good, and it has a particular purpose, namely to justify coercion on the part of the state. An exclusive principle of public reason serves as a route toward this justification; it is not designed to assess whether a particular conception of the good is correct or even plausible. Thus, those who care about justifying their choices to others must avoid replicating the deeper disagreement that exists in a society such as our own. Although Rawls tries to do so by relying on a workable distinction between political and nonpolitical values, the obvious problem with this approach is that shared political values, such as those that involve the equal right to vote, to participate in political life, and to run for public office, do not get us very far when we must decide real cases. In addition, an approach that relies heavily on political values underestimates the depth and breadth of the plurality of such values found in the American political tradition and even in liberal political thought.[41]

For these reasons, as I see it, it makes more sense to interpret the Rawlsian project in the following way. An exclusive principle of public reason should strictly restrict the kinds of considerations that can count as legitimate reasons for actions that are likely to affect others in more than a trivial

---

[41] Rogers M. Smith, *Liberalism and American Constitutional Law* (Cambridge, MA: Harvard University Press, 1985), esp. 1–17.

manner. This principle should incorporate a presumption that most of the reasons that people offer to others to justify their actions are inadequate. That basic idea is found not only in deontological accounts of ethics but also in those where the right has priority over good. By definition, a sufficiently public reason is one that fully respects the equal right of each person to form, revise, and pursue his or her own conception of the good. The claims that citizens put forth to pursue ends transgressing these limits, as Rawls puts it, have no weight.[42] Within the constraints of right, citizens are left free to pursue their more or less self-regarding ends. Each person is entitled to an equal share of freedom, and a state action that violates this principle is illegitimate. The priority of the right also is premised on the epistemic difficulty of qualitatively or quantitatively comparing the worth of different human life plans and rejects the view that these kinds of distinctions are a matter of public concern.[43] The priority of the right implies that all persons, provided that their pursuit of their respective conceptions of the good does not unreasonably interfere with those of others, have a fundamental right to make their own choices about how they ought to live. In a liberal democracy, then, lawmakers are supposed to eschew any conception of the good as the moral basis for legislation.

This normative claim underlies the modern understanding of American constitutionalism and is fundamental to all versions of antiperfectionist liberalism. Yet liberal neutrality does not mean that the state, through its laws and policies, must be morally indifferent to injustice, crime, economic prosperity, public health, the environment, or national security. It would be a mistake to equate the principled refusal of the state to pass judgment on a particular reasonable life plan with that of not making any moral judgments at all about what actions are right or wrong.[44] The government has the constitutional authority to create and to maintain the conditions that make the realization of people's life plans possible. That is another way of saying that such state actions are based on sufficiently public reasons. The reduction of crime, for example, is an end that all reasonable people share. But that does not mean that all reasonable people would agree that a particular measure designed to serve that end is publicly justified when they also care about preventing law-enforcement officers from using morally unacceptable tactics like racial profiling or coercing confessions. Any liberal theory worthy of our consideration will have a normative vision of social justice and a blueprint for its realization but also will place limits on what the state may do to achieve it. In doing so, any theory will try to draw a defensible

---

[42] Rawls, *Political Liberalism*, 209.

[43] John Rawls, "The Right and the Good Contrasted," in *Liberalism and Its Critics*, ed. Michael J. Sandel (New York: New York University Press, 1984), 49–51.

[44] See Stephen Holmes, *The Anatomy of Antiliberalism* (Cambridge, MA: Harvard University Press, 1993), esp. 232–46.

line between the public and private spheres to ensure that the state does not abuse its authority. A state that did not do so or that failed to promote tolerance or to protect individual rights would be illiberal. But liberal neutrality means that the state must be as indifferent as possible toward the content of reasonable conceptions of the good when it exercises its coercive power. The vast majority of competent adults can be trusted to know what ends they want to pursue and how they should go about pursuing them without paternalism or supervision on the part of the state.

Here, it is imperative to see that there is a crucial difference between personal autonomy as constitutive of the good life and the kind of political autonomy that underlies reasonableness as a civic attitude.[45] Indeed, this difference is basic to political liberalism.[46] The plausibility of any liberal principle of public justification turns on the extent to which a person with a nonliberal conception of the good nevertheless could live a good life free from unnecessary state interference. Naturally, many liberals would prefer a society in which most people were disposed to critically reflect on their lives, to disavow superstitions, to renounce violence and cruelty, to privatize religion, to welcome intellectual challenges, to make their own choices rationally, to have the courage to be unconventional, to acknowledge the rights of others, and to accept responsibility for the consequences of their actions. For most of them, though, that preference is not the equivalent of supporting a state that is designed to inculcate a strong sense of personal autonomy in its members. As Brian Barry notes, "In a liberal society, people who do not wish to devote themselves to Socratic questioning are perfectly free not to do so."[47] The equal freedom for each citizen that political liberalism promotes means that citizens can have whatever beliefs they please and also the freedom to associate with whomever they please. After all, it is their life, and whether it goes well affects them more than anyone else. Their deeper beliefs must be reasonable only in the sense of respecting the right of their fellow citizens to live their own lives according to their own standards of what is most worthwhile.

The liberal refusal to use the power of the state to impose a more liberal conception of the good on those who are committed to nonliberal ways of life should not be construed as tacit moral approval of those ways of life

---

[45] Although there are different conceptions of autonomy, all of them emphasis the indispensability of the agent's making informed choices on the basis of good reasons. See, e.g., George Sher, "Liberal Neutrality and the Value of Autonomy," 12 *Social Philosophy and Policy* (1995), 139. Joseph Raz believes that autonomy is a life of uncoerced choices that requires (1) adequate mental abilities to form sufficiently complex intentions and (2) an adequate range of options to choose from. Joseph Raz, *The Morality of Freedom* (Oxford, U.K.: Clarendon Press, 1986), 371–4.

[46] See John Tomasi, *Liberalism beyond Justice: Citizens, Society, and the Boundaries of Political Theory* (Princeton, NJ: Princeton University Press, 2001), 25.

[47] Brian Barry, *The Liberal Theory of Justice* (Oxford, U.K.: Clarendon Press, 1973), 121.

or as revealing skepticism about the possibility of making such evaluations rationally.[48] A liberal often, but not always, believes that people have a legal right to do what is morally wrong or self-destructive. A person who believes that premarital sex or adultery is morally wrong, for example, is not then committed to the view that there should be a law that prohibits such conduct. The best explanation for the liberal attitude toward nonliberal beliefs lies in the strong reluctance on the part of liberals to use legislation or threat of force to accomplish what they cannot bring about through an exchange of ideas. There is a moral obligation to persuade rather than to use threats or disincentives. This is the case even for those who advocate different versions of liberal perfectionism.[49] For a liberal, it is wrong to impose an idea on another human being even when that person is living a life that leaves a lot to be desired in terms of liberal standards of human flourishing. It is a tragedy when coercion is the only option after rational persuasion has failed. Everyone is familiar with the high costs of coercion, but there is more to it than that. There would be something deeply unsettling about a political philosophy that claimed to value individual freedom and at the same time had no qualms about using the coercive power of the state to force people to do what is purportedly in their best interests, even if the state were more competent and more impartial than it is and probably ever will be. From the standpoint of public justification, whether a person lives well according to a perfectionist standard of liberal flourishing is not, and cannot be, a matter of law. Those who try to apply an exclusive principle of public reason to real cases have to be committed to the legal irrelevance of such a question if public reasoning is to result in public justification.

None of the foregoing implies excessive optimism about human abilities. Real people make poor choices, and those choices not only will hurt themselves but also may hurt others who are close to them. That is the downside of freedom. Nonetheless, these choices are their own even when they are based on reasons that are barely intelligible or that they would have rejected if they had been more mature, more thoughtful, or better informed. Rational reflection is an important good; it can help us to detect inconsistencies in our thinking, to decide what ends matter most to us, and to determine whether we have adopted the most appropriate means to our ends. No one wants to live a bad life. At the same time, that does not mean that citizens must reflect thoroughly on their deepest beliefs to live well or to live autonomously. If that were the standard, very few of us would ever approximate any kind of autonomous life. When we separate autonomy as constitutive of a good

---

[48] Roberto Unger mistakenly believes that liberal neutrality is based on the skeptical belief that there is no rational way of determining that one kind of life is better than another kind of life. Roberto Unger, *Knowledge and Politics* (New York: Free Press, 1975), 76.

[49] See, e.g., Steven Wall, *Liberalism, Perfectionism and Restraint* (Cambridge: Cambridge University Press, 1998), 77.

human life from the sort of minimal political autonomy that would enable reasonable citizens to develop what Rawls calls a capacity of justice and to apply an exclusive principle of public reason, we can see that most people are more or less autonomous or have the potential to be so.[50]

III. EXCLUSIVE CONSTITUTIONAL PUBLIC REASON

A. Constitutional Judgment

Adherence to an exclusive principle of public reason would minimize the likelihood that reasonable people would be coerced on the basis of reasons that they would be justified in rejecting. In this respect, my position is close to that of Charles Larmore, who maintains that the principle of respect for persons lies at the core of the ideal of public reason.[51] This ideal reflects an attempt to find minimal moral common ground without convergence on a controversial conception of human flourishing such as Kantian autonomy or Millian individuality. The basic idea is that coercion on the part of the state should be justified to everyone who is subject to it, and all reasonable persons would accept this moral proposition without having to give up their deepest convictions. That is not to say that all actual persons would accept the requirements of being reasonable or my interpretation of it, but that most people could most of the time when everyone has an overarching interest in living the best possible life. Thus, in Rawlsian terms, everyone should want to live in a society where their share of primary goods is as large as possible and the benefits and burdens of social cooperation are fairly distributed.

As we know from everyday politics, the exchange of reasons in the effort to reach mutual understanding, consensus, or even compromise is considerably more complicated than simply establishing institutions that foster face-to-face deliberation or increase popular participation. That deliberators are allowed to speak does not ensure that anyone will listen to them or appreciate the significance of what they have said. For this reason, listening skills are as important as speaking skills are. Being able to deliberate with others in the weighing of reasons for and against a course of action and being able to discriminate among them requires additional qualities that cannot be captured by the notion of deliberation as mere conversation or discussion. One of the main weaknesses of nearly every account of citizenship in the vast scholarship on deliberative democracy is that scholars have too little to

---

[50] For an argument that Catholics should endorse a Rawlsian political conception of justice, see Leslie Griffin, "Good Catholics Should Be Rawlsian Liberals?" 5 *Southern California Interdisciplinary Law Journal* (1997), 297–373.

[51] Charles Larmore, "Political Liberalism," 18 *Political Theory* (1990), 347–9. There is a voluminous literature on political liberalism, but Larmore's article is one of the clearest expositions of the minimally moral basis of a political conception of justice that anyone has ever written.

say about how citizens would identify the relevant particulars of individual cases and assign the appropriate weight to them.

The operation of the moral judgment of individual citizens – what they do when they reflect on what to do after they have been exposed to the best arguments – is essential to the practice of democratic citizenship. The ultimate success of public deliberation according to an exclusive principle of public reason turns on their ability to entertain the possibility that their initial assessment of a fundamental political question may have been wrong or incomplete.[52] There are three main reasons why people who are sincerely motivated to deliberate may change their minds: (1) they were not aware of facts that were relevant to the disposition of the case, (2) they missed or did not fully appreciate their significance, or (3) they had not weighed competing considerations carefully or struck an appropriate balance among them. Deliberation can disseminate information, clarify the underlying causes of their disagreement, and lay the groundwork for future deliberation that may narrow the initial differences of the deliberators. Their ability to appreciate the obstacles in the path of agreement, furthermore, is likely to lead an increased awareness of what makes hard cases hard in the first place. As such, on a case-by-case basis, deliberators learn the extent to which the burdens of judgment limit the possibility of agreement even among deliberators who are appropriately motivated.[53]

Waldron notes that Rawls expects issues of justice to be "dealt with on the basis of public reason."[54] The problem with this expectation, he alleges, is that "to sustain the idea of public reason as a basis for an argument about justice, Rawls must deny that the burdens of judgment affect such argumentation."[55] Waldron then concludes that, for Rawls, such burdens preclude the use of public reason in some areas, suggesting the absurd conclusion that reasonable disagreement in politics is impossible.[56] If reasonable disagreement about fundamentals of justice exists, as Waldron insists, then an appeal to public reason as common ground would beg the question. Rawls would be relying on a consensus on basic political values that in fact is disputed. This skeptical objection, however, is belied by the existence of widespread agreement in the United States on political morality and

---

[52] I am assuming that processes of public deliberation have some epistemic value. On this point, see Carlos Santiago Nino, *The Constitution of Deliberative Democracy* (New Haven, CT: Yale University Press, 1996), 117–19.

[53] For Rawls account of the burdens of judgment, see *Political Liberalism*, 54–8; *The Idea of Public Reason Revisited*, 177; *Justice as Fairness*, 35–7.

[54] Waldron, *Law and Disagreement*, 152.

[55] Ibid.

[56] Ibid., 152–3. Shortly thereafter, Waldron adds that he is "reluctant to attribute this [absurd] conclusion" to Rawls and claims that "the idea of public reason is incompatible at most with the existence of disagreement about *the fundamentals* [his emphasis] of justice." Ibid., 153.

constitutional principles at least at an abstract level. Here, the meaning of *fundamentals* must be clarified. If by "fundamentals," Waldron means that reasonable people can disagree over whether women should have the right to vote, to own property, or to earn a living, he is clearly mistaken. If he means that we disagree in more difficult cases, like that of affirmative action and abortion, then he is obviously right.

Waldron's claim that the burdens of judgment do not affect the practice of public reasoning is wrong because he assumes that the burdens of judgment either apply to a particular kind of disagreement or do not apply at all. However, the severity of these burdens will vary depending on the particularities of the question to be answered. A question about the human good, such as whether a life of pleasure is superior to a life of contemplation, is likely to differ markedly from the question of whether gay and lesbian persons should have the rights to marry, to adopt children, or to teach in public schools. Similarly, whether commercial speech ought to be afforded the same constitutional protection that political speech receives differs from the question of whether hate speech deserves such protection. To lump all such questions together is to fail to appreciate their uniqueness.

Waldron also alleges that the ultimate power that Rawls attributes to public reason to resolve disagreements about justice suggests that initial disagreement was not reasonable after all. The problem with this interpretation is that it trades on an ambiguity. For Rawls, a citizen who is reasonable has the psychological disposition to reach fair terms of social cooperation with others who are similarly motivated. By "reasonable disagreement," though, Rawls refers to an epistemic condition under which unanimity is unlikely for reasons that have nothing to do with improper motives or with irrationality. The inherent difficulty of the case is built into the case itself independent of the motives or intellectual abilities of those who have encountered it. Nevertheless, the nature of such a case does not mean that evidence and reasons cannot ultimately resolve it to the satisfaction of everyone. In the antebellum period, the case of slavery was thought to be hard, and thus was the subject of repeated political compromises.[57] Waldron's interpretation of public reason erroneously assumes that such reason is supposed to dictate answers to real cases, including hard ones, as if it were a decision procedure. Even from the standpoint of the public justification, some cases are bound to be difficult because it will not be obvious which facts are most relevant and which considerations ought to be decisive. The implications of an exclusive principle of public reason in the real world must be worked out on a case-by-case basis in which judges decide each case on its own merits. The relevant inquiry is not whether the burdens of judgment affect the practice

---

[57] James M. McPherson, *Battle Cry of Freedom: The Civil War Era* (New York: Oxford University Press, 1988), esp. 6–169.

of public reason but *how* they may affect the likelihood of consensus in individual cases.

B. The Accessibility of Public Reasons

It is not hard to see why so many people consider public deliberation both instrumentally and intrinsically good, and why many contemporary political theorists make such deliberation an integral part of their theories of liberalism and deliberative democracy. Although it is easy to agree with the importance of such deliberation in principle, many theorists have not adequately addressed the issue of whether arguments made on the basis of some principle of public reason can meet the minimal standard of public justification under conditions of moral pluralism. As I explained in the previous chapter, different people have different ideas about which kinds of reasons would meet the standard, and meeting such a principle more often than not cannot be beyond the abilities of most real people. We do not expect ordinary citizens to become philosopher-kings or to devote their lives to a civic republican ideal of active citizenship. Any theory of democratic citizenship that demands too much of their time or asks them to sacrifice their deepest convictions would not be viable under the conditions that characterize modern liberal democracies. A minimal conception of liberal democratic citizenship is our best bet for achieving a political life in which the freedom and equality of everyone in the political community is respected. One of the advantages of the practice of public reasoning is that it is likely to be less exclusionary than the kind of richer deliberation that some deliberative democrats recently have put forth.

Seyla Benhabib denies that Rawlsian democracy is sufficiently deliberative in that it is not truly open public debate.[58] She would have us believe that Rawls has little or no use for rigorous public deliberation and that now he is skeptical about the existence of moral truth. The problem is that Benhabib misses the main purpose of the practice of public reasoning: to render democratically legitimate decisions under conditions of moral pluralism. This does not mean, as she alleges, that Rawls wants to remove controversial political issues from the public agenda for the sake of civility. Rather, what Rawls is skeptical about is the usefulness of claims to moral truth in our politics. It matters whether the reasons that the state puts forth on behalf of its laws are acceptable to most reasonable people. That most people would not accept reason X is a reason not to use reason X as justification for the legislation in question. Respecting the freedom and equality of those who disagree with us at deeper levels requires us not only to converse

---

[58] Seyla Benhabib, "Liberal Dialogue versus a Critical Theory of Discursive Legitimation," in *Liberalism and the Moral Life*, ed. Nancy L. Rosenblum (Cambridge, MA: Harvard University Press, 1989), 143–56.

with them in a shared language but also not to coerce them without proper justification; they have the same self-imposed duty toward us. As such, we must be prepared to resist the temptation to say many things that we believe to be true and right and to give those beliefs the force of law. A principle of public reason is more likely to be accessible to more Americans and to encourage them to take responsibility for the choices that otherwise would be made only in their name.

In a representative democracy, ordinary citizens must understand the reasons that underlie the laws that their elected representatives enact. That a reason or argument is too complex to be understood by the vast majority of the population cuts against using it as a means of public justification. That is one of the main reasons why the laissez-faire and inclusive principles of public reason will not serve as the best means to public justification. Other things equal, assuming reasonable levels of education and attention, we ought to prefer reasons that are widely accessible to reasons that only a minority of the most intellectually gifted citizens can grasp. Actual people cannot accept a reason if they cannot understand it. Reasons that only the highly educated can understand occupy an awkward spot in a democracy because ordinary citizens, on their own, must accept them as well.

If real people cannot grasp these reasons, we cannot really say that we have respected the autonomy of each citizen, that is, his or her ability to understand and accept reasons that are supposed to legitimize the laws that he or she must live under. When we do not treat citizens in this way, we do not treat them as political equals. This publicity requirement – that for public reasons to have real justificatory force they must be sufficiently accessible – raises a difficult question about what kinds of reasons ought to be excluded on the ground that they are too complex to be comprehended by an adult of average intelligence. I cannot address this matter here, but there is room for debate concerning whether a particular reason or argument falls on one side of the line or on the other. The point is that to legitimize public laws, the reasons that underlie public laws must not only be fair to all of those who are affected. These reasons must also be as transparent as possible when they accept or reject them.

Allowing voters to cast their ballots on the basis of their personal preferences, as many advocates of pluralist forms of democracy would have them do, is bound to be less taxing. Each voter has to figure out only what she wants and then vote accordingly, without necessarily taking into account other-regarding considerations. Although this way of making collective decisions would be fair in the sense that everyone is allowed to vote their preferences, it falls far short of the ideal that we owe others adequate reasons when we want those reasons to justify a law. Citizens in a democracy should be able to explain their vote with some appreciation for its potential adverse effects on others. The aggregation of votes determines either the content of the legislation itself or who will have the power to make such decisions for a certain period of time. The reasons that citizens provide need not be sophisticated, but they ought to be minimally moral and based on relevant facts. The moral reasons that are offered to justify public laws ought to legitimize, in other words, what otherwise would be unjustified coercion. They must be fair to everyone in the sense that they respect the right of each citizen to formulate and pursue his or her own morally permissible ends. Even when sincere deliberators cannot reach consensus in hard cases, a vote that takes place after such deliberation is more likely to be legitimate in the eyes of deliberators who have been exposed to all of the relevant arguments and who have had a fair opportunity to be heard.

B. Reasonableness

I now want to go into more detail about what it means to be reasonable in the sense of complying with an exclusive principle of public reason. For Rawls, a comprehensive doctrine or conception of the good is reasonable "if it acknowledges the freedom and equality on which political liberalism rests."[59] That definition implies that many conceptions of the good are compatible with some sort of political conception of justice. That raises the question of whether Rawls believes that such a political conception of justice is true, which I cannot address here, but I suspect that Rawls believes that an overlapping consensus "is never seriously mistaken."[60] When a political conception of justice is approximately true or stands a good chance of turning out to be true, reasonable people in a more or less well-ordered society would not reject it. Such a consensus would be the product of the meeting of the minds of reasonable people. For Rawls, such consensus of reasonable comprehensive doctrines would form around one of these political conceptions of justice, not necessarily his own, thereby motivating most people to want to live in a society that honors the two principles of justice. Reasonable persons would have more or less reasonable comprehensive doctrines, but their being fully reasonable, in the Rawlsian sense, requires quite a bit more in terms of moral psychology. Rawls writes that when constitutional essentials and matters of basic justice are at stake, such persons must be able to "explain their vote to one another in terms of a reasonable balance of public reasons."[61] They must also exhibit a "willingness to listen to others and a fairmindedness in deciding when accommodations to their views should reasonably be made."[62] They are also tolerant: "Reasonable persons

---

[59] Kent Greenawalt, "On Public Reason," 64 *Chicago-Kent Law Review* (1994), 671.
[60] I owe this idea to David Estlund, "The Insularity of the Reasonable: Why Political Liberalism Must Admit the Truth," 108 *Ethics* (1998), 263–4.
[61] Rawls, *Political Liberalism*, 243.
[62] Ibid., 217.

will think it unreasonable to use political power, should they possess it, to repress comprehensive views that are not unreasonable, though different from their own."[63]

Reasonableness is the primary civic virtue of democratic citizens who are committed, at the appropriate times, to the practice of public reasoning in politics. As Samuel Freeman explains, "Reasonableness involves a readiness to politically address others of different persuasions in terms of public reasons."[64] Rawls lists five attributes of reasonable persons:

1. (a) They have the two moral powers (the capacities for a sense of justice and for a rationally defensible conception of the good), (b) they possess the intellectual powers of judgment, thought, and inference, (c) they have a determinate conception of the good based on some comprehensive view or views, and (d) they can be normal, fully cooperating members of a well-ordered society.[65]
2. They are willing to propose and abide by fair principles of social cooperation, provided that others will do likewise.[66]
3. They recognize the burdens of judgment.[67]
4. They have a reasonable moral psychology.[68]
5. They recognize the five essential elements of a conception of objectivity.[69]

These five features define an ideal reasonable person, which is not to say that most reasonable people are perfectly reasonable or meet each criterion equally well. At minimum, the reasonable person regards others as political equals who have a fundamental right to make their own decisions about their own lives.

As it turns out, a lot is packed into that seemingly simple idea. Reasonable persons care about public justification and approach constitutional choices in the following way. They imagine that they are a judge who must resolve a legal conflict that will not have a happy ending for one of the litigants. They are sitting in a room with the litigant, who is going to dissent from the decision the judge is about to reach. The task is to explain to that person why he or she is about to come out on the losing end. In some instances, this explanation will mean that the person will be legally forbidden to do what he or she wants to do or be put at a legal disadvantage. What would reasonable persons say to that person? What sorts of reasons would be

---

[63] Ibid., 60.
[64] Samuel Freeman, "Deliberative Democracy: A Sympathetic Comment," 29 *Philosophy and Public Affairs* (2000), 401.
[65] Rawls, *Political Liberalism*, 15–35, 81.
[66] Ibid., 48–54.
[67] Ibid., 54–8.
[68] Ibid., 81–6.
[69] Ibid., 110–12.

good-enough reasons, say, to incarcerate a person who disobeys the legal ruling that they are about to make? The basic idea of public justification holds as much for a custody dispute, restraining order, or bail revocation as for a legal challenge involving a putative constitutional right. To claim that they take pleasure in stamping out vice, superstition, worthless ways of life, or barbaric cultural practices or that they know what is best for another's physical or psychological well-being would not come close to being a reason that the litigant could accept. Nor would they, if the positions were reversed, accept those kinds of reasons. That helps to explain why the view that error has no rights or that the weak suffer what they must is not a view that a reasonable person would have. All persons could find themselves in a legislative minority on an important political issue and would not want to be vulnerable just because the majority believes them to be mistaken.

Reasonable persons imagine what it would be like to see the world through a different pair of eyes and are not going to accept a reason as good enough simply because they like that reason or because that reason is consistent with their deepest convictions. They try to imagine what it would be like to see the conflict from the standpoint of a person whose convictions may be diametrically opposed to their own. If the law in question restricts a constitutional right, then there must be a strong presumption against that restriction. When sufficiently public reasons do not clearly support the restriction, they must defer to what that person wants.[70] That may mean that they have to accommodate nonliberal beliefs and practices that they believe to be mistaken. As I said earlier, whether a reasonable person should accept or reject a reason turns on the details of the case. But the approach to each case is the same: a reason is not good enough simply because someone prefers it or believes it to be good or even excellent. Rather, you have to ask yourself whether you would accept that reason if your freedom to pursue your conception of the good were at stake but you had different but sincere deeper convictions. If you have reasonable doubts, then that reason is not good enough to justify the decision.

As one commentator observes, a person who accepts the burdens of judgment is "epistemically charitable."[71] When that person offers a reason to others, it is not enough that he she is convinced that that reason is correct. Instead, that person must also sincerely believe that others, who are equally reasonable, could also acknowledge that reason as sufficient to do the required justificatory work. What it would mean to satisfy this requirement is not as straightforward as it might seem. Rawls never went into detail about what it means for a person to be justified in reasonably accepting or reasonably rejecting a reason. No person wants to be subject

[70] See Lawrence B. Solum, "Faith and Justice," 39 *DePaul Law Review* (1990), 1102.
[71] Wall, *Liberalism, Perfectionism and Restraint*, 73.

to a law that he or she believes to lack proper justification, but surely that person can be wrong about whether the law in question is unjustified. It is possible for a law to be sufficiently publicly justified without all reasonable persons, as a matter of fact, recognizing it as such.

This puts Rawls and others, like Thomas Nagel and Charles Larmore, who seek to develop a workable principle of reciprocity, into an awkward position. On the one hand, Rawls cannot foreclose the possibility that certain reasons are correct or most rationally justified under the circumstances. If he denies this possibility, then he would be committed to a kind of skepticism about moral and political truth that many people would rightfully reject. On the other hand, if he tries to draw as bright a line as possible between what is reasonable and what is unreasonable and insists that one can be correct but not justified in imposing that political view on others, he encounters another difficulty. It would be wrong, for example, to criminalize abortion if those who disagree and who are reasonable could not accept the justification of such criminalization. Likewise, it would be wrong for the state to permit abortion if those who are reasonable but who oppose the practice could reasonably reject the reasons that support the availability of the procedure. The implication is that the ultimate correctness of any reason is beside the point; what matters is whether the dissenters are justified in reasonably rejecting the reasons that those who favor the law have offered in support of it.

It is hard not to feel the pull of this objection. When the state has to take a position on a controversial matter like abortion, physician-assisted suicide, capital punishment, or affirmative action, it should not be too easy for dissenters to maintain that their dissent is reasonable, and therefore be able to veto the proposed legislation. If the pool of incorrect but good-enough reasons is too large, then that would lead to state inaction in cases where the state would probably be justified in intervening. Richard Arneson has argued that the crucial distinction that Rawls relies on between beliefs that are reasonable for everyone and beliefs that are justified from a private standpoint is untenable.[72] If a reason is a good reason for one person, when he or she makes a personal decision, then it is a good reason in principle for others as well. If a reason is bad for one person, then in principle it is bad for others as well. Arneson uses the example of taking precautions against a "dread disease."[73] If one has reason to take such precautions, then that reason is also relevant in deciding whether to force others to take the same precautions to "avoid a comparable risk."[74] Arneson concedes that a decision maker must "factor in costs of coercion" but insists that "a reason

[72] Richard J. Arneson, "Neutrality and Utility," 20 *Canadian Journal of Philosophy* (1990), 215–40.

[73] Ibid., 235.

[74] Ibid.

that counts as nothing when it comes to justifying my coercive imposition on another person [cannot] still count for something in justifying my own self-regarding conduct to myself."[75] As Arneson puts it elsewhere, "Either it is the case that the others' objections to one's views neutralize or defeat them or not. If the latter is the case, then one is reasonable to continue to believe in the superiority of one's own views. But then one's own views, rationally deemed superior, are available to justify both the conduct of one's life and the choice of public policy. If the former, then I do not see how a rational person could continue to insist on the superiority of her own views."[76]

The asymmetry that Arneson identifies between reasons that are good for me and reasons that are good for others is based on the premise that a consideration that is relevant for one person in one context is equally relevant for another person in the same context. The relevance of a reason cannot be contingent on whether the person in question recognizes it as such. If that reason is relevant but he or she fails to recognize its relevance, then that person has made a mistake. This is the classic understanding of "reasonable rejectability," in which a belief should be rejected if it is inconsistent with right reason.[77] For Rawls, to be reasonable is to be committed to the criterion of reciprocity in collective decision making, but such a criterion cannot help here because Arneson's position is that someone can meet this criterion by introducing the right reasons, even if those reasons are controversial. This is a serious objection because Rawlsian public reason is premised on the fundamental distinction between what is true and what is reasonable.

Rawls could respond, I think, in the following way. Take Arneson's example of avoiding a dread disease. It is true that most people would want to avoid such a disease, especially if the costs of taking such precautions are minimal compared with the likely benefits, and it would be odd for someone to insist that he or she wants cancer or heart disease. It is also true, though, that people might have their own reasons for not taking such precautions. They might enjoy taking risks, see the taking of such precautions as manifesting a lack of faith in divine protection, or value the enjoyment that they receive from smoking over the risks to health. Or they may not want a life-saving blood transfusion because such a medical procedure would conflict with their religious faith. Those reasons may not make any sense to you and me, but they may be integral to the pursuit and realization of that person's conception of good.

Apart from the concern that the most divisive questions of political morality are not analogous to avoiding a dread disease, the force of a particular

---

[75] Ibid.

[76] Richard J. Arneson, "Liberal Neutrality on the Good: An Autopsy," in *Perfectionism and Neutrality: Essays in Liberal Theory*, ed. Steven Wall and George Klosko (Lanham, MD: Rowman and Littlefield, 2003), 208.

[77] Wall, *Liberalism, Perfectionism and Restraint*, 38–9.

reason is bound to vary with the conception of the good that that person adheres to. If each of us has only a nonpublic reason, derived from our deeper convictions, to support the law in question, then we have two choices: either we can subject that person to coercion or unequal treatment on the basis of a reason that we know that he or she does not accept, or we can conclude that that reason is inadequate. If we know that the person does not accept that reason, and furthermore may be justified in rejecting it, it seems to be even more morally problematic for us to impose that law on him or her. One's reasons are good enough within his or her own belief system, and they also may justify that person's rejection of the law that we seek to publicly justify. The latter is our primary concern. That person's beliefs are true for him or her, but we also want to know whether we should acknowledge whether those beliefs give us an adequate reason for not imposing a law on him or her.

It is clear, I think, from numerous political examples in the contemporary United States, that what is a reason, and perhaps a good reason, for us is not necessarily a reason or a good reason for others. A conservative Roman Catholic and a utilitarian would disagree about the comparative strength of the reasons for and against birth control but would see each other's reasons as intelligible. Both of them also might conclude that the other has good reasons, just not reasons that trump his or her own reasons. A theory of public justification should allow us to reject the rationality of a belief system and nevertheless, despite its falsity, permit us to conclude that it is not unreasonable. We can understand why someone would adhere to those beliefs and why those beliefs would be part of a life that is meaningful to that person. For me, religious beliefs fall into this category, and I have no doubt that religious persons would say the same about my secular beliefs. This state of affairs indicates why the idea of the burdens of judgment has such an important place in Rawls's more recent political thought. Reasonable persons, even when they believe that their reasons are superior to those of others, recognize that their deeper beliefs have colored their judgment and thus try to see their force from the standpoint of someone who does not and never will share their deepest beliefs. It is possible that, ultimately, one person really has reason on his or her side, but the burdens of judgment make it nearly impossible to be confident enough to know where the truth lies. Even if it were easier, under better epistemic conditions, to make such judgments, we still might not want to coerce people who are mistaken.

A moral proposition about right action such as "it is wrong to rape people" is either true or false. By contrast, someone might believe that a life of pleasure is the best human life. Such a belief is intelligible, and we can understand why someone might want to live that kind of life. However, a claim that life X is superior to its rivals is not likely to be true or false in the way that a claim about the most basic moral requirements is. Whether a certain kind of life is the best kind of life may turn out to be more a matter of taste or preference than anything else. In addition, it is not clear what kind of evidence or what kind of argument would establish the truth of the proposition that life X captures the essence of the human good, whereas one could more easily adduce evidence and reasons that explain what makes certain sorts of behaviors, such as rape and homicide, morally impermissible.

One of the problems here is that people often confuse the good and the right; they treat the question of what it is good as if it were the equivalent of what people may do to others. I suspect that part of the explanation for why so many undergraduates are moral relativists or at least express that view in the classroom is that some of them believe that it is wrong to judge the content of the lives of others, which is sensible most of the time, but then they also extend this refusal to pass judgment to all of the actions of others, which is often not as defensible. People may lie or cheat to get what they want, and that may be more common today than it was in the past.[78] But from an impersonal standpoint, it would not be obvious how one could defend the claim that one may fake a disability to get more time when taking the Law School Admissions Test (LSAT). No doubt, limiting ourselves to public reasons will be psychologically and intellectually difficult. Naturally, we believe that the balance of reasons favors the political positions that we hold, or else we would not hold those positions in the first place.

As one commentator has observed, such acceptance of the burdens of judgment is incompatible with the current teachings of the Roman Catholic Church.[79] In addition, certain kinds of fundamentalism are at odds with any requirement that counsels believers to eschew the whole truth in political argumentation. But that does not mean that such a demand could not be met by a wide variety of people who have been able to reconcile their faith with democratic ideals.[80] Rawlsian citizens must think critically about their own deeper convictions, appreciate the wide range of reasonable disagreement that characterizes their society, and understand the difference between what is reasonable and what may be right or true. A shared recognition of the inherent limits of the capacity of human reason to evaluate different reasonable conceptions of the good on their merits makes it possible for such citizens to observe the criterion of reciprocity that lies at the core of an exclusive principle of public reason.

Just as there are postmodernists who are inherently suspicious of concepts like reason and truth, there are those who have more confidence in the

---

[78] On different kinds of dishonesty in contemporary America, see David Callahan, *The Cheating Culture: Why More Americans Are Doing Wrong to Get Ahead* (Orlando, FL: Harcourt, 2004).

[79] Leif Wenar, "Political Liberalism: An Internal Critique," 106 *Ethics* (1995), 44–5.

[80] For instance, many American Catholics do not accept official church teachings on divorce, abortion, masturbation, and birth control.

power of human reason to serve as our moral compass even in the midst of what appears to be an intractable moral disagreement. Robert George has been a vocal and persistent critic of Rawlsian public reason, and I want to use him as an example of someone who is unreasonable in the Rawlsian (and my own) sense of the term. Not surprisingly, George considers himself reasonable because he and others like him "defend their views precisely by offering public justification, that is, rational arguments in support of the principles and propositions on the basis of which they propose political action. Their arguments are either sound or unsound. If sound, there is no reason to exclude the principles and propositions they vindicate as 'illegitimate' reasons for political action."[81] A person who is committed to public justification, then, tries to assess each argument offered in support of a particular political conclusion, such as permitting abortion or same-sex marriage, on its merits.

It is clear that George is using the word *reasonable* differently than Rawls does, and he has in mind something like this: a person is reasonable when he or she is sincere and offers reasons that can ultimately be substantiated true even when others cannot recognize their truth. George insists that human reason should push those who disagree over the most important questions of political morality toward the same answer, and their disagreement usually indicates that they do not recognize what is true or right. Naturally, George believes that the positions that he takes on certain issues are correct and ought to be adopted, even by those who are secular: "Those of us who promote natural law doctrines believe that our views are based on 'political values everyone can reasonably be expected to endorse.'"[82] George advocates a laissez-faire principle of public reason, insisting that deliberators should feel free to appeal to the truth as they see it. In questions of human rights, "there are uniquely morally correct beliefs that are, in principle, available to every rational person."[83] He cites John Finnis's remark that "[p]ublic reasoning should be directed at overcoming the relevant mistakes, not pre-emptively surrendering to them."[84] George writes that "law and policy in this area [consensual same-sex sex acts and relationships] should be shaped in accordance with the truth."[85] With respect to marriage, "society's obligation [is] to 'get it right,' that is, to embody in its law and policy a morally sound conception of marriage."[86]

---

[81] Robert P. George, "Public Reason and Political Conflict: Abortion and Homosexuality," 106 *Yale Law Journal* (1997), 2484.

[82] Robert P. George and Christopher Wolfe, "Natural Law and Liberal Public Reason," 42 *American Journal of Jurisprudence* (1997), 32.

[83] George, "Public Reason and Political Conflict," 2485.

[84] Ibid., 2486.

[85] Ibid., 2499–500.

[86] Ibid., 2501.

The glaring difficulty with George's position is that he denies what Rawls calls the facts of reasonable pluralism and the burdens of judgment, or at least he believes that operation of human reason over time can overcome these two sources of reasonable disagreement. As I explained earlier, that is probably overly optimistic. It is true that certain questions of political morality, which used to be considered intractable, are no longer thought to be so. Today, no morally literate person would defend an institution like slavery or coverture, and we should not underestimate the capacity of human reason to illuminate and to answer our most challenging moral questions. In two hundred years, it may turn out that we were as morally obtuse as our ancestors were with respect to some of our personal, social, and political behaviors. At the same time, collective decisions that will have the force of law have to be made, and we cannot wait for human reason to speak audibly. In our current and perhaps permanent epistemic predicament, one could argue that we have a higher-order reason "for not acting on the basis of some set of valid first-order reasons."[87] For example, one could be convinced that belief in God is not rationally justified and still realize that that belief should not be the basis of laws that everyone is subject to. After all, it is not as if all contemporary philosophers of religion have converged on a single proof for the existence of God that they believe is sound and that, thus, a person who is an agnostic or atheist must be mistaken.[88] George believes that it is more important to act on personal convictions that are true, at least in some circumstances, than to meet his duty of civility to others. "Acting according to right reason," as he puts it, is "precisely what natural law is all about."[89] That may be what natural law is all about, but it is not what public reason is all about, especially when it is almost always unclear what right reason requires in hard constitutional cases. As Rawls writes, "The zeal to embody the whole truth in politics is incompatible with an idea of public reason that belongs with democratic citizenship."[90] To adopt George's principle of right reason would be to leave people at the mercy of sectarian comprehensive doctrines that reasonable people would have good grounds for rejecting.

"There is," George writes, "no reason to suppose that people can or should attempt to prescind from their 'comprehensive views' in determining their obligations to those with whom they find themselves in morally charged political conflict."[91] In fact, there is an excellent reason. As Charles

[87] Micah Schwartzman, "The Completeness of Public Reason," 3 *Politics, Philosophy and Economics* (2004), 213.

[88] See *The Cambridge Dictionary of Philosophy*, ed. Robert Audi (New York: Cambridge University Press, 1995), 607–11.

[89] George and Wolfe, "Natural Law and Liberal Public Reason," 32.

[90] Rawls, *The Idea of Public Reason Revisited*, 132–33.

[91] George, "Public Reason and Political Conflict," 2502.

Larmore puts it, "On fundamental issues about the meaning of life, we have come to expect that reasonable people tend naturally to disagree with one another."[92] He continues, "On these matters, being reasonable – that is, thinking and conversing in good faith and applying, as best we can, the general capacities of reason that pertain to every domain of inquiry – tends not to produce agreement but to spark controversy."[93] Anyone could be wrong, and if we have a false belief, then as it turns out, it appears to us that we have a reason when, in fact, we do not. Even when we believe that a moral or empirical proposition is true, it is possible that we are mistaken, and everyone should be able to admit this possibility. From the standpoint of public justification, the reason for eschewing controversial views of the good life is not that we cannot think that superior reasons support our own views but that other reasonable people believe that their reasons are superior with respect to the most controversial matters, and they are just as likely to be right. Or at least the probability of their being right is high enough so that we should assume that there is a good chance that we are wrong. George will continue to maintain that those who disagree with him over the morality of abortion and consensual same-sex sex acts must be in error, but it is just as likely that the burdens of judgment are the primary cause of reasonable disagreement about such matters.

The case for an exclusive principle of public reason, however, need not be based on skepticism. A rational person could continue to insist on the superiority of his or her own views and at the same time believe that others have sufficient reasons for affirming a different conception of the good. As I see it, one who is reasonable is not necessarily in the awkward position of having to acknowledge that that the reasons of others for living as they do are equally strong. A person may believe that the proposition "God does not exist" is true beyond a shadow of a doubt and thus live as a secular humanist. Nevertheless, that person can understand why people who are religious believe that this proposition is false, and more important, he or she can appreciate why beliefs, which he or she is convinced are false, may have great value in the lives of others. That is not some sort of utilitarian point but reflects the fact that the nature of a good human life, even if it is not entirely subjective or relative to a particular time and place, is bound to have a lot to do with the distinct socialization, individual talents, unique experiences, and personal preferences of the person in question. As such, a reason could be bad for one person and good for another depending on his or her conception of good; its force, to some degree, would be a function of that person's deeper convictions.

---

[92] Charles Larmore, "The Moral Basis of Political Liberalism," 116 *Journal of Philosophy* (1999), 600.
[93] Ibid.

Normally, we can agree to disagree about many things, and the more often that we can do so, the better. At the same time, this option is not available when a collective decision has to be made, and to be reasonable is to resist the temptation to equate reasons that one would act on in one's own life with those that others also should act on, even when one is convinced, beyond a shadow of a doubt, that those reasons are correct and any reasonable person would see them as such. That attitude reflects a commitment to the view that even if others are mistaken, they are entitled to make up their own minds about the quality of the reasons that they act on when they form, revise, and pursue their respective conceptions of the good. There is an important connection, then, between respecting people and respecting their beliefs.[94] From the standpoint of public justification, the challenge is to evaluate the reasons of others as fairly as possible and to determine whether those reasons call into question the justification of the legislation at issue. Although another reasonable person's reasons are entitled to a fair hearing, with a presumption in their favor, those reasons still may not turn out to be good enough to render that law insufficiently publicly justified or unconstitutional. The most challenging part of meeting the criterion of reciprocity that lies at the heart of an exclusive principle of public reason is to know when another person's reason is not good enough and to not make this judgment too hastily.

[94] Charles Larmore, *Patterns of Moral Complexity* (New York: Cambridge University Press, 1987), 62.

SIX

The Limits of Public Justification

In the previous chapter, I spelled out how an exclusive principle of public reason differs from a laissez-faire principle and Rawls's more inclusive principle and showed how it requires people to exercise as much self-restraint as possible when they offer reasons to those who are likely to reasonably disagree with them. I also stressed that following an exclusive principle of public reason is more likely to produce reasons that are more easily understood in a society like our own. In this chapter, I want to shift my focus from those who try to publicly justify public laws and constitutional decisions to those who are asked to accept the public justification in question. Public justification has two sides, and those who care about justifying the most important laws not only give reasons but also receive them. I then explain how a reasonable person should go about determining whether the justification that someone else has offered is good enough to legitimize the decision at issue.

This approach also requires good faith and competence. Just because someone sincerely believes a reason to be sufficiently public does not make it so. At the same time, that belief ought to prompt others to scrutinize their own reasons more carefully and be willing to revise them when necessary. The more complicated the case, the more likely reasonable persons will dispute whether particular reasons have met the standard of public justification, and the burden of proof is on those who seek to restrict the freedom of others or treat them unequally. At times, reasonable disagreement is to be expected, and as long as those who have the burden of proof have come close to meeting it, dissenters should accept the decision that the Court has reached even though they would have decided the case differently.

I. THE LIMITS OF PUBLIC JUSTIFICATION

A. Reasonable Disagreement

From the standpoint of public justification, the most difficult cases will involve distinguishing public arguments that seem to meet the standard of public justification equally well but lead to opposite conclusions. David Reidy has raised the concern that public reason will not be able "to resolve all or nearly all fundamental political questions" without appeal to nonpublic reasons.[1] As such, Rawls must widen his principle of public reason to include the nonpublic reasons that may resolve issues like abortion, animal rights, and the taking of private property. When citizens, their elected representatives, and judges are limited to a principle of public reason that is too exclusive, they will not have the resources to answer the most contentious political questions, and thus to publicly justify the most important laws. If Rawls widens his principle of public reason any further, however, he may have to give up the possibility that widely shared, shallow reasons could settle the most challenging constitutional questions under conditions of moral pluralism.[2] In the end, it may be true that an exclusive principle of public reason, like my own, cannot settle certain intrinsically difficult questions that involve determining the moral status of a fetus, a person who is brain dead, or a chimpanzee.[3]

Public reasons may run out, and deliberators may not be able to rank them conclusively. For any political decision, when there are a plurality of criteria and no impartial means of ordering them, the criteria may be indeterminate in their application.[4] This may mean that even those who agree on the relevant reasons may rank them differently, producing different outcomes, each of which appears to be rationally justified.[5] Thus, it still may not be clear what a commitment to an equal share of freedom implies when there are, or at least appear to be, strong public reasons on each side of a particular constitutional question and reasonable people rank them differently. A reasonable person may not know when one public reason should trump another public reason. Part of what makes affirmative action a hard case is that those who support and those who oppose such plans seem to have equally compelling public reasons for their respective positions. Each

---

[1] David A. Reidy, "Rawls's Wide View of Public Reason: Not Wide Enough," 6 *Res Publica* (2000), 52, 64.

[2] Ibid., 72.

[3] Kent Greenawalt also contends that in challenging cases such as those involving animal rights, abortion, and human cloning, deliberators may have resort to nonpublic reasons to "settle" the disagreement. See Kent Greenawalt, *Religious Convictions and Political Choice* (New York: Oxford University Press, 1988), 147.

[4] Gerald F. Gaus, *Contemporary Theories of Liberalism: Public Reason as a Post-Enlightenment Project* (Thousand Oaks, CA: Sage Publications, 2003), 12.

[5] Ibid.

side appeals to what it believes to be the most appropriate understanding of equal treatment, but it is not immediately evident whose understanding is superior. On the one hand, it would seem to be wrong, in law school admissions, to require better numbers from white or Asian applicants and, in effect, ask some of them to bear the costs of an affirmative action plan. On the other hand, such a plan that is designed to compensate for past and present societal discrimination or seeks to ensure a critical mass of underrepresented students to increase the racial diversity of the law school would also seem to be justified.

The foregoing oversimplification suggests that both sides of the affirmative action debate seem to have sufficiently public reasons that support their respective positions. When it is not clear where the balance of public reasons lies, Reidy concludes that deliberators who seek a rational resolution of their disagreement must rely on nonpublic reasons.[6] He assumes that the introduction of nonpublic reasons would allow the conversation to continue. At best, these reasons will end the stalemate, and at worst, the deliberators will be no worse off than they were before they expanded the pool of reasons. This assumption is understandable. People can be convinced by many different kinds of arguments, and if certain kinds of arguments, such as those limited to premises based on public reasons have failed, it stands to reason that another route toward public justification may turn out to be more successful. After all, what do the deliberators have to lose? It is not clear, however, why these kinds of deeper reasons stand a better chance of breaking the deadlock. According to Andrew Williams, "[S]uch indeterminacy need not be eliminated by recourse to comprehensive doctrines."[7] In standoffs, where there are at least two reasonable but incompatible answers to a fundamental political question, there are a number of options that do not involve reliance on nonpublic reasons. As Williams points out, in such situations, deliberators can try "to identify the *most* reasonable political conception [of justice]."[8] That would not require them to invoke their deepest beliefs or other controversial reasons prematurely.

According to Williams, there are two basic problems with Reidy's thesis that public reason is too thin or incomplete. First, Reidy has not shown that public reason cannot solve problems like fetal and animal rights.[9] The practice of public reasoning should be dynamic, and we cannot know that public reasons have been exhausted in individual cases ahead of time. With respect to animal rights, for example, one could argue that such rights are

---

[6] Reidy, "Rawls's Wide View of Public Reason," 69.

[7] Andrew Williams, "The Alleged Incompleteness of Public Reason," 6 *Res Publica* (2000), 203.

[8] Ibid.

[9] Ibid., 207.

implied by a more expansive understanding of equality that is not limited to the human species. Laws that prohibit animal cruelty are predicated on the assumption that animals like dogs and cats are not the moral equivalent of rocks; they can suffer and thus have a right not to be abused. Surely, laws that prohibit cruelty to animals are publicly justified. A reasonable person can immediately recognize the validity of the reasons that underlie them. What I have just said is not intended to be an argument in favor of animal rights or welfare but is simply designed to show that it is possible for someone, who is limited to basic concepts like equality, pain, and cruelty, to develop a sufficiently public argument to support the conclusion that people can be prohibited from treating animals in certain ways.

Whether public reasons have been exhausted must be determined on a case-by-case basis.[10] At the outset, with respect to a particular constitutional question, it may be hard to predict how large the pool of potentially public reasons will be. It may turn out to be larger than deliberators anticipate, especially when they are sincerely searching for such reasons and are not tempted to cross the border into the land of nonpublic reasons. The content of public reason itself is not fixed, and it does not provide an algorithm for deciding the most difficult constitutional questions. As Micah Schwartzman puts it, "We demand too much of public reason if we expect it to have answers waiting in the wings."[11]

Second, there are decisive reasons for not allowing deliberators in certain situations to invoke their deepest beliefs. Usually, we do not want judges to do so, even when we are sympathetic to their point of view. Reidy himself acknowledges that the Supreme Court should not use nonpublic reasons in cases of conflict.[12] Indeed, more than two hundred years of constitutional practice in our country indicates that most constitutional controversies can be resolved without invoking deeper reasons and arguments. As Williams suggests, it might even be better to employ a randomizing device to break ties.[13] Schwartzman puts forth five different ways of doing so that do not involve recourse to nonpublic reasons.[14] If someone can show that public reason cannot identify a single correct or most reasonable answer, then instead of introducing nonpublic reasons, deliberators could invoke one of these procedures. In such a situation, my preference would be for them

[10] On this point, see Jonathan Quong, "The Scope of Public Reason," 52 *Political Studies* (2004), 244.
[11] Micah Schwartzman, "The Completeness of Public Reason," 3 *Politics, Philosophy, and Economics* (2004), 207.
[12] Reidy, "Rawls's Wide View of Public Reason," 56.
[13] Williams, "Alleged Incompleteness of Public Reason," 210.
[14] He lists intrapersonal delegation, deference to others, moral accommodation, democratic procedures, and arbitrary decision procedures. Schwartzman, "Completeness of Public Reason," 209–14.

to defend their positions as cogently as possible with respect to how their reasons are more consistent with freedom and equality than those of others. That approach would have the advantage of remaining faithful to the commitment not to subject one's fellow citizens to coercion on the basis of reasons that they could not be expected to share, and it would keep the conversation going.

In the context of CUUS679-06.xmlconstitutional decision making, ultimately judges will have to vote, and voting is a defensible way of deciding when there is reasonable disagreement about which answer to an important constitutional question is most reasonable. I confess that I simply do not understand how appeal to deeper beliefs will accomplish what Reidy and others, like Kent Greenawalt, hope it will accomplish, especially when those beliefs are bound to be even more controversial. As Schwartzman puts it, "[U]sing nonpublic reasons to break deadlocks...contravenes values central to the ideal of public reason."[15] That claim does not beg the question in favor of public reason but reflects the inherent difficulty of achieving agreement on the most important constitutional essentials on the basis on nonpublic reasons. More often than not, appeal to a much wider class of reasons opens the floodgates to all sorts of divisive nonpublic reasons that will drive a morally diverse nation like our own even farther apart.

Public reason is "indeterminate" when it is silent with respect a particular constitutional question, and it is "inconclusive" when there are multiple and conflicting solutions that seem to be equally justified.[16] It is possible that, in too many cases, public reasons will run out too quickly, and it is also possible that such reason will not be able to do enough heavy lifting in novel cases. The concern is that without recourse to nonpublic reasons, the most important constitutional questions will go unanswered, and this solution is premised on the view that the exercise of practical reason should be able to yield uniquely correct answers. As I see it, though, under conditions of moral pluralism and the burdens of judgment, deliberators must not aim for such answers but for reasons that all reasonable people can accept or at least not reject. The method matters more than the outcome, and reasonable people who have been given adequate public reasons in a particular case have no complaint even though they disagree with the outcome.

Most people have a tendency to think that their deeper convictions are less controversial than they really are, and I do not see how resort to deeper religious reasons, for example, would increase the chances of agreement any more than resort to deeper secular reasons would. Today, quite a bit of the moral disagreement that pervades our politics is religious in

---

[15] Ibid., 213.
[16] Gerald F. Gaus, *Justificatory Liberalism: An Essay on Epistemology and Political Theory* (New York: Oxford University Press, 1996), 151–8.

nature.[17] An exclusive principle of public reason could accomplish more than Reidy believes it could, on a case-by-case basis, especially when deliberators acknowledge the downside of appealing to the nonpublic reasons that they happen to prefer. If they value continued social cooperation, they will make a more sincere effort to converge on reasons that everyone can share. Suppose that in a hard constitutional case, after the first round of deliberation, two arguments appear to be equally sufficiently public but lead to different results. After further discussion, it still is not clear which argument is more publicly justified. More discussion will not push reasonable people, who are already divided, toward the position that those who disagree with them hold. A vote is then taken. Because more people believe that argument A is more publicly justified than argument B, argument A carries the day. How should a person respond who sincerely believes, and has good reasons for believing, that argument B is the better argument? Ideally, that more reasonable people chose A over B would reflect the fact that A was more public justified. That might be rare or more common than anticipated, but which conclusion was more publicly justified would depend on the details of the particular case and the strength of the public reasons that deliberators put forth. Those who found B to be more convincing could give those who found A more convincing the benefit of the doubt, not only with respect to their sincerity but also with respect to the quality of the judgment that they actually made.

The standpoint of the person who is the target of those reasons and who is sincerely willing to accept reasons that meet the standard of public justification is as important as that of the person who puts forth the argument in question. The practice of public reasoning is not a one-way street where deliberators have assigned roles, either as givers or receivers of reasons. In one way or another, the people and their elected representatives will respond to what the Court has done. In such matters, there is no higher authority than an exclusive principle of public reason, and deliberators may invoke it by casting their argument in the language of public reasons to convert those who initially disagree with them, even though they acknowledge the likelihood that they will not be successful. Ideally, everyone would understand that a good argument is a sufficiently public argument and that deliberation is an opportunity not only to advance one's own views but also to learn from others and perhaps modify those views as a result of the force of the sufficiently public arguments of others. Participants in public deliberation have to care more about the reasons that they give to others than about the results that they hope others would reach. A person who is committed to the exchange of public reasons does not simply seek to have his or her position

[17] See, e.g., James Davison Hunter, *Culture Wars: The Struggle to Control the Family, Arts, Education, Law and Politics in America* (New York: Basic Books, 1992).

on a constitutional essential prevail at the end of public deliberation. Such people also want their position to carry the day for the right reasons, and that means that they must explain to those who initially disagree with them why a certain decision would better respect the freedom and equality of everyone than the alternatives would.

In most public deliberations, those who participate will assume both roles. At the same time, it is useful to separate these two roles not only for conceptual clarity but also because of the dynamics of judicial review, where the Court renders decisions and the rest of us assess the quality of the opinions that the justices offer. Historically, the Court's decisions rarely have settled constitutional controversies once and for all, and other political actors, including the people themselves, are often not passive. As one commentator observes, "[W]e should not expect the Court generally to have an overwhelming effect."[18] The key to achieving public justification involves the willingness of reasonable citizens to settle for less than consensus on the reasons that support a particular outcome. It is extremely unlikely that everyone will be perfectly satisfied with the answer to a particular fundamental constitutional question or its rationale when there appears to be equally good arguments on both sides of that question. In the interest of minimal legitimacy, though, there is an enormous difference between an outcome that is based on reasons that are too controversial and an outcome that is based on reasons that are at least arguably sufficiently public and, as such, good enough. The objective of public deliberation within the limits of public reason is to find the balance of reasons that is least unreasonable.

This attitude on the part of the vast majority of deliberators – agreeing to accept a public law or judicial decision as legitimate even when they have reached a different result on their own – reveals a weaker but more realistic conception of legitimacy than that of unanimity. This conception takes into account the inherent difficulty of putting together arguments of political morality that would convince all or most reasonable persons. A dissenter can dispute the correctness of the outcome and nevertheless accept that the outcome is provisionally legitimate because it is not clearly unreasonable. This charitable attitude would reduce the likelihood that dissenters would be justified in disputing the legitimacy of the most controversial judicial decisions and would refuse to comply with them after a court has confirmed that the state has put forth sufficiently public reasons in defense of the law in question. After all, dissenters' reasons receive consideration even if others do not ultimately accept them. That addresses the concern that mere procedural fairness is a weak reason to obey a collective decision that a citizen sincerely believes to be morally mistaken. The mere rejection of

[18] Lawrence Baum, *The Supreme Court*, 2nd ed. (Washington, D.C: Congressional Quarterly Press, 1985), 229.

such reasons in itself does not manifest a lack of respect for those persons or their beliefs. Otherwise, dissenters would be justified in questioning the legitimacy of all majoritarian outcomes, no matter how procedurally fair and well debated they might have been. Surely, unreasonable objections should not prevent the enactment and enforcement of law.

In the absence of consensus, deliberators must narrow the scope of reasonable disagreement to a set of reasons that is not obviously insufficiently public. A legitimate collective decision, which binds everyone who must live under it, then becomes possible in the absence of a shared understanding of the correct outcome in particular constitutional controversies. In other words, legitimacy need not be an "all-or-nothing affair."[19] The deliberative process must end in a vote, by citizens themselves, by their elected representatives, or by judges when they must render a decision. The final tabulation lets citizens know which solution won the approval of the largest number of the members of the decision-making body and reflects the greater strength of one set of public reasons compared with others in the minds of a majority of the voters. This does not mean, though, that the reasons that won the day necessarily were the strongest possible relative to the normative standard of public justification. Those who engage in public reasoning are aware that there may have been good or even better reasons that supported a different conclusion and that they may have to change their minds in the future. Hopefully, the practice of exchanging public reasons over time would make citizens less certain about the correctness of their own positions in the hardest of hard cases. They will be more willing, then, to be more charitable to their fellow citizens and less inclined to impose their own beliefs on them if they are not sure that their reasons have the intersubjective validity that public justification requires.

Like Reidy, Kent Greenawalt is skeptical that, even under the best of conditions, "shared standards of decision" could resolve many political questions.[20] This kind of indeterminacy – in which no set of reasons is clearly superior – is probably inevitable in the most difficult constitutional cases. Oddly enough, this is not one of the defects of public reason, but as it turns out, it is one of its strengths. Those who lose on a particular issue had what they sincerely believed to be stronger public reasons, but the majority found these reasons to be less compelling than others. The point is not that the decision is true or right beyond a shadow of a doubt, but that it is acceptable under the imperfect epistemic conditions of the real world.[21] As long as the reasons were close enough to meet the standard of public justification,

---

[19] I borrow this phrasing from Harry Brighouse, "Civic Education and Liberal Legitimacy," 108 *Ethics* (1998), 736.

[20] Greenawalt, *Religious Convictions and Political Choice*, 12.

[21] See Catharine Z. Elgin, *Considered Judgment* (Princeton, NJ: Princeton University Press, 1996), ix.

the decision that the Court reaches is legitimate in that everyone has a prima facie political obligation to comply with it. That is the kind of resolution of a constitutional controversy that is possible under conditions of moral pluralism and the burdens of judgment.

In an ideal deliberative democracy, the state would ensure that all reasonable persons are able to take part in the deliberative process, to put forward their best public arguments, to choose freely among them, and to reach a decision that everyone can live with. Thus, dissenters could not claim that others ignored their best arguments; they could accept collective decisions as legitimate and be justifiably coerced to comply with them. When the vast majority of voters recognize that reasonable people in good faith have identified the relevant considerations but have weighed them differently, that very fact might lend more legitimacy to a controversial decision than it otherwise would have. The purpose of public justification is to limit the reasons that permit the majority to force dissenters to submit to its will, thereby maintaining a less morally problematic relationship between political authority and personal freedom. That is the kind of resolution that those who care about public justification must aim for, and that is as close as our society can come to justifying its most important constitutional choices.

C. Publicly Justified Laws

I have already established that judges must limit themselves to public reasons in deciding hard constitutional cases. As Greenawalt puts it, for Rawls, judges have not fulfilled their duty if they have "self-consciously determined their decisions by a comprehensive view . . . and then have offered entirely different public reasons in the majority opinion."[22] As I explained earlier, especially when our democracy is not particularly deliberative and our public officials do not disclose their real reasons, the Court must also play the role of gatekeeper by limiting law-making bodies to sufficiently public reasons. This raises the question of which reasons the Court must evaluate. I believe that the Court should have the discretion, as it already does in a number of areas of constitutional law, to examine both the legislative purpose and the foreseeable effects of the law in question. As such, the justices may look not only at the reasons given in the legislature but also at those given in defense of the statute in court. First, they must search the legislative history to see whether the legislators have sufficiently public reasons. Second, they must assess the reasons that the state offers in court in defense of the statute in question. That implies that, when the underlying reasons differ, the same statute could be constitutional in one context and unconstitutional in another. As I see it, that is not a problem because the reasons matter more than the outcome. It would be more convenient to avoid an inquiry into the

---

[22] Kent Greenawalt, "On Public Reason," 69 *Chicago-Kent Law Review* (1994), 677.

actual motives of those who legislate when there are bound to be multiple legislators with multiple purposes. At the same time, there is a lot to be said for compelling legislators to be more candid about the reasons that underlie their votes. If a number of legislators, for example, have racist motives in either supporting or opposing an affirmative action plan, then the Court should not ignore them. Nevertheless, the Court should focus primarily on the reasons that the government's attorneys advance. It is true that there are reasons for one to be skeptical of the post hoc reasons offered during the litigation.[23] It is also clear that the Court should not go out of its way to develop its own sufficiently public reasons in defense of the law in question. From the standpoint of public justification, the onus must be on the state to do so.

D. Weighing Public Reasons

But what happens when a judge has to weigh conflicting public reasons? As Stephen Macedo states, "Just because we all agree on the authority of public reason, that is not going to mean we are going to agree on where it leads, or how public reasons should be weighed."[24] Consider the Court's decision in the *Bob Jones University* case, where the Court upheld the Internal Revenue Service's denial of tax-exempt status to the private university because of its whites-only admission policy.[25] On the one hand, the university claimed that the Bible prohibits interracial dating and marriage. In theory, a ban on the admission of African American students would prevent such dating and marriage by minimizing contact between students of different races on campus. On the other hand, despite the sincerity of the religious beliefs that underlie the discriminatory admissions policy, the Court gave more weight to the state's interest in preventing such racial discrimination. If a person believes that *Bob Jones University* was wrongly decided, he or she will have to begin by showing that the Court failed to assign the weight to the interest of the university in maintaining an all-white student body that it deserved.

There are plenty of examples like the preceding one in constitutional cases where the Court must balance competing considerations, and standards of review are useful because they already do a lot of the balancing. The idea of weighing reasons is omnipresent in theories of adjudication but underdeveloped because the metaphor of a balance scale mistakenly suggests a quantitative approach, as if a reason could be assigned a numerical value. In his earlier jurisprudential writings, Dworkin tried to solve the problem

---

[23] U.S. Railroad Retirement Board v. Fritz, 449 U.S. 166 (1980) (Brennan, J., dissenting).
[24] Stephen Macedo, "In Defense of Liberal Public Reason: Are Slavery and Abortion Hard Cases?" in *Natural Law and Public Reason*, ed. Robert P. George and Christopher Wolfe (Washington, D.C.: Georgetown University Press, 2000), 44.
[25] Bob Jones University v. United States, 461 U.S. 574 (1983).

of weighing principles by referring to their "institutional support" or prevalence in cases and statutes.[26] An ideal judge, like Dworkin's Hercules, would count the number of times that the conflicting principles appear in the recognized legal sources of that society to determine their weight relative to one another. The obvious problem with this approach is that it is too mechanistic. The exercise of judgment requires the person who must choose to make qualitative distinctions as well.[27] After he or she has identified the relevant reasons, a judge does not simply assign them a numerical value and add them up to figure out where the balance of reasons lies, as an accountant or a policy analyst engaged in cost-benefit analysis would. Nor would the judge tally up the reasons of each side and let the numerical majority dictate the result.[28] The normative force of the relevant reasons is bound to depend on the unique facts of the case, and their force can be affected by the presence or absence of other reasons. In the opening passages of *The Nicomachean Ethics*, Aristotle tells us that to choose well is to ask the right questions in identifying the particulars that the agent ought to consider in the decision-making process.[29] Aristotelian practical reasoning is not deductive in the sense that a conclusion is entailed by the major premise of a practical syllogism.[30] To see a real situation of choice accurately is not to deduce conclusions from premises as in formal logic but to appreciate the relationship between the various relevant considerations and to strike a reasonable balance among them. The practically wise person knows when one consideration, as a possible reason for an action, affects the relative strength of other reasons and may override them.

Although the practically wise person usually makes the best choice under the circumstances, the appropriate standard is not certainty. The weight of one reason might increase, decrease, or stay the same depending on the relative force of the other relevant reasons. For instance, one might firmly believe that racial segregation is almost always unjustified. However, in the context of county jails and state prisons, because of racial animosity that leads to violence and jeopardizes the safety of prisoners and prison employees, one might reasonably give prison officials the benefit of the

---

[26] Ronald Dworkin, *Taking Rights Seriously* (Cambridge, MA: Harvard University Press, 1977), 14–45.

[27] One of the best and underappreciated accounts of the nature of choosing wisely under conditions of uncertainty is F. H. Low-Beer, *Questions of Judgment: Determining What's Right* (New York: Prometheus Books, 1995).

[28] Steven J. Burton, *Judging in Good Faith* (New York: Cambridge University Press, 1992), 57.

[29] See Martha Nussbaum, *The Fragility of Goodness: Luck and Ethics in Greek Tragedy and Philosophy* (Cambridge: Cambridge University Press, 1986), 10.

[30] See Martha Nussbaum, "The Discernment of Perception: An Aristotelian Conception of Private and Public Rationality," in *Aristotle's Ethics: Critical Essays*, ed. Nancy Sherman (New York: Rowman and Littlefield, 1999), 145–6.

doubt and assume that they do not have the wrong motives, absent evidence to the contrary. If judges were to give more weight to safety, however, they would have to explain why they would permit prison officials to practice such segregation and why all of the less drastic alternatives would fail. In the end, their reasons probably would not convince those who insist that such segregation will propagate the notion that people should stick with their own kind and reinforce racist attitudes and practices on the part of inmates and those with whom they interact. Securing the agreement of those who disagreed initially would be preferable, but that is outside of judges' control. What they can do, though, is to defend the weight that they have assigned to the importance of safety inside the prison and to not believing that any of the alternatives would be equally or more effective.

Consider a case like *Florida Star v. B.J.F.*, in which the Court invalidated a Florida law that made it illegal to print, publish, or broadcast the name of the victim of a sexual offense.[31] The Court ruled that the state may not prohibit the publication of truthful information about a matter of public significance "absent a need to further a state interest of the highest order."[32] In his majority opinion, Justice Thurgood Marshall acknowledged that the state had three "closely related" interests: to protect the privacy of victims, to ensure their physical safety, and to encourage them to report such crimes.[33] At the same time, he concluded that the legislative means that the state used in trying to serve these ends indicated that Florida lacked a state interest "of the highest order."[34] Florida could have chosen more effective means to advance its legislative end.[35] Marshall conceded that it would be possible, under different circumstances, for the state to impose civil sanctions for the publication of the name of a victim of a sexual assault.[36] What is disappointing is that Marshall fails to explain why the state's interests, taken together, are not important enough to reach the level of a state interest of the highest order. As Justice Byron White pointed out in his dissent, "I would find a place to draw the line higher on the hillside: a spot high enough to protect B.J.F.'s desire for privacy and peace-of-mind in the wake of a horrible personal tragedy. There is no public interest in publishing the names, addresses, and phone numbers of persons who are victims of crime – and no public interest in immunizing the press from liability in the rare cases where a State's efforts to protect a victim's privacy have failed."[37]

---

[31] Florida Star v. B.J.F., 491 U.S. 524 (1989).
[32] Ibid., 533.
[33] Ibid., 537.
[34] Ibid.
[35] Ibid., 540–1.
[36] Ibid., 537.
[37] Ibid., 553 (White, J., dissenting).

The foregoing is a good example of the failure of the Court to weigh public reasons appropriately. There is no doubt that usually there is at least some value in permitting the dissemination of truthful information about matters of public concern, like a crime that has occurred in a particular community. Most people would want to learn about such events. At the same time, rape is a brutal crime and some victims may never be able to fully recover from the trauma of such an experience. Marshall does not deny this point; he mentions the "tragic reality of rape."[38] However, he not only fails to appreciate how important the interests of the state are but also does not distinguish between knowing that a crime took place and identifying the victim of the crime. Surely, the name, address, and phone number of the victim need not be included in a story about such a crime. At most, what people in that community have a right to be informed about is the crime itself, so that they can take precautions. The point is not that no one could give more weight to the public's interest in knowing all of the details but that a thoughtful person would imagine what it would be like to be a victim of a sexual assault and whether he or she would want such highly personal information disseminated.

Although reasonable persons may weigh different reasons differently, that does not entail that the weight that a person assigns to a particular public reason is beyond criticism. That a person has assigned a certain amount of weight to a public reason that may be disputed is not the end of a conversation but the beginning of one that deliberators can conduct only in the language of public reasons. If a person believes that the privacy of the alleged victim outweighs the public's right to know all of the information, then he or she must explain why the privacy interest implicated in such crimes is so important and differs from that of other felonies. If a person believes that the privacy interest of the alleged victim is not strong enough, then he or she must address each concern that a person in disagreement has expressed. An exchange of reasons with others in an effort to persuade them enables the decision maker to describe the circumstances of choice more completely and yields provisional reasons that hopefully point to the most defensible answer. The decision maker then must sort through all of the remaining relevant reasons before rendering a decision. At this point, considerable room would still exist for deliberation, reflection, and correction of initial impressions, because all of the relevant considerations are only potential public reasons, which is to say that, ultimately, they may not be good enough when compared with the alternatives.

For judges who must decide, the significance of reasons becomes apparent only when they see their connection to the material facts of the case. When a particular fact implicates a constitutional principle such as censorship is

---

[38] Ibid., 537.

wrong, for example, then the judge has a reason, which must be weighed and balanced against other reasons, in deciding on the most appropriate course of action.[39] For instance, in *New York Times v. Sullivan*, Justice William Brennan devotes a substantial part of his majority opinion to explaining why an actual malice standard of fault is constitutionally required when public officials seek damages for defamation.[40] It is plausible that requiring actual knowledge of the falsity of the defamatory statement or reckless disregard for its truth or falsity on the part of the defendant is less likely to have a chilling effect on those who want to criticize the actions of the government. Still, there is no doubt that there is also something to be said on behalf of using a negligence standard, especially when one gives more weight to the interest of the state in protecting the reputations of public officials. Indeed, the Court weighed different considerations differently in *Gertz*, where it permitted juries to award compensatory damages when the plaintiff, as a private figure, could prove that the defendant had acted negligently in not verifying the truth of a defamatory statement.[41] It makes sense to believe that the state has a stronger interest in protecting private figures than public figures from defamation. One could understand why the Court reached the conclusion that it did in *Gertz* but at the same time, like Justice Brennan, still believe that what really matters is whether the matter in question is a public concern. If it is, then the actual malice standard should also apply even though the plaintiff is a private figure and only is seeking compensatory damages.

In constitutional cases more generally, the judge must determine the strength of these reasons relative to the others. Merely bringing a fact or its significance with respect to public justification to another judge's attention does not create a conclusive reason for a particular outcome. This act merely makes the judge aware of its existence and makes it possible for that person to take it into account in making a good decision if he or she recognizes its relationship to the principle that each person is entitled to an equal share of freedom. The more closely a reason is tied to freedom and equality, the more likely it is to be a better reason, but whether it is, in fact, a better reason will be determined by the specific arguments that deliberators advance on its behalf. As Macedo remarks, "The American Constitution is an aspirational document that provides . . . ideals to strive for and argue about."[42] The facts of a particular case become conclusive reasons for a decision only when they implicate the strongest public reasons and defeat other conflicting public reasons.

---

[39] In applied ethics, the "stringency" of a moral rule refers to its weight relative to other considerations. Russ Shafer-Landau, "Moral Rules," 107 *Ethics* (1997), 585.

[40] New York Times v. Sullivan, 376 U.S. 254 (1964).

[41] Gertz v. Robert Welch, Inc., 418 U.S. 323 (1974).

[42] Stephen Macedo, *Liberal Virtues: Citizenship, Virtue, and Community in Liberal Constitutionalism* (New York: Oxford University Press, 1990), 76.

The attempt to comply with an exclusive principle of public reason provides a means of moving forward in the face of constitutional uncertainty because judges know what kinds of reasons they must find before they make a decision, namely reasons that an ideal reasonable dissenter would not reject, if they are going to uphold the law. The challenge for anyone who is committed to public justification more generally is not only to separate public from nonpublic reasons but also to weigh the remaining public reasons appropriately in reaching the conclusion that is most publicly justified. From the standpoint of public justification, a hard case is one in which the sufficiently public reasons for and against a particular outcome do not tip the balance scale one way or the other. In such a case, one would expect judges to devote a significant portion of their opinions to explaining why they believe certain public reasons to be stronger than other public reasons. In doing so, they make a sincere effort to defend their decision to reasonable dissenters by explaining why they ought to accept the public reasons that the state has offered on its behalf and hope that these reasons, all things considered, will be good enough, after they have done their best to address their concerns. Judges assume that the reasonable dissenter is receptive to public reasons that they did not recognize or did not weigh properly. Judges have achieved their objective when an imaginary reasonable dissenter says, "Personally, I believe that the balance of public reasons reveals the unconstitutionality of the statute in question. However, I also see why a reasonable person would reach the opposite conclusion and I cannot reasonably reject the public reasons that have been given because they are not bad. I see why another reasonable person would have weighed the relevant public reasons differently and reached the opposite conclusion. Thus, the decision is legitimate, which is not to say that I fully agree."

If judges decide to strike down the law, they also should be able to explain to those who will disagree with their decision why the reasons that the state offered fell short of the standard of justification. But it is important to recall that, in such cases, the burden of proof lies with the state, and when they invalidate legislation, they simply have to defend their conclusion that the state has not met its burden, which typically will be easier to do. This practice over time might encourage law-making bodies to adhere to some kind of standard of public justification as well. Macedo is right when he calls for the other branches of government to take their constitutional responsibilities more seriously.[43] In terms of public justification, that would include some sort of attempt at public justification on the part of other political actors. For example, a legislator would not support a bill that he or she believes to be based on reasons that reasonable dissenters could not possibly accept,

[43] Ibid., 147.

such as one that made it a felony for noncitizens to stay in the United States illegally, regardless of the circumstances.

Whatever the founders may have intended or hoped for, American history suggests that it is naive to expect that our interest-group-driven politics can be more principled than they currently are. In the "Federalist No. 10," James Madison claims that the cause of factions can never be eliminated because they are a part of human nature. As such, political institutions must be designed to minimize their divisive effects. Historically, those who care about constitutionality have put their faith in judges, and those who care about public justification hope that a judge can imagine what it would be like to be a reasonable dissenter and write his or her opinion accordingly. Oddly enough, a hard case like abortion or affirmative action can be a blessing in disguise because it provides an opportunity for reasonable people to see that those who disagree with them on the most important constitutional questions are not crazy or evil but also may have their own sufficiently public reasons. At the same time, even the most competent deliberators with the best of intentions cannot weigh public reasons precisely or read other people's minds. The result is that there will always be a considerable amount of indeterminacy in hard cases that will frustrate those who seek a reason that will trump all of the others conclusively. After all, weighing reasons is only a metaphor and, hopefully, a useful way of thinking about what a judge is supposed to be doing in a hard case. The judge puts each set of reasons on a balance scale and those that are heaviest outweigh the reasons that support the opposite conclusion.

We should not take this metaphor too literally or assume that this process can be algorithmic. Before he or she votes, a judge must determine the strength of all of the relevant public reasons relative to one another for or against a particular decision with a presumption in favor of freedom and equality. After the judge has ruled out insufficiently public reasons, there is likely to be a continuum of prima facie public reasons, ranging from the very strong to the very weak. The judge then exercises his or her own best judgment in determining how strong the remaining reasons really are, with close attention to how an ideal reasonable dissenter would weigh them. Prima facie public reasons can be overridden by stronger public reasons. Whether they yield a particular conclusion on how to resolve a particular constitutional question is to be determined through the best efforts of the judge at making a rational comparison among the relevant sufficiently public reasons.

Deliberation and reflection must eventually come to an end, and at the moment of choice, the judge has the unenviable responsibility of selecting the argument that strikes him or her as most publicly justified. The judge makes this choice, however, only after he or she has been exposed to the arguments that indicate that the weight initially planned for a particular reason may not be appropriate. In trying to publicly justify a decision to an ideal reasonable dissenter, the judge explains not only why he or she gives more weight to one public reason than to others but also why the weight that a reasonable dissenter would give to different reasons is inappropriate under the circumstances. The more successful the judge is at this task, the better that opinion is likely to be, which is not to say that reasonable dissenters will be fully convinced. A hard case is hard precisely because there are sufficiently public reasons that support different conclusions. The notion of a prima facie public reason is premised on the assumption that, in some cases, people only appear to have certain reasons that support a particular conclusion, and those reasons may not turn out to be as public as others are after due consideration.

II. THE PROBLEM OF POLITICAL LEGITIMACY REVISITED

A. The Rationale of Public Justification

So far, I have tried to explain what public justification is, why it is important, and how it could be accomplished, but I have said little about why a reasonable person would care about such justification or want to live in a society that is committed to it. Here, I want to articulate its rationale by explaining why someone would want to limit lawmakers to public reasons when they seek to justify the most important laws. Unlike *A Theory of Justice*, Rawls's *Political Liberalism* deals with political legitimacy: the conditions under which someone will properly accept a law as morally binding even when he or she disagrees with it.[44] Moral pluralism and the burdens of judgment dramatically increase the likelihood of reasonable disagreement, and this is why the search for reasons on a case-by-case basis that an ideal reasonable person would not reject becomes imperative. Such an approach to justification will not be amenable to those who seek to impose their sectarian doctrines on their fellow citizens or seek to take advantage of their superior bargaining positions in the legislative process, but it reflects the principle that the life plan of each person counts equally in the eyes of the law.[45]

I believe that a rational person, who sees society as a scheme of social cooperation and expects to benefit from such a scheme, would also care about public justification. Rational persons cannot be reasonable and at the same time indifferent to public laws that undermine their own freedom and equality and that of others. By definition, governments that are legitimate have the authority to rule, that is, to demand obedience from

[44] Burton Dreben, "On Rawls and Political Liberalism," in *The Cambridge Companion to Rawls*, ed. Samuel Freeman (Cambridge: Cambridge University Press, 2003), 316–17.

[45] I borrow this term from Seyla Benhabib, "The Democratic Moment and the Problem of Difference," in *Democracy and Difference: Contesting the Boundaries of the Political*, ed. Seyla Benhabib (Princeton, NJ: Princeton University Press, 1996), 9.

their subjects.[46] In the liberal tradition, the duty to obey the law is supposed to arise from some kind of act of consent or implied promise to obey.[47] People alienate some of their control over their own lives to enhance ordered liberty, to facilitate social cooperation, and to provide collective goods that would otherwise not be available. What justifies the rule of some over others is one of the canonical questions in the history of political thought. Such a question about political legitimacy naturally emerges in human societies that must make collective decisions about how they are going to mediate conflicts, allocate benefits and burdens, distribute scarce resources, and use the power of the state to enforce the laws that serve these ends. The most appropriate source of political legitimacy is a question that every decent society must address, and the answer that it gives is bound to affect the lives of its members. Liberal accounts of legitimacy usually require either the hypothetical consent of the governed or the actual consent of at least a simple majority of the governed, and that actual consent cannot come about through coercion or manipulation.[48]

Some historical and cultural variance is to be expected. Ancient and medieval political thinkers assumed that some persons were naturally or divinely ordained to rule others. A question about the legitimacy of political rule, for them, would have to be addressed only when those who appeared to be naturally inferior exercised political power. By contrast, early modern political thinkers were convinced that the basis of political legitimacy could not be found in hierarchies built into the cosmic order. The legitimacy of the state would have to be explained by the reasons that the people who were to be governed would have for preferring the existence of civil society to a prepolitical state of nature. The question became whether it was rational for everyone to leave the apparent insecurity or inconveniences of the state of nature and to form political relationships for mutual benefit. As Robert Nozick once put it, they have to decide "whether the remedy is worse than the disease."[49] The absence of adequate reasons for moving from one condition to the other would mean that the government could not rightfully demand obedience from its citizens even if it might be able to compel their compliance through brute force.

Social contract theorists such as Thomas Hobbes and John Locke tried to close the gap between the purported authority of the state to rule and

[46] In other words, "[t]he right to rule entails a duty to obey." Joseph Raz, "The Obligation to Obey: Revision and Tradition," in *The Duty to Obey the Law: Selected Philosophical Readings*, ed. William A. Edmundson (Lanham, MD: Rowman and Littlefield Publishers, 1999), 160.

[47] Kent Greenawalt, "Legitimate Authority and the Duty to Obey," in *The Duty to Obey the Law: Selected Philosophical Readings*, ed. William A. Edmundson (Lanham, MD: Rowman and Littlefield, 1999), 178.

[48] Harry Brighouse, "Civic Education and Liberal Legitimacy," 108 *Ethics* (1998), 720–1.

[49] Robert Nozick, *Anarchy, State, and Utopia* (New York: Basic Books, 1974), 11.

the right of the people not to be ruled by arguing that citizens voluntarily agree to submit to the authority of the state. For Hobbes, because everyone fears death, each person has at least one very good reason to alienate his or her personal decision-making power to the sovereign and to obey its commands under nearly all circumstances. It would be unwise, in other words, not to submit to political authority and to take your chances in the state of nature. Much less bleakly, Locke maintains that coercive political institutions could protect personal freedom, preserve property rights, and avoid other social problems, such as the private enforcement of law, associated with the state of nature. As Stephen Holmes writes, "The crucial difference between the state of nature and civil society is that members of society are sometimes politically coerced to do what they do not want to do."[50] Both Hobbes and Locke insist that legitimate political authority arises only through the actual or hypothetical consent of human agents. As a self-interested, rational agent, a person must have better reasons to submit to the authority of the state than to remain in the state of nature, where he or she is subject to the coercion of others. This consent legitimizes what would otherwise be a morally troubling relationship between the state and the individual citizen.

On the surface, that explanation should make some sense, but as many critics of the social contract have pointed out, the concept of consent is laden with serious practical and theoretical difficulties.[51] Although Locke maintains that a person's presence in a particular country constitutes tacit consent, there is a long list of reasons why someone might choose to stay in a particular place that has nothing to do with acquiescence to the political authority that he or she lives under.[52] Others argue that there is a "duty of fair play" under some circumstances.[53] Others maintain that such consent can be inferred from the benefits that citizens receive from the existence of the state.[54] It is not clear, though, how one could reject those benefits. Such worries about the nature of consent raise the deeper question, which lies at the heart of the anarchist challenge to political authority: why would anyone willingly hand over political power to anyone else in the first place?

[50] Stephen Holmes, *The Anatomy of Antiliberalism* (Cambridge, MA: Harvard University Press, 1993), 236.

[51] However, some commentators have argued that political obligation need not be based on consent. For instance, a utilitarian theory of political obligation is premised on considerations of the general welfare. See Russell Hardin, "Political Obligation," in *The Good Polity: Normative Analysis of the State*, ed. Alan Hamlin and Philip Pettit (New York: Basil Blackwell, 1989), 103–19.

[52] On the "argument from tacit consent," see A. John Simmons, *Moral Principles and Political Obligations* (Princeton, NJ: Princeton University Press, 1979), esp. 75–100.

[53] See, e.g., John Rawls, "Legal Obligation and the Duty of Fair Play," in *Law and Philosophy*, ed. Sidney Hook (New York: New York University Press, 1964), 3–18.

[54] This could be called the argument from gratitude. See Simmons, *Moral Principles and Political Obligations*, 157–90.

The concept of citizenship implies a prima facie moral obligation to obey the authority of the state. Threats and inducements can bring about the desired behavior, but they cannot serve as the moral basis of political obligations. At minimum, each citizen should have adequate reasons to submit to the coercive power of the state. In one way or another, he or she has to benefit from the arrangement. The existence of a government has to be, on balance, an improvement over the person's condition in the state of nature; the benefits must outweigh the burdens. The problem is that it is far from self-evident why everyone benefits enough from centralized political authority to accept it or more to the point, to consent to the particular political arrangements that are forced on them. Thus, citizens may not have a moral obligation to comply with laws when those laws do not distribute the benefits and burdens of social cooperation fairly and those people have had no meaningful opportunity to object to them. It is even more disturbing when the state demands that they comply with laws that violate their conscience.

As anarchists continue to point out, the moral autonomy of the individual citizen is not easily squared with the legitimate authority of the state.[55] Truly autonomous citizens, in this view, should refuse to be ruled.[56] The raison d'être of the state, however, is the authority to rule. How can the laws of the state, then, ever be morally binding on those who live under them? One possible solution to this apparent paradox, which Jean-Jacques Rousseau first recognized, is unanimous direct democracy. In small political units, citizens participate directly in collective self-rule, preserving their autonomy by authoring the laws that they themselves must follow; through their participation, they command themselves. As Rousseau remarks, "each one, while uniting himself with all, nevertheless obeys only himself and remains as free as before."[57] In this way, the unanimous self-legislation of the general will reconciles the authority of the state to command and the right of each citizen to obey his or her own will. As Aristotle would have said, "[C]itizens rule and in turn, are ruled."[58] Notoriously, Rousseau also thinks that the majority is always right in its opinion concerning the general will.[59] This belief has

---

[55] I borrow this characterization of the problem of political legitimacy from Robert Paul Wolff, *In Defense of Anarchism* (Berkeley: University of California Press, 1970), xxvii.

[56] Wolff has a very strong or demanding conception of autonomy. As Gerald Dworkin explains, liberty is "concerned with promoting or inhibiting first-order desires; it ignores the unique human ability to reflect upon them." By contrast, autonomy is the "second-order capacity of persons to reflect critically upon their first-order preferences, desires, wishes, and so forth and the capacity to accept or to attempt to change these in light of higher-order preferences." See Gerald Dworkin, *The Theory and Practice of Autonomy* (New York: Cambridge University Press, 1997), 15–18.

[57] Jean-Jacques Rousseau, *The Social Contract*, ed. and trans. Donald A. Kress (Indianapolis, IN: Hackett Publishing, 1987), 24.

[58] Aristotle, *The Politics*, trans. T. A. Sinclair (London: Penguin Books, 1992), 362.

[59] Rousseau, *Social Contract*, 82.

less totalitarian implications when readers differentiate the (moral) authority to command obedience from the brute power to force compliance. The individual will can be autonomous only in the midst of other wills when it freely conforms itself to them. Those who refuse to conform their individual wills to the general will, Rousseau tells us, "will be forced to be free" to do what they ought to do as a member of a political community.[60]

The failure to solve this paradox has led a few political philosophers to conclude that a morally legitimate state is a logical impossibility.[61] Even majority rule under perfect conditions falls short of the ideal of unanimous self-rule, because those who find themselves in the minority on a particular issue have not authored the particular legislation that they are expected to obey; they are not commanding themselves but are being commanded by others. Nor does it make much sense, as Rousseau thought, that one must be wrong when one's individual will does not conform to the will of the majority. Rousseau believed that private interests would corrupt the general will.[62] For him, it was conceptually impossible for the general will to conflict with the real will of each citizen. If individuals oppose the general will, their opposition indicates that their private will has overcome their real will, which is always oriented toward the public good. Obviously, this argument is flawed because moral disagreement is not necessarily a matter of repressing illegitimate self-interest in the name of the common good.

However, as many critics also have pointed out, more direct, participatory forms of democracy, which aim at consensus, face numerous difficulties. Unanimous consent is extremely unlikely to be achieved, undercuts pluralism, renders dissent illegitimate, and would seem to be unrealistic today because of problems of scale. Securing the actual consent of all citizens on a large number of highly detailed political issues would also place extraordinary demands on their time if they were expected to become informed and vote on every single issue on the public agenda. Furthermore, real people have vastly different abilities to form rational views, to evaluate empirical evidence, to reason correctly, and to articulate their beliefs. Many of them appear to be too poorly informed to make reasonable decisions about public affairs or to make useful contributions to public debate.[63] As such, one might not be optimistic about the prospects of a democracy that incorporates high levels of popular participation.

Nonetheless, the question of how to constitute the will of a political community of individuals who have different conceptions of the good without violating their fundamental right to pursue them is as important as it was in

[60] Ibid., 26.
[61] See, e.g., Wolff, *In Defense of Anarchism*, vii.
[62] Rousseau, *Social Contract*, 26, 55.
[63] See, e.g., Rick Shenkman, *Just How Stupid Are We? Facing the Truth about the American Voter* (New York: Basic Books, 2008).

Rousseau's time. Politics will always be the arena in which differences are supposed to be resolved to the satisfaction of those who inhabit that political community. Although political conflict cannot be wished away, unanimity is out of the question because reasonable people can be expected to have reasonable differences over a wide range of political questions. Historically, most political thinkers have been much less optimistic than Rousseau was about the possibility of the achieving anything close to unanimity even in smaller political units.[64] As a result, they were more willing to settle for alternatives that did not require the actual consent of everyone who might be subject to coercive public laws.

For the foregoing reasons, I share the sentiment, articulated by Randy Barnett, that "because the [actual] consent of the governed is impossible on a national scale . . . a constitution must provide protection for the preexisting rights retained by the people.[65] As human beings, people have natural rights, and that means that they have a right not to be treated in certain ways by others or by the state. At the very least, they have negative rights not to be interfered with unless what they would like to do harms others or infringes on others' equally important right not to be interfered with. Laws that restrict personal freedom infringe on these rights, but that would not be a source of moral concern if people actually consented to such restrictions; their consent would bind them. This is one of the reasons our society will never see victimless crimes like prostitution or gambling as being on par with crimes like sexual assault or murder. The trouble is that unanimous consent cannot be secured under the conditions that characterize the contemporary United States. That leaves two options. A person could simply deny that the Constitution is (or ever could be) legitimate or that person could predicate constitutional legitimacy on hypothetical consent, that is, on the idea that that people would consent to a constitution that protects the most basic rights of everyone. Such legitimacy is possible, then, on the assumption that the "lawmaking power of the government must be constitutionally limited" to protect them.[66]

As a solution to this problem of unanimity, contemporary contractualists distinguish among reasons that actually convince real people and reasons that ought to convince them if they were ideally rational and fair minded.[67] Their strategy is to base justification on reasons that are

---

[64] Rousseau only requires unanimity for the original social contract. However, "the more important and serious deliberations are, the closer the prevailing opinion should be to unanimity." Ibid., 81–2.

[65] Randy E. Barnett, *Restoring the Lost Constitution: The Presumption of Liberty* (Princeton, NJ: Princeton University Press, 2004), 4.

[66] Ibid., 30.

[67] Rawls regarded all of the major social contract theorists – Hobbes, Locke, Rousseau, and Kant – as advancing the social contract as a hypothetical thought experiment. See Samuel Freeman, *Rawls* (New York: Routledge, 2007), 16.

sufficiently impartial to be accepted by everyone who might be affected. As such, political arrangements can be justified even when they have not actually been justified through direct democratic mechanisms. The idea is that the principal justification of the use of coercive political power is the preservation of the external freedom of each citizen consistent with the exercise of that same freedom by others. Even today, this Kantian characterization of how all of persons could live together on mutually acceptable terms is a fruitful way of understanding the imperfect solution to the problem of political legitimacy. Ideally, such legitimacy is based on sufficiently public reasons that the inhabitants of the political community could endorse. Their sufficiency justifies their binding character without requiring that all citizens actually be persuaded by the arguments that support such justification. Otherwise, unreasonable people, on the basis of bad reasons, would not have a prima facie obligation to obey the law. Political authority or the authority to use coercion is based on a promissory note: when they ask for them, citizens would receive adequate reasons that account for why they have a moral obligation to comply with public laws.

As I have explained, contractualists point out that, as a practical matter, securing the consent of all persons is not a realistic option in the modern nation-state. The point of hypothetical consent through a hypothetical contract is to solve the problem created by the impossibility of sampling the opinion of every citizen on every political matter. Whereas Hobbes and Locke may not have provided compelling reasons for leaving the state of nature and for entering civil society, contemporary contractualists have tried to meet this challenge by showing that such reasons do exist on more careful reflection. The modern adaptation of the social contract is supposed to explain why an ideally rational person would accept the legitimacy of the state in making peaceful coexistence, social cooperation, and the pursuit of different conceptions of the good possible.

In contemporary political theory, the most famous example of this kind of contractualist approach is found in Rawls's *A Theory of Justice*. Rawls argues that despite circumstances of justice – scarce material resources, limited benevolence on the part of most human beings, and deep disagreement about the human good – rational and reasonable people could endorse political principles that would regulate the basic institutions of their collective life. He begins with three very general moral intuitions that he takes to be uncontroversial: (1) citizens are free in the sense that they can set, revise, and pursue their own ends, (2) they are equal in terms of the two moral powers – that is, a capacity for a conception of the good (a coherent system of values that defines our first-order aims in life) and a capacity for a sense of justice (to be able to understand, apply, and act from the principles of justice that specify fair terms of social cooperation in a well-ordered society); and (3) society is a scheme of social cooperation for mutual advantage. Next, he lays out a fair initial choice situation, known as the original position, which reflects these assumptions. This initial choice situation is structured to ensure that everyone who must live under the regulatory principles that are selected, despite their disparate ends, would accept them. Hypothetical persons have an interest in acquiring as many primary goods (all-purpose means) as possible to maximize their chances of flourishing.

Because the parties in the original position deliberate behind the veil of ignorance, Rawls believes that they would achieve unanimity on principles of justice. Strictly speaking, the parties do not deliberate in the sense of exchanging reasons with one another but instead, under conditions of ignorance, deduce the two principles from their shared moral commitments to freedom, equality, and social cooperation. The purpose of choosing under conditions of ignorance is to prevent natural and social contingencies from affecting how the principles are chosen. The attempt to justify them through recourse to the idea of a hypothetical social contract prevents the parties that will be subject to the agreement from tailoring the proposed principles to their advantage. A thick veil of ignorance blocks knowledge of probabilities and forces the deliberators to be risk averse because they could turn out to be the worst-off members of their society. In selecting the principles of justice that they must live under, they indemnify themselves against future loss. A thought experiment can satisfy this basic moral requirement of impartiality in resolving problems of collective choice because it can be formulated in a way that screens out morally irrelevant considerations.

It is far less certain how a real social contract could work out fair answers to fundamental political problems, and it is unsatisfactory to assert that an invisible hand would lead real deliberators to the optimal outcome. The original position precludes the human temptation to capitalize on superior bargaining positions either to advance self-interested or sectarian projects. Rawls does not believe that make-believe promises in a hypothetical world bind us in the way that a real contract or a promise might create a moral or legal obligation.[68] Alternatively, on reflection, real people could accept the conditions of choice that the original position is predicated on inasmuch as they are fair or at least are fairer than other options are. He refers to the original position as a device of representation because it is designed to model the way in which an ideal moral agent would reason about the requirements of social justice under ideal circumstances. We begin with very general moral intuitions about human worth and about how people should live together, and we end up with the much more substantive conclusions embodied in

---

[68] For a much more detailed account of why a hypothetical contract is not contract at all, see Ronald Dworkin, "The Original Position," in *Reading Rawls: Critical Studies on Rawls's "A Theory of Justice,"* ed. Norman Daniels (Stanford, CA: Stanford University Press, 1989), 16–53.

the two principles of justice that regulate the basic structure of a well-ordered society. This hypothetical choice under conditions of ignorance, which results in unanimity and substitutes for actual consent, is the first step toward full justification of the principles of justice.

As I mentioned earlier, hypothetical consent is a second-rate alternative. A reasonable person could be justified in rejecting the reasons that he or she is supposed to have for accepting political authority and everything that follows from it. As I see it, it is not clear what one could say to people who deny that they would consent if they were ideally rational and have good reasons for their dissent. Just because they think that they have good reasons does not make them good, but their insistence that they have not consented and that this refusal is rationally justified cannot be summarily dismissed. That is another way of saying that it is not clear what kind of argument would answer the anarchist challenge to the legitimacy of all political arrangements. Nonetheless, there are plenty of good reasons independent of legitimacy not to go down the anarchist path. There is an expression that the best is the enemy of the good, and when we have to settle for something less than unanimity, we have to try to make the best of our circumstances. If the kind of political legitimacy that Rousseau had in mind is out of the question, what are the second- and third-best alternatives that are practicable in a society like our own? This is why I believe that there is a lot to be said on behalf of hypothetical consent as a solution to the problem of political legitimacy. As long as the state treats each person fairly, which is the objective of the practice of public reasoning, those who are coerced without their actual consent still have reasons to continue to participate in the scheme of social cooperation. The challenge will be to explain to dissenters why it is in the best interest of everyone to accept a government with constitutional limits.

A natural or human right not to be treated in certain ways usually entails a right to personal freedom and a presumption against state action that compromises it. A law that prohibits me from doing what I would like to do is coercive, and thus lawmakers must justify it to me, and to others like me, in the following way: no reasonable person could reject its underlying rationale.[69] Without such public justification, the exercise of the coercive power of the state amounts to an attempt to secure compliance on the basis of a threat, thereby violating the Kantian principle of never treating others exclusively as means.[70] None of that should be controversial, but what I have tried to show in this chapter is that none of us would agree, if we cared about the success of our life plans, to let the state to produce laws that are not

---

[69] Gerald F. Gaus, "Liberal Neutrality: A Compelling and Radical Principle," in *Perfectionism and Neutrality: Essays in Liberal Theory*, ed. Stephen Wall and George Klosko (New York: Rowman and Littlefield, 2003), 138.

[70] Charles E. Larmore, "The Moral Basis of Political Liberalism," 96 *Journal of Philosophy* (1999), 600–7.

sufficiently publicly justified. In effect, we make a hypothetical agreement with one another not to use nonpublic reasons as the basis of legislation that either deprives a person of an important right or treats a group of persons unequally. A commitment to public justification on the part of all persons who live in the same society under the same laws involves a principled refusal to legislate based on nonpublic reasons even when they have the political clout do to so. We would commit ourselves to such self-restraint inasmuch as we care about treating all of the members of our political community as equals who have a fundamental right to form, revise, and pursue their respective conceptions of the good. Such a thought experiment is a useful way of understanding the moral basis of legal obligation under conditions of moral pluralism. The exclusive principle of public reason that I favor is designed to force those who legislate to imagine what it would be like to be adversely affected by such a law and to strictly limit themselves to widely acceptable reasons.

B. Good-Enough Legitimacy

A judge cannot determine the exact strength of a reason in any case a priori. He or she must have a detailed understanding of all of its relevant particulars and their implications with respect to the freedom and equality of everyone. That alone would not determine the outcome of any hard case, but it would create parameters for meaningful constitutional discourse and further inquiry before the final decision. That someone knows how to proceed in the face of uncertainty and that others more or less share this approach does not ensure that reasonable people will converge on the same public reasons as the best public reasons, but it increases the likelihood that they will be clearer on the nature of their reasonable disagreement if they reach different conclusions. That one reason has priority over another reason under certain circumstances does not necessarily mean that it also would have priority under different circumstances. Typically, the context will limit the weight that a judge can reasonably assign to a particular reason. After deliberation and reflection, it is still possible that two different specifications of the same abstract constitutional provision or principle are equally compelling. Under such circumstances, reasonable people may disagree, but it does not follow that the existence of equally compelling specifications always puts into doubt the legitimacy of a particular decision. Instead, provided that the particular specification falls into a narrow range of plausible specifications, that application is sufficiently publicly justified. In terms of legitimacy, there is a crucial difference between specifications that fall within and those that fall outside of that range, and the judge should ensure that the rationale for the decision in question falls within that range. If it does, then it is legitimate, and the judge has done all that can be asked of him or her.

Ideally, judges would base their votes on what they take to be the strongest set of public reasons. All of them should be genuinely motivated by what they honestly believe an exclusive principle of public reason implies. There is world of constitutional difference between a decision that is arguably publicly justified and one that is clearly not. It may be true that no one knows what counts as the best argument in a constitutional controversy, but what matters is whether reasonable people know what counts as a bad argument; that is, an argument based on insufficiently public reasons, and whether this knowledge would allow them to distinguish between an argument that crosses the threshold of public justification and one that falls a bit short.

Ideologues or those who care only about results will not welcome this approach to resolving the most difficult constitutional questions because they will insist that the moral correctness of their views is the only consideration that should be decisive in politics and in law. This is something that many people on both ends of the political spectrum have in common. Because they perceive their deepest convictions as right and those of others who disagree with them as wrong, they are not as concerned as they should be about whether dissenters do, or should be able to, accept their reasons. As they see it, their reasons are the best reasons, even when those who disagree with them do not recognize them as such, and thus their reasons should carry the day. As I have tried to show, that is not the right way to think about public justification when the state enacts laws and judges exercise the power of judicial review. No one is omniscient, and at times, even bright, well-educated people can be obtuse when they fail to see what they ought to see. That is not only one source of tragedy in human life but also a challenge for even the wisest of judges who try to hold the state to an exclusive principle of public reason. Judges who care about public justification must recognize that past understandings, including their own, may have to be revised, especially when they acknowledge the fallibility of their judgment and the limitations of their life experience. New cases stimulate constitutional discourse and help to determine the meaning of abstract constitutional principles like freedom and equality. Although some constitutional issues are settled beyond a shadow of a doubt, that does not preclude someone from trying to defend a new application that may ultimately be accepted as the best understanding of what public justification requires.

Hard cases may seem like a curse, but they enable Americans to become aware of how abstract principles like freedom and equality can be extended into new territory. We understand the implications of the free speech clause, for instance, only when we confront new problems that clarify how its language might cover new phenomena. It would be hard to explain why *Brown* is universally regarded as rightly decided without recourse to the more abstract principle of moral equality and the less abstract principle of racial equality. In the end, we can ask only so much from any constitutional standard that is supposed to mediate between the constitutional text (and the cases that have glossed it over time) and the unique facts of particular cases. Such a standard cannot tell a judge what to do in all cases; it can only be faulted for providing insufficient guidance or promoting the wrong constitutional vision.

Although there is no substitute for good faith or for good judgment, such a standard can help those who exchange reasons with one another to restrain themselves appropriately and recognize when an argument has come close to being publicly justified when they care about the views of others. Whether ordinary people can be reasonable enough for the purposes of public justification is an empirical question, and it is a question that I do not address in this chapter. It is not too much, though, to expect judges, who make some of the most important constitutional choices in the name of the American people, to live up to an exclusive principle of public reason, especially when they have to hold the state accountable to it. That real judges would fall short of an ideal of strict self-restraint goes without saying, but to insist that they explain why the state has offered or has failed to offer sufficiently public reasons to reasonable dissenters in defense of the law in question is not too much to ask of those who have the primary responsibility in our political system of articulating constitutional meaning.

SEVEN

Standard Objections to Public Reason

In the first part of this chapter, I defend public reason against a number of well-known objections and then try to explain its appeal in a society like our own. An ideal of public justification cannot be too controversial if it is to serve as the mode of public reasoning that will help us to resolve constitutional disputes as fairly as possible. Those who are reasonable but have different conceptions of good must use the same principle of public reason when they exchange reasons with one another to narrow the range of their initial disagreement. I shall show that none of these objections is compelling and that some of them rest on misconceptions about the nature of Rawlsian public reason.

In doing so, I deviate from Rawls's own view by insisting that people who are not judges should not feel obligated to limit themselves to public reasons when they deliberate and vote on the most important political questions. Public deliberation should be as participatory and open ended as possible to enable everyone to express their sentiments and articulate their deepest convictions. My position is distinct, then, from that of Rawls, who believes that citizens and public officials should have a self-imposed duty to limit themselves to sufficiently public reasons in certain circumstances. Instead, I believe that judges should limit themselves and others to public reasons when they exercise the power of judicial review. That alone should take some of the sting out of the practical objections to public reason, which usually are premised on the claim that ordinary people and public officials could not live up to its demands. The primary objective of this chapter is to show that the standard objections to a broadly Rawlsian principle of public reason are far from decisive and that judges can apply it without discriminating against any particular reasonable conception of the good.

I. OBJECTIONS TO PUBLIC REASON

There is no shortage of critics of public reason, and they come from both ends of the political spectrum. In this section, I will not rehearse all of the objections to public reason. Instead, I will focus on what I take to be the seven strongest objections to public reason and attempt to rebut them. In constitutional adjudication, the function of the constitutional text and precedent is to frame constitutional issues and to facilitate constitutional discourse. However, these constraints alone cannot tell us what is the correct answer in a hard case or what should count as a good constitutional argument. Reasonable people may differ on which reasons are adequate, and that is why, in the preceding chapters, I have defended an exclusive principle of public reason as the most appropriate normative standard for deciding whether public laws and judicial decisions are justified. But if that principle is biased against any reasonable conception of the good, then a reasonable person would be justified in rejecting it.

A. The Distinction between Public and Nonpublic Reasons Is Untenable

For Rawls, the authority nonpublic reasons come from sources that people may reasonably reject, whereas the authority of public reasons comes from sources that reasonable people must accept. A nonpublic reason is too controversial to do the required justificatory work, and a reason that is too controversial is one that a person could reasonably reject. Rawls deliberately leaves the content of public reason vague so that deliberators can work out the implications of this principle on their own. As such, public deliberation in a society governed by such a principle will be more discursive than some critics have imagined it to be. There are public reasons all around us, even when we do not notice them immediately. For Rawls, standard public reasons would include political values like freedoms of conscience, speech, and association, and the rights to vote, run for public office, and participate in political life. Not only are these values widely accepted and an essential part of our constitutional heritage, but also it is hard to see how a constitutional democracy could survive without them.

Ronald Dworkin is not sympathetic to an approach to public justification that eschews nonpublic reasons that are likely to be true from the standpoint of a liberal who believes that an autonomous life is the best kind of human life. He finds "the doctrine of public reason difficult to define and defend" for two main reasons. First, he does not see what the principle of reciprocity implicit in public reason excludes other than religious convictions.[1] Second,

---

[1] Ronald Dworkin, *Justice in Robes* (Cambridge, MA: Harvard University Press, Belknap Press, 2006), 252–3.

he takes the distinction between political and nonpolitical (comprehensive or deeper) convictions to be problematic.[2]

None of the foregoing should be surprising. Dworkin is the most famous proponent of a moral reading of the Constitution, and a judge who is not trained in moral and political philosophy is unlikely to have the wisdom to answer the most difficult constitutional questions. He does not believe that Rawls's conception of public reason "can help us much in filling out . . . a conception of legality and adjudication.[3] At the same time, he expresses great admiration for Rawls as a legal philosopher.[4] I suspect that Dworkin's ambivalence can be traced to the fact that, on the one hand, Rawls's standard of public justification, like my own, is a principle-based approach to constitutional deliberation that is predicated on a commitment to the freedom and equality of all persons. That standard resembles Dworkin's principle of equal concern and respect where a liberal democracy recognizes the dignity of all persons and treats them accordingly. On the other hand, Dworkin worries that an inclusive or exclusive principle of public reason may not produce the political results that he and others who are like-minded hope for, such as the constitutionality of affirmative action and the protection of abortion rights. Dworkin is right to have mixed feelings about a Rawlsian approach to judicial review. A judge who cares about public justification is not free to turn his or her preferred principle of distributive justice into a constitutional principle unless he or she is convinced that an ideal reasonable person would have no reasonable doubts about its merits. Dworkin would not be pleased with some of the results that a sincere attempt at public justification might produce.

As I previously discussed, the test of reciprocity implicit in public justification excludes appeals to all kinds of perfectionist standards of human flourishing or deeper convictions. Typically, perfectionist arguments qualitatively distinguish between the ends that people pursue on the ground that some ends are intrinsically more valuable than others are and include beliefs about which human capacities should be cultivated, which activities and projects are most worthwhile, which impulses should be resisted, and which behaviors must be avoided. They specify what people should care about and why they should care about some things and not others. An exclusive principle of public reason covers not only religious conceptions of good but secular ones as well. That means that liberals cannot appeal to their own conceptions of the good, such as Millian individuality, Kantian autonomy, Lockean self-ownership, Emersonian self-reliance, or a combination of them. Nor should they make antireligious arguments that religion

[2] Ibid., 253.
[3] Ibid., 254.
[4] Ibid., 261.

is harmful to humankind or that it perpetuates superstition. Nonbelievers do not want to be coerced in the name of a nonexistent deity, nor do they want to be forced to comply with a moral code that they do not believe to be divinely inspired. But they should also realize that believers would not want to be forced to accept a secular conception of the good as the basis of political life that would undermine their religious practices. As such, liberals must exercise the same sort of restraint as everybody else in publicly justifying particular exercises of coercive state power.

For almost all liberals, a liberal conception of the good based on autonomy or individuality not only is normatively superior to nonliberal alternatives but also should guide one's life decisions. As Brian Barry remarks, "Liberalism rests on a vision of life: a Faustian vision. It exalts self-expression, self-mastery . . . the active pursuit of knowledge and the clash of ideas; the acceptance of personal responsibility for the decisions that shape one's life. For those who cannot take the freedom, it provides alcohol, tranquilizers, wrestling on television, astrology, psychoanalysis, and so on, endlessly, but it cannot by its nature provide certain kinds of psychological security."[5] A person who adheres to a liberal conception of the good will try to live a life that meets the preceding criteria. That person will also try to perfect the intellectual and moral capacities that would enable him or her to lead this kind of life and secure the resources that would enable him or her to do so. But a political liberal like Rawls cannot simply take his own side in an argument when he is trying to publicly justify his position to others, especially to those who do not share his deepest convictions about the nature of the good. From the standpoint of public justification, an argument that a reasonable person should not reject under conditions of moral pluralism must be sufficiently independent of the liberal perfectionist claim that an autonomous life is the best kind of human life.

There are religious, secular, and mixed conceptions of the good, and provided that they respect the freedom and equality of others, they are equivalent. A liberal state can treat almost all conceptions of the good as matters of individual taste or preference, whereas it cannot be neutral with respect to the right, that is, to the actions of its citizens that harm others or infringe on their equally important rights to achieve their ends.[6] The choice of a particular reasonable conception of the good is not a political or legal concern; it is best left to individual judgment. A choice that is not self-regarding, though, may be treated differently. A conception of the good that requires or permits its adherents to stamp out heresy is a political and

---

[5] Brian Barry, *The Liberal Theory of Justice* (Oxford, U.K.: Clarendon Press, 1973), 127.

[6] See Stephen Holmes, *The Anatomy of Antiliberalism* (Cambridge, MA: Harvard University Press, 1993), 244.

legal concern. That is the case because a liberal state cannot be indifferent to behaviors that undermine the commitment to equal shares of freedom. A political liberal can doubt that a life of athletic achievement is superior to that of artistic or intellectual accomplishment, but he or she cannot be skeptical about all moral matters, and certainly not about the wrongfulness of unreasonable actions. Within the domain of the reasonable, the practice of public reasoning is supposed to lead toward public justification under conditions of religious, moral, and cultural pluralism. Thus, it would make little sense to exclude only appeals to religious convictions; that exclusion would unfairly discriminate against religious people in favor of those who are secular.

The more serious difficulty would involve defining a conception of the good, agreeing on that definition, and identifying arguments that are directly derived from such conceptions in real constitutional controversies. These obstacles are not insurmountable, because it would be easier to agree on the formal criteria of a conception of the good, way of life, or life plan than to agree on its value. The liberal tradition recognizes that a plurality of ways of life is not only inevitable, but desirable in any society that values individual freedom over order, solidarity, salvation, virtue, and tradition. A conception of the good charts what goods should be pursued, how they should be pursued, and what evils should be avoided. Some conceptions of the good are bound to be more religious, theistic, or spiritual, and will incorporate the importance of faith or following divine commands. Others are bound to be more systematic in how much excruciating detail they contain concerning how one is supposed to live: what one may not eat, how one must dress, how one should treat one's family members, which holidays one must celebrate, and so on. More often than not, the conceptions of the good of real people are partially comprehensive or eclectic in that they mix bits and pieces from a variety of different traditions.

All of that should be expected in pluralistic societies that permit the flourishing of a wide variety of ways of life. A good life could consist in Platonic self-mastery, where reason governs desire, or could be Aristotelian in the sense of pursuing a number of distinct goods and trying to integrate them, in the right amounts, into a coherent life plan. A good life could involve the Stoic emphasis on minimizing the impact of external goods on one's well-being, or such a life could aspire to the Buddhist elimination of the passions, attachments, and delusions that cause human beings to suffer. Less philosophically, a good life could involve being a good partner, parent, child, friend, or colleague and leave time for hitting a golf ball well, training for a bodybuilding contest, collecting designer athletic shoes, playing fantasy-league baseball, doing volunteer work, working for a political campaign, or repairing antique electric trains. What all of these diverse activities have in common is that they help to form the identities of the people who engage in them, and their value reflects the significance that the person who engages in them attaches to them.[7]

People can try and have tried to judge conceptions of the good on their merits, depending on whether they value the pursuit of higher spiritual or intellectual ends or the fulfillment of lower bodily desires. In both the West and the East, a significant number of ethical and political thinkers, especially ancient ones, were preoccupied with the character of a good human life and attempted to explain why one conception of the good life was superior to its rivals. In the beginning of *The Nicomachean Ethics*, Aristotle sets out to show that the best human life is not a life of bodily pleasure and begins to defend the claim that a good human life involves contemplation or rational activity done well.[8] Today, that definition would be malleable enough to cover a wide range of human activities. A number of first-rate contemporary political theorists still care about articulating the nature of the good and correcting the flaws of the modern self, and their inspiration, arguably, is theistic.[9] At times, most people cannot help but make such judgments about the direction of their own lives and those of others and often measure success in terms of whether they have achieved or have come close to achieving their personal or professional goals. Parents are particularly judgmental when they disagree with the lifestyles of their children, and the same can be said of their children with respect to the quality of parenting that they received. Such criticism would make no sense, however, if they were not, at least implicitly, relying on a perfectionist standard of human flourishing.

We give advice to others because all of us believe that self-improvement is possible, and we take advice from others because we realize that we could live a better life. A good life is purposeful, and a person who does not seriously question the direction of his or her life from time to time is rare. Although they come in many shapes and forms, conceptions of the good incorporate qualitative distinctions about what is good and bad, better and worse, important and unimportant, and orient the life plan of the adherent accordingly. That does not mean that a person will live up to the requirements or even come close. In fact, considerable failure is probably the norm. In a democracy, most people will look skeptically on the idea of wisdom about how to live. For better or for worse, Americans are supposed to rule themselves, and they are likely to respond to claims of

---

[7] For a concise and nontechnical discussion of the personal aspects of the meaning of life, see Anthony T. Kronman, *Education's End: Why Our Colleges and Universities Have Given Up on the Meaning of Life* (New Haven, CT: Yale University Press, 2007), esp. 9–35.

[8] Aristotle, *The Nicomachean Ethics*, trans. J.A.K. Thomson (London: Penguin Books, 1988), 68.

[9] See, e.g., Charles Taylor, *Sources of the Self: The Making of Modern Identity* (Cambridge, MA: Harvard University Press, 1989), esp. 495–521.

moral expertise by insisting that no one is qualified to say what is better and what is worse and so on. Today, there is no equivalent of a Stoic Sage who lives an exemplary life. At the same time, they seek advice about how to live from others like friends, colleagues, priests, rabbis, therapists, and talk-show hosts. Just about everyone agrees that parents should serve as role models. That makes sense to the extent that we can agree on the basics of what it means to be a decent human being, and most of us have intuitions about such basics. Surely, we do not want parents to exhibit selfish, dishonest, or intolerant behavior that their children will emulate. It is perfectly intelligible to claim that someone is wasting his or her life or valuing the wrong things because human biology and psychology limit what is good and bad for normal people. Unadulterated subjectivism or relativism with respect to the human good would also belie our intuitions that, in rare instances, even adults need to be saved from themselves. One would be hard pressed to argue that the life of a crystal-meth addict is a good human life.

Instead, within a wide range of possible conceptions of the good, what one decides to do with one's life is a deeply personal matter, and competent adults are better situated than anyone else to determine where their talents lie, which goods are most important to them, how they want to prioritize them, and how they want to pursue them.

Dworkin's worry about the distinction between a comprehensive (or non-political) reason and a noncomprehensive (or political) reason could be taken as a concern about the difficulty of separating the right from the good or doing so with sufficient precision to make the distinction workable. The basic principles of the right "concern how society should respond to and arbitrate the competing demands of individuals."[10] Unfortunately, the phrase "the priority of the right over the good" has generated confusion.[11] This phrase should not be interpreted as an ontological claim or as a kind of perfectionism.[12] Politically, the priority of the right describes the place of principles of justice in regulating the collective decision making of people that inhabit the same social space.[13] When the right is prior to the good, an individual is also committed to acting on reasons that constrain what he or she would like to do out of respect for the autonomy of others. That

---

[10] Charles Taylor, "Cross-Purposes: The Liberal-Communitarian Debate, in *Philosophical Arguments* (Cambridge, MA: Harvard University Press, 1995), 186.

[11] See Richard J. Arneson, "The Priority of the Right over the Good Rides Again," 108 *Ethics* (1997), 169–96.

[12] For examples of the misinterpretation, see Michael J. Sandel, "Justice and the Good," in *Liberalism and Its Critics*, ed. Michael J. Sandel (New York: New York University Press, 1984), 159–76; Roberto Alejandro, "Rawls's Communitarianism," 23 *Canadian Journal of Philosophy* (1993), 78–9.

[13] See Immanuel Kant, "The Doctrine of Virtue," in *The Metaphysics of Morals*, ed. and trans. Mary Gregor (New York: Cambridge University Press, 1996), 147.

someone wants to do something very badly and sincerely believes that doing so will advance his or her conception of the good does not always justify what he or she plans to do. That person must also determine whether the end is morally permissible or consistent with the equal rights of others to pursue their morally permissible ends. There are simply some things that we cannot do to others, however much we may desire to do them, and a morally competent person recognizes the importance of this kind of self-restraint when he or she interacts with others.

That principle strikes me as a fundamental moral requirement. If we are unsure about whether what we want to do is morally permissible, then we can ask the person who is likely to be affected for permission. In the penal code, mutual consent would distinguish a professional mixed martial arts match from assault and battery and sexual harassment from legally acceptable sexual advances. Indeed, that someone refuses to consent to a proposed activity is usually a morally decisive reason for not going ahead with it. We might challenge their reasons for their refusal, but the quality of their reasons is almost always beside the point. This view parallels the principle of free exercise of religion that the Court will only investigate the sincerity of the person whose religious belief is in question and will not address its merits. The importance of such consent in everyday life is revealed by the fact that all of us share notions about what kinds of reasons we could offer to others to justify our decisions to them. The point is not that we cannot assess a person's reasons on their merits but that his or her assessment of them, in the end, is what matters morally.

There will be borderline cases, but their existence does not mean that there is no such thing as a perfectionist reason or argument, no more than it would be impossible to distinguish a religious argument from a secular one. An argument that referred to a divine command or the salvation of the soul would be undeniably religious.[14] An argument that women should not have careers because they should be wives or mothers is premised on qualitative judgments about proper or natural gender roles, and thus is clearly perfectionist. An argument that women with advanced degrees should not be mothers because they have a duty to integrate male-dominated professions would be equally perfectionist. By contrast, an argument that women should put their careers on hold when they become mothers because their children need their care during the first few years of their childhood would not be obviously perfectionist. In this example, the difference would be that in the perfectionist arguments, one of the premises is a normative claim about what women should do because of what it is better to be, whereas the nonperfectionist argument relies on a claim that the children would be

---

[14] Robert Audi, *Religious Commitment and Secular Reason* (Cambridge: Cambridge University Press, 2000), 70.

denied parental care that is owed to them. In principle, that is a reason that everyone could recognize as relevant, which again, is not to say that it would necessarily override other reasons that conflict with it.

Politically, perfectionism means that the state should advance worthwhile conceptions of the good life. It is difficult to distinguish the more deontological approach that I have defended here from a thin or moderate perfectionism that seeks to provide people with the primary goods that would enable them to flourish, whatever their respective conceptions of the good happen to be.[15] As Peter De Marneffe puts it, "[A]ny plausible justification of social institutions, liberal or otherwise, must presuppose some conception of human good, however general."[16] I am tempted to say that the difference is terminological; that is, I have no beef with a moderate perfectionism that attempts to secure the conditions that a minimally decent life requires. Surely, some conception of value will animate any normative political theory. Americans may disagree about a lot of things, but they want decent jobs, a satisfactory standard of living, clean air and water, safe neighborhoods, affordable energy, and good schools for their children. The list does not end there, and a reason that implicates such basic goods or services is likely to be sufficiently public.

Joseph Chan has raised the legitimate concern that Rawls and others, in adopting an antiperfectionist approach, have responded to what he calls an "extreme" version of perfectionism.[17] As Chan points out, "noncoercive" perfectionism does not raise the same concerns as those associated with more coercive forms that permit the state to induce compliance through force or threat of force.[18] Nonetheless, one has to be worried that a kinder, gentler perfectionism can morph into a more extreme form that goes beyond all-purpose primary goods and therefore infringes on the rights of at least some people to form, revise, and pursue their own conceptions of the good. Conceptually, Chan is right, but historically, Rawls and others are on firm ground when they use a more extreme form of perfectionism on the part of the state, the kind that leads to religious intolerance and political instability, as their primary political example of what must be avoided. The example of extreme perfectionism is not a straw man but a real possibility in a society like our own that has always struggled with the proper place of religion in public life.

---

[15] There could be reasonable disagreement over what counts as a primary good, but the basic idea is that regardless of his or her conception of the good, a rational person would want to have such resources to increase the likelihood of realizing his or her life plan.

[16] Peter De Marneffe, "Liberalism, Liberty, and Neutrality," 19 *Philosophy and Public Affairs* (1990), 254.

[17] Joseph Chan, "Legitimacy, Unanimity, and Perfectionism," 29 *Philosophy and Public Affairs* (2000), 8, n.8.

[18] Ibid., 14–15.

B. Public Reason Is Rigged

The next objection is that public reason fixes the outcome in advance before deliberators actually deliberate. As Thomas Nagel writes, "[T]he suspicion remains on the part of many critics that such views are a kind of liberal camouflage for much more partisan arguments."[19] As two critics allege, "Public reason is a doctrine devised and promoted by Rawls and other liberals... and it almost always has the effect of making the liberal position the winner in morally charged political controversies."[20] Peter Berkowitz writes, "The obscurity of [public reason's boundaries] and the authority with which Rawls and his followers endow it allow it to serve as a magical incantation for use in the heat of the debate – or in the leisure of scholarship – to advance partisan causes by cutting off discussion, shutting down questioning, and stopping the inquiring mind dead in its tracks."[21] Berkowitz accuses Rawls of doing just that in Rawls's notorious footnote concerning the implications of public reason with respect to abortion.[22] Others have taken a similar tack by showing that the political conclusions that Rawls and Nagel reach with respect to abortion, allegedly on the basis of public reasons, are unduly sectarian.[23] As another commentator writes, "[I]t is remarkable how predictable and unified are their conclusions about major issues like abortion, assisted suicide, campaign finance reform, and its relation to free speech."[24]

There are two obvious responses. First, Berkowitz's allegation is an ad hominem attack. His claim has less to do with public reason itself and more to do with how Rawls and his followers purportedly have used public reason to beg questions in favor of their own preferred political conclusions. Unless the practice of public reasoning in good faith predetermines certain political conclusions, then the main thrust of Berkowitz's criticism has to be directed at those who have tried to apply public reason to real political controversies and have done so in a self-serving, results-oriented manner. Surely, that a standard can be misapplied or has been misapplied by those who act in bad faith cannot be grounds for dismissing that standard. That Jacobins murdered thousands of counterrevolutionaries during the French Revolution in the name of liberty, equality, and fraternity does not eviscerate the importance of these values. Nor does the fact that a substantial number

---

[19] Thomas Nagel, "Rawls and Liberalism," in *The Cambridge Companion to Rawls*, ed. Samuel Freeman (New York: Cambridge University Press, 2003), 77.

[20] Robert P. George and Christopher Wolfe, "Natural Law and Liberal Public Reason," 42 *American Journal of Jurisprudence* (1997), 31.

[21] Peter Berkowitz, "The Ambiguities of Rawls's Influence," 4 *Perspectives on Politics* (2006), 124.

[22] John Rawls, *Political Liberalism* (New York: Columbia University Press, 1996), 243, n.32.

[23] See, e.g., Robert Westmoreland, "The Truth about Public Reason," 18 *Law and Philosophy* (1999), 283–4.

[24] Ibid., 287.

of the founders of the United States owned slaves taint the ideal of moral equality that is espoused in the Declaration of Independence. If anything, the existence of chattel slavery revealed the hypocrisy of its author, Thomas Jefferson, and the moral shortcomings of a society that could not live up to its professed political ideals. In retrospect, it is clear that the framers misunderstood the implications of the principle of moral equality that they claimed to adhere to with respect to nonwhite persons and women. Even today, we may still be morally obtuse by misunderstanding its implications with respect to nonhuman animals.[25]

Second, Rawls's application of public reason to a particular constitutional controversy is not necessarily authoritative. As we have seen, an exclusive principle of public reason sets stricter limits on the kinds of reasons that judges can allow lawmakers to rely on when they exercise the power of judicial review. Rawls himself later clarified that he had not intended his footnote about public reason and abortion to be an argument in favor of the pro-choice position.[26] Even if he had made such an argument, those who are committed to public reason still have to apply its norms themselves and are not bound by how Rawls or his followers would have applied them; that is their own civic responsibility. Public reason is democratic in that it is accessible to all rational persons. What makes public reason both useful and interesting is the extent to which it does not provide obvious answers to hard cases but provides a vocabulary and mode of reasoning that may produce reasons that everyone can live with.

However, Berkowitz may have another point in mind, namely that those who try to follow norms of public reason will exclude legitimate ideas and preach to the choir, thereby stifling self-expression and undermining the search for truth in the free marketplace of ideas. Thus, not only is freedom of expression compromised, but also those who engage in public reasoning will not be exposed to the different points of view that would enable them to change their minds when appropriate or have more epistemic confidence in their initial political positions. Exposure to a diversity of views would also help people to detect and correct their mistakes.[27] Recently, Cass Sunstein has exposed the dangers of "ideological amplification" when like-minded persons deliberate together and more or less preach to the converted.[28] Clearly, Berkowitz has a valid point if deliberation constrained by a principle of public reason would invariably function the way in which

[25] See, e.g., Peter Singer, *Animal Liberation* (New York: Harper Collins, 1975); Tom Regan, *The Case for Animal Rights* (Berkeley: University of California Press, 1983).
[26] John Rawls, "The Idea of Public Reason Revisited," in *The Law of Peoples* (Cambridge, MA: Harvard University Press, 1999), 169n80.
[27] Cass R. Sunstein, *Why Societies Need Dissent* (Cambridge, MA: Harvard University Press, 2003), 177.
[28] Ibid., 167.

he thinks it would function. As Mill noted long ago, self-censorship due to the tyranny of public opinion is as much of a threat to free expression as government censorship.[29]

What Berkowitz also assumes is that that those who are sincerely trying to publicly justify their constitutional choices will reach the same conclusion, but I do not see why this is so. Any principle of public reason is schematic; it is supposed to function as a "kind of grammar" for political discourse about constitutional essentials.[30] As such, public reason does not decide all constitutional essentials in advance. That is not to say that public reason does not point to certain answers in easy cases. Someone who argues that women should be disenfranchised because they lack rational capacities would not have made an argument that can be squared with a commitment to the freedom and equality of all persons. In more difficult cases, what would happen would depend on who is doing the deliberating and what they are deliberating about, but that hardly means that there would not be sincere disagreement over whether the reasons on the table were sufficiently public. All deliberations are minimally constrained in the sense that the participants have already decided that certain reasons are not relevant in the decision-making process. This is a precondition of communication that aims at persuasion in any discursive context and is not unique to the exclusive principle of public reason that I have defended.

Although even reasonable people who are committed to an exclusive principle of public reason could disagree over the relevance of a particular reason, an exchange of reasons aimed at mutual understanding could not take place if all possible reasons were relevant. As I explained earlier, that is the main trouble with a laissez-faire principle of public reason, where public deliberation is essentially unrestricted. What Berkowitz would have to establish is that a discourse constrained by public reason is necessarily a discourse where, in hard cases, there is only one argument that is sufficiently publicly justified and only a few reasons that are sufficiently public to serve as its premises. In that instance, there is only one uniquely correct answer and only one sound argument that would lead to that answer. Not only has Berkowitz not shown this to be the case; he also fails to see that there are likely to be a number of sufficiently public arguments that compete for our allegiance in any difficult constitutional controversy. Even more important, he does not recognize that what matters is not the result but the kinds of reasons that deliberators offer on behalf of that result. One has to wonder whether public reason settles too little in advance, that is, whether it can

---

[29] John Stuart Mill, *On Liberty and Other Writings*, ed. Stephan Collini (Cambridge: Cambridge University Press, 1989), esp. 5–18.

[30] Patrick Neal, "Is Public Reason Innocuous?" 11 *Critical Review of International Social and Political Philosophy* (2008), 140.

provide the resources that would enable a morally divided society to solve its most difficult constitutional problems.

C. Public Reason Unwisely Restricts Public Deliberation

Other critics of Rawlsian public reason insist that citizens should be able to introduce any reason or argument that they like into public deliberation.[31] Although I have already explained the strengths and weaknesses of a laissez-faire principle of public reason in the fourth chapter, these critics are less concerned about the search for truth and more concerned about its adverse political effects. Richard Bellamy contends that not allowing people to express all of their reasons, including their deepest ones, would protect unreasonable views from criticism and deny those with reasonable views the opportunity to hear the other side of the argument.[32] As he remarks, public reason "leads to a woefully impoverished political discourse that alienates citizens from the state rather than attaching them to it."[33] John Horton writes, "[T]here does not in general seem any great cause of optimism about the potential of public reason to find a way through the many disagreements that characterize a modern pluralistic society."[34] Seyla Benhabib claims that "all contestatory, rhetoric, affective, impassioned elements . . . with all of their excesses and virtues" are missing from public reason.[35] The most promising response to these sorts of criticism is that the scope of public reason is limited; it applies only to constitutional essentials and matters of basic justice, and only to certain persons in certain situations, and thus does not cover the background culture. But Benhabib also has another concern in mind, namely that the neutrality or impartiality implicit in public reason will lead to a lack of creativity, flexibility, and perhaps open-mindedness on the part of those who participate in public discussions. Thus, it would impoverish the kind of deliberation that should take place in the public sphere of a democracy.

Again, this objection would have more bite if it were true that Rawlsian public reason is as fixed or static as Benhabib believes it to be. As Lawrence Solum has explained, though, Rawlsian public reason is not limited to reasons that people already share but also permits the introduction of reasons that "may be available to the public, even if [they are] not yet accepted by

---

[31] See, e.g., Iris Marion Young, "Difference as a Resource for Democratic Communication," in *Deliberative Democracy: Essays on Reason and Politics*, ed. James Bohman and William Rehg (Cambridge, MA: MIT Press, 1997), 383–406.

[32] Richard Bellamy, *Liberalism and Pluralism: Towards a Politics of Compromise* (New York: Routledge, 1999), 58.

[33] Ibid., 43.

[34] John Horton, "Rawls, Public Reason and the Limits of Liberal Justification," 2 *Contemporary Political Theory* (2003), 18.

[35] Seyla Benhabib, *Situating the Self: Gender, Community and Postmodernism in Contemporary Ethics* (New York: Routledge, 1992), 102.

the public."[36] That would leave space for experimentation with novel reasons that others may accept over time and would address Jeremy Waldron's concern that Rawls's conception of public reasoning would preclude "the novel or disconcerting move in political argumentation."[37]

William Galston attacks public reason from a different angle: "[W]e show others respect when we offer them, as an explanation, what we take to be our true and best reasons for acting as we do."[38] This approach would be more appropriate if the people in a morally pluralistic society such as our own were likely to share such reasons after exchanging their best reasons with one another. In a more morally homogeneous society, public deliberation would most likely lead to widely acceptable conclusions. A society in which most persons were Roman Catholic, for instance, would be more likely to be less divided over the moral and legal permissibility of abortion. If Andy offers his best reasons to Betty as justification for a particular law, and Betty can be expected to accept Andy's best reasons and make them her own, then Galston's version of public justification would be defensible.

The foregoing is not what Rawls means when he speaks of respecting one's fellow citizens, but more to the point, I do not see how one respects others by giving them reasons that they could not possibly share. Above all, the point of public justification is that self-serving or sectarian reasons should not be allowed to dominate politics. Galston does not explain why giving one's sectarian convictions the force of law would evince reasonableness on the part of the person who offers such reasons, which entails a willingness to cooperate with others and to find as much common ground with them as possible to avoid unjustified coercion. The most serious difficulty with Galston's position is that he is overly optimistic that Andy's best reasons will coincide or overlap with Betty's best reasons or that Galston does not seem to care whether those reasons are accepted or rejected. Presumably, the purpose of public deliberation is not only to exchange reasons with others out of politeness but also to find reasons that can be shared from a much wider range of perspectives. After all, such reasons will be the basis of public laws. Galston's understanding of public justification is predicated on a common pool of deeper reasons that deliberators, who are motivated appropriately, can draw from.[39] That is not out of the question in easy cases, but he never defends the premise that each person's best reasons are likely

---

[36] Lawrence B. Solum, "Novel Public Reasons," 29 *Loyola of Los Angeles Law Review* (1996), 1477.

[37] Jeremy Waldron, "Religious Contributions in Public Deliberation," 30 *San Diego Law Review* (1993), 838.

[38] William A. Galston, *Liberal Purposes: Goods, Virtues, and Diversity in the Liberal State*, (Cambridge: Cambridge University Press, 1991), 109.

[39] William A. Galston, *Liberal Pluralism: The Implications of Value Pluralism for Political Theory and Practice* (Cambridge: Cambridge University Press, 2002), 116.

to be shared by others, and thus could legitimize public laws, especially in the cases that divide Americans.

This outcome is highly improbable, especially when these best reasons almost always derive from the plurality of deeper convictions that currently exist in the United States. If most people actually shared these best reasons in the first place, then public deliberation within the parameters of public reason would be less urgent or perhaps not even necessary. When they vote on fundamental political questions, they must restrain themselves in respecting the freedom and equality of their fellow citizens.[40] Otherwise, reciprocity is not possible. Under conditions of moral pluralism, citizens must exercise self-censorship with respect to many of the reasons that ultimately provide the moral basis of public laws. But usually, to offer one's best reasons is to avoid such self-restraint and to be insensitive to how others would respond to them. In contrast, by observing the limits of public reason, people form a political relationship based on mutual respect and trust despite their deeper differences. Whether an outcome is justified according to a principle of public reason, then, is left to public deliberation suitably constrained. The intuition underlying Rawlsian public reason reflects a common thought: if we really want to convince someone that a particular proposal is justified, then we must appeal to reasons that already exist or should exist in the moral vocabulary of a reasonable person, regardless of his or her conception of the good. Whether an exclusive principle of public reason offers the most promising means of persuading people, as I see it, turns on whether there are more plausible alternatives under current conditions and those of the foreseeable future.

Nonpublic reasons are "of an epistemic class unsuited for public life" because they cannot possibly have the kind of widespread appeal that would permit them to underwrite public laws under conditions of moral pluralism.[41] Rawls is not claiming that we cannot give deep reasons or deep arguments in nonpublic forums that might justify or motivate us to act on its behalf. In the midst of some kind of overlap of reasonable comprehensive doctrines on some kind of political conception of justice, we should be able to do so. Reasons or arguments that are too deep will never bring about sufficient agreement in political life. By opting for epistemic abstinence, Rawls seeks to avoid predicating his political conception of justice on controversial metaphysical assumptions about the good. This way, despite their deeper disagreement, citizens might still be able to affirm a political conception of justice in a principled way.

---

[40] See Evan Charney, "Political Liberalism, Deliberative Democracy, and the Public Sphere," 92 *American Political Science Review* (1998), 101.

[41] I borrow this phrase from Joseph Raz, "Facing Diversity: The Case of Epistemic Abstinence," 19 *Philosophy and Public Affairs* (1990), 4.

D. Public Reason Discriminates against Citizens of Faith

Another well-known objection is that Rawlsian public reason discriminates against certain religious points of view. Not only should citizens be able to say whatever they want to say in the public realm, but citizens also should be able to vote according to their deepest religious convictions. As Nicholas Wolterstorff writes:

> Is it equitable to ask everyone that, in deciding and discussing political issues, they refrain from using their comprehensive perspectives...? [This] seems to me not equitable. [For it] belongs to the *religious convictions* of a good many religious persons in our society that *they ought to base* their decisions concerning fundamental issues of justice on their religious convictions. They do not view it as an option whether or not to do so. It is their conviction that they ought to strive for wholeness, integrity, integration, in their lives; that they ought to allow the Word of God, the teachings of the Torah, the command and example of Jesus, or whatever, to shape their existence as a whole, including, then, their social and political existence. Their religion is not, for them, *something else* than their social and political existence; it is also about their social and political existence.[42]

It is true of course, descriptively, that some if not most Americans feel this way. Their religious beliefs are not independent of their identity, and these beliefs have political and legal implications. Thus, forcing citizens to limit themselves to public reasons is unfair in the sense that religious people may not appeal to their deepest, most sincere beliefs in deciding difficult political questions. The allegation is that Rawlsian public reason excludes from dialogue those groups that are unwilling to accept the deliberative virtues of fallibilism and pluralism and the consequent distinction between religious and nonreligious belief.[43]

In the preceding passage, Wolterstorff seems to be suggesting that citizens who have secular beliefs are not under the same constraints and would immediately embrace an ideal of public reason because it would enable them to advance their sectarian humanist agenda more effectively. For him, public reason is secular reason in disguise. However, Rawls explicitly denies this claim.[44] It is important to understand the basis for this denial because such an understanding weakens Wolterstorff's position and those that are similar to it. Whether the criterion of reciprocity, which lies at the core of any principle of public reason, is satisfied is to be determined on a case-by-case basis; its fairness in a particular instance cannot be determined beforehand. As Kent Greenawalt points out, one could support aid to religious education

---

[42] Nicholas Wolterstorff, "The Role of Religion in Political Issues," *Religion in the Public Square*, ed. Robert Audi and Nicholas Wolterstorff (Lanham, MD: Rowman and Littlefield, 1997), 104–5.

[43] Although he is responding to Michael Perry, I borrow this characterization from David M. Smolin, "Regulating Religious and Cultural Conflict in a Postmodern America: A Response to Professor Perry," 76 *Iowa Law Review* (1991), 1067.

[44] Rawls, *Idea of Public Reason Revisited*, 143.

or prayer in public schools on a number of arguably public grounds.[45] It is possible that Rawlsian public reason may turn out to be far too accommodating of religious ways of life from the perspective of those who are deeply committed to secularism.

For Wolterstorff, religious reasons must be permitted access to public deliberation because it would be unfair to allow only secular reasons to be candidates for being adequate reasons. On its face, that seems fair, but the problem with this contention is that the notion of fairness that he employs is ambiguous. Wolterstorff claims that it is unfair not to permit religious persons to appeal to their deepest convictions when nonreligious persons have the freedom to do so. But clearly, this is not the case. Those who are unreasonable, even if they are secular, have no right to interject antireligious reasons into public discourse. Comprehensive liberals who may be atheists or agnostics also have a duty of self-restraint. If a citizen sincerely believes that homosexuality is a positive good, for instance, he or she is not supposed to vote on the basis of this reason in deciding the legality of same-sex marriage. The relevant distinction, then, is not between religious and nonreligious reasons but instead lies between public and nonpublic reasons, paralleling Rawls's distinction between the reasonable and unreasonable. The criterion of reciprocity also excludes deeper secular beliefs about the human good from the practice of public reasoning.

Other critics also worry that it is unfair to ask religious citizens to refrain from introducing their theological views into public debate or from appealing to them when they decide how to vote.[46] Privatizing religion does not permit them, these critics maintain, to remain faithful to the requirements of their religious tenets. To insist that religion should not play a public role is to ask religious citizens to deny who they are.[47] Both Stephen L. Carter and Richard John Neuhaus have contended that the liberal commitment to separation of church and state undermines the way of life of religious citizens.[48] These critiques have the appeal that they do to believers because

---

[45] Kent Greenawalt, "On Public Reason," 69 *Chicago-Kent Law Review* (1994), 683.

[46] See, e.g., Nicholas Wolterstorff, "Why We Should Reject What Liberalism Tells Us about Speaking and Acting in Public for Religious Reasons," in *Religion and Contemporary Liberalism*, ed. Paul J. Weithman (Notre Dame, IN: University of Notre Dame Press, 1997), 162–81.

[47] This objection has been called the integrity objection. Gerald Gaus and Kevin Vallier, "The Roles of Religious Convictions in a Publicly Justified Polity: The Implications of Convergence, Asymmetry, and Public Institutions," 8, unpublished paper, http://publicreason.net/2008/09/26/ppps-the-roles-of-religious-conviction-in-a-publicly-justified-polity/.

[48] Stephen L. Carter, *Culture of Disbelief: How American Law and Politics Trivializes Religious Devotion* (New York: Anchor Books, 1993); Richard John Neuhaus, *The Naked Public Square: Religion and Democracy in America*, 2nd ed. (Grand Rapids, MI: William B. Eerdsmans, 1994).

privatization of religious belief may be the final step toward secularization. The consequences of the restrictions of public reason, furthermore, are hardly neutral when citizens with nonliberal conceptions of the good and their children are likely to feel pressure to assimilate into an increasingly secular culture.

Patrick Neal claims that Rawls is asking too much of "citizens of faith" by demanding that they rely on public reasons when they reflect on constitutional essentials and matters of basic justice.[49] Religious persons have an allegiance to something higher, the will of God, and may care more about the salvation of their own soul and the souls of others. Neal also suggests that a person who is committed to public reason would better understand the standpoint of a citizen of faith if he or she were asked to endorse an ideal of political justice based on religious presuppositions. Presumably, the point of this thought experiment is to show political liberals that they would be equally unwilling to commit themselves to a conception of justice that would be at odds with their deepest convictions. As such, they would better understand the perspective of someone who is theistic. There is nothing particularly fair, then, about public reason, and those who reject it are not, by that very fact, unreasonable.

Neal's criticism must be taken seriously because it challenges the claim that public reason does not discriminate against those who are religious. However, could a more religion-friendly alternative be offered in the place of public reason be fairer to everyone? Neal is understandably concerned that the practice of public reasoning would demand too much of citizens of faith insofar as they are asked to put their identities at risk or to violate their consciences. As a matter of both decency and fairness, citizens of faith should not be asked to sacrifice their conceptions of the good at the altar of public reason, nor should they be asked to compromise if secular persons are not willing to do likewise. At the same time, Neal cannot ignore the existence of those who cannot be considered citizens of faith. That is why even an ecumenical religious ideal of justice could not serve as the moral basis of coercive laws, and that also would be one justification for a high wall of separation between church and state. Neal would have to offer his own theory of public reason that not only would be friendlier to citizens of faith but also would accommodate those who are not citizens of faith or reject the idea of public justification altogether. Until then, we cannot know whether a more religious form of public reasoning could compete with Rawlsian public reason on the merits without wishing reasonable pluralism out of existence. The criterion of reciprocity implicit in public reason must be agnostic toward

---

[49] Patrick Neal, "Political Liberalism, Public Reason, and the Citizen of Faith," in *Natural Law and Public Reason*, ed. Robert P. George and Christopher Wolfe (Washington, D.C.: Georgetown University Press, 2000), 184.

reasonable conceptions of the good to serve as the normative standard of public justification. If Rawlsian public reason were biased against religious conceptions of the good, then it could not perform this function.

Such reason is biased against those who are unreasonable, whether they are religious or secular, and I do not see how people who refuse fair terms of social cooperation with others can complain when they have not been treated with the respect that they refuse to extend to others. In the end, everyone who wants to enjoy the benefits of a well-ordered society has to give up the desire to use the law to impose his or her deeper convictions on others. As Samuel Freeman writes, "Rawls does not seek to incorporate into society's overlapping consensus on justice either unreasonable people or unreasonable doctrines."[50] That is not because of intolerance of difference but because of the unwillingness to those who adhere to such doctrines to treat others as equals. At minimum, that is what the criterion of reciprocity requires, and it is not clear to me why it would be unfair to exclude the unreasonable when they refuse to treat others fairly. By definition, unreasonable people refuse to cooperate according to mutually acceptable terms.[51] There have to be limits as to what counts as reasonable, even in the midst of worries about excluding people who should not be excluded.[52]

A commitment to public justification reflects a willingness to make moral compromises when necessary. Each of us must make a sincere effort to meet the criterion of reciprocity if we expect others to do likewise and if we want to continue to live together as political equals. An additional problem with Neal's criticism, then, is that it is not evident why it would be more unfair to ask citizens of faith to bracket their deepest convictions when secular citizens must also do the same. As Peter De Marneffe has explained, "Adherence to Rawls's idea of public reason will thus impose a considerable cost from the liberal point of view if there are important liberal positions on the scope of basic liberty that cannot be adequately defended in terms of such values alone."[53] This claim is supported by the fact that perfectionist liberals, especially those who are strongly committed to autonomy and egalitarianism and who raved about *A Theory of Justice*, have not been nearly as enthusiastic about *Political Liberalism*.[54] Although De Marneffe does not have religious and secular reasons in mind, he uses the case of abortion to show that the principle of public reason, which limits appeals to uncontroversial

[50] Samuel Freeman, *Rawls* (New York: Routledge, 2007), 371.

[51] Ibid.

[52] See, e.g., Erin Kelly and Lionel McPherson, "On Tolerating the Unreasonable," 9 *Journal of Political Philosophy* (2001), 39.

[53] Peter De Marneffe, "Rawls's Idea of Public Reason," 75 *Pacific Philosophical Quarterly* (1994), 234.

[54] See, e.g., Brian Barry, "John Rawls and the Search for Stability," 105 *Ethics* (1995), 874–915.

political values, may prevent liberals from putting forth a "full" defense of the liberal position on the moral permissibility of abortion.[55] Liberals would like to make deeper arguments in support of their interpretation of constitutional essentials and matters of basic justice or at least have the option of bringing out the heavy artillery. Some of them may want to advance traditional antireligious arguments against religious authority, but a person committed to an exclusive principle of public reason cannot simply claim that "a religious way of life is inferior or misguided."[56] As Solum points out, "[T]he religious/secular reason distinction does not map directly onto the public/nonpublic distinction."[57]

The moment one realizes that secular persons are as deeply attached to their conceptions of the good as religious persons are, and how most of them would prefer to live in a society where religion did not have such a visible place in the public realm, it is not obvious that citizens of faith are being asked to sacrifice more than secular citizens are. Neal must explain why asking citizens of faith to let a commitment to public reason override their deeper beliefs when fundamental political questions must be addressed differs from asking the same of secular persons. He seems to believe that either the nature of religious and secular convictions differ significantly or that, psychologically, these beliefs are held different markedly. He is welcome to question the fairness of both the practice and the results of applied public reason from a religious perspective. But it is equally important to understand that secular persons are also asked to compromise some of their deepest convictions in the name of tolerance for the beliefs of others, and that indicates that public reason may be fairer than he believes. As Rawls himself has made clear, moral autonomy fails to satisfy the constraint of reciprocity.[58] By comparison, openly perfectionist forms of liberalism, which deliberately and unapologetically promote a distinctly liberal conception of the good, probably pose more of a threat to religious ways of life.[59]

E. Public Reason Excludes the Unreasonable

Other critics have challenged Rawls's definition of reasonableness on the grounds that it excludes too many citizens from the "legitimation pool," the

---

[55] De Marneffe, "Rawls's Idea of Public Reason," 240–1.

[56] See, e.g., Richard Dawkins, *The God Delusion* (New York: Houghton Mifflin, 2006), esp. 317–87.

[57] Lawrence Solum, "Constructing an Ideal of Public Reason," 30 *San Diego Law Review* (1993), 741.

[58] See Rawls, "Public Reason Revisited," 146.

[59] See, e.g., Joseph Raz, *The Morality of Freedom* (Oxford: Oxford University Press, 1986); Thomas Hurka's *Perfectionism* (New York: Oxford University Press, 1993); George Sher, *Beyond Neutrality* (New York: Cambridge University Press, 1997); Steven Wall, *Liberalism, Perfectionism and Restraint* (New York: Cambridge University Press, 1998).

group of persons whose endorsement would legitimize collective decisions made within the limits of public reason.[60] Greenawalt believes that "nonreligious liberal comprehensive views," like those of Kant and Mill, "will suffer much less from self-censorship than will nonliberal comprehensive views and religious liberal comprehensive views."[61] Bellamy worries that "[m]any non-liberals could embrace Rawls's political morality only by sacrificing some of their core commitments."[62] In response to such challenges, Erin Kelly and Lionel McPherson have argued for a wider or more inclusive understanding of public reason, what they refer to as "wide public justification," to avoid excluding unreasonable persons from the consensus that would form around a political conception of justice in a well-ordered society.[63] If successful, such an approach has a noteworthy practical advantage: more people in a society like our own, despite their deeper unreasonable views, would still see others as free and equal persons and, therefore, as Rawls had hoped, would appeal to sufficiently public reasons when necessary.

It is true that some conceptions of the good, namely unreasonable ones, might do better under alternative political arrangements. As one commentator remarks, "The manifold blessings of liberal social orders come at a price, and we should not be surprised that those who pay the most occasionally grow restive."[64] The likelihood that some comprehensive doctrines will not thrive under a regime of public reason – a possibility that Rawls himself acknowledges – might weaken his claim that all reasonable persons could support it for their own reasons. The presupposition of public justification is that life plans that that do not respect the freedom and equality of the other members of the political community cannot be used to determine what kinds of reasons justify coercion on the part of the state.[65] That is so because reasonable people do not have to give reasons to those in their political community who refuse to treat them as equals. As a result, reasonable persons may legitimately oppose giving the force of law to conceptions of the good that are intolerant of the reasonable life plans of others.

---

[60] I borrow the term *legitimation pool* from Marilyn Friedman, "John Rawls and the Political Coercion of Unreasonable People," in *The Idea of Political Liberalism: Essays on Rawls*, ed. Victoria Davion and Clark Wolf (Lanham, MD: Rowman and Littlefield, 2000), 16.

[61] Kent Greenawalt, *Private Consciences and Public Reasons* (New York: Oxford University Press, 1995), 84.

[62] Bellamy, *Liberalism and Pluralism*, 57.

[63] Kelly and McPherson, "On Tolerating the Unreasonable," 39.

[64] William Galston, "What Is Living and What Is Dead in Kant's Practical Philosophy?" in *Kant and Political Philosophy: The Contemporary Legacy*, ed. Ronald Beiner and William James Booth (New Haven, CT: Yale University Press, 1993), 222.

[65] That does not mean that the state can persecute unreasonable people or that unreasonable people have no constitutional rights. Beyond that, it is not clear exactly how a well-ordered society is supposed to treat such people, and I leave that question to another day.

The issue, then, is whether the exclusion or restriction of certain ways of life can be defended as being as fair as possible to the others who reside within the political community. An exclusive principle of public reason, as I have presented it, reflects an ideal of equal respect for all persons, however unconventional or bizarre their conceptions of the good turn out to be.[66] To say that a particular reason is irrelevant is to say that, whether it is true or false, that consideration should not be permitted to influence the decision that must be made. The benchmark cannot be an ideal communitarian world in which all ways of life are perfectly compatible with one another and political conflict has ceased to exist. It is not enough to insist that one's life plan would be disadvantaged by the result of public reasoning in a particular case. A person who enjoys the thrill or benefits of crime will resent the enforcement of the penal code, but that does not mean such laws are unfair or could not be justified to that person if he or she were reasonable. Because no political conception of political morality can be perfectly neutral in its effects, what makes it reasonable to reject an exclusive principle of public reason is that it leaves a person too badly off compared with others or that it demands too much of that person.[67]

Stephen Macedo has characterized perfect fairness as a "mirage."[68] The impact of the laws and policies of the state are bound to be nonneutral; some conceptions of the good will fare better than others will. Whether the differential impact is unfair depends on whether the baseline from which the difference is measured is unfair. The unfairness objection presupposes what needs to be demonstrated: that the appropriate baseline for assessing even-handedness is public deliberation unrestricted by public reason.[69] As I have explained in previous chapters, anyone who cares about the quality of his life has a reason to want to live in a society that is dedicated to public justification. Those who believe that Rawlsian public reason leaves inadequate room for diversity must offer an alternative of their own that is fairer to all conceptions of the good, yet at the same time does not foreclose the possibility of public justification. One cannot simply wish moral pluralism out of existence, ignore the burdens of judgment, and then put forth a utopian vision that assumes that people's ends will not conflict. Not all conceptions of the good, including secular ones, will survive the competition of the marketplace of ideas. It is hard to imagine a human society

---

[66] Cf. Charles Larmore, "The Moral Basis of Political Liberalism," 96 *Journal of Philosophy* (1999), 608.

[67] I borrow this definition from Thomas Nagel, *Equality and Partiality* (New York: Oxford University Press, 1991), 38.

[68] Stephen Macedo, *Diversity and Distrust: Civic Education in a Multicultural Democracy* (Cambridge, MA: Harvard University Press, 2000), 188–211.

[69] Andrew Lister, "Public Reason and Democracy," 11 *Critical Review of International Social and Political Philosophy* (2008), 285.

that did not marginalize at least some conceptions of the good, especially those that could not peacefully coexist with others, and this reminds us of the costs of living together. It is not as if any political morality can include all conceptions of the good when the very problem in the first place is that such conceptions, even reasonable ones, are bound to conflict at times – and as Isaiah Berlin once put it, "there is no social world without loss."[70]

The more appropriate question is whether such marginalization is legitimate in the sense of using criminal or civil sanctions against those refuse to comply. Fundamentalist Christians may have a right to pass on their religious beliefs to their children, but that right does not mean that they also may use the coercive power of the state to impose their religious convictions on others in the name of what is best for them. Likewise, liberals do not have the right to force their values, such as self-realization and autonomy, onto others who have religious understandings of the place of humans in the universe. Being unreasonable involves a failure to appreciate that coercive laws should not be based on sectarian doctrines that cannot be justified to those who do not adhere to those doctrines. Because of the unwillingness of unreasonable citizens to extend civic respect to others, unreasonable persons can be legitimately coerced, provided that the reasons offered for such coercion are sufficiently public, even when unreasonable persons do not actually accept them. Whether a citizen is reasonable on a particular constitutional question is to be determined on a case-by-case basis, and those who care about public justification must be careful not to label a particular viewpoint unreasonable without due consideration.

In principle, the exclusive principle of public reason that I favor should encourage the flourishing of different ways of life because it does not attempt to assess life plans on their merits. Such a principle would rule out reliance on any thick conception of the good as the moral basis of the most important public laws. Rawls's political liberalism might even be challenged on the ground that his refusal to rank particular conceptions of the good reveals a distinct, and arguably controversial, antiperfectionist tolerance for individual inclinations.[71] A life plan that appears to be silly or eccentric to you or me, provided that it is reasonable in the sense of not unjustifiably interfering with those of others, should not fare any worse than other reasonable life plans would fare; people are free to take it or leave it. The thought is to permit citizens to pursue their diverse ends because the beauty of such ends is in the eye of the beholder. Rawlsian public reason is designed only to settle conflicts among the plurality of ends that inevitably arise in political

---

[70] See Isaiah Berlin, "The Pursuit of the Ideal," in *The Crooked Timber of Humanity* (New York: Alfred Knopf, 1991), 13; see also Rawls's interpretation of Berlin on this point in *Political Liberalism*, 197, n.32.

[71] See Thomas Nagel, "Rawls on Justice," in *Reading Rawls: Critical Studies on Rawls' A Theory of Justice*, ed. Norman Daniels (New York: Basic Books, 1989), 9.

life, and any theory of political morality worthy of our praise must be able to do just that. Individuals have a fundamental right to reach their own conclusions about how they ought to live, and only sufficiently public reasons can override that most fundamental of fundamental rights. As long as citizens decide to form political communities, they must construct regulatory principles that allow them to make the most difficult collective choices as fairly as possible. That requires not only fair decision-making procedures but also a more substantive commitment to the freedom and equality of everyone who is a member of that community. One cannot simply object that such principles are unnecessary in an ideal society that is beyond justice or political conflict.

Those who are critical of Rawls's approach must show that their alternatives would accommodate more reasonable conceptions of the good than Rawls's theory of public reason would accommodate and still meet the minimal requirements of public justification. Even if they claim to reject such an ideal, they still must explain how clashes of ideals can be settled in a mutually acceptable manner to avoid unjustified coercion. Appeals to unregulated public deliberation seem to deny the importance of public justification, the existence of moral pluralism and the burdens of judgment, or that such pluralism and such burdens pose a challenge to political legitimacy. Whether diversity would grow under Rawls's scheme, or under any other liberal scheme for that matter, remains to be seen. In principle, though, the case for Rawlsian public reason looks more promising than vague appeals to ideals of diversity, tolerance, or community because the reciprocity implicit in an inclusive or exclusive principle of public reason would not reduce a morally acceptable political relationship to a shared liberal conception of the good.[72]

Once one realizes that applied public reason does not predetermine political outcomes that all liberals would favor, and that antireligious arguments are ruled out as well, public reason would serve as a road to the public justification of laws, whatever other difficulties it may have. The practice of exchanging public reasons is supposed to allow people who have nonliberal life plans to pursue them without compromising the equally important rights of others to do the same. Under any liberal scheme, people are given considerable latitude to determine what makes their lives meaningful even if they make those determinations in accordance with religious beliefs or cultural traditions that regard freedom as a curse, an invitation to sin, or an excuse to be selfish and deny one's obligations to one's family or community. The reasons that various members of religious minorities in the United States often put forth as an explanation for why they want to limit their children's exposure to secular values in public school, for example, often reflect the fact that they do not value autonomy, critical reflection, and

---

[72] Rawls, *Political Liberalism*, 98.

individuality.[73] A society committed to public justification is not dismissive of the way in which those who have nonliberal convictions understand their identities. At the same time, they cannot expect to have their way all of the time. It would seem, then, that the apparent incommensurability between the deeper normative commitments of liberalism to a particular vision of the good and nonliberal ways of life is less serious than it initially appeared to be, especially when the practice of public reasoning would leave sufficient room for a wide variety of ways of life.

The primary prudential reason for preferring some sort of political liberalism as the basis of political morality is not only that comprehensive or perfectionist liberalisms, which rely on controversial liberal conceptions of the good, are more likely to precipitate political conflict among reasonable citizens. More important, acceptance of reasonable moral pluralism also requires a political morality that does not employ a strong conception of autonomy so that all reasonable citizens can endorse the same political institutions for minimally moral reasons.[74] Brian Barry writes, "[A] liberal cannot coherently believe that liberal principles should themselves be compromised to accommodate the demands of anti-liberals."[75] But the real challenge is to specify the meaning of those principles of freedom and equality in real situations to accommodate those who do not and never will have fully liberal convictions.

Barry has nothing nice to say about Rawls's idea of political liberalism.[76] He is right to identify the dangers of what we might call excessive tolerance for nonliberal practices that are based simply on the claim that they are a part of a particular culture or tradition, and therefore entitled to special protection.[77] Although political liberals cannot be willing to uncritically embrace all differences all of the time, they also cannot dismiss the value that real people attribute to the norms of their culture. As I interpret it, Rawls's political liberalism is not simply a compromise of liberal principles in the face of a variety of nonliberal ways of life but a principled attempt to tolerate as much difference as possible and, in doing so, avoid unjustified coercion. The coercion in question may be unjustified not because others do not accept it but because it may be based on reasons that a reasonable person could reject. For any principle of public reason to regulate public deliberation and voting decisions on fundamental political questions, the vast majority of citizens must be motivated to apply it without having to sacrifice their

---

[73] See, e.g., Mozert v. Hawkins County Board of Education, 827 F.2d 1058 (6th Cir. 1987).

[74] Cf. Gerald Dworkin, *The Theory and Practice of Autonomy* (Cambridge: Cambridge University Press, 1988), 9 (arguing that autonomy need not be an all-or-nothing affair).

[75] Brian Barry, *Culture and Inequality* (Cambridge University Press, 2001), 283.

[76] See, e.g., Barry, "John Rawls and the Search for Stability," 874–915.

[77] See Brian Barry, *Culture and Equality: An Egalitarian Critique of Multiculturalism* (Cambridge, MA: Harvard University Press, 2001).

deeper convictions. This may mean that liberals may have to stomach ways of life that they find to be deeply misguided or even repugnant. Today, religious, moral, and cultural differences about how human beings ought to live extend far beyond the relatively narrow sectarian differences that existed in Locke's or even in Mill's time. A version of liberalism that takes the breadth and depth of this kind of moral pluralism seriously is likely to be the most successful candidate as a theory of political morality because it has the best chance of being accepted by a diverse audience for the right reasons.

Nevertheless, those who are skeptical of the political part of political liberalism and voice the following concern. The political liberal, who is committed to public reason, is likely to be impaled on one or the other horn of a dilemma.[78] On the one hand, "liberalism with a spine" is likely to be too sectarian to serve as a vehicle of public justification.[79] A more perfectionist liberalism would be too closely connected to the deeper liberal principle of autonomy, and therefore be unacceptable to those who are reasonable but justifiably reject liberal ideals of human flourishing. On the other hand, a more antiperfectionist liberalism is likely to tolerate ways of life that undermine the freedom and equality of all persons; doing so would permit too much injustice in an understandable but misguided attempt to accommodate too many religious and cultural differences. In such a case, there could be too many public reasons and none of them would be decisive.[80] As I have already explained, political liberalism, and the ideal of public reason on which it is based, is not as sectarian as critics would have us believe. With regard to the concern that the public reason is too thin to provide guidance when it is most needed, one could respond that we cannot know which reasons are sufficiently public without knowledge of the particulars of the case. What such a critic should be able to show is that a political liberal is always impaled on one or the other horn of this dilemma when he or she seeks to find a mutually acceptable solution. After all, it is easier to move forward on a case-by-case basis, and deliberators can meet the standard of public justification only when they pay close attention to the details of individual cases.

F. Public Reason Is Undemocratic

Another objection is that public reason is hostile to democracy.[81] Democratic critics alleges that Rawls displaces participatory politics with his

---

[78] For the characterization of this dilemma, I am indebted to Westmoreland, "The Truth about Public Reason," 280.

[79] I borrow the phrase from Macedo, *Diversity and Distrust*, 5.

[80] See Joseph Raz, "Facing Epistemic Diversity: The Case of Epistemic Abstinence," 19 *Philosophy and Public Affairs* (1990), 40.

[81] For an argument that Rawlsian political liberalism is too "totalizing," see Iris Marion Young, "Survey Article: Rawls's *Political Liberalism*," 3 *Journal of Political Philosophy* (1995), 181–90.

theory, that the original position reveals the impoverished nature of politics in the well-ordered society, and that philosophy has no special standing in democratic politics.[82] The charge leveled at Rawls is also part of a more general indictment of political philosophers' purported attempt to find a critical standpoint outside of the shared values of particular societies or traditions.[83] In Rawls's scheme, they charge, political philosophy usurps the role that citizens are supposed to play in reaching collectively binding decisions.[84] They insist that Rawls's new political turn does not answer any of their initial objections nor solve any of the practical problems with his theory of justice more generally.[85]

As Sheldon Wolin writes, "Despite frequent reference to 'liberal democracy' and 'constitutional democracy,' democracy is not a distinctive presence in [*Political*] *Liberalism*, and one can say that *Liberalism* does less for democracy than it does for liberalism."[86] Wolin indicts Rawls for not being a real democrat. Rather, Rawls is committed to individual liberty, judicial supremacy, and constitutionalism, and as Wolin sees it, Rawls tries to settle too much ahead of time.[87] A Rawlsian political conception of justice would render politics irrelevant, and for Wolin, the practice of public reasoning not only would have undemocratic consequences but also would be inherently undemocratic because it would not – and more to the point, could not – be participatory. At its best, Rawls's "guardian democracy" would still be elitist by silencing the voices of the marginalized and preventing them from challenging their oppression.[88] Wolin accuses Rawls of trying to establish a "liberal political hegemony."[89]

It is hard to take all of Wolin's polemic too seriously because in a number of places he simply misinterprets Rawls's views or puts them into the worst possible light. Rawls is hardly the defender of the status quo that Wolin makes him out to be. Nevertheless, the possible antidemocratic implications of Rawlsian public reason ought to be addressed, and Wolin is justified in worrying that certain political matters, like class structures, bureaucracy,

---

[82] See Stephen M. Griffin, "Political Philosophy versus Political Theory," 69 *Chicago-Kent Law Review* (1994), 692.

[83] See Lyle A. Downing and Robert B. Thigpen, "Beyond Shared Understandings," 14 *Political Theory* (1986), 451–2; Michael Walzer, *Spheres of Justice: A Defense of Pluralism and Equality* (New York: Basic Books, 1983).

[84] See, e.g., Benjamin Barber, *The Conquest of Politics: Liberal Philosophy in Democratic Times* (Princeton, NJ: Princeton University Press, 1988).

[85] See, e.g., Bonnie Honig, *Political Theory and the Displacement of Politics* (Ithaca, NY: Cornell University Press, 1993), 12.

[86] Sheldon Wolin, "The Liberal/Democratic Divide: On Rawls's *Political Liberalism*," review, 24 *Political Theory* (1996), 98.

[87] Ibid., 98–9.

[88] Ibid., 100.

[89] Ibid., 104.

military power, and capitalism, seem to be off the table.[90] The best response to such a critique, I believe, is to show that the practice of public reasoning is not too philosophical or elitist for ordinary people and that their participation on some level would be required. Rawls has made clear that deeper, complex philosophical argumentation is inappropriate when a society like our own tries to resolve its most difficult constitutional questions to the satisfaction of all reasonable people. Many theorists who are sympathetic to Rawls's approach have tried to show how liberalism can be made more democratic.[91] Some of them have argued that democracy presupposes a commitment to certain substantive individual rights.[92] Amy Gutmann has argued that Rawlsian liberalism is "both democratic and liberal at its core" because it is "fundamentally committed to securing *both* substantive political and personal liberties.[93]

My concern here is not to establish that democracy is prior to liberalism, or vice versa, or to distinguish democratic rights from liberal ones. Instead, a society like our own, which is committed to freedom and equality, also has to be committed to the judicial protection of these values. Under current conditions, outside of judicial forums, I simply do not see where public justification is supposed to take place. In the end, how compatible any principle of public reason is with a particular conception of democracy is bound to turn not only on the content of that vision but also on the limits of real people and real political institutions. Those who insist, like Wolin, that public reason poses a barrier to popular participation and precludes radical critiques that would challenge the power relations that constitute the status quo will not be convinced by anything that I have just said.[94] We simply have different normative political theories, and if we ever have to settle those differences, it will have to be within the bounds of democratic theory and a rational exchange of ideas. At the same time, I believe that a well-ordered democracy must be deliberative, and public deliberation presupposes a commitment to a principle of public reason that is accessible to everyone.

G. Public Reason Is Unrealistic

Although Rawls intends his political liberalism to be a serious political proposal for our liberal democracy, many of his critics are convinced that it

---

[90] Ibid., 106.

[91] See, e.g., Joshua Cohen, "A More Democratic Liberalism," 92 *Michigan Law Review* (1994), 1503–47.

[92] See, e.g., Corey Brettschneider, *Democratic Rights: The Substance of Self-Government* (Princeton, NJ: Princeton University Press, 2007).

[93] Amy Gutmann, "Rawls on the Relationship between Liberalism and Democracy," in *The Cambridge Companion to Rawls*, ed. Samuel Freeman (New York: Cambridge University Press, 2003), 174.

[94] As Wolin remarks, Rawls's political liberalism would lead to an "idealization of the status quo." Wolin, "The Liberal/Democratic Divide," 100.

remains hopelessly utopian. They allege that a commitment to public reason cannot bring about the kind of long-term stability that he envisions because it could not effectively regulate deliberation or voting on fundamental political questions.[95] In particular, most ordinary citizens would not be able to resist the temptation to vote according to their self-interest, personal preferences, or deeper convictions. His critics then conclude that he has not been able to close the gap between his political conception of justice and the real world. This kind of indictment of Rawls's work is not new. Initially, many political theorists, echoing Hegel's critique of Kant, maintained that Rawls's approach to political philosophy was too abstract.[96] Those who are skeptical about the viability of public reason usually claim that such reason is too formal or abstract to engage the will of real human beings. Yet if it can be shown that a public reason in one way or another is already embedded in our particular political heritage or constitutional tradition, then we can be more confident that it is not as abstract or utopian as his critics imagine it to be.

In *Political Liberalism*, Rawls does not start from scratch. He thinks that the seeds of public reason have been sown in the development of our political institutions over time. Articulating an ideal of citizenship based on public reason is his way of capturing our moral intuitions about political equality and their implications, of which we may not be fully aware. Political actors who are concerned with persuading others must refer to principles that are widely held. It is normal to want to discuss things in a language that is acceptable to everyone. The difficult part is trying to preserve the consensus on political principles that exists at higher levels of abstraction when citizens must address concrete cases but these principles can no longer be of service due to their abstractness.

One also could object that no ideal of democratic citizenship could motivate us to listen to others and to compromise when necessary, especially when we do not seem to have any deeper reasons to be reasonable. Isn't the problem that real people are not very principled or that benevolence is in short supply? If that is the case, then we should worry about the prospects of any more participatory form of democracy. Rawls responds to this sort of objection by offering an account of why citizens would learn to honor the limits of public reason that goes beyond mere appeal to the values of our political heritage. A widespread commitment to public reason would

---

[95] Other critics argue that by relying on overlapping consensus and public reason, Rawls has detached social justice too much from moral philosophy. See, e.g., Jean Hampton, "Should Political Philosophy Be Done without Metaphysics?" 99 *Ethics* (1989), 806.

[96] See, e.g., Barber, *The Conquest of Politics*; James W. Ceaser, *Liberal Democracy and Political Science* (Baltimore, MD: Johns Hopkins University Press, 1990); John G. Gunnell, *Between Philosophy and Politics: The Alienation of Political Theory* (Amherst: University of Massachusetts Press, 1986); Honig, *Political Theory and the Displacement of Politics*.

eventually develop as its norms become fully actualized in our political institutions and practices. What Rawls has in mind here is some sort of reflective equilibrium in which people come to recognize the both the utility and the fairness of public reason as they oscillate back in forth between higher-level theory and lower-level practice in their shared political life. These norms speak to us because they square with our considered judgments about the kinds of rights and duties that the practice of democratic citizenship requires.

This kind of political constructivism displays Rawls's philosophical affinity with Hegel by maintaining that public reason becomes less abstract when it expresses itself in our politics. By encouraging people to develop a desire to realize an ideal of democratic citizenship and to be motivated to honor its requirements, his hope is that over time we would not experience the limits that public reason imposes on us as constraints on freedom. Rather, we would come to see them as the necessary conditions that make a well-ordered society possible. The practice of public reasoning is a kind of civic education; it is supposed to shape the moral psychology of free and equal citizens and to generate the kind of moral disposition that would underwrite good citizenship in a well-ordered society even when at times we are at odds with one another. This self-understanding provides the primary motive for following a political conception of justice, thereby reducing that motivational strain that citizens with nonliberal conceptions of the good might experience.[97] Rawls's thought is that justification need not go any deeper for people who are already committed to an abstract notion of democratic citizenship. But without feeling the pull of public reason to some degree, they could not fulfill their civic duties for the right reasons.

In the spirit of the Rawlsian project, there should be no strict separation between the theory of public reason and its practice. Unfortunately, Rawls adds to confusion surrounding the character of public reason when he claims that his ideal of citizenship is "philosophical" and not "psychological."[98] This characterization makes it seem as if his conception is not concerned with empirical facts about human beings or with the limits of their moral psychology. Still, Rawls explains that any political conception of justice must be "practicable" insofar as "its requirements and ideal of citizenship must be ones that people can understand and apply, and be sufficiently motivated to honor."[99] Rawls also remarks that this ideal of citizenship "specifies the most reasonable conception of the person that general facts about human nature and society seem to allow."[100] He is not saying that empirical facts about human beings are irrelevant in formulating a viable political conception of justice. In contrast, and equally important,

[97] Rawls, *Political Liberalism*, 87.
[98] Ibid., 86–7.
[99] Ibid., 87.
[100] Ibid.

our alleged limitations should not be used as an excuse to set the bar too low. We do not know what we are capable of until we have fully opened ourselves to the kind of moral growth that the practice of public reasoning makes possible.[101]

When Rawls argues for the necessity of attaching ourselves to a principle of public reason in a morally pluralistic society, he is not only saying that incommensurable comprehensive doctrines tend to undermine civility and that consensus, as a modus vivendi, tends to be unstable. Instead, there is an essential connection between the actual practice of public reasoning and political stability. When we feel that we have been treated fairly because of the reasons that we have been given, we develop respect for others and are more likely to treat them with the same respect. An essential part of our civic development, then, includes learning to give acceptable reasons to those with whom we disagree in the spirit of fairness and future cooperation. Thus, for Rawls, actual political discourse conducted in the appropriate way teaches us how to interact with those who have different deeper beliefs. As we cultivate the appropriate type of civic character by mastering "the concepts and principles of practical reason" in our political lives, we learn to be the kind of citizen who honors public reason even when we are tempted not to honor it.[102]

Because I have argued that courts should be the primary vehicle of public justification, it might be thought that it does not matter whether real people comply with an exclusive principle of public reason. After all, the ultimate responsibility of public justification is in the hands of those who exercise the power of judicial review. It is true that judges, who are supposed to hold the people and their elected representatives to the standard of public justification, must have certain intellectual abilities and psychological dispositions if they are to perform their jobs well or even competently. At the same time, public justification is an independent normative standard, and just because the Court says that a particular public law meets it does not make it so. There should be plenty of opportunities for others to challenge the reasoning that the justices offer on behalf of their opinions. As I see it, the kind of reasoning that an exclusive principle of public reason requires should make judicial opinions as accessible as they can be to those who are not lawyers or academics. In that sense, public reason is democratic, and it is the responsibility of all of us to ensure that an ideal of public justification guides judicial decision making.

---

[101] Ibid.
[102] Ibid., 112, 71.

EIGHT

Easier Cases

In the next two chapters, I concern myself with the details of how judges should hold lawmakers to the standard of public justification. In doing so, I refer to some of the best-known constitutional issues to render my exclusive principle of public reason less abstract: freedom of religion, same-sex marriage, affirmative action, and abortion. I use particular cases as examples of when the Court met or failed to meet the standard of public justification, and then in some instances, I explain why the concurring or dissenting opinion was more publicly justified. When none of the opinions is sufficiently publicly justified, I offer my own thoughts as to how such an opinion could have been written. The point is not to claim that these hypothetical opinions are necessarily correct but to illustrate the kinds of opinions that could be publicly justified, and therefore could guide future judicial decision making.

I. RELIGIOUS FREEDOM

In *Wisconsin v. Yoder*, three Amish men, Wallace Miller, Jonas Yoder, and Adin Yutzy, were charged with violating a Wisconsin law that made school attendance compulsory until the age of sixteen.[1] The crime was a misdemeanor, with penalties ranging from a minimum of a $5 fine to a maximum of a $50 fine and three months in jail.[2] The defendants were convicted and fined $5 each but were reluctant to appeal their convictions because of the Christian principle of not "going to law" to resolve disputes.[3] Initially, during junior high school, Yoder had been uncomfortable with his daughters' participation in physical education classes because he felt that their

---

[1] Wisconsin v. Yoder, 406 U.S. 205 (1972).
[2] Shawn Francis Peters, *The Yoder Case: Religious Freedom, Education, and Parental Rights* (Lawrence: University Press of Kansas, 2003), 36.
[3] Ibid., 54–6.

mandatory uniforms were "inappropriately modern and worldly."[4] He also objected to his daughters' having to change and shower in front of other girls after physical education class.[5] The Amish in the community of New Glarus, Wisconsin, had mixed feelings toward formal education.[6] Although they conceded that their children would benefit from learning basic skills in reading, writing, and math, they also believed that education that went beyond the basics was likely to undermine their religious faith.[7] For them, the eighth-grade cutoff for school attendance was sensible because excessive exposure to the sinfulness of the world, when as adolescents they were most impressionable, would put their salvation at risk and increase the chances that the Amish community would not survive.[8]

The case was complicated by a number of facts. First, not only did the state have an interest in compulsory education that conflicted with the free exercise of religion claims of the Amish, but also Amish children had an interest in not being pushed into the Amish way of life despite their parents' wishes. Second, the Amish were prosecuted in the first place because the school superintendent retaliated against them for refusing to enroll their children in the public high school for only the first few weeks of the academic year so that they would be counted for the purpose of state funding.[9] However, school officials were also concerned that an exemption for one religious group would lead to a slippery slope of exemptions for others groups.[10] Third, the Amish were not, as popularly believed, being forced by law to send their children to public schools but, in fact, had already formed their own private schools.[11] What Yoder and the other defendants were claiming, in effect, was that they had a constitutional right not to send their children to any high school at all, public or private.

There are as many critics as supporters of the Court's decision in *Yoder*, and some of these critics insist that the case sets a bad precedent by making it too easy for other cultural or religious minorities to obtain exemptions

---

[4] Ibid., 22.

[5] Ibid.

[6] A number of conflicts between different Amish sects and school authorities occurred in the 1950s and 1960s. Although some Amish in some states opened their own schools, others had to pay fines for not sending their children to public schools and serve jail terms. See Steven N. Nolt, *A History of the Amish* (Intercourse, PA: Good Books, 1992), 300–4.

[7] Peters, Yoder *Case*, 27–8.

[8] Part of the process of achieving adult membership in the Amish community involves accepting the Ordnung, the social rules that are supposed to guide the behavior of all of the members and clarify the basic principles of separation, nonresistance, apostasy, and exclusion. Some of these rules have direct biblical support, but others do not. See John A. Hostetler, *Amish Society*, 4th ed. (Baltimore, MD: Johns Hopkins University Press, 1993), 82–3.

[9] Peters, Yoder *Case*, 32.

[10] Ibid., 125.

[11] Ibid., 111.

from generally applicable laws.[12] Amy Gutmann is perhaps the most famous and trenchant critic, maintaining that to be a liberal is to believe that *Yoder* was wrongly decided. She claims that her (and our) interest in this case is "not one of American constitutional law but rather one of liberal democratic theory."[13] Her concern is that a liberal state cannot tolerate or accommodate all forms of religious, moral, and cultural pluralism when it has a very important interest in ensuring that all children are prepared for their future civic responsibilities. The indiscriminate multiculturalist embrace of difference overlooks cultural practices that retard the development of the critical-thinking skills of future citizens, and thus are incompatible with the promotion of civic attitudes that would help to create a more just, more democratic society. Under a liberal scheme, people are given considerable latitude to determine what makes their lives meaningful even if they make these determinations in accordance with their religious beliefs or cultural traditions. It would seem, then, that the apparent incommensurability between the deeper normative commitments of liberalism to a particular vision of the good and of nonliberal ways of life is not inevitable. The people who threaten the stability of a liberal state can become good citizens provided that they can be persuaded that a liberal conception of human flourishing leaves sufficient room for their own moral, religious, or cultural practices. Compared with communitarian or civic republican alternatives that leave even less room for difference, there is a lot to be said in defense of a more comprehensive liberalism and its ability to accommodate a wider range of conceptions of the good. As much as possible, liberal regimes committed to liberal neutrality must try to leave religious and cultural minorities well enough alone.

Nonetheless, the problem with this kind of approach to the challenge of moral pluralism is that, even in the name of better citizenship, it still favors the kinds of lives that are autonomously chosen over ones that cannot be justified in terms of the overriding value of choice, introspection, reflection, contemplation, and experimentation in human life. It still is too sectarian, despite its civic veneer, to secure the moral support of all reasonable persons. This may mean that the political effects of a public culture based on a liberal conception of the good would not be sufficiently neutral because those who have nonliberal life plans are tolerated only insofar as their respective life plans do not conflict with the liberal commitment to autonomy, individuality, and self-expression. In such circumstances, a minority group may not receive the recognition that it deserves. As Charles Taylor writes, "[W]ith

---

[12] There is a voluminous literature on multicultural themes: the nature and value of culture, group rights, the appropriateness of accommodation, gender inequality, and so on. One of the best recent books in this area is Sarah Song, *Justice, Gender, and the Politics of Multiculturalism* (New York: Cambridge University Press, 2007).

[13] Amy Gutmann, "Civic Education and Social Diversity," 105 *Ethics* (1995), 566.

the politics of difference, what we are asked to recognize is the unique identity of this individual or group, their distinctness from everyone else."[14] Thus, the liberal solution seems to be dismissive of the way in which those who have nonliberal convictions understand their identities and the value of their own lives. The reasons that various members of religious minorities in the United States put forth as an explanation for why they want to limit their children's exposure to secular values in public school, for example, often have to do with their rejection of autonomy, critical reflection, and individuality.[15] For political liberals, their values may be wrong according to a liberal standard of human flourishing, but that is beside the point. For the sake of political legitimacy under conditions of moral pluralism, the concern is that liberals should not use the state to advance autonomy as a conception of the good.[16] The reason for preferring some sort of political liberalism as the basis of political morality is not only that comprehensive liberalisms, which rely on controversial liberal conceptions of the good, are more likely to precipitate political conflict. Respect for reasonable moral pluralism also requires a political morality that does not employ a strong conception of autonomy so that all reasonable persons can endorse the same political morality for minimally moral reasons.

In such situations, the dilemma that liberals are bound to find themselves in is that if they adhere to a theory of civic education that is premised on the value of autonomy, then they will be seen as an advocate of a sectarian ideal.[17] But if they reject this theory in favor of a more tolerant alternative, then they will be accused either of not having the courage of their convictions or of advancing an ideal that undermines the state's interest in ensuring that future citizens possess the minimal skills that active democratic citizenship presupposes. There is no obvious escape from this dilemma, and Gutmann deserves credit for clearly articulating where a liberal, who is fully committed to the value of autonomy, must stand. Instead of focusing on the limits of liberal toleration, I want to use the kinds of arguments found in *Yoder* to illustrate how I believe the Court should have decided that case. Let us assume that the conflict that Gutmann addresses is genuine in the sense that the inculcation of democratic values would undermine the ways of life of some religious or cultural minorities, and that toleration of these ways of life therefore might require exemptions for children whose parents are

---

[14] Charles Taylor, "The Politics of Recognition," in *Multiculturalism: Examining the Politics of Recognition*, ed. Amy Gutmann (Princeton, NJ: Princeton University Press, 1994), 38.

[15] See, e.g., Mozert v. Hawkins County Board of Education, 827 F.2d 1058 (6th Cir. 1987).

[16] Perfectionist liberals come in many shapes and forms. For example, William Galston argues for the value of a full theory of the good that he believes is latent in liberal practice. William Galston, "Defending Liberalism," 76 *American Political Science Review* (1982), 627.

[17] See Will Kymlicka, *Multicultural Citizenship: A Liberal Theory of Minority Rights* (Oxford, U.K.: Clarendon Press, 1995), 162.

members of those minorities.[18] Let us also assume not only that the Amish way of life is incompatible with an education in autonomy or individuality, as Gutmann herself claims,[19] but also that this case represents the kind of claims about free exercise of religion that the Court will have to deal with in the future when other religious or cultural minorities demand exemptions from generally applicable laws.

In a morally pluralistic society such as our own, an ideal of civic education should try to strike an appropriate balance between tolerance for different ways of life and cultivation of the skills and virtues that make good citizenship possible in a liberal democracy.[20] Although the aim of civic education is civic competence, Americans still must decide what such competence encompasses and the most appropriate means to that end. They also must pursue the end of civic education in a manner that does not unnecessarily antagonize those who adhere to nonliberal conceptions of the good. For example, school officials should try to respect the wishes of parents who do not want their daughters to wear shorts during physical education classes. In an era of educational choice, school officials have to proceed with caution; they do not want to drive such students into home, charter, or private schools where they might become even less civically literate. Most of the time, these requests can be accommodated, but in some instances, liberals have to draw a line in the sand. A parent who is opposed to the teaching of evolution in biology class or does not believe that boys should take a home-economics class should not expect that a public school will agree to his or her request to have a child exempted from the required curriculum.

There are limits on what parents may ask school officials to do in the name of tolerance, and at times it will be challenging to determine where these limits lie. Surely, tolerance of difference cannot mean that public schools should not teach children the value of rationally assessing evidence on the ground that all methods of acquiring truth are equally reliable. Even highly religious people want their choices to cohere with their preferences. Invariably, as a by-product of their civic education, children would learn that rational evaluation is more reliable than irrational alternatives, such as reading tea leaves or the entrails of dead animals, as the path toward the realization of their conceptions of the good. A reasonable person must tolerate the different reasonable conceptions of the good that exist in society. Thus, liberals are also committed to promoting an ideal of citizenship that

---

[18] Amish children, when they reach physical maturity and demonstrate sufficient knowledge of the Amish religion, are baptized into the Amish community. Their willingness to suffer persecution or death is made explicit during their baptism. See Hostetler, *Amish Society*, 172.

[19] Gutmann, "Civic Education and Social Diversity," 566–8.

[20] See, e.g., Stephen Macedo, *Diversity and Distrust: Civic Education in a Multicultural Democracy* (Cambridge, MA: Harvard University Press, 2000).

enables people to respect the freedom and equality of their fellow citizens. As a result, even among liberals themselves, the content of civic education is bound to be somewhat controversial.[21] Unless one is convinced by Lockean arguments that the personal freedom of parents entails an absolute parental right to pass on their way of life to their children,[22] the state must exercise some kind of educational authority over children in the name of their future citizenship. A society that seeks to create competent, tolerant citizens cannot always defer to the wishes of parents or leave the development of civic virtues to chance.[23]

It would seem to be obvious that to function well, democracies must rely on the character of their citizens. The right habits, attitudes, and principles are easier to instill in children than in adults. For the sake of civic education, governments are more justified in treating children paternalistically before their deliberative abilities have fully matured. More generally, at times, the freedom of children ought to be restricted to enable their rational abilities to develop; that is one of the reasons why being a parent is so challenging. Although many institutions are educative, public schools must play a central role in the inculcation of civic virtues in children. The purpose of civic education is to foster the skills and attitudes that enable future citizens to propose fair terms of cooperation with others, to settle differences in mutually acceptable ways, to tolerate dissent, to participate in collective decision making, and to abide by agreed-on terms of social cooperation provided that others reciprocate.

For Gutmann, in a conflict between autonomy and religious freedom that has illiberal consequences, a liberal must take her own side in an argument. Thus, the right of Old Order Amish parents to teach their way of life to their children does not entail a "right to deny their children an education adequate for liberal democratic citizenship."[24] Gutmann then wonders why there is so much disagreement, even among liberals, over this case.[25] The vast majority of Amish are "part-time" citizens because they conscientiously refuse both the benefits and the burdens of social cooperation in American society.[26] For Gutmann, that only a single year of schooling was at issue also makes this case less difficult than it otherwise would have been.[27] As I interpret her, she also is contending that reasons of civic education or

---

[21] Harry Brighouse, "Civic Education and Liberal Legitimacy," 108 *Ethics* (1998), 719.

[22] See, e.g., Milton Friedman, *Capitalism and Freedom* (Chicago: University of Chicago Press, 1962), 85–107.

[23] On the latter, see Macedo, *Diversity and Distrust*, 10.

[24] Gutmann, "Civic Education and Social Diversity," 568.

[25] Ibid.

[26] On this point, see Stephen Macedo, "Liberal Civic Education and Religious Fundamentalism: The Case of God v. John Rawls?" 105 *Ethics* (1995), 471–2.

[27] Amy Gutmann, "Children, Paternalism, and Education: A Liberal Argument," 9 *Philosophy and Public Affairs* (1980), 348.

reasons of future democratic citizenship are public reasons, whereas reasons based on the value of autonomy or individuality as conceptions of the good are not. Anyone who cares about the quality of American democracy cannot be indifferent to the development of the democratic character of its future citizens. Today, there are probably many phenomena that would undermine democratic education, such as poverty, poor public education, pervasive advertising, crass consumerism, obsession with the lives of celebrities, and excessive debt. Parents who induce their children to care only about professional success, wealth, or physical appearance would be unlikely to produce future citizens who care about the freedom and equality of others and are sensitive to the disadvantages that the less-privileged often face through no fault of their own. In a multicultural world, the nonliberal ways of life of relatively insulated minority groups tend to be easy targets because regulating them is likely to affect fewer people, and thus be easier to implement without public outcry.

Gutmann is right when she insists that the right of children "to think about their own lives" is no more partisan than the right of parents to prevent them from doing so."[28] Both positions are based on value choices, and indeed on choices that can be justified in liberal terms. Is this a public or a nonpublic argument? How would an Old Order Amish person see it? There is no question about whose side Gutmann is on. As future democratic citizens, children must learn the critical-thinking skills that would enable them to cooperate with the other members of the political community and share the benefits and burdens of such cooperation. Surely, there is a lot to be said on behalf of a more value-laden form of civic education, especially when one is convinced that it not only is based on the right value(s) but also will improve the prospects of American democracy. Because Gutmann is an outspoken proponent of deliberative democracy, she is preoccupied with the development of deliberative skills on the part of future citizens who are supposed to exchange reasons with one another in the public sphere.[29]

Gutmann also is right to frame *Yoder* as a question of who ought to have educational power over children.[30] On the one hand, the state must prepare children for the practice of democratic citizenship. On the other hand, on grounds of free exercise of religion, parents would seem to have a qualified right to raise their children as they please and to pass on a particular way of life to them. What is the appropriate balance between the two considerations? There was no doubt that the Old Order Amish rejected conceptions of the good based on autonomy or individuality and believed that

[28] Gutmann, "Civic Education and Social Diversity," 575.
[29] Amy Gutmann, *Democratic Education* (Princeton, NJ: Princeton University Press, 1987), esp. 50–2.
[30] Gutmann, "Children, Paternalism, and Education," (1980), 338.

mandatory secondary school education would undermine the Amish way of life.[31] Gutmann openly relies on the overriding importance of autonomy and concludes that when push comes to shove, comprehensive or perfectionist and political liberals will close ranks and present a united front against a nonliberal point of view. As such, their differences are not differences of kind but rather of degree; the political implications are the same. In *Yoder*, there is no Solomonic solution. If one were to side with the Old Order Amish, that one would be reducing the likelihood that Amish children would ever live the kind of life, full of experiments in living, that John Stuart Mill had envisioned. Furthermore, from the standpoint of deliberative democracy, such children, when they grow up, would be much less likely to be able to deliberate with their fellow citizens over the most important political questions or to be able to assimilate into other communities if they were shunned by the Amish community. In Rawlsian terms, they would be more prone to behaving unreasonably in political life. The social costs of a poor civic education may be significant, and non-Amish would have to bear them as well.

There are two responses to Gutmann's position that a liberal has to be opposed to *Wisconsin v. Yoder*. First, Gutmann herself concedes that a liberal state could not require an exclusively secular education.[32] This concession implies that there may be more room for nonliberal ways of life than she imagines, and the challenge is to draw lines in the appropriate places. In the end, Gutmann's position on how *Yoder* should have been decided boils down to giving more weight to children's rights to develop their autonomous capacities and the state's interest in producing good democratic citizens than to the interest of parents in passing on a way of life and sustaining a particular community over time. A choice has to be made, and a liberal who opposes granting an exemption to the Amish or to any other religious minority similarly situated should be candid about the content of his or her value judgment. Gutmann's position would not be intelligible if she did not value an autonomous life, think that such a life was better than the Amish way of life, and believe the development of autonomous capacities was essential to future democratic citizenship.

In terms of public justification, the problem is that an Amish person could not possibly accept an argument that was premised on an autonomous way of life being the best kind of human life or an argument about future democratic citizenship that is predicated on perfectionist liberalism. That suggests that a reasonable person could be justified in rejecting Gutmann's position on the ground that autonomy is a controversial conception of the good. Alternatively, one might believe that we should presume that the Amish way of life is of "equal worth" or at least is "almost certain to have

---

[31] Wisconsin v. Yoder, 406 U.S. 210–11 (1972).
[32] Gutmann, "Children, Paternalism, and Education," 352.

something that deserves our admiration and respect, even if it is accompanied by much that we have to abhor and reject."[33]

Yoder is complicated by the fact that children do not have the same rights as adults. That is not to say they have no rights whatsoever or that those of their parents are absolute. Surely, parents do not own their children and parents could not prevent their children from being educated at all even on the basis of sincere religious beliefs. Is it possible, then, to still be a liberal but to side with the Amish? Unlike Gutmann's focus, one could argue that Yoder has less to do with a minimal civic education and more to do with basic life and job skills. A person who has no formal education is unlikely to be able to function in the contemporary United States, where even relatively insular religious communities have plenty of contact with the outside world. Nor would it be easy for such people to exit the Amish community if their upbringing is so narrow that they are not be able to adjust to a different environment. As I see it, from the standpoint of public justification, Gutmann relies far too much on an ideal of democratic citizenship that is predicated on an undeniably liberal conception of the good. In her account, autonomy and good democratic citizenship have an incestuous relationship. Such a conception cannot serve as the moral basis of laws in a pluralistic society. Gutmann insists that comprehensive liberals like herself and political liberals like Stephen Macedo are not so different after all with respect to the demands of civic education.[34] Even political liberals will have to take their own side in an argument at times, as much as they wish they could avoid doing so.

I believe that political liberals not only could reject autonomy or individuality as the basis of democratic citizenship on antiperfectionist grounds but also would not accept Gutmann's conception of citizenship, and thus her conception of civic education. Part of the problem with her demanding conception of democratic citizenship is that is unrealistic for the following three reasons: (1) it requires too much time and effort from ordinary persons, (2) it would ask many people to sacrifice the commitments that help to constitute their identities, and (3) it would push the limits of their cognitive capacities. If Gutmann were in a room with a member of the Old Order Amish, she could not expect that person to accept the argument that she made in trying to justify her opposition to Yoder, and that failure suggests that she has fallen short of the standard of public justification.

That is not because the premises of her argument are necessarily false or do not support the conclusion. Rather, a reasonable person would see that there is something to be said for the Amish way of life and a hands-on education that would prepare children for their lives in Amish communities.

---

[33] Charles Taylor, "The Politics of Recognition," in *Multiculturalism: Examining the Politics of Recognition*, ed. Amy Gutmann (Princeton, NJ: Princeton University Press, 1994), 72.

[34] Gutmann, "Civic Education and Social Diversity," 558.

In the majority opinion in *Yoder*, Chief Justice Warren Burger explains that the Old Order Amish sincerely believed that by complying with Wisconsin's compulsory school attendance law, they would be endangering their own salvation and that of their children.[35] However, he does not dwell on theological questions such as Amish ideas of salvation and adult baptism, as one might expect in a typical free exercise case. Instead, he focuses on the values at stake – such as cooperation, living in harmony with nature and the soil, and the rejection of material success – that characterize the Amish way of life.[36] These values could just as easily form the basis of a secular conception of the good. As Burger puts it, "[The Amish] view secondary school education as an impermissible exposure of their children to a 'worldly' influence in conflict with their beliefs. The high school tends to emphasize intellectual and scientific accomplishments, self-distinction, competitiveness, worldly success, and social life with other students. Amish society emphasizes informal learning-by-doing; a life of 'goodness,' rather than a life of intellect; wisdom, rather than technical knowledge; community welfare, rather than competition; and separation from, rather than integration with, contemporary worldly society."[37] Burger also points out that not attending school past the eighth grade would help to integrate Amish adolescents into the Amish community.[38]

Although he does not make an explicit antiperfectionist argument, Burger frames the constitutional question as a conflict of values or of ways of life that requires a value judgment on the part of the state, and then he proceeds to explain why the Amish way of life is sufficiently worthy of respect even though autonomy or individuality is not a part of it. He explains that the Amish are "productive and very law-abiding members of society" and reject public assistance.[39] Here, Burger seems to be suggesting that there is value in the Amish way of life, and he could be faulted for making a judgment about that way of life on the merits. After all, what if the Amish hadn't been productive or law abiding? However, presumably, his intention is to show that the Amish adhere to a particular conception of the good and, in the eyes of the law, that their conception of the good is reasonable because it did not deny the rights of others to pursue their life plans. As he states, "There can be no assumption that today's majority is 'right' and the Amish and others like them are 'wrong.' A way of life that is odd or even erratic but does not interfere with the equal rights of others is not to be condemned because it is different."[40]

---

35 Wisconsin v. Yoder, 406 U.S. 208 (1972).
36 Ibid., 210.
37 Ibid., 211.
38 Ibid.
39 Ibid., 222.
40 Ibid., 223–4.

Burger is correct that we cannot assume that the Amish way of life is inferior to other more secular or more liberal ways of life but wrong if he also means that no such argument could be made. Indeed, many theorists since Plato and Aristotle have tried to explain why a certain kind of life was the best life for human beings, including liberals who would describe themselves in perfectionist terms. Such a philosophical enterprise always has been and always will be important in understanding the role of the good in human life and its possible political ramifications. That is not to say, though, that we would know a good argument about the human good if we saw one. Again, Burger's intuition is that it is not the proper role of the state to make such judgment on the merits. By implication, it is a proper use of judicial review to strike down a statute that compromises the survival of the Amish way of life. By contrast, Justice William Douglas's dissent in *Yoder*, even though it emphasizes the rights of Amish children and teenagers, is a paradigmatic example of a perfectionist argument.[41] Douglas has a point that the interests of Amish children deserve consideration: "If a parent keeps his child out of school beyond the grade school, then the child will be forever barred from entry into the new and amazing world of diversity that we have today."[42] Mill would have agreed with this sentiment, and this position presupposes the value not only of choice but also of critical reflection in living a good life. For Douglas, the child must be heard from before an exemption is granted.[43] As such, Frieda Yoder, because she testified in favor of the exemption, should be exempted, but exemptions for the other two teenagers, Vernon Yutzy and Barbara Miller, should not have been granted until they had also testified and explained their opposition to a high school education.[44]

There is something to be said on behalf of Douglas's position. Parents' rights to free exercise of religion may have to be qualified if they conflict with the rights of their children. Still, one has to come to terms with the implications of Gutmann's and Douglas's similar views. Presumably, any way of life that significantly conflicts with a minimalist civic education in a democracy is not to be tolerated. According to Gutmann's standard, many parents do a poor job of raising their children, but no one believes that that failure alone would justify the state's removal of those children from their homes; quite a bit more would be required, such as physical or psychological abuse. In their concurring opinion, both Justices Potter Stewart and William Brennan admit that *Yoder* would be very different if the Amish were to

---

[41] As Martha Nussbaum notes, it is not realistic to expect children to express their real feelings in such circumstances. Martha C. Nussbaum, *Liberty of Conscience: In Defense of America's Tradition of Religious Equality* (New York: Basic Books, 2008), 143.

[42] Wisconsin v. Yoder, 406 U.S. 245 (1972).

[43] Ibid., 246.

[44] Ibid., 243.

forbid their children from ever attending school at any time or to refuse to comply with the most minimal educational standards.[45] In this case, only a few Amish were concerned with the adverse effects that attendance at public schools would likely have on their children during the crucial adolescent period before their initiation as full members in the Amish community. One has to recognize the need for basic reading, writing, and arithmetic skills in any industrialized society. In the end, judges have to resist the temptation to assess ways of life on their intrinsic merits because they are not simply choosing for themselves and their family but also for their neighbors and fellow citizens. In terms of public justification, Gutmann's view ought to be treated as an external preference about how others should live and raise their children. A commitment to public justification is a commitment to appeal to sufficiently public reasons when the coercive power of the state is used to limit the freedom of others. Here, not only were Amish parents who failed to comply with compulsory education subject to criminal sanctions, but even more important, their reasonable way of life was put in jeopardy. Even perfectionist liberals have to admit that the kind of freedom that exists in liberal societies means that autonomy and individuality may be undermined in the midst of social and economic pressures to conform.[46] Liberal societies use coercion as a last resort, and most of them know that the state, short of draconian measures, will not be able to force autonomy onto those who reject it.

At the same time, most people recognize the mistake of assuming that just because a particular cultural practice has existed over time, it should continue to exist. Chattel slavery was a part of the traditional way of life in the antebellum South, and even today, domestic violence is more "acceptable" in some cultures than in others. Brian Barry has pointed out the dangers of romanticizing the way of life of the Amish.[47] I doubt that too many of us would want to defend the practice of shunning as a means of compelling the wayward back into the fold. Barry is also right that not every exemption that some Amish seek should automatically be granted. A state law that requires, out of a concern for public safety, that all slow-moving vehicles, including Amish ones, have a red or orange reflective triangle on its back would be publicly justified.[48] At times, the desire to accommodate certain religious or cultural practices can produce intolerable results.[49] Very few

---

[45] Ibid., 238.

[46] See, e.g., Benjamin R. Barber, *Consumed: How Markets Corrupt Children, Infantilize Adults, and Swallow Citizens Whole* (New York: W. W. Norton, 2007).

[47] Brian Barry, *Culture and Equality* (Cambridge, MA: Harvard University Press, 2001), 181.

[48] State v. Hershberger, 444 N.W.2d. 282 (Minn. 1989).

[49] As Nussbaum observes, the decision in *Yoder* had a different (and worse) impact on young women than on young men in terms of their options of exiting the community in the future. However, the Court never addressed this issue. Nussbaum, *Liberty of Conscience*, 143.

people support the position that parents, with sincere religious convictions, could physically or emotionally abuse their children or refuse to educate their daughters.[50] Nor are they sympathetic to the claim that a generally applicable statute that banned cruelty to animals would be unconstitutional simply because members of a particular religious group wanted to torture an animal as a part of a religious ritual.[51] Although the decision in *Hialeah* was unanimous and the Court struck down the ordinance that prohibited the sacrifice of any animal on free exercise grounds, it was clear that the city had passed the law in question because it disliked the practice of Santeria and wanted to abolish its sacrificial rituals. This case illustrates an important point about public justification. If the city of Hialeah had justified its prohibition of animal sacrifice on the grounds, say, of public health or prevention of cruelty to animals, its ordinance would have been much more likely, in the eyes of the Court, to be publicly justified. By contrast, the facts indicated that city had a discriminatory motive and was acting on reasons that an ideal reasonable person would not find to be sufficiently public.

In cases where the state is not acting on the wrong kinds of reasons, a reasonable person is likely to have reservations about how much accommodation is justified, particularly when the practice in question is central to its practitioner's identity or way of life. The most obvious reason against compromise or some sort of accommodation, in the example of the Amish and fluorescent triangles on their slow-moving vehicles, is that respect for or tolerance of these religious beliefs should not be used to justify endangering the lives of others who also use public roads.[52] Presumably, these beliefs were sincere, and some Amish saw the triangles as "worldly symbols." Nevertheless, most Amish did not reject this law.[53] Many Amish did not share the belief of those who brought the lawsuit that alleged that the presence of such triangles on their vehicles conflicted with their free exercise rights, indicating that the refusal of the state to accommodate the request by some Amish for an exemption was not unreasonable.

The Rehnquist Court repudiated the approach used in *Yoder*, and I believe that doing so was a mistake. The Court was not so willing to grant such exemptions and curtailed free exercise rights in cases that involved the right of an Air Force officer to wear a yarmulke on duty and the rights of prisoners to have their work schedules modified to make room for their religious

---

[50] Perhaps the most concise, thoughtful overview of the problems that cultural difference raises for those who are concerned with gender equality is that of Susan Moller Okin, "Is Multiculturalism Bad for Women?" in *Is Multiculturalism Bad for Women?* ed. Joshua Cohen, Matthew Howard, and Martha C. Nussbaum (Princeton, NJ: Princeton University Press, 1999), 9–24.

[51] Church of the Lukumi Babalu Aye, Inc. v. Hialeah, 508 U.S. 520 (1993).

[52] See Barry, *Cultural and Equality*, 185.

[53] Ibid., 184.

services.[54] *Yoder* is probably no longer good law after the Court's decision in *Employment Division v. Smith*.[55] In that case, the Court ruled that as long as the state does not intend to discriminate against particular religious beliefs, then the impact of the law on particular persons or religious groups is neither here nor there. There was no doubt that the respondents in *Smith* had sincere religious reasons for the use of peyote in their religious rituals. *Smith* represents a rejection of the *Yoder* approach in which a generally applicable rule may not be enforceable when its enforcement seriously interferes with an individual's free exercise of religion. The free exercise clause no longer requires the state to carve out an exemption for Native Americans or any other group from a law that does not have a discriminatory purpose. The state no longer has to balance the competing interests between the right to practice one's religion and the authority of the state to prohibit the possession and use of certain controlled substances. That decision indicates that laws that burden the free exercise of religion are no longer subject to strict scrutiny standard of review.

As Justice Harry Blackmun writes in his dissent in *Smith*, "A state statute that burdens the free exercise of religion ... may stand only if the law in general, and the state's refusal to allow a religious exemption in particular, are justified by a compelling interest that cannot be served by less restrictive means."[56] In the language of public reason, the Court made it too easy for the state to offer reasons as justification for such laws that reasonable people would be justified in rejecting. Of course, for most people, the use of a hallucinogenic drug is not an essential aspect of the quality of their lives. No thoughtful person equates liberty with license (to do whatever one pleases) but a reasonable person is open to the possibility that unconventional or uncommon behavior may warrant constitutional protection depending on its importance to the life plan of the person who is challenging the law. It is difficult to explain why some liberties are more important than others, and it is just as difficult, at times, to explain why what some people want to do is not as important as what other people would like to do.

I have no doubt that for so-called potheads, smoking marijuana for recreational purposes is not only an important part of their lives but also an important part of their identities.[57] Although a standard of public justification cannot turn every want or desire people happen to have into a constitutional right, courts should look more carefully at the reasons that the state offers in defense of laws that prohibit the use of marijuana. The

---

[54] Goldman v. Weinberger, 475 U.S. 503 (1986); O'Lone v. Shabazz, 478 U.S. 342 (1987).

[55] Employment Division v. Smith, 494 U.S. 872 (1990).

[56] Ibid., 907 (Blackmun, J., dissenting).

[57] On the costs and benefits of different federal regulatory schemes involving the so-called marijuana problem, see Mark A.R. Kleiman, *Marijuana: Costs of Abuse, Costs of Control* (New York: Greenwood Press, 1989).

case of peyote in religious ceremonies is bound to be easier because most of us immediately recognize that most of a person's religious practices are likely to be an essential component of her conception of the good. A law that prohibited the wearing of yarmulkes would be unequivocally unconstitutional, and a law that prohibited the wearing of all head coverings would also be unconstitutional, even if it did not have an underlying discriminatory purpose. After all, the wearing of a yarmulke is not an option for an Orthodox Jew. If the use of peyote in *Smith* were nonessential to the practice of the religion in question, then it would have been much more difficult for the defendants to maintain that the free exercise clause requires the state to exempt them. It may seem silly to speak of a right to smoke pot or a right to drink, but in the latter case, the nationwide prohibition of alcohol consumption required a constitutional amendment.

II. SAME-SEX MARRIAGE

In this section, I would like to explain why there is a constitutional right to same-sex marriage or, alternatively, why laws that prohibit same-sex marriage are not publicly justified. At the tail end of the 1960s, consensual same-sex intercourse was legal in only one state, Illinois.[58] At that time, no legislation protected gays and lesbians from being fired or denied housing because of their sexual orientation.[59] At present, the Defense of Marriage Act prohibits federal recognition of same-sex marriage.[60] In 2004, President George W. Bush endorsed the Federal Marriage Amendment.[61] By 2005, forty states had enacted statutes or constitutional amendments that prohibited same-sex marriage.[62] With the exceptions of Massachusetts, Connecticut, Vermont, and Iowa, it does not appear that the states, on their own, will extend the right of marriage to same-sex couples anytime soon.[63] Recently, the California Supreme Court recognized a constitutional right to same-sex

[58] David Carter, *Stonewall: The Riots that Sparked the Gay Revolution* (New York: St. Martin's Press, 2004), 1.

[59] Ibid.

[60] Defense of Marriage Act, Pub. L. No. 104–199, 110 Stat. 2419 (Sept. 21, 1996) (codified as 28 U.S.C. §1738 (1996)).

[61] Daniel R. Pinello, *America's Struggle for Same-Sex Marriage* (New York: Cambridge University Press, 2006), 20.

[62] Ibid., 29.

[63] *Goodridge v. Department of Public Health*, 798 N.E.2d 941 (Mass. 2003); Kerrigan v. Commissioner of Public Health, 289 Conn. 135, 957 A.2d. 407 (2008). In addition, the Iowa Supreme Court has recently recognized the right to same-sex marriage under the Iowa Constitution. Varnum v. Brien, Docket No. 07-1499 (2009). Vermont was the first state to create civil unions for same-sex couples, and it is also the first state to create a right to same-sex marriage through legislation.

marriage, under the California Constitution, but California voters over-turned that decision by approving Proposition 8.[64]

Many of those who support the right to same-sex marriage confine them-selves to legal premises, insisting that there is a fundamental right to marriage for everyone, irrespective of sexual orientation, or that denial of marriage licenses to same-sex couples violates "equal protection of the laws."[65] Oth-ers rely on predictions about the social benefits that would result if states were to recognize legally same-sex marriage.[66] Some commentators main-tain that the denial of equal rights to same-sex couples constitutes gender discrimination.[67] Others try to dispel the conservative fear of social change by explaining why equal rights for same-sex couples would not require the complete rejection of traditional morality.[68] Others have compared sexual identity to religious identity to equate unjustified discrimination on the basis of sexual orientation with that of religious belief.[69] Others have argued that straight people will benefit from the legal recognition of same-sex marriage.[70]

None of these arguments is obviously bad. In fact, some of them are prob-ably as sound as any moral or legal argument can be. However, I believe that we should focus on the reasons that underlie laws that ban same-sex marriage. My contention is that even the best reasons of those who oppose same-sex marriage are too controversial to be shared by everyone in the political community; therefore, for constitutional purposes, they are unrea-sonable. The problem with the typical argument that opponents of same-sex marriage advance is that it relies on premises that could not possibly be accepted by those who do not already share their particular deeper convic-tions. In this section, I will argue that this kind of political argumentation, which is based on appeals to perfectionist ideals of human flourishing, is not suited to the political task at hand: to find reasons for public laws that all fair-minded citizens cannot reasonably reject.

---

[64] In re Marriage Cases, 43 Cal. 4d 757, 183 P. 3d 384, 76 Cal. Rptr. 3d 683 (2008). Proposition 8, the "California Marriage Protection Act," appeared on the November 4, 2008 California election ballot and was approved by 52 percent of voters.

[65] See, e.g., *Baehr v. Lewin*, 852 P.2d 44 (Haw. 1993).

[66] See, e.g., Mark Strasser, "The State Interests in Recognizing Same-Sex Marriage," in *Marriage and Same-Sex Unions: A Debate*, ed. Lynn D. Wardle (Westport, CT: Praeger Publi-cations, 2003), 33–4.

[67] See, e.g., Andrew Koppelman, "Discrimination against Gays Is Sex Discrimination," 69 *New York University Law Review* (1994), 197–287.

[68] Stephen Macedo, "Homosexuality and the Conservative Mind," in *Marriage and Same-Sex Unions: A Debate*, ed. Lynn D. Wardle (Westport, CT: Praeger Publications, 2003), 98.

[69] See, e.g., David A. J. Richards, *The Case for Gay Rights: From* Bowers *and* Lawrence *and Beyond* (Lawrence: University Press of Kansas, 2005), 108.

[70] See, e.g., Jonathan Rauch, *Gay Marriage: Why It Is Good for Gays, Good for Straights, and Good for America* (New York: Henry Holt, 2004), esp. 72–85.

In what follows, my aim is to show that only certain kinds of reasons would justify the unequal treatment of same-sex couples with respect to civil marriage and that those reasons do not exist. There is likely to be reasonable disagreement about the fairness of the most important laws in any constitutional democracy.[71] Nevertheless, not every disagreement qualifies as reasonable, and not every case is bound to be so hard that the balance of reasons does not support one conclusion over its opposite. If the reasons that attempt to publicly justify unequal treatment are inadequate, then that law is insufficiently publicly justified. Not every argument is good enough, despite the intensity of the feelings of those who find themselves on different sides of a particular political controversy. On a case-by-case basis, the difficulty lies in distinguishing a reasonable from an unreasonable argument that purports to justify unequal treatment.

Recently, the California Supreme Court ruled that the failure to "designate the official relationship of same-sex couples as marriage" violates the California Constitution.[72] The dissenters made a number of different arguments: (1) the lack of a constitutional right to same-sex marriage, (2) the use of rational-basis standard of review for legislative classifications based on sexual orientation, (3) the constitutional adequacy of substitutes for marriage like domestic partnerships for gays and lesbians, (4) the traditional definition of marriage, (5) the facial neutrality of Proposition 22, and (6) the importance of separation of powers, where courts exercise restraint in the midst of social disagreement over a controversial political issue. I want to focus on the separation-of-powers argument because I believe that is it the best one that the dissenters advanced in this case, and those who advocate judicial restraint more generally are fond of it. Justice Marvin Baxter claimed that the majority had overstepped its bounds by not permitting the meaning of marriage to change through ordinary democratic processes.[73] The problem with the majority's decision, as he wrote, is that "a bare majority of this court, not satisfied with the pace of democratic change, now abruptly forestalls that process and substitutes, by judicial fiat, its own social policy views for those expressed by the People themselves."[74] In her dissent, Justice Carol Corrigan also made clear that Proposition 22, the popular initiative that banned same-sex marriage prior to the passage of Proposition 8 in 2008, reflects the recent will of California voters.[75] She then emphasized

---

[71] See Jeremy Waldron, *Law and Disagreement* (Oxford: Oxford University Press, 1999).

[72] In re Marriage Cases, 43 Cal. 4d 757, 780 (2008) (George, J., majority).

[73] In re Marriage Cases, 43 Cal. 4d 757, 860-878 (2008) (Baxter, J., dissenting).

[74] In re Marriage Cases, 43 Cal. 4d 757, 863 (2008) (Baxter, J., dissenting).

[75] In re Marriage Cases, 43 Cal. 4d 757, 878-885 (2008) (Corrigan, J., dissenting). In a field poll on September 18, 2008, about two months before the election on November 4, 2008, 55 percent of registered California voters opposed Proposition 8, whereas 38 percent were in favor of it. http://field.com/fieldpollonline/subscribers/RIs2287.pdf.

the extent to which statutory alternatives to marriage for same-sex couples, such as civil unions or domestic partnerships, satisfy equal protection requirements and implied that this case would have been different in the absence of such partnerships.[76]

What both of the dissenting opinions have in common is the belief that the judiciary should restrain itself and let democratic processes take their course for better or for worse. This position could be called the argument from democracy, or the argument from majority rule. As a practical matter, this view is sensible. In principle, no one thinks that it is a terrific idea for the judiciary to get too far ahead of public opinion on controversial issues or to circumvent the legislative process, especially when that process is headed in the right direction, and invite a backlash. The trouble with this approach is that it permits the state to act on the wrong kinds of reasons. There are at least a number of ways to describe the reasons that underlie Proposition 8 or other laws in other states that limit marriage to opposite-sex couples: those based on external preferences about what others should be allowed to do; sectarian convictions about the sinfulness of homosexuality or same-sex marriage; or controversial empirical claims, which are closely tied to theological positions, about how a broader definition of marriage would undermine the traditional understanding of marriage and would have, as Justice Baxter characterized it, "such a cataclysmic transformation of this venerable institution."[77]

The reality is that the sky is not going to fall when states begin to create a constitutional right to same-sex marriage. In the recent California case, that right is also premised on the view that substitutes for same-sex marriages, such as civil unions and domestic partnerships, are not only inadequate but also inherently demeaning. Unlike Justice Corrigan, who argued that such alternatives reflect a commitment to equality,[78] the existence of such substitutes could be interpreted to indicate that same-sex couples are not entitled to the same kind of legal recognition that traditional, opposite-sex couples are. Unquestionably, a statutory substitute for marriage for interracial couples would not save a ban on interracial marriage. It may be unfair to insist that such an alternative sounds too much like separate but equal and too little like "there is no caste system here," but it is legitimate to inquire into why such a legal distinction should be made, and someone who responds that we have to protect the traditional definition of marriage still would have to explain why doing so would justify discriminatory treatment, although it is possible to imagine discriminatory treatment that is even worse. A sincere response would have to include an explanation of why the state has the authority to

[76] In re Marriage Cases, 43 Cal. 4d 757, 880 (2008) (Corrigan, J., dissenting).
[77] In re Marriage Cases, 43 Cal. 4d 757, 866 (2008) (Baxter, J., dissenting).
[78] In re Marriage Cases, 43 Cal. 4d 757, 879 (2008) (Corrigan., J., dissenting).

put its imprimatur on some legal relationships but not on others. One also might believe that neutrality on the part of the state requires the abolition of same-sex marriage and the creation of a regime of private contract in which couples formulate their own legal rights and duties.[79] After all, the state could be violating the principle of liberal neutrality by endorsing marriage as a better way of life than, say, cohabitation.[80]

A. Academic Arguments against Same-Sex Marriage

In academic writings, there are more sophisticated arguments against same-sex marriage that do not involve disputed claims about protection of the family. Lynn Wardle has put forth a number of arguments against same-sex marriage.[81] He writes, "The heterosexual dimension of the relationship is at the very core of what makes 'marriage' what it is, and why it is so valuable to individuals and to society."[82] "[T]he union of a man and a woman," he claims, "is part of the very nature and *reality* of the marriage relationship itself."[83] Historically, "The legal status of marriage has been reserved exclusively for special covenant heterosexual unions because those unions are unique and uniquely beneficial."[84]

There are at least two noticeable problems with these kinds of arguments. First, Wardle comes dangerously close to begging the question by defining marriage in a way that presupposes heterosexuality. A tautology, such as marriage is exclusively for opposite-sex couples because marriage is exclusively for opposite-sex couples, will not put this issue to rest for us. No one thinks that the argument that "by definition, marriage is between people of the same race" would be sound if the issue were the constitutionality of a law that banned interracial marriage.[85] No important legal, political, or moral question can be settled by definition when the core issue is normative: not what has been the case but what should be the case now and in the future. Burkean conservatives are still fond of appealing to the accumulated wisdom of tradition.[86] However, there is good reason to be skeptical of the claim, which seems to be based on Providence or some sort of evolutionary theory, that institutions that survive over time are morally justified by the

---

[79] For this argument, see Tamara Metz, "Why We Should Disestablish Marriage," in Mary Lyndon Shanley, *Just Marriage* (New York: Oxford University Press, 2004), 99–105.

[80] See Ralph Wedgewood, "The Fundamental Argument for Same-Sex Marriage," 7 *Journal of Political Philosophy* (1999), 227.

[81] See, e.g., Lynn D. Wardle, "Legal Claims for Same-Sex Marriage: Efforts to Legitimate a Retreat from Marriage by Redefining Marriage," 39 *South Texas Law Review* (1998), 736–68.

[82] Ibid., 748.

[83] Ibid., 749.

[84] Ibid., 750.

[85] See Loving v. Virginia, 388 U.S. 1 (1967).

[86] See Russell Kirk, *The Conservative Mind: From Burke to Eliot*, 7th ed. (Washington, D.C.: Regnery Publishing, 1953), 8–11.

very fact of their existence. Just because something has been the case does not mean that it ought to be the case, and just because something is not the case does not mean that it should not be the case.[87] As such, a different kind of argument is required, one that is not circular and one that does not assume the moral correctness of the practices of the past.

Second, the naturalness of any human activity may be open to dispute even after we have been able to distinguish between what is a product of nature and what is a product of nurture. Indeed, dozens of other sorts of nonreproductive sexual practices, including same-sex intimacy, have existed and continue to exist in different cultures at different times. Also, there are plenty of human characteristics (e.g., body odor, bad breath) and plenty of human behaviors (e.g., selfishness, callousness, narrow-mindedness) that are natural in that they are widespread in one form or another in all human societies. But that does not mean, of course, that they are good or should be considered a norm; conventional morality should not be confused with critical morality.

Surely, that is not how Wardle intends to use the word *natural*. He is not making a mere observation or statistical generalization about how often acts of same-sex intimacy occur around the world. Rather, his argument about the unnaturalness of homosexuality is based on an appeal to natural law that is premised on a neo-Aristotelian theory of natural purposes or functions built into the nature of the universe.[88] "Homosexual behavior is directly related to the fundamental purposes of marriage laws," Wardle claims, "that is, regulation of sexual behavior and protection of mores that define the core identity, boundaries, and basic structure for the moral order of a society."[89] These purposes are not contingent on time and place but rather built into the structure of the universe. For Wardle, opposite-sex and same-sex marriages are not morally equivalent because they do not equally advance "the social purposes for which the state has established the preferred legal institution of marriage."[90] In addition, Wardle maintains that opposite-sex marriages advance these social interests much more than same-sex unions do.[91]

I admire Wardle's willingness to expose the real foundations of arguments against same-sex marriage. Compared with the "Yes on Prop 8" campaign here in California, where voters were led to believe that overturning the

---

[87] For an argument that, historically, marriage has not always been a heterosexual institution, see William N. Eskridge, *The Case for Same-Sex Marriage* (New York: Free Press, 1996).

[88] For a short explanation of the confusion between descriptive and prescriptive laws common to claims about the unnaturalness of certain sorts of behavior, see Jeffrie G. Murphy and Jules L. Coleman, *Philosophy of Law: An Introduction to Jurisprudence*, rev. ed. (New York: Westview Press, 1990), 7–8.

[89] Wardle, "Legal Claims for Same-Sex Marriage," 752.

[90] Ibid., 754.

[91] Ibid., 755.

California Supreme Court's decision in favor of same-sex marriage would "protect" opposite-sex marriage, not to mention other tactics that misled voters into thinking that churches that refuse to perform same-sex marriage ceremonies would lose their tax exemptions or that children would be taught about same-sex marriage in public schools, Wardle's candor makes it possible for those who disagree to know what they are disagreeing about. Normally, attorney generals would prefer not to articulate the grounds for moral disapproval of same-sex marriages with the knowledge that not only courts but also the voters frown on such arguments. That is why the "Yes on Prop 8" campaign went to such great lengths to frame the issue in a way that made it seem as if the traditional institution of marriage were under siege, or alternatively, why those who were opposed to the proposition were intolerant of their religious beliefs.[92]

At their best, though, Wardle's claims are highly questionable. First, the cause-effect relationship between the institution of opposite-sex marriage and the social interests that Wardle lists are bound to be empirically controversial.[93] Second, each of these social interests, assuming that they are legitimate social interests in the first place, must be assigned different weights in formulating public policy because trade-offs are inevitable. Third, at present, legally recognized same-sex marriages have come into existence only recently and only in four states. Thus, there is simply no basis for comparison. Until same-sex marriages are legalized and each group to be compared is large enough to provide a random sample, no empirical judgments about the relative merits of opposite-sex and same-sex marriages can be made. One cannot simply extrapolate from the same-sex relationships that currently exist largely without equal legal rights and benefits because those rights and benefits are likely to change the character of those relationships. Same-sex and opposite-sex marriage might turn out to be quite a bit more similar than Wardle imagines. Fourth, it is not clear why same-sex marriages would have to provide the same social benefits that heterosexual marriages purportedly provide to be treated equally in the eyes of the law. If interracial marriages did not contribute equally to the social interests specified, compared with same-race marriages, that would not mean that interracial couples would not have a right to marriage. Similarly, that statistically children who are adopted by parents of a different race may have a more difficult time growing up because of racial prejudice does not mean that the right to adopt such children, for this very reason, should not exist. Fifth, Wardle may be dead wrong about the consequences. Laws that permit

---

[92] See www.protectmarriage.com.

[93] These social purposes include safe sex relations; procreation; child rearing; the status of women; the stability, strength, and security of the family; the integrity of the basic unit of society; civic virtue; public morality; interjurisdictional comity; and government efficiency. Wardle, "Legal Claims for Same-Sex Marriage," 754.

same-sex marriage may inculcate values such as tolerance, understanding, and mutual respect in children and young adults that will make American society more humane in the future.

B. Why Opposition to Same-Sex Marriage Is Unreasonable

The foregoing responses are more or less obvious. The most sophisticated opponents of same-sex marriage will argue that same-sex marriage harms the participants and undermines the social function of marriage. They might even insist, like Robert George and John Finnis do, that all reasonable persons, who respond to the dictates of right reason, will acknowledge the harmfulness of homosexual conduct. It is clear that this position is religious. This kind of harm cannot be detached from the particular theistic conceptions of the good of those who advance such claims. Plenty of people do not believe that consensual same-sex sex is harmful, and they probably believe that it is a part of a healthy long-term same-sex relationship. Obviously, the kind of harm that opponents of same-sex marriage have in mind here differs from that of murder or of sexual assault.

This is why such arguments are problematic. Those who think that they provide sufficient justification for the state to refuse to recognize such marriage can continue to tell themselves that those who disagree with them are simply mistaken, but that rings hollow when those who disagree with them can come up with exactly the same response and show that those who disagree with them are offended or bothered by the immoral conduct in question. The very notion of moral harm is bound to be more controversial than the examples of more tangible harm that I have just offered.[94] From the standpoint of public justification, the burden is on those who advance such reasons to show that they are sufficiently independent of their deeper convictions, and so far, they have not been able to do so. Just about any view can be based on the claim that it is justified according to a common conception of right reason that is supposed to be available to all normal humans. More important, it is evident that the use of such a standard has its limits in a morally pluralistic society such as our own.

George and Finnis have an argument, but not one that can be cast in terms of public reasons, and that is where the problem lies. In the end, the primary argument against same-sex marriage is that a society may legitimately enact public laws that are based on the moral convictions of the majority.[95] The baseline question, then, is whether moral disapproval is a good-enough reason to justify laws that treat same-sex couples unequally. Wardle makes no

---

[94] See Joel Feinberg, *Harm to Others: The Moral Limits of the Criminal Law* (New York: Oxford University Press, 1984), 1:65–70.

[95] For an example of this argument, see Lord Patrick Devlin, "Morals and the Criminal Law," in *The Philosophy of Law*, ed. Ronald Dworkin (New York: Oxford University Press, 1977), 66–82.

effort to explain why gay and lesbian citizens, who are negatively affected in so many ways by laws that define marriage so narrowly, could accept the reasons that he offers against same-sex marriage. Presumably, to him, it does not matter what they, or more generally those who disagree with him, think about the truth of his deeper beliefs, and that is problematic. For gay and lesbian persons, what is at stake is more than symbolic: inheritance rights, Social Security benefits, income tax, welfare payments, adoption, division of property on dissolution of the relationship, alimony, custody, medical benefits, insurance benefits, immigration, and testimonial privilege.[96] The absence of these rights, which puts gays and lesbians at a distinct legal disadvantage, would make it more difficult for them to live a good life and sends a message that their lives are inferior compared with those who are straight. Even if such a right to civil unions did exist, under a domestic partnership law like that of California, one still has to wonder what protecting the traditional understanding of marriage really amounts to.

Wardle finds it odd that those who are in favor of same-sex marriage appeal to a moral value like equality but at the same time reject "traditional moral opposition" to homosexuality as the appropriate basis for marriage laws.[97] Of course, many of those who support same-sex marriage are not moral subjectivists or relativists, including myself.[98] That is the case because a person who maintains that values are mere tastes or preferences, and thus cannot be rationally justified, cannot turn around and make moral judgments of his or her own, claim that they are rationally justified, and then expect others to accept them. But Wardle misses an important point. In terms of public reason, the right question is not about whether same-sex intimacy is immoral or based on a misunderstanding of what it means to live a good human life. This question would be appropriate in personal matters or when a voluntary association, such as the Roman Catholic Church, formulates the rules that govern its inner life and the conduct of its members. No one is arguing that, by law, the Catholic Church should be forced to ordain women as priests or to condone homosexuality, abortion, stem-cell research, birth control, or euthanasia. Those matters are properly left to Catholics. The

---

[96] Richard A. Posner, "Homosexuality: The Policy Questions," in *Same-Sex Marriage: Pro and Con*, ed. Andrew Sullivan (New York: Vintage Books, 1997), 187–8. On the legal consequences of same-sex marriage, see David Chambers, "What If? The Legal Consequences of Marriage and the Legal Needs of Lesbian and Gay Male Couples," 95 *Michigan Law Review* (1996), 447–91.

[97] Wardle, "Legal Claims for Same-Sex Marriage," 756.

[98] Wardle believes that claims in favor of same-sex marriage are morally relativistic and that the legal recognition of such marriages might set a precedent for polygamous marriages. Ibid., 760–1. Although he may be right about what might follow, what matters is consent on the part of the adults who seek unconventional marital relations. Obviously, a person could not marry a child because a child is not old enough to give consent. The same would be true for someone who wanted to marry his or her favorite pet; an animal cannot consent.

rationale behind public justification is that some reasons are inappropriate to invoke in the name of the public justification of coercion, whereas those same reasons would be perfectly appropriate in other contexts.

As I see it, the question of whether there is a constitutional right to same-sex marriage is about whether sectarian moral or religious convictions can legitimize the unequal legal treatment of gays and lesbians who would like to be married. Recall that Rawlsian public reason is public with respect to a particular audience, namely all reasonable persons, and is a response to the difficulty of publicly justifying laws to everyone who must live under them. Reasonable people may have very different ideas about the kinds of public laws that would be legitimate. Public reason is a political morality because it outlines how they ought to treat one another – with equal concern and respect – when they must resolve fundamental political matters that cannot be left to individual choice. Not only do they not vote their interests, tastes, or preferences; they also do not appeal to what they believe to be right or true according to their own deeper convictions out of respect for the equal rights of others to pursue their respective conceptions of the good.

At first glance, the virtues of public reason may not be evident. Wouldn't it be better to try to ascertain the truth of the matter? Wouldn't it also be fair for everyone to deliberate and vote on the basis of their deeper convictions? John Finnis insists that "homosexuals" who are out of the closet are "deeply hostile to the self-understanding of those members of the community who are willing to commit themselves to real marriage."[99] Robert George writes,

In fact, however, at the bottom of the debate is a possibility that defenders of traditional marriage law affirm and its critics deny, namely, the possibility of marriage as a one-flesh communion of persons. The denial of this possibility is central to any argument designed to show that the moral judgment at the heart of the traditional understanding of marriage as inherently heterosexual is unreasonable, unsound, or untrue. If procreative-type acts in fact unite spouses interpersonally, as traditional sexual morality and marriage law suppose, then such acts differ fundamentally in meaning, value, and significance from the only types of sexual acts that can be performed by same-sex partners.[100]

In this passage, George claims that critics of traditional marriage law deny the possibility that marriage "is a one-flesh communion of persons." This simply is not true. A person committed to an exclusive principle of public reason, like myself, is not denying that possibility. Instead, that person is denying the relevance of the "truth" of George's proposition, for purposes of

[99] John Finnis, "Law, Morality, and Sexual Orientation," 69 *Notre Dame Law Review* (1994), 1069–70.

[100] Robert P. George, "Neutrality, Equality, and 'Same-Sex Marriage'," in *Marriage and Same-Sex Unions: A Debate*, ed. Lynn D. Wardle (Westport, CT: Praeger Publications, 2003), 123.

public justification, because of its theological underpinning. If the political aim is to legitimize public laws under conditions of moral pluralism, then appeals to truth, given the existence of reasonable moral pluralism and the burdens of judgment, are not likely to be accepted by most reasonable persons as the proper basis of public laws.

George also claims that for proponents of the so-called liberal view, there is no moral difference between homosexual sex acts and heterosexual marital intercourse.[101] Again, this claim is not necessarily true because a political liberal could believe that there is a moral difference but that it is not significant enough to warrant different legal treatment or that the state must be as neutral as possible toward different conceptions of the human good, and thus should eschew evaluating consensual sexual practices on their alleged merits. To permit someone to live out a sexual fantasy premised on domination and subordination with another consenting adult is not necessarily to approve of that behavior. For the most part, that two people would like to do X is usually a good enough reason for allowing them to do it even when one is convinced that doing X is unhealthy, demeaning, or not something that one would want to do. It is hard to understand why any person would agree in the first place to be a member of a society that did not plan to respect his or her right to pursue his or her own way of life even when the majority had moral objections to it.

Although George believes that we would be better off without public reason,[102] he never offers a plausible alternative of his own that would accomplish what the practice of public reasoning is designed to accomplish: to legitimize public laws under current conditions. It is surprising that he does not recognize that some of the deeper arguments that he makes with respect to same-sex marriage would ring hollow to those who are not theistic. Instead, he wishes moral pluralism and reasonable disagreement out of existence and suggests that a genuine idea of public reason would include all kinds of nonpublic arguments, including natural law ones.[103] As I explained in the fourth chapter, the obvious difficulty with this laissez-faire principle of public reason is that it will not accomplish what it is supposed to accomplish in the midst of reasonable disagreement about the character of a good human life. The exchange of deeper reasons has not worked in the past and may even drive a morally pluralistic society even farther apart. George's essentially unrestricted principle of public reason is designed "to identify and embody in law and public policy truths available to rational inquiry, understanding, and judgment."[104]

---

[101] Ibid.
[102] Robert P. George and Christopher Wolfe, "Natural Law and Public Reason," in *Natural Law and Public Reason* (Washington, D.C.: Georgetown University Press, 2000), 70.
[103] Ibid.
[104] Ibid.

His expansive definition of public reason, which appears to be fair on its face, does not excuse him from explaining why he believes that a morally pluralistic society like our own could share his particular theory of natural law when so many of us are not Roman Catholics, Thomists, or theists. Indeed, some who are secular are convinced that belief in the supernatural is not rationally justified and that a fully rational person would not be religious when the balance of evidence cuts against the existence of God. Any principle of public reason must contain a standard of reciprocity for that society; it must identify the kinds of reasons that reasonable people may offer others and expect them to accept. A secular person who is reasonable could reject religious reasons as justification for limiting same-sex marriage to opposite-sex couples.[105] George thinks that deliberators can meet the criterion of reciprocity by offering reasons that are "true" according to their deepest convictions. What the reader should immediately notice is how far George is from the position of comprehensive or perfectionist liberals on so many of the most important constitutional issues. Surely, he is aware of the distance, and he could defend his position on each issue on the ground that he is more likely to be right than those who disagree with him. I do not know what else a political liberal could say to him other than, "I am equally convinced that you are more likely to be wrong than I am. Your position ought to take into account how difficult it is to verify the truth of deeper convictions, regardless of whether they are theistic or not. Unless you believe they are stupid or insincere, you can understand why those who disagree with you may have good reasons for that disagreement. You might even concede that the existence of what appears to be reasonable disagreement indicates that you should have less confidence in the truth of your deepest convictions."

I believe that this attitude toward the existence of reasonable disagreement makes more sense than maintaining that others who disagree are probably wrong in disputed matters of public morality. They could be wrong, of course, but they could say the same about your views, and they could be right. As such, the practice of public reasoning requires considerable self-restraint on the part of all participants, not just from those who happen to be religious, to increase the likelihood of publicly justifying public laws. With respect to the controversy over same-sex marriage, those who are in favor of it should not appeal to the virtues of same-sex relationships.[106] This self-restraint allows a morally pluralistic society like our own to make collective

---

[105] Cf. Stephen Macedo, "In Defense of Liberal Public Reason: Are Slavery and Abortion Hard Cases?" *Natural Law and Public Reason*, ed. Robert P. George and Christopher Wolfe (Washington, D.C.: Georgetown University Press, 2000), 22.

[106] For an example of this kind of argument, see Andrew Koppelman, "Homosexual Conduct: A Reply to the New Natural Law Lawyers," in *Same Sex: Debating the Ethics, Science, and Culture of Homosexuality*, ed. John Corvino (Lanham, MD: Rowman and Littlefield, 1997), 44–57.

decisions on fundamental political questions without convergence at deeper levels.[107] Public reason is not secular reason, and it does not always lead to recognizably liberal results.[108] A commitment to an exclusive principle of public reason narrows our deeper differences and renders them more manageable when collective decisions have to be made to the satisfaction of every reasonable person.

Not surprisingly, George believes that public reason is rigged; when applied to real political controversies, such reason "almost always has the effect of making the liberal position the winner in morally charged political controversies."[109] According to him, this occurs because nonliberals have been deprived of their heavy artillery, so to speak, namely their best substantive moral arguments.[110] What he fails to note is that liberals have been deprived of their heavy artillery as well. Surely, perfectionist liberals would like to appeal to their deepest convictions, namely Kantian autonomy, Millian individuality, Emersonian self-creation, or Lockean self-ownership, when they seek to justify particular applications of political power. It would not be hard to put together a deeper liberal argument to support the right of same-sex marriage. Above all, that is what separates political liberals from perfectionist liberals, and that is not a mere semantic difference. An exclusive principle of public reason also rules out those sorts of appeals; thus, there is no guarantee that applied public reason will always produce so-called liberal results. A person could be minimally reasonable and still adhere to a nonliberal conception of the good. As I shall show in the next chapter, the issue of abortion is a more open question than it may appear to be.[111]

George will respond that, in practice, political liberals retain their heavy artillery; their conception of political autonomy is not sufficiently independent from autonomy as an ideal of the good. Again, this move works only if the practice of public reasoning only produces liberal conclusions that are biased in favor of autonomy. As I explained in the previous chapter, the content of Rawlsian public reason is not fixed, and deliberators can

---

[107] This interpretation of Rawlsian public reason finds additional support in Rawls's idea of "decent nonliberal peoples" in which "decent" is an even weaker constraint than "reasonable." See Rawls, "The Law of Peoples," in *The Law of Peoples* (Cambridge, MA: Harvard University Press, 1999), 60–7.

[108] Ibid., 131, 143.

[109] George and Wolfe, "Introduction," in *Natural Law and Public Reason*, 1–2.

[110] Ibid., 2.

[111] In a notorious footnote in the first edition of *Political Liberalism*, Rawls speculated that applied public reason would lead to a woman's right to abort an unwanted fetus during the first three months of pregnancy (243, n.32). Later, he clarified his position, explaining that he had not intended what he said in the earlier footnote to be an argument in favor of a right to abortion. He then stated that he did not know whether the balance of public reasons would support such a right or the denial of such a right. Rawls, "The Idea of Public Reason Revisited," 169, n.80.

determine whether the law in question is publicly justified only on a case-by-case basis. In addition, the exclusive principle of public reason that I have defended as the best understanding of public justification requires considerable self-restraint on the part of those, like myself, who would like to see our society become more secular. The raison d'être of public reason is intractable moral disagreement about the nature of the best human life. As such, reasonable people should not draw inferences from premises that are too deeply embedded in particular secular or perfectionist liberal doctrines when they are trying to convince others. This also means that atheists and agnostics may not put theists at legal disadvantages. A citizen who is committed to public justification would also deny political authority to anyone who seeks to treat opposite-sex couples unfairly.[112] Those who disapprove of homosexuality have no more right to express their disapproval of it in public law than non-Catholics would have to express their moral disapproval of Roman Catholicism and to enact laws that reflect such disapproval.

In terms of an exclusive principle of public reason, the denial of the right to marry for same-sex couples is a relatively easy case. Among other things, what is at stake is the right of same-sex couples to live without legal disadvantages and to be treated with equal concern and respect without judgment by the majority about the intrinsic merits of their sexual identity and way of life. That does not mean that the content of some human lives may not be qualitatively better or worse than others. A perfectionist principle of some kind is likely to guide most people when they make their most important, self-regarding personal choices. That is appropriate in most contexts of choice but not in all of them. From the standpoint of public justification, the quality or worth of the lives of others is politically irrelevant. When public laws must be enacted, citizens should not give their own secular or religious beliefs the force of law because of the inherent difficulty of justifying these beliefs to others who are bound to find them too controversial to support unequal treatment. That is what it means to live in a political community with others in the absence of a shared understanding of the human good. Everyone should be prepared to cast their positions on fundamental political questions to one another in terms of reasons that all reasonable persons could be expected to accept as fair enough for purposes of making a final decision. That means that those who oppose same-sex marriage have the burden of explaining to their fellow gay and lesbian citizens why same-sex couples are so differentially situated, vis-à-vis civil marriage, that the right to enter into such a legal relationship is properly denied to them. So far, opponents of same-sex marriage have been able to offer only nonpublic reasons in

---

[112] Cf. Macedo, "Liberal Civic Education and Religious Fundamentalism?" 480. Macedo claims that political liberals would deny decision-making authority to those who would create principles of justice based on their view of the whole truth.

support of limiting the definition of marriage to opposite-sex couples; thus, they have failed to publicly justify unequal treatment of gays and lesbians.

At times, compromise may be politically expedient. The notion of civil unions or domestic partnerships as a proxy for marriage has the appeal that it does because it is less likely to antagonize social conservatives who oppose same sex-marriage on religious grounds and consider same-sex marriage a threat to the traditional institution of opposite-sex civil marriage.[113] Still, tactical considerations should not blind us to the fact that laws that limit marriage to same-sex couples are unreasonable inasmuch as gay and lesbian citizens would never deny the right to marriage to opposite-sex couples even if they had the political power do to so. Those who oppose same-sex marriage on religious grounds need not support laws that discriminate against gay and lesbian citizens. After all, to believe that a certain act should be legally permissible is not to morally approve of that act.[114] One could believe that divorce is wrong and still believe that the dissolution of civil marriages should be permitted. One could believe that a particular kind of sexual activity is depraved or degrading and still not believe that such behavior should be illegal. There are other ways of expressing moral disapproval in a free society. It hardly follows from the fact that a person morally disapproves of a particular way of life that that way of life should be proscribed or that its adherents should be treated unequally. In a liberal society, a presumption in favor of individual liberty and equal treatment means that personal choices about human flourishing must be separated, as much as possible, from the moral basis of state coercion.[115] In the case of same-sex marriage, religious reasons must be excluded from this basis. A reason that would serve as the rationale for a ban on same-sex marriage must not only be mutually intelligible; it also must be good enough to be accepted by all reasonable persons.

Because all reasonable persons do not share the reasons that opponents of same-sex marriage have offered and, more important, are justified in not sharing them, a law that does not extend the same right to gays and lesbians is insufficiently publicly justified. That is not to say that some of those who oppose same-sex marriage here in California do not recognize that their

---

[113] Not all religious groups oppose same-sex marriage. See Eskridge, *The Case for Same-Sex Marriage*, 46–7. Many Americans favor protecting homosexuals from discrimination in employment and housing, yet they are not ready to say that their intimate relationships should be treated identically to those of gays and lesbians. See Andrew Sullivan, "The Conservative Case," in *Same-Sex Marriage: Pro and Con*, ed. Andrew Sullivan (New York: Vintage Books, 1997), xxii.

[114] See Posner, "Homosexuality," 186.

[115] William Galston's idea of a "rebuttable presumption in favor of liberty" is a useful way of understanding where the burden of proof lies. William A. Galston, *Liberal Pluralism: The Implications of Value Pluralism for Political Theory and Practice* (Cambridge: Cambridge University Press, 2002), 19.

primary reasons are nonpublic. In their defense of a yes vote on Proposition 8, they claimed that the legal recognition of same-sex marriage would undermine opposite-sex marriage and have all sorts of horrible consequences. However, they did not specify the cause-and-effect relationship, and the divorce rate in California has not gone up since the California Supreme Court's ruling. Their additional effort to frame the issue in a manner that makes it seem as if one could be tolerant and still oppose same-sex marriage on religious grounds made political sense, but it revealed something else as well: most of those who do not see such marriage as a civil rights matter do not believe that is it morally acceptable to impose their views on others without adequate justification. The "Yes on Prop 8" campaign went out of its way to try to convince California voters that public reasons underlie their opposition and to conceal their real reasons.

As I have explained, those public reasons do not exist. A reasonable person is not going to vote yes on Proposition 8 because the Catholic Church would be forced to marry same-sex couples or because priests would be sued for discrimination. The strategy of those who supported Proposition 8 reflects the fact that, at some level, most California voters endorse the principle that a conception of the good should not be forced on others. After all, few of them would ever consent to live in a political society in which the majority would be able to restrict their personal freedom without adequate justification. This may be asking a lot of ordinary persons, but this is the civic duty of tolerance that we owe to our fellow citizens, even when we believe their life choices to be foolish, misguided, or morally suspect. That is an essential part of what it means to live with others who do not share, and cannot ever be expected to share, the same ideas about what is most worthwhile in human life. Opponents of same-sex marriage must try harder to understand gays and lesbians as they understand themselves and then produce reasons that gay and lesbian persons could not reasonably reject. They expect, and probably take for granted, that those who disagree with their religious convictions at a deeper level would not put them at a legal disadvantage even if nontheists constituted a legislative majority.

We should not forget that opposite-sex couples have a fundamental right to marry, and that right will never be taken away. Moreover, it does not require a lot of imagination or empathy to appreciate how important marriage may be to the happiness of all human beings, including those who are not straight.[116] Nor does one have to be perceptive to recognize that gay, lesbian, bisexual, and transgender persons are still discriminated against but it may be very difficult to identify and prove in a legal proceding.[117] It is nearly impossible to avoid the conclusion that those who oppose same-sex marriage do so primarily because they believe homosexuality to be morally wrong on religious grounds. From the standpoint of public justification, moral disapproval by itself is not a sufficiently public reason. Such disapproval would have to be coupled with reasons that went beyond such disapproval, such as harm to others.[118] Without a religious basis, fewer people would be opposed to same-sex marriages.

[118] See Sonu Bedi, *Rejecting Rights* (New York: Cambridge University Press, 2009), 111–112.

NINE

Harder Cases

In the previous chapter, I explained why *Yoder* and same-sex marriage are relatively easy because those on the wrong side use nonpublic reasons to underwrite their respective positions. What is missing from their accounts is an explanation of why an ideal reasonable dissenter would not reject their reasons. In enacting public laws, everyone has a very good reason not to act for certain reasons, namely those based on their deepest convictions, provided that others do likewise, and the Court must ensure that lawmakers do not rely on those kinds of reasons. In the case of religious freedom, the state may not rely on judgments about religious practices and ways of life on the merits, and there should be a strong presumption in favor of free exercise of religion and in favor of personal freedom more generally. In the case of same-sex marriage, moral disapproval of same-sex intimacy or reasons closely related to this view should not serve as the basis of denying marriage licenses to gays and lesbians. The cases of *Yoder* and same-sex marriage would have been more difficult if both sides had offered sufficiently public reasons of more or less equal strength.

In this chapter, I explain how a judge, who is committed to public jus-tification, should go about deciding harder cases, namely those involving affirmative action and abortion, and then I use the difficulty of those cases to illustrate the limits of public justification. At the outset, the reader should keep in mind that the mere existence of hard cases, where no answer is clearly publicly justified, is not a decisive objection to the use of an exclusive principle of public reason. The reader should be suspicious of any theory of constitutional adjudication that purports to employ a decision procedure that spits out clear-cut answers to hard constitutional questions. Meeting the standard of public justification happens only when the person offering such justification acts in good faith with sensitivity to all of the relevant details of the case and awareness of their implications with respect to freedom and equality. Such a standard cannot save a judge who has the wrong motives or lacks wisdom.

My descriptions here of how judges should approach harder cases are only attempts to offer guidance. The reader can take them or leave them, but that does not relieve readers or anyone else of the duty of explaining which kinds of reasons they believe to be good enough to justify the law in question. Above all, a judge who tries to hold lawmakers to an exclusive principle of public reason must be prepared for the likelihood of reasonable disagreement in such cases. A judge who does not anticipate such disagreement or cares too much about the result is less likely to address the legitimate concerns of reasonable dissenters. Thus, the best answer in such cases is not the best "because it is certainly true but because it is reasonable in the epistemic circumstances."[1] It may turn out that there is no most publicly justified answer to a very hard constitutional question that all reasonable persons would or should accept. In addition, provided that the majority opinion has shown why the state has met its burden of proof by crossing the threshold of public justification, a reasonable dissenter ought to accept its reasoning and the conclusion that follows from it, even when he or she does not fully agree.

Although most of us speak of affirmative action and abortion as if they were single issues, each consists of a number of overlapping but distinct issues that merit individualized attention. It is misleading to lump all affirmative action or abortion cases into a category like "affirmative action" or "abortion," as if the details of the cases were beside the point. Without being inconsistent, one could believe that a particular affirmative action plan is sufficiently publicly justified but that another one with different features falls short of the standard, depending on the particulars. One could believe that abortion should be legally permitted in some circumstances, to save the life of the mother or to preserve her health, but not in others. In a common law system, courts do not only try to decide cases on their individual merits but also try to establish rules or principles that lower courts are supposed to use as precedent in similar cases in the future. At the same time, the strength of public reasons is bound to vary with the unique facts of each case, and it is up to judges to discern their relative strength and explain to reasonable dissenters why they weighed those reasons the way that they did.

I. AFFIRMATIVE ACTION

A. Overview

The constitutional text does not ban affirmative action.[2] The Fourteenth Amendment does not mention the practice by name or refer to any of its

---

[1] I borrow this wording from Catharine Z. Elgin, *Considered Judgment* (Princeton, NJ: Princeton University Press, 1996), ix.

[2] Cass R. Sunstein, *One Case at a Time: Judicial Minimalism on the Supreme Court*, (Cambridge, MA: Harvard University Press, 1999), 125.

synonyms, such as "preferential treatment."[3] President John F. Kennedy first used the term *affirmative action* in an executive order in 1962 as a means of ending discrimination in employment by the government and contractors.[4] Furthermore, equal protection of the laws cannot mean identical treatment, or else the state could never make legislative classifications at all. Obviously, the state may discriminate on the basis of certain reasons, and under rational basis standard of review, just about any reason that the state relies on will suffice. The state would not be acting unconstitutionally if it charged out-of-state residents more for tuition than in-state residents at public universities or if it set the driving age at sixteen. Therefore, one cannot simply argue that so-called preferential treatment for a person of an underrepresented minority group is automatically unconstitutional, as if he or she were deducing that conclusion from a premise in the text. It is easy to blame the Court for unnecessarily complicating affirmative action, but a closer look at what the Court has said in the most important affirmative action cases reveals a more charitable interpretation: the Court found itself in the unenviable position of having to produce an answer to a constitutional question that would be wrong in the eyes not only of many people but also of many reasonable people. As a compromise over a divisive political issue, perhaps there is something to be said on behalf of what the Court did in its most recent affirmative action cases involving higher education, but my concern lies in determining whether the arguments that the state put forth in them were sufficiently publicly justified.

In *Bakke*, the Court produced a number of opinions that did little to clarify the constitutionality of affirmative action plans.[5] Four of the justices believed that the set-aside program for racial and ethnic minorities, sixteen out of one hundred seats in the first-year class at the University of California, Davis, Medical School, should be subject to only intermediate scrutiny standard of review and therefore was constitutional. This conclusion was predicated on the reasonable belief that white persons, who have not been victimized by racial discrimination, should not be able to take advantage of the highest standard of review, strict scrutiny for racial classifications, and

---

[3] It is fairly clear that the original public understanding of equal protection of the laws meant something like "equal protection of individuals by equal enforcement of the generally applicable laws and equal executive action to protect individuals from violations of their legal rights." The function assigned by the modern case law was originally understood to be performed by the privileges or immunities clause. However, during Reconstruction, in a 5–4 decision, the Court ruled that this clause only prohibited state infringement of the rights of national citizenship, which did not include many of the most basic civil rights, like the right to work. See the Slaughterhouse Cases, 83 U.S. (Wall) 36 (1873). I am indebted to an anonymous reviewer of the book manuscript for this point.

[4] Steven M. Cahn, "Introduction," in *The Affirmative Action Debate*, 2nd ed., ed. Steven M. Cahn (New York: Routledge, 2002), xi.

[5] Regents of the University of California v. Bakke, 438 U.S. 265 (1978).

benefit from its very strong presumption of unconstitutionality. The effect of applying strict scrutiny to such a racial classification would be to reject the difference between invidious and benign discrimination by treating a white applicant as a member of a suspect or quasi-suspect group that deserves as much special judicial protection as a "discrete and insular minority"[6] that had suffered discrimination in the past, continued to be discriminated against in the present, and was likely to be politically vulnerable. Oddly enough, in the context of gender discrimination, then-Associate Justice Rehnquist made a similar point years earlier when he argued, in his dissent in *Craig v. Boren*, that men, as a class, should not receive the added constitutional protection of intermediate scrutiny.[7]

Even when one is not convinced that so-called benign discrimination in favor of underrepresented racial and ethnic minorities is so benign after all, at least for those who do not benefit from the affirmative action plan in question and may be put at a competitive disadvantage by it, one is hard pressed to consider affirmative action the constitutional equivalent of the kind of racial discrimination that the equal protection clause was designed to prevent. In Justice Brennan's words, "[W]hites as a class [do not] have any of the traditional indicia of suspectness: the class is not saddled with such disabilities, or subjected to such a history of purposeful unequal treatment, or relegated to such a position of political powerlessness as to command extraordinary protection from the majoritarian political process."[8] Brennan could have added that the traditional rationale for using strict scrutiny in the first place would not seem to apply to racial classifications that are not premised on the inferiority of one racial group and the superiority of another racial group.

No critic of affirmative action has ever argued that reverse discrimination stigmatizes white persons as second-class citizens or reinforces notions of white inferiority. Typically, those who oppose affirmative action claim that such programs are unfair to applicants who do not receive extra points or a plus in the admissions process due to their race; their race functions as a minus factor. In addition, critics often take out of context Justice John Marshall Harlan's famous quotation from *Plessy*, that "Our constitution is color-blind," and use it to support the conclusion that all racial classifications, regardless of their underlying purposes, are unconstitutional. In the end, this claim may be true, but it is not too much to ask from those who advocate a color-blind approach to affirmative action cases to explain why white persons, as a racial group, would qualify as members of a suspect class, given how race has affected the allocation of the benefits and burdens

[6] U.S. v. Carolene Products Co., 304 U.S. 144, 152, n.4 (1938) (Stone, J., majority)
[7] Craig v. Boren, 429 U.S. 190 (1976) (Rehnquist, J., dissenting).
[8] Regents of the University of California v. Bakke, 438 U.S. 265 (1978).

of social cooperation over time in our society. Someone who disagreed with this approach would be entitled to such an explanation, and someone who cared about public justification would try to offer such an explanation, which is not to say that it would convince those who disagree.

In *Bakke*, four of the justices believed that the set-aside program was illegal racial discrimination under Title VI of the 1964 Civil Rights Act. As everyone knows, Justice Lewis Powell cast the pivotal vote, writing that a quota system – the explicit reservation of seats that only underrepresented racial and ethnic minorities could fill – was not narrowly tailored, whereas the Harvard Plan, where the admissions committee used race only as a plus factor in more individualized review of each applicant's file, was narrowly tailored to serve the legislative objective of non-racial diversity. Perhaps this was an example of splitting the difference, and thus was politically expedient; subsequently, lower federal courts were divided over whether Powell's opinion counted as the law of the land. Five of the justices, including Powell, believed that an admissions committee could take race into account in the admissions process as one variable among others that might make an application more attractive. Four of the other justices believed that such a quota was illegal under federal law. In *Croson*, five of the justices finally agreed on what standard of review race-conscious affirmative action programs would precipitate, namely strict scrutiny, but the majority opinion still left a number of important questions unanswered with respect to programs that were less vulnerable than that of *Croson*, such as one based on adequate legislative findings of past racial discrimination by the state.[9] The Court reaffirmed strict scrutiny as the appropriate standard of review for affirmative action in *Adarand* when it ruled that a federal affirmative action program that gave contractors on highway construction projects a financial incentive to hire minority-owned firms as subcontractors was unconstitutional.[10] As Justice Sandra Day O'Connor also noted, foreshadowing what was to come in the two University of Michigan affirmative action cases, strict scrutiny is not necessarily "strict in theory, fatal in fact."[11] That was the first step toward the confusion that still surrounds the constitutionality of affirmative action.

B. The University of Michigan Cases: *Grutter* and *Gratz*

In *Grutter v. Bollinger*, in a 5–4 decision, the Court upheld the race-conscious affirmative action plan at the University of Michigan Law School, where the admissions committee treated undergraduate grade point

---

[9] Richmond v. Croson, 488 U.S. 469 (1989).
[10] Adarand Constructors v. Pena, 515 U.S. 200 (1995).
[11] Richmond v. Croson, 488 U.S. 469 (1989).

average and LSAT score as hard variables and treated race as a soft variable, like enthusiasm of the recommenders, quality of undergraduate institution, and difficulty of undergraduate curriculum.[12] Whether the committee really treated race as a soft variable is in dispute, but the law school sought to enroll a critical mass of underrepresented racial and ethnic minority students in the name of racial and ethnic diversity so that such students would not feel isolated and could participate meaningfully in classroom discussions. A wider variety of perspectives in the classroom would break down negative stereotypes that white students might have about nonwhite students, facilitate interracial understanding, and enhance the learning experience for all students. As a result, law students would become more sensitive to cultural differences and be better able to serve their clients and cooperate with their colleagues when they worked as lawyers. Although Justice Scalia mocked those in the majority who believed that diversity, because of its educational benefits, was a compelling state interest, it is clear that a variety of perspectives in the classroom would not only improve the quality of classroom discussions but also challenge the preconceptions that many law students, especially those who come from privileged backgrounds, might have about others. The law school was using race and ethnicity as a proxy for life experience on the assumption that, as a statistical generalization, those who are members of underrepresented minority groups are likely to have different and valuable perspectives on, say, the racial biases of the legal system. At the very least, white students might become more racially sensitive after being exposed to ideas that nonwhite students might express, which is bound to have some educational value in a diverse society like our own. It is hard to see how someone could practice law competently in certain fields, such as immigration law, without an extensive knowledge of the norms of the cultures of his or her clientele. That would count as a public reason.

Justice O'Connor cast the deciding vote, and she ostensibly applied strict scrutiny to the racial classification in question but found that the state (1) had a compelling interest in ensuring such diversity in the law school and in the legal profession, and (2) that the means used – "holistic" or individualized review – were narrowly tailored. With respect to (2), O'Connor believed that means-end fit was not the functional equivalent of a constitutionally forbidden racial quota because some white students, with less impressive numbers, had been accepted over some nonwhite applicants and the number of applicants who benefited from the affirmative action plan fluctuated from year to year.[13] For O'Connor, this meant that the admissions committee was really doing what it claimed: using race as one soft variable among others in the admissions process.

[12] Grutter v. Bollinger, 539 U.S. 306 (2003).
[13] Terry H. Anderson, *The Pursuit of Fairness: A History of Affirmative Action* (New York: Oxford University Press, 2004), 271.

There is little point, I think, to going over the obvious criticisms of her position in much detail. As Justice Kennedy noted in his dissent, holistic review in the name of achieving a critical mass of underrepresented minority students was indistinguishable in its effects from unconstitutional quotas. Unless one is more concerned with appearances, it is hard to make the principled distinction that O'Connor tries to make between assigning a certain number of points to race and assigning a certain amount of weight to it when its form should be constitutionally irrelevant. In admitting every academically qualified African American or Latino, the University of Michigan was admitting students with much lower GPAs and LSAT scores who would have been rejected if they had been white.[14] What should matter is how the admissions committee is taking into account the race of an applicant in the admissions process, that is, how much race actually increases an applicant's chances of being accepted. Presumably, the concern that Powell had in *Bakke* was that the admissions committee was assigning far too much weight to race through a quota system whose effect was for white students to compete for eighty-four of the one hundred seats in the first-year class and for nonwhite students to compete for the remaining sixteen in a two-track admissions system. That use of race was not narrowly tailored to the end or non-racial diversity. The best interpretation of Powell's plurality opinion is that a two-track admissions system turned race into what would later be called a hard variable, especially when applicants who were accepted through the affirmative action program had significantly lower numbers than their white counterparts. Those of Allan Bakke, for instance, were much better than those who had been accepted under Davis's affirmative action program.[15]

In *Grutter*, the director of admissions stated that there was no number, percentage, or range of numbers or percentages that constitute a critical mass. But she also testified that the critical mass of underrepresented minority students could not be achieved if admissions decisions were based primarily on LSAT scores and undergraduate grade point averages. In other words, the admissions committee had to use race as more than a soft variable to ensure a critical mass of underrepresented minority students. As the expert for the law school stated, had the admissions committee not used race as a variable, underrepresented minority students would have constituted only 4 percent of the entering class of 2000, as opposed to 14.5 percent.[16] Those figures indicate that, at least in some years, the admissions committee used race as more than one factor among many others. That should not be surprising when the purpose of the affirmative action program was to ensure that the law school was sufficiently racially diverse.

[14] Ibid., 269.
[15] Barbara A. Perry, *The Michigan Affirmative Action Cases* (Lawrence: University Press of Kansas), 22.
[16] Ibid.

It is hard to reconcile O'Connor's position in *Gratz* with that of *Grutter*, where she joined the majority and struck down the University of Michigan's affirmative action program for undergraduate admissions on the ground that an additional 20 points for race out of a possible 150 points functioned too much like a forbidden quota because it meant that qualified minority applicants were almost always admitted under the plan.[17] As Justice David Souter explained in his dissent, the twenty-point bonus for race does not differ substantively from the law school's practice of using race as a factor in its holistic review of each applicant's file, especially when nonminority applicants could receive an extra twenty points on the basis of athletic ability or socioeconomic disadvantage. In making a comparison between a more quantitative approach like the assignment of points and holistic review, one would have to know how much weight the admissions committee typically assigned to the race of an applicant who qualified for the affirmative action program. That the number of such applicants who were admitted varied over time suggests that membership in an underrepresented minority group was a more significant variable in some years than in others. That may have been because of the composition of the admissions committee or statistical variation in the pool of qualified underrepresented minority applicants, which was more rarefied in some years than in others.

Although it would have looked worse, the undergraduate admissions committee could have taken away twenty points from those who were members of overrepresented racial groups to increase diversity on campus. The point is that there is no way to know whether using a twenty-point bonus is any worse than using race as a soft variable in the holistic review of an applicant's file without being privy to all of the details of how the law school admissions committee made its decisions. It makes even less sense to claim that racial or ethnic diversity is a compelling state interest and that a university may use race, but not too much, in trying to achieve this interest. If a law school has a compelling interest in ensuring a racially diverse student body, then it should be able to use race as a variable in the admissions process and assign a numerical value to it when doing so would be expedient. Otherwise, it may fall short of its goals. In this context, affirmative action is about race, and the Court has announced that ensuring racial diversity is a compelling interest. Even the most effective outreach programs are unlikely to accomplish what can be accomplished through race-conscious measures.[18] At the same time, the Court cannot overlook the extent to which being a member of an overrepresented racial group may disadvantage an applicant in the admissions process. As Justice Scalia pointed out during oral argument, that

---

[17] Gratz v. Bollinger, 539 U.S. 244 (2003).

[18] Bob Laird, *The Case for Affirmative Action in University Admission* (Berkeley, CA: Bay Tree Publishing, 2005), 161–6.

"very few people are being treated unconstitutionally" would not render an unconstitutional statute constitutional.[19]

The less charitable interpretation of O'Connor's apparently inconsistent positions in the two cases is that she was simply looking for a political compromise that would not upset either side too much. It is harder to be upset in the aftermath of any Court decision when its implications are not clear. The more charitable interpretation is that she recognized the inherent difficulty of such a case and the inevitability of reasonable disagreement about its proper outcome. She does not use the technical language of Rawlsian public reason or public justification, but she deserves some credit for her approach – looking for reasons that all reasonable persons should be able to share – even if she failed to find them. One could even argue that most employers expect college and law school graduates to work effectively with those from different backgrounds, and that is an important public reason.[20] If holistic review worked the way that it was supposed to work, where race really was one variable among many others, such an affirmative action plan would be arguably sufficiently publicly justified. The trouble in *Grutter* is that the law school was using race as more than a soft variable, which is not surprising given its aim of increasing racial diversity, but this fact formed the basis of the dissent's claim that the affirmative action plan in question functioned like a constitutionally forbidden quota. True, O'Connor left herself vulnerable to the charge that she cares only about results and not about the quality of the legal argument(s) that support that result. As a matter of fact, that may be accurate, and we may never know what was going through her head when she decided which side to take in all of the affirmative action cases that she has participated in.

Still, a public justification rationale is available for both cases. Quotas and mechanical points do not provide a reason to denied applicants that at least some of them could accept as reasonable. They could not accept that race alone is a good-enough reason for their unequal treatment. Holistic evaluation in light of the value of diversity to all students is a reason that they could accept because each candidate is assessed on the totality of his or her merits, and one of those merits is race, because of its educational value. The same could be said on behalf of admitting a white applicant with lower numbers because of her unique background, such as growing up on a farm, serving in the military, or being a community organizer. A reasonable person, then, might accept the fairness of such a plan. A white applicant who was not admitted would not have a better complaint than an applicant who did not have unique life experiences or terrific letters of recommendation.

---

[19] Perry, *Michigan Affirmative Action Cases*, 123.

[20] See Derek Bok, *Our Underachieving Colleges: A Candid Look at How Much Students Learn and Why They Should Be Learning More* (Princeton, NJ: Princeton University Press, 2006), 74.

The outcome may be the same, but the reasons provided for that outcome will differ.[21] A reasonable person knows a hard case when he or she sees it, and thus will not make it seem as if there is little or nothing to be said on behalf of the position that he or she disagrees with. It is hard to read Scalia's cavalier dismissal of the educational benefits of diversity, dripping with sarcasm, and not conclude that he just does not see why a reasonable person would disagree with him. O'Connor can be faulted for not writing an opinion in *Grutter* that can be easily squared with her position in *Gratz*, but a judge who cares about public justification will look for these kinds of reasons that everyone can share in finding a solution.

C. The Challenge of Affirmative Action

Cass Sunstein believes that the task of judges would be easier if they had a better understanding of the consequences of real affirmative action programs.[22] That would be helpful, no doubt, but more unrealistic than he seems to believe. One does not have to be a social scientist to recognize the challenge of trying to disaggregate variables in determining what affirmative action programs actually do. Also, it is unlikely that most judges would have sufficient sophistication in social science methodologies to be able to make accurate empirical judgments and causal inferences. Recently, Richard Sander has tried to show that affirmative action in law school admissions decreases the number of African American lawyers because African American applicants, who receive a boost in the admissions process due to their race, are misplaced at law schools that exceed their academic abilities, resulting in bad grades and lower bar-passage rates.[23] If his mismatch hypothesis is correct, then those findings would count as public reasons, and the question, then, would be how judges ought to weigh them. In the past, without the support of statistical evidence, Justice Thomas has made a similar point about the costs of affirmative action programs for African American applicants. It is not evident how researchers could test the hypothesis that "racial preferences reinforce the dreadful stereotype that blacks just aren't academically talented."[24] As one commentator remarks, "The empirical situation remains too complex to assess with any confidence."[25] Even if that situation changes, and we learn that Sander is right, the negative consequences that he makes so much of are not dispositive of the constitutional

---

[21] I owe all of this point to an anonymous reviewer of the book manuscript.

[22] Sunstein, *One Case at a Time*, 255.

[23] Richard Sander, "The Tributaries to the River," 25 *Law and Social Inquiry* (2000), 557–63.

[24] See Stephan Thernstrom and Abigail Thernstrom, "Does Your 'Merit' Depend on Your Race: A Rejoinder to Bowen and Bok," in *The Affirmative Action Debate*, 2nd ed., ed. Steven M. Cahn (New York: Routledge, 2002), 187.

[25] George Sher, "Diversity," in *The Affirmative Action Debate*, 2nd ed., ed. Steven M. Cahn (New York: Routledge, 2002), 192.

permissibility of affirmative action admission plans in law schools. One could accept those unintended consequences as a cost of affirmative action policies, yet still believe that, on balance, the benefits outweigh the costs. Or one could simply point out, as proponents and opponents of affirmative action programs often do, that such programs either are fair or unfair, and that question cannot be reduced to empirical claims about their positive or negative consequences. There is no escape from the moral question of whether a law school may take race into account in admissions decisions.

Affirmative action is a hard case for a number of empirical and normative reasons. First, the disagreement involves who has been wronged, what is due to them, who should pay the costs, and what should be done to reduce racial inequality. How many generations must elapse before claims of compensation for past racial discrimination lose their force? How does one measure the effects of past injustice on specific individuals? There are three main justifications for affirmative action: (1) to offset past discrimination (compensation), (2) to counteract present unfairness (a level playing field), and (3) to achieve future equality (diversity).[26] Second, the concept of a "preference" is ambiguous.[27] A preference could be used to break ties, as a plus factor, to trump all other factors, or serve as quota. Third, affirmative action programs may be more justified with respect to some ethnic and racial groups than with respect to others and may be more justified in some contexts than in others. For example, an affirmative action program that attempted to increase the number of Latino and African American law enforcement officers in a community with large numbers of these groups, in the midst of cultural and language barriers, would be unequivocally justified in a way that an affirmative action program, say, in hiring faculty in law schools might not be. Those officers might be less likely to commit or be charged with police brutality, improving the relationship between law enforcement officers and the communities in which they serve and reducing the number of civil rights lawsuits filed against the police department. Such officers also might have more credibility on the witness stand in the eyes of some of the jurors during a trial. It would be much more difficult for a defense attorney to insinuate that his or her client was the victim of racial profiling or a racist conspiracy if the investigating officers were of the same race as the defendant.

In *The Shape of the River*, William Bowen and Derek Bok point out that just because applicants have a better academic record, based on grades in high school and SAT scores, does not necessarily mean that they worked

---

[26] Steven M. Cahn, "Introduction," in *The Affirmative Action Debate*, 2nd ed., ed. Steven M. Cahn (New York: Routledge, 2002), xiii.

[27] Ibid.

harder in high school and thus, are more deserving of admission.[28] Any kind of academic record will be the product of many different factors, a large number of which will be outside the control of the applicant. Bowen and Bok put their finger on the issue in a footnote where they write that one cannot define merit in the context of higher education without determining "the mission of the educational institution involved."[29] In defining *merit*, one must have a theory of the purpose(s) of public universities and more often than not, reasonable people are going to have different ideas about what this purpose(s) should consist of. Ronald Dworkin observes that merit cannot be defined in the abstract and that the race of an applicant might be a legitimate consideration in the admissions process.[30] As such, one could not simply play the merit card and beg the question with respect to the proper definition of merit, without assuming that one's race is never a relevant characteristic of those who might contribute to the quality of a first-year class or who are successful in the medical or legal professions.

At the same time, reasonable people will have different ideas about the educational mission of state universities, and as such, they may have different but reasonable conceptions of merit. If one is more concerned with cultivating the minds of those who have the highest grades and test scores, on the assumption that these figures exhibit academic potential or predict likely academic success, then one is going to define merit differently than a person does who is skeptical that grades and test scores reflect academic achievement or potential, disturbed by the unfairness of the educational system and its implications for those who are socioeconomically disadvantaged, or convinced that the racial integration of certain professions is a prerequisite of racial harmony. A reasonable person would acknowledge that grades and test scores are relevant in the process of determining which applicants will be admitted, given what is expected academically from a typical college student. No supporter of affirmative action believes that the members of certain underrepresented racial and ethnic minorities with the lowest grades and test scores should routinely be admitted over those who have much better numbers. Likewise, no reasonable person is comfortable with the fact that one's race is correlated with one's socioeconomic status, and thus bound to affect one's educational opportunities.

Ultimately, in terms of public justification, what makes determining the constitutionality of affirmative action in higher education so challenging is not that there are no sufficiently public reasons but that there are too many of them, and it is not evident where the balance of such reasons lies. On the

---

[28] William G. Bowen and Derek Bok, "The Meaning of 'Merit'," in *The Affirmative Action Debate*, 2nd ed., ed. Steven M. Cahn (New York: Routledge, 2002), 177.

[29] Ibid., 182, n.3.

[30] Ronald Dworkin, *A Matter of Principle* (Cambridge, MA: Harvard University Press, Belknap Press, 1985), 299.

one hand, there seem to be sufficiently public reasons that justify at least some race-conscious affirmative action plans. The benefits might include producing more role models, breaking down attitudes of white superiority, enhancing opportunity for those who are members of groups that have been victimized in the past, ensuring a greater plurality of alternative life experiences and their accompanying perspectives, reducing racial misunderstanding, and racially integrating the legal profession so that lawyers are better able to serve all of their clients and that the law works for all persons and not only for the rich and famous. One might be convinced, as I am, that a lack of culturally diversity in the classroom detracts from the quality of classroom discussions in some classes more than in others. In a less diverse classroom, students are less likely to be exposed to different perspectives or unconventional views that they ought to encounter sooner rather than later in their lives. Surely, during a discussion of racial profiling or racial bias in capital cases, a more racially diverse class is more likely to produce the comments that will help all of the students to appreciate the seriousness and complexity of such problems. Whether they realize it or not, the more limited their life experiences, the more narrow their understandings are bound to be, and people who come from culturally homogeneous environments are less likely to be racially sensitive.

On the other hand, equally important, there seem to be sufficiently public reasons that support the opposite conclusion, leading to a standoff. The costs might include losses of efficiency when less academically qualified applicants are selected over more qualified ones, backlash from applicants who rightly or wrongly believe that they would have been admitted but for affirmative action, reinforcement of the stereotype that certain persons are less academically prepared and intelligent than others, and exacerbation of racial conflict. My own view is that one could make a sufficiently public argument for either conclusion: that, in principle, affirmative action is or is not constitutional. Thus, the Court would be justified in giving the state the benefit of the doubt by letting most affirmative programs stand, subjecting them to the intermediate scrutiny standard of review. In terms of public reasons, there is enough to be said for continuing to rectify the effects of past racial injustices and to offset the benefits that white persons received when "affirmative action was white."[31] Coupled with the likely educational benefits of greater cultural diversity in the classroom, these considerations cut in favor of the view that a law school may take race into account in the admissions process. Those affirmative action programs that do not treat race as a hard variable are more likely to be sufficiently publicly justified.

---

[31] I borrow the phrase from Ira Katznelson, *When Affirmative-Action Was White: An Untold History of Racial Inequality in Twentieth Century America* (New York: W. W. Norton, 2005).

For these reasons, I believe that courts should defer to legislative judgments about the need for most race-conscious affirmative action plans in higher education, which is not to say that a particular affirmative action could not fall short of the standard of public justification. These days, politically, the question is almost moot, but a reasonable person could have reached either conclusion concerning the constitutionality of most affirmative action plans. A reasonable person not only recognizes the obvious reasons for treating certain nonwhite persons differently in the admissions process but also is concerned that certain applicants, who are not the beneficiaries of affirmative action plans, are likely to bear the costs, which arguably is unfair to them, especially when they are not socially and economically privileged. In summary, neither side is right or wrong in the sense that the balance of public reasons clearly supports each side's position.

II. ABORTION

A. Overview

The constitutionality of laws that prohibit or restrict abortion is perhaps the paradigmatic example of a hard case but for different reasons than those that make affirmative action a hard case. This is so not because of the intensity of feelings on the part of those who would describe themselves as pro-choice or pro-life but because of the need to settle the issue of the moral status of a fetus. That question must be answered, but it is not clear that public reasoning would be of any use. Many Americans still believe that *Roe v. Wade* was wrongly decided and should be overturned.[32] *Roe* will never come to enjoy the consensus that surrounds *Brown*, the greatest civil rights decision of the past century. In the eighteenth and early nineteenth centuries, abortion was illegal only after quickening, the stage at which the pregnant woman could feel the movement of the fetus.[33] Prior to the decriminalization of abortion laws in the United States, most doctors who performed abortions were not "dirty and dangerous back-alley butchers."[34]

The issue of abortion in the United States is complicated because it seems to be about so many different things: the place of religion in politics and law, states' rights, the limits of legislative authority, the proper role of the

---

[32] Jack M. Balkin, "Preface," in *What* Roe v. Wade *Should Have Said: The Nation's Top Legal Experts Rewrite America's Most Controversial Decision*, ed. Jack M. Balkin (New York: New York University Press, 2005), x.

[33] Leslie J. Reagan, *When Abortion Was a Crime: Women, Medicine, and Law in the United States 1867–1973* (Berkeley: University of California Press, 1997), 8.

[34] Rickie Solinger, "Introduction: Abortion Politics and History," in *Abortion Wars: A Half Century of Struggle 1950–2000*, ed. Rickie Solinger (Berkeley: University of California Press, 1998), 4.

judiciary, the rights of parents, and reproductive freedom. Others have called attention to the relationship between the availability of legalized abortion and gender equality.[35] As Justice Blackmun wrote in his dissent in *Webster*, without legalized abortion, there would not be "full participation of women in the economic and political walks of American life."[36] There are a wide variety of positions with respect to the moral permissibility of abortion, ranging from extreme to moderate on both sides.[37] One could believe that abortion is an absolute right, and thus that the state could never prohibit or even regulate it under any circumstances, even during the third trimester. Alternatively, one could believe that abortion is always wrong, and thus that the state may prohibit it, even in cases of rape, incest, severely deformed fetuses, or when the mother's life or health is in jeopardy. The beliefs of most Americans fall in between these two extremes.[38] In this section, I am not going to rehearse all of the arguments put forth for or against either the morality or the legality of abortion or try to interpret public opinion. Rather, I am concerned with whether any arguments cross the threshold of public justification and what those arguments tell us about the limits of such justification.

B. Does *Roe* Lack a Constitutional Basis?

In *Roe v. Wade*, the holding is about as specific as any holding in an important constitutional case could be. In the beginning of his majority opinion, Justice Blackmun rejects two traditional arguments in favor of legal prohibitions on abortion: that such laws discourage so-called illicit sexual conduct and reduce the dangers associated with abortion as a medical procedure. These interests are no longer strong enough to justify such prohibitions. He then asserts that the state's interest in protecting "prenatal life" also is not strong enough and explains why a woman's right to privacy includes a right to abortion during the first two trimesters of pregnancy. Blackmun writes that during the first trimester, the state may not ban or closely regulate abortions, even to protect the mother's health. In the second trimester, the state could advance its interest in protecting her health by regulating abortion procedures, but only in ways that are reasonably related to her

---

[35] See, e.g., Laurence H. Tribe, *Abortion: The Clash of Absolutes* (New York: W. W. Norton, 1990), 105. In addition, some scholars maintain that the politics of the abortion controversy has been a referendum on the meaning of motherhood and the proper role of women. Barbara Hinkson Craig and David M. O'Brien, *Abortion and American Politics* (Chatham, NJ: Chatham House Publishers, 1993), 46; As Kristin Luker writes, "The abortion debate is actually about the meaning of women's lives." Kristin Luker, *Abortion and the Politics of Motherhood* (Berkeley: University of California Press, 1984), 193–4.

[36] Webster v. Reproductive Health Services, 492 U.S. 490, 557 (Blackmun, J., dissenting).

[37] Ronald Dworkin, *Life's Dominion: An Argument about Abortion, Euthanasia, and Individual Freedom* (New York: Vintage Books, 1994), 31.

[38] www.gallup.com/poll/1576/Abortion.aspx.

health. Blackmun lists a number of examples of permissible means to this end: ensuring that the person who performs the medical procedure is qualified and that the place where the procedure is to take place is appropriate. The state has a compelling interest in protecting fetal life only after viability, that is, at that beginning of the third trimester, "except when it is necessary to preserve the life or health of the mother."[39]

The holding of *Roe* is predicated on the right to privacy, found in the due process clause of the Fourteenth Amendment and spelled out in more detail in a number of important constitutional cases like *Pierce v. Society of Sisters*, *Meyer v. Nebraska*, and *Griswold v. Connecticut*. The best-known objection to the proposition that abortion is a constitutional right is that such a right lacks a constitutional basis.[40] This right allegedly lacks such a basis in two senses. First, the constitutional text does not contain the word *privacy*.[41] Nor, as Robert Bork has observed, is the enumerated right to abort a fetus to be found in the Constitution.[42] Critics of *Roe* also deny that the plain language of the due process clause can support the idea of substantive due process.[43] For example, Michael Stokes Paulsen insists that "[t]here is no remotely plausible argument" that supports the claim that a right to abortion can be found in the constitutional text.[44] Second, the judicial interpretations that have glossed the constitutional text over time do not support the claim that abortion is a fundamental right. In *Roe*, Rehnquist begins his dissent with the words: "I have difficulty in concluding, as the Court does, that the right of 'privacy' is involved in this case."[45] That is so, he insists, because people do not normally use the word *privacy* in the way Blackmun does in his majority opinion, and the notion of privacy, found in Fourth Amendment search and seizure cases, is not applicable. Blackmun merely asserts that the right of privacy "is broad enough to encompass a woman's decision whether or not to terminate her pregnancy."[46] As John Hart Ely pointed

---

[39] Roe v. Wade, 410 U.S. 113 (1973).

[40] Tribe, *Clash of Absolutes*, 80.

[41] See, e.g., Michael W. McConnell, "*Roe v. Wade* at Twenty-Five: Still Illegitimate," in *The Ethics of Abortion: Pro-Life vs. Pro-Choice*, 3rd ed., ed. Robert M. Baird and Stuart E. Rosenbaum (Amherst, NY: Prometheus Books, 2001), 135–8.

[42] Robert H. Bork, *The Tempting of America: The Political Seduction of the Law* (New York: Simon and Schuster, 1990), 112.

[43] Sophisticated defenders of *Roe* then move to the privileges or immunities clause or the Ninth Amendment, but the plain language of these alternative constitutional sources also does not provide clear-cut support for a constitutional right to abortion. As such, some kind of constitutional construction will be required. I owe an anonymous reviewer of this manuscript for this insight.

[44] Michael Stokes Paulsen, "Dissenting," in *What Roe v. Wade Should Have Said: The Nation's Top Legal Experts Rewrite America's Most Controversial Decision*, ed. Jack M. Balkin (New York: New York University Press, 2005), 196.

[45] Roe v. Wade, 410 U.S. 113 (1973).

[46] Ibid., 153.

out more than thirty years ago, Blackmun and the other justices in the majority never defended this assertion.[47] At the very least, dissenters are entitled to an explanation of why the state's interest in protecting fetal life prior to viability is not compelling or significant enough to override a woman's right to have an abortion. Furthermore, the right to abortion in the second trimester is almost absolute. The state "may only regulate the abortion procedure to the extent that the regulation reasonably relates to the preservation and protection of maternal health."[48]

For other reasons, Ely also believed that *Roe* was wrongly decided: "[The decision] is bad because it is bad constitutional law, or rather because it is *not* constitutional law and gives almost no sense of an obligation to try to be."[49] For him, *Roe* is a paradigmatic example of the abuse of judicial power. Instead of interpreting the Constitution, the justices in the majority rewrote it and invented a right to abortion. Ely's belief is predicated on the claim that the Constitution says nothing explicit about abortion in particular or about abortion-related and privacy issues more generally. He is right that the word *abortion* does not appear anywhere in the text and when he claims that more is involved in the decision to abort a fetus than "control over the woman's body."[50] But he is wrong to understand the scope of judicial power so narrowly in seeing lawmakers as free to do what they please in the absence of express prohibitions in the constitutional text. Such a view would give the state far too much authority and would not be consistent with the idea of limited government. There are lots of things that the state may not do that are not explicitly spelled out in the constitutional text. Does anyone really believe that the state could force women to abort their fetuses after they had already given birth to one child in the name of population control? There is no question that abortion implicates the abstract principles of freedom and equality. Thus, a legal prohibition of abortion raises a constitutional issue, even if Ely and other critics of *Roe* believe that the Court should have stayed out of this thicket. The key to understanding Ely's position is its underlying value relativism. Ely claims that the decision to give more weight to either the woman's interest or the fetus's interest involves a nonrational judgment.[51] No rational balancing of these conflicting interests is possible: neither preference is right or wrong but merely reflects the tastes or feelings of different persons. Ely then insists that the real problem is the Court's usurpation of legislative authority in the sense of exercising the power of judicial review when it should have declined

---

[47] John Hart Ely, "The Wages of Crying Wolf: A Comment on Roe v. Wade," 82 *Yale Law Journal* (1973), 924.

[48] Roe v. Wade, 410 U.S. 113 (1973).

[49] Ely, "Wages of Crying Wolf," 947.

[50] Ibid., 931.

[51] Ibid., 943.

the invitation. These two positions are not mutually exclusive. When one believes that neither conclusion is rationally justified in a particular case, it is much easier to leave such questions to legislatures, which are presumably better at aggregating the preferences of the electorate than courts are. But public reasons are the only relevant reasons in important constitutional cases, and constitutional discourse must be about why such reasons are sufficiently public and why judges should give such reasons more or less weight.

In *Casey*, the Court partially overturned *Roe* in paving the way for the state to regulate abortion more strictly during the first six months of pregnancy but reaffirmed the "essential holding of *Roe*."[52] After *Casey*, the state may restrict abortion during the first six months of pregnancy, provided that it does not put an "undue burden" on the woman's right to choose abortion.[53] One's reaction to this decision is bound to turn on the meaning of an undue burden, which O'Connor defines as a "substantial obstacle in the path of the woman who seeks an abortion."[54] What exactly an undue burden is supposed to cover is not clear, and its vagueness invites states to test its limits, and some of them have done exactly that. In *Casey*, the Court saw Pennsylvania's spousal consent provision to be such a burden, unlike legal requirements such as the twenty-four-hour waiting period, parental consent, and record keeping and reporting. What is clear, though, is that *Casey* made it easier for restrictions of abortion to survive constitutional challenges. There is a lot to criticize in the plurality opinion, but unlike Blackmun's opinion in *Roe*, the plurality did a much better job of capturing the perspective of the woman who might want an abortion: "the liberty of the women is at stake in a sense unique to the human condition and so unique to the law. The mother who carries a child to full term is subject to anxieties, to physical constraints, to pain that only she must bear.... Her suffering is too intimate and personal for the State to insist, without more, upon its own vision of the woman's role."[55] That pregnancy affects the woman who carries the fetus more than anyone else is beyond dispute, and that is probably the strongest public reason in favor of leaving the decision to abort the fetus to the woman. She is burdened by a pregnancy in a way that others are not, or at least she might experience an unwanted pregnancy in that way. A state law that gave veto power over the decision to abort to the father of the fetus would not be publicly justified because a man is not similarly situated.[56]

---

[52] Planned Parenthood of Southeastern Pennsylvania v. Casey, 505 U.S. 833, 846 (1992).

[53] Ibid., 877.

[54] Ibid., 877.

[55] Ibid., 852.

[56] The Court may have had this concern in mind when it struck down as an undue burden the part of the Pennsylvania statute that required spousal notification.

C. Stalemate

In the remainder of this chapter, I do not deal with factors that would needlessly complicate my analysis, such as rape, incest, fetal deformity, and so on. But I should add that even those who believe that abortion is morally impermissible are not eager to embrace the conclusion that rape victims who are impregnated should be forced by law to have the child of her assailant.[57] Although such cases are rare, if one sincerely believes that a zygote is a person at the moment when the sperm fertilizes the egg or when the zygote implants itself in the wall of the uterus, it should not matter whether the fetus is the product of rape or incest. A woman could not be permitted to kill her one-year-old son simply because he is the by-product of a sexual assault. As Francis Beckwith writes, "For if the unborn is fully human, then we must ask whether the relieving of the woman's mental suffering justifies the killing of an innocent human being. *But homicide of another is never justified to relieve one of emotional distress.*"[58]

That example reveals that most of us cannot but help to think in terms of public reasons from time to time and hope that we can draw from the same pool of common reasons. John Noonan tries to limit himself to reasons that theists and secularists can share.[59] As another pro-life writer puts it, "The contribution of this book is that it...searches for and presents grounded reasoning...using universal argumentation common to any person of faith or to a person of no faith."[60] In the next sentence, however, the author adds, "Religious principles must not be abandoned, or replaced, or deleted." The trouble is that reasonable people will not necessarily share these principles. A person who is opposed to abortion on moral or religious grounds but who nevertheless believes that the law should make exceptions under certain circumstances, such as rape, is not necessarily inconsistent. For most Americans, it would be unthinkable to put a woman through such an ordeal, especially when she is not responsible for the unwanted pregnancy. One could not maintain that she had assumed the risk of pregnancy by having sexual intercourse. A woman who was forced to carry her fetus to term under such conditions would suffer irreparable psychological harm and most likely would not be willing to take care of the child. Someone might respond that either abortion is immoral in all circumstances or it is not. If one really believes that abortion is the taking of human life, then it should

---

[57] Only one in five persons polled believes that there should be no exception for pregnancies that result from rape or incest. http://www.pollingreport.com/abortion.htm. N = 900 registered voters nationwide, margin of error +/– 3 percent, October 23–24, 2007.

[58] Francis J. Beckwith, *Defending Life: A Moral and Legal Case Against Abortion Choice* (New York: Cambridge University Press, 2007), 106.

[59] See John Noonan, "An Almost Absolute Value in History," in *The Morality of Abortion: Legal and Historical Perspectives* (Cambridge, MA: Harvard University Press, 1970), 51–9.

[60] Carol Crossed, "Foreword," in Vasu Murti, *The Liberal Case against Abortion* (R.A.G.E. Media, 2006), 4.

not matter how the child was conceived. But this response misses something important: reasonable people are willing to look carefully at the details and make exceptions when exceptions are warranted under the circumstances. In the case of rape, it is understandable why someone who believes that abortion is immoral might give more weight to the woman's interest in her psychological well-being. It is hard to imagine that a reasonable person would not feel the pull of this argument for an exception in cases of rape and perhaps in other cases as well.

Others may see state regulations of abortion procedures as motivated not by a concern for informed consent but by the desire to reduce abortions. At the same time, abortion is more than a typical surgical procedure, and removal of a fetus is not the moral equivalent of removing an appendix. Even liberals who are sympathetic to the result that the Court reached in *Roe* have had doubts about the quality of its reasoning. Today, they are more likely to seek refuge in the equal protection clause and maintain that the absence of legalized abortion reinforces gender inequality in a number of ways. Obviously, restrictions on abortion affect women in a way that such restrictions do not affect men.[61] As Jack Balkin writes, "[R]estrictions on abortion require pregnant women to bear children and become mothers whether or not they wish to. They force women either to devote themselves to traditional roles and responsibilities of child care that lack both status and economic remuneration or else suffer the stigma and shame of admitting their inability to care for their own children by placing them up for adoption. Restrictions on abortion thus employ basic social expectations about the duties and responsibilities of motherhood as a lever to pressure women into traditional roles of child care."[62] By contrast, women who are able to "control their reproductive destiny" are more likely to be able to escape traditional gender roles if they so desire.[63] Comparatively, it would be easier for women who do not have the primary responsibility of child care to take advantage of career opportunities.

In *Political Liberalism*, Rawls got himself into hot water in a footnote when he seemed to be arguing that due respect for human life; the ordered reproduction of political society over time, including the family in some form; and finally the equality of women as equal citizens would lead to a right to abortion, at least during the first trimester.[64] Clearly, some

---

[61] However, there are self-described pro-life feminists who insist that permissive abortion laws do not enhance reproductive freedom or social equality. See, e.g., Sidney Callahan, "Abortion and the Sexual Agenda," in *The Ethics of Abortion: Pro-Life vs. Pro-Choice*, 3rd ed., ed. Robert M. Baird and Stuart E. Rosenbaum (Amherst, NY: Prometheus Books, 2001), 172.

[62] Balkin, *What* Roe v. Wade *Should Have Said*, 45.

[63] Tribe, *Clash of Absolutes*, 33.

[64] Rawls writes, "Now I believe that any reasonable balance of these values will give a woman a duly qualified right to decide whether or not to end her pregnancy during the first trimester.

arguments against abortion are nonpublic: abortion is wrong because it frustrates God's creative gift of life, because a fetus has a soul at the moment of conception, because all life is sacred, or because the pope has declared that abortion is a sin. The strongest public argument in favor of a constitutional right to abortion would rely on the wrongfulness of the state's compelling a woman to remain pregnant against her will. Andrew Koppelman has argued that forcing a woman to carry her fetus to term can be likened to slavery.[65] More generally, it is not unreasonable to believe that allowing a woman to make her own most personal decisions about her own body and her future should trump the lesser importance of protecting the life of a entity whose moral status, at least in the early stages of pregnancy, can be reasonably disputed. Therefore, one might conclude that the balance of public reasons cuts in favor of a right of abortion prior to the viability of the fetus. Justice Blackmun reached the same conclusion in *Roe*: the state's interest in protecting fetal life prior to viability was weaker than the interest of the woman in deciding whether she was going to have the child.

Laurence Tribe characterizes *Roe* as a compromise.[66] In the trimester framework, a woman does not have an absolute right to abortion. Still, the Court cannot really balance interests in the sense that the fetus has an interest in not being killed. After all, there is no right to commit infanticide. The trouble is that those who favor more restrictive laws that would more strictly regulate or eliminate the right to abortion believe that the right to life of the fetus is more important than the woman's right to reproductive autonomy. As such, there is no obvious way to determine which public reasons, on balance, are most compelling. It is very difficult to determine whether an entity has rights or interests based on its potentiality, but that view is not obviously unreasonable.[67] One might argue that killing a fetus is not wrong or at least is less wrong than killing a mature human being. Michael Tooley has argued that an entity cannot have a right to life unless it can have an interest in its continued existence, and it must be capable of conceiving a continued self.[68] Tooley may be right, but it is not self-evident that he is, especially when a fetus is at least a potential person that may deserve the benefit of the doubt.

The reason for this is that at this early stage in pregnancy the political value of the equality of women is overriding and this right is required to give it substance and force." John Rawls, *Political Liberalism* (New York: Columbia University Press, 1996), 243n32.

[65] Andrew Koppelman, "Forced Labor: A Thirteenth Amendment Defense of Abortion," 84 *Northwestern University Law Review* (1990), 480.

[66] Tribe, *Clash of Absolutes*, 78.

[67] See Joan C. Callahan, "The Fetus and Fundamental Rights," in *The Ethics of Abortion: Pro-Life vs. Pro-Choice*, 3rd ed., ed. Robert M. Baird and Stuart E. Rosenbaum (Amherst, NY: Prometheus Books, 2001), 307.

[68] Michael Tooley, "Abortion and Infanticide," 1 *Philosophy and Public Affairs* (1972), 37–65.

As Kent Greenawalt writes, "The abortion issue is so intractable because of the sharp divergence over the moral status of the fetus."[69] The exchange of public reasons does not seem to help as much here as it does in most other constitutional cases. At what stage of development does a zygote, embryo, or fetus have a right not to be killed? As Greenawalt has also pointed out, the question of when human life begins is not inherently religious.[70] The issue of the moral and legal permissibility of abortion cannot be stripped down to the imposition of religious views, which might be prohibited under the establishment clause but involves deeper, and more difficult, philosophical questions about what it means to be a person. In the end, public reasons do not seem to be able to resolve "the point at which the fetus is entitled to particular degrees of moral consideration."[71] As Stephen Macedo states, there are many reasonable arguments on both sides of the abortion debate.[72] In *Roe*, Blackmun was right to single out the severity of the potential medical and psychological harm that might result from forcing a woman to have a child and the numerous difficulties associated with having an unwanted child.[73] Without question, those are public reasons. Many women will continue to have abortions regardless of whether the procedure is legal, and their socioeconomic status is bound to affect their relative access to this procedure. No one wants to see women die as a result of illegal abortions or for there to be more unwanted or neglected children. Children should be wanted and cared for, and we know that not every person is cut out to be a parent. Those who want to see *Roe* overturned should be able to explain how the state would go about prosecuting women and physicians who violate, attempt to violate, or conspire to violate the law and what kinds of punishments they would receive. It would be hard to imagine that the state would charge a woman who intentionally had an abortion with first-degree murder and sentence her to life imprisonment without possibility of parole or to death.

Michael Perry believes that *Roe* was wrongly decided because Americans are divided on the moral permissibility of abortion except in cases of rape, incest, or fetal deformity.[74] The trouble is that popular consensus, even if it exists, cannot settle the issue, and judges have other ways of deciding morally difficult cases. Although Justice White referred to the

---

[69] Kent Greenawalt, *Religious Convictions and Political Choice* (New York: Oxford University Press, 1991), 121.

[70] Ibid., 255.

[71] Ibid., 126.

[72] Stephen Macedo, "In Defense of Liberal Public Reason: Are Slavery and Abortion Hard Cases?" in *Natural Law and Public Reason*, ed. Robert P. George and Christopher Wolfe (Washington, D.C.: Georgetown University Press, 2000), 29.

[73] Roe v. Wade, 410 U.S. 153 (1973).

[74] Michael J. Perry. *Morality, Politics, and Law* (New York: Oxford University Press, 1988), 174–8.

"convenience, whim or caprice of the putative mother" in his dissent in *Roe*, which surely understates the reasons why most women have abortions, he has an important, if poorly articulated, point: the Court could not simply value the right or interest of the mother over the potential life of the fetus without a substantive defense of that premise. Blackmun attempts to put together such a defense by showing that on historical grounds, the fetus was not a legal person, but it seems that a historical inquiry alone does not get us very far. The constitutional text does not mention nonhuman animals, but surely the federal government could pass laws to protect endangered species, and a city could prevent its inhabitants from killing dogs and cats.

Historical inquiries are not irrelevant, but at the same time, even clearcut answers to them could not resolve the most important question: at what stage of its development does a fetus have a right not to be killed? Intuitively, it would seem that as the fetus approaches fuller development, its claim not to be killed is stronger and it may have this right before viability. It would be incomprehensible to believe that the moral status of the fetus declines as the fetus matures, absent some kind of disease or birth defect.[75] Personhood is a moral concept that implies criteria such as brain activity, consciousness of external objects, self-awareness, sentience, and capacities to reason and communicate. Even if reasonable people did not dispute these criteria, they still might disagree over whether a fetus meets the criteria well enough to qualify as a human being. As Don Marquis puts it, "Fetuses seem to be like arbitrarily chosen human cells in some respects and like adult humans in other respects."[76] There seems to be no escaping the deeper metaphysical questions that must be addressed before one can conclude, with some confidence, that a fetus is close enough to being a person to have the prima facie right not to be killed. That is what makes the constitutional question so intractable. Even if one does not believe that killing a ten-week-old fetus is the moral equivalent of infanticide, he or she is probably less than comfortable with the procedure. After all, a fetus may be "a human being in the making."[77]

Reasonable people should be able to discuss the issue dispassionately and be willing to exchange reasons with one another to determine which argument is the best of the plausible arguments for and against the moral acceptability of abortion, but that is often not the case in the United States. As one scholar writes, "One of the distinguishing features of the abortion conflict compared to other social debates of our times is the level of

[75] Greenawalt, *Religious Convictions and Political Choice*, 136.
[76] Don Marquis, "Why Abortion Is Immoral," 86 *Journal of Philosophy* (1989), 202.
[77] Warren Quinn, "Abortion: Identity and Loss," in *Morality and Action* (New York: Cambridge University Press, 1994), 36.

protest, harassment, and violence generated over this issue."[78] Paulsen feels so strongly about the immorality of abortion that he describes those who agree with the result of *Roe* as "embrac[ing] constitutionalized private mass murder."[79] Paulsen is entitled to his opinion, of course, and he is also free to accuse those who believe that abortion should not be criminalized of being complicit in an evil practice. But this shrill rhetoric exhibits the kind of attitude of unreasonableness that I have been warning against throughout this book. What is striking about Paulsen's position is his certainty; he simply cannot conceive of how a reasonable person could disagree with him, even though so many smart people have disagreed with the pro-life position over time and have articulated good reasons for their disagreement. In a number of places in his article, he conflates being human, which is a biological category, with personhood, which is a moral category.[80] Even bright people are not immune from making logical errors or overestimating the strength of their arguments when they are emotionally wedded to particular conclusions. The same could be said of those who take abortion rights as an article of faith and cannot fathom how other Americans could possibly disagree with them.

It is important to acknowledge what can be said on behalf of positions like Paulsen's. There are times when we do not want people to cave into majority sentiment, even when those in the majority insist that they are reasonable, especially in the midst of grave injustice. That a person believes him- or herself or a position to be reasonable does not make it so. Just because a slave owner believes the institution of chattel slavery to be dictated by the will of God or by nature does not mean that it is. Just because a segregationist believes that his or her way of life justifies the racial segregation of public facilities does not make it so. At particular moments in American history, unfortunately, many people have been unreasonable, and even today, with respect to some issues, that will be the case. We would not have wanted abolitionists to give up their moral crusade during the antebellum period or Freedom Riders to have concluded that white resistance to racial integration was reasonable. Nothing that I have said here or earlier should be taken as an excuse to ignore social injustice or to defer uncritically to the judgment of others. An exclusive principle of public reason serves as an independent standard of assessment. Thus, what matters is the quality of the reasons that those who hold a particular position have. If those reasons are incompatible with a commitment to the freedom and equality of everyone, like those who supported slavery or opposed civil rights, then they can be reasonably rejected.

---

[78] Alesha E. Doan, *Opposition and Intimidation: The Abortion Wars and Strategies of Political Harassment* (Ann Arbor: University of Michigan Press, 2007), ix.

[79] Michael Stokes Paulsen, "Dissenting," 212.

[80] Ibid., 196, 207.

I believe that abortion is not as obviously morally wrong as slavery is. Not everyone would agree with that statement, but no one committed to equality can maintain any longer that the latter is morally acceptable or reasonable. By contrast, history will probably never settle the question of the moral permissibility of abortion. At most, a society like our own will be able to minimize the political conflict that such a question generates. Even Judith Thomson has acknowledged that the pro-life view of the moral status of the fetus is not unreasonable.[81] She concedes that those who believe abortion to be immoral have good reasons for their belief that the fetus is a being with a prima facie right not to be killed. At the same time, the pro-choice position, where a nonviable fetus is not a being with a prima facie right not to be killed, is at least equally reasonable. Because neither side has presented superior reasons, a reasonable person could believe that abortion is morally permissible or immoral and have good reasons to support either conclusion. So far, no sound argument, which a rational person must accept inasmuch as he or she is rational, has fallen from heaven. Thomson then concludes that aborting nonviable fetuses should be legally permitted because of the effects that restriction or regulation would have on women's freedom.[82] For her, if no one really knows what the moral status of a fetus should be, and it is not evident how one could assign probabilities to the two possibilities, then the woman's interest in reproductive control over her body tips the scale in favor of a right to abortion, not to mention the bad consequences of recriminalizing abortion.

Francis Beckwith responds, "Thomson does not seem to appreciate the...implications of conceding the reasonableness of the pro-life position."[83] He then insists that even if Thomson is correct about the equal reasonableness of the pro-choice and pro-life positions, it does not follow that abortion cannot be criminalized.[84] It may be wrong to err on the side of liberty in such a case, Beckwith claims, because "the odds of the unborn being a human person are [50–50]."[85] Therefore, it makes just as much or even more sense to err on the side of life by assuming that a fetus counts as a person.[86] The obvious difficulty with this argument is that it is not clear whether Thomson's or anyone else's belief that the pro-life position is not unreasonable entails that there is a 50–50 chance that a one-week-old fetus is a full-fledged member of the human community. Surely, Thomson would reject this characterization of her position. One could believe that the pro-life position is not unreasonable and still have very strong reasons for

---

[81] Judith Thomson, "Abortion: Whose Right?" 20 *Boston Review* (1995), 11–15.
[82] Ibid., 8.
[83] Beckwith, *Defending Life*, 59.
[84] Ibid., 60.
[85] Ibid., 61.
[86] Ibid.

thinking that a nonviable fetus is not a person. The odds could favor the possibility that such a fetus is not entitled to the rights that an infant would be entitled to.

However, the reverse is true as well. A person who believes that the pro-choice position is not unreasonable need not believe that the odds are even. Beckwith is wrong to assume that the reasonableness of a position on abortion is synonymous with the fetus's having a 50–50 chance of being a person with a prima facie right not to be killed. A position is only unreasonable when there are no good reasons that underlie it, that is, reasons that an ideal reasonable person would not reject. In principle, a person who is, say, 80 percent sure that a position that he or she is assessing is wrong may still believe that that position is not unreasonable given the complexity of the question and the possibility that he or she is wrong. Beckwith is right, though, that if one doubts that the fetus is nothing more than a mass of cells, then the freedom of the woman would not necessarily trump the state's interest in protecting fetal life prior to viability. One might even conclude that many of the reasons that women have for abortions, when the moral status of the fetus is uncertain, are not compelling enough. No one thinks that a mother may kill her six-month-old child so that she can reenter the workforce or take a vacation to Cabo San Lucas. Nor could one position's be "I believe abortion is the taking of innocent human life but I will let others do so because it is not my business." If murder is wrong, then others cannot be allowed to do it.

In 1971, Judith Thomson introduced the most famous analogy in the vast literature on abortion: a woman who becomes pregnant is like a person who, against her will, is hooked up to a famous violinist who has a life-threatening kidney ailment and needs to use her body for nine months.[87] Thomson employs this analogy to try to show that no person should be morally required to render aid to another person even if not rendering aid would result in the person's death. There are a number of more or less obvious problems with this analogy. A woman who aborts a fetus does not simply unplug it but has another person, usually a physician, kill it, and most women who become pregnant can foresee that sexual intercourse may result in pregnancy. In other words, they may have assumed the risk and have been responsible for the fetus's coming into existence. A better analogy would involve her engaging in some activity that she knows carries a small risk that she may be attached to a famous violin player who needs to use her kidney for at least nine months. The point of this analogy is that a woman's right to protect her body from invasions overrides the fetus's right not to be killed, even if the fetus does not threaten the life or health of the woman

---

[87] Judith Jarvis Thomson, "A Defense of Abortion," 1 *Philosophy and Public Affairs* (1971), 47–66.

carrying it. Thomson goes for a knockout by trying to show that even if a fetus is a person with a prima facie right not to be killed, a woman could still be permitted to abort her fetus on the ground that no one should be forced to be a Good Samaritan for the duration of a normal pregnancy. She hopes to avoid the deeper metaphysical question of the moral status of the fetus by granting the most important premise of the pro-life argument: at conception, a fetus, despite its appearance, is a full-fledged member of the human community with a prima facie right not to be killed.

The trouble is that one's position on the moral and legal permissibility of abortion is bound to turn on what one believes about the moral status of a fetus at different stages of its development. Robert George is right when he insists that "even a 'duly qualified' right to abortion 'in the first trimester' [cannot] be established without engaging the deep and metaphysical questions on the basis of which people divide over the question of abortion."[88] Almost everyone believes that a fetus that is viable or has been born is the equivalent or at least is closer, morally speaking, to being a person with the basic rights that any person is entitled to by virtue of his or her humanity.[89] Alison Jaggar declares that she would like to defend the right to abortion on political grounds and avoid the "vexed question of fetal moral status."[90] This move is natural, but one cannot simply bracket the issue of the moral status of the fetus and focus on who should make the decision on whether to abort the fetus and under what circumstances without taking an implicit position on the prior question. It would not make nearly as much sense for someone to claim that he or she is going to focus on whether a woman has a right to kill her six-month-old son. Jaggar's desire to focus on the aspects of the question of abortion that she cares most about as a feminist is understandable but at the same time frustrating inasmuch as she neglects to engage an issue that she must engage if she is going to convince others, who are skeptical, that abortion under most circumstances is morally permissible. One cannot simply frame the issue of abortion as a mere matter of choice or gender equality without an explanation as to why a fetus lacks the moral status of a being that has a prima facie right not to be killed.

This brief discussion shows, I think, the intractability of the abortion question; it looks like there is not, and never will be, an argument that is so

---

[88] Robert P. George, "Public Reason and Political Conflict: Abortion and Homosexuality," 106 *Yale Law Journal* (1997), 2495.

[89] But see Peter Singer and Helen Kuhse, "On Letting Handicapped Infants Die," in *The Right Thing to Do: Basic Readings in Moral Philosophy*, ed. James Rachels (New York: Random House, 1989), 146.

[90] Alison M. Jaggar, "Regendering the U.S. Abortion Debate," in *Abortion Wars: A Half Century of Struggle 1950–2000*, ed. Rickie Solinger (Berkeley: University of California Press, 1998), 342–3.

compelling that all rational persons must acknowledge its soundness. Even Tribe admits that a reasonable person could object to *Roe v. Wade* on the ground that the Court "gave insufficient weight to the value of fetal life."[91] Anyone who has read some of the philosophical literature on abortion is struck by both the quantity and the quality of arguments presented to support both sides of the abortion debate. How is someone supposed to assign a probability to the possibility that a nonviable fetus has achieved personhood? Most of us do so in exercising our own best judgment with respect to the moral and legal permissibility of abortion, but the trouble is that a reasonable person could easily be justified in rejecting those probabilities.

There will always be critics of *Roe*, and there would be critics of this decision even if the Court had tried to explain why a nonviable fetus does not have the moral status of a viable fetus or infant and had done a better job. To not expect a knockdown argument in any hard case is to expect too much, but to not expect the majority opinion to address the issues that must be addressed is to demand too little from an institution that is not democratically accountable. Kermit Roosevelt writes that *Roe* "lacks an explanation as to why the Court has the authority to second-guess the legislative judgment."[92] If only religious reasons underlie a law that prohibits abortion, then the Court does have the authority to strike down such a law or any law that is predicated on clearly nonpublic reasons. As I have tried to show, the real trouble with *Roe* is that Blackmun never adequately articulates why the woman's right to choose to terminate her pregnancy trumps the fetus's right not to be killed. That is not to say that a more convincing argument could not have been made, but it is to say that, Blackmun failed to provide sufficiently public reasons to those who disagreed with the decision.

Nor did the Court do much better in *Casey*. In the end, I am convinced that the Court could have improved in this respect: it could have explained to likely dissenters why the moral status of a nonviable fetus is not that of a viable fetus or infant. Likewise, if the Court reaches the opposite conclusion, it has to articulate why the state may protect a fetus from being killed on the ground that it is a person or at least close enough to be treated as such. A defense of the right to abortion requires a nonpublic argument about the moral status of the fetus, and that is the main reason why the issue continues to resist adjudication. Dissenters are entitled to such an explanation, even if they will never accept it, which the Court has never provided and has explicitly tried to avoid. That does not mean that all reasonable dissenters would accept such an explanation if the Court had put forth one. A person

[91] Laurence H. Tribe, *God Save This Honorable Court: How the Choice of Supreme Court Justices Shapes Our History* (New York: New American Library, 1985), 118.
[92] Kermit Roosevelt, *The Myth of Judicial Activism* (New Haven, CT: Yale University Press, 2007), 114.

who believes that a fetus is a person at conception is also committed to the belief that abortion is infanticide and, for that reason, may not be willing to grant exceptions in cases of rape or incest. Like that of affirmative action, the constitutional case for abortion rights is contestable and a reasonable person should recognize it as such, which is another way of saying that those who oppose *Roe* are right that the Court should not have invalidated all laws forbidding abortion during the first six months of pregnancy.

TEN

The Case for Judicial Review

Scholars who write about public justification and deliberative democracy usually have little to say about judicial review.[1] This neglect may be due to their preoccupation with citizenship. Rather than putting institutions front and center, as many empirical political scientists do, they write about how ordinary people must think and behave in certain ways when they participate in politics. There is nothing wrong with this focus, and those who hope that Americans politics can become more principled and more deliberative have come up with some ingenious plans for adapting the "ideal of face-to-face democracy to the large nation-state."[2] As I see it, the prominence of the judiciary in our contemporary politics also merits an account of the proper relationship between judicial decision making and the ideal of public deliberation that deliberative democrats envision. Any theory of deliberative democracy that is premised on the notion that citizens are supposed to deliberate in the public sphere cannot pretend that courts do not exist and overlook the fact that most Americans continue to put their faith in them.

According to many accounts, the framers were republicans who rejected more populist forms of democracy and believed that the wisest men should exercise political power subject to institutional checks and balances.[3] That sounds unacceptably elitist to contemporary democratic ears, and few of us today would be comfortable with the notion that our elected representatives should feel free to ignore public opinion because they are more virtuous, more disinterested, more intelligent, or more knowledgeable than the people. Like it or not, though, Americans are stuck with constitutional democracy, and constitutionalism still entails limiting the power of legislative

---

[1] A notable exception is Cass R. Sunstein, *One Case at a Time: Judicial Minimalism on the Supreme Court* (Cambridge, MA: Harvard University Press, 1999).

[2] James S. Fishkin, *The Voice of the People: Public Opinion and Democracy* (New Haven, CT: Yale University Press, 1995), 5.

[3] Stephen Macedo, *The New Right v. the Constitution* (Washington, D.C.: Cato Institute, 1987), 42.

majorities. That has meant that judges have played and will continue to play an important role in determining where these limitations lie. Any constitutional theory that denied the place of judicial review in American politics would have to sever itself from our tradition of constitutional practice.

In this chapter, I will argue that courts, as opposed to the people themselves or their elected representatives, should have the primary responsibility of striking down unconstitutional legislation. In doing so, I will describe the appeal of popular constitutionalism but make the case that it is both untenable and undesirable under current conditions. My contention is that the judiciary is capable of assessing and offering the kinds of reasons that might meet the exclusive principle of public reason that I have defended in this book; it is the institution that is best equipped to ensure that the state does not act on the wrong kinds of reasons.

I. JUDICIAL REVIEW

A. Overview

The foregoing contention about the role of the judiciary as a gatekeeper might not seem to be controversial to most Americans, but it is at odds with the spirit of critiques of judicial review that insist that its scope ought to be restricted so that the people and their elected representatives can participate more actively in the process of making of constitutional choices. Recently, Justice Stephen Breyer has defended a civic republican theory of judicial review.[4] Cass Sunstein's idea of "incompletely theorized agreements" is designed to encourage other political actors to develop constitutional principles democratically.[5] These critiques of judicial review, and by implication judicial power, do not only come from the Left. Conservative critics of judicial review continue to insist that activist judges with liberal political agendas illegitimately invent new rights.[6] They allege that the Warren Court and the early Burger Court abused their authority by grounding their most controversial decisions in the substantive value choices of individual justices.[7] These days, that may sound more like political rhetoric and less like a principled objection to judicial review itself, especially when

---

[4] Stephen Breyer, *Active Liberty: Interpreting Our Democratic Constitution* (New York: Alfred A. Knopf, 2005).

[5] Cass R. Sunstein, *Legal Reasoning and Political Conflict* (New York: Oxford University Press, 1996), 7.

[6] Lino A. Graglia, "Constitutional Law without the Constitution: The Supreme Court's Remaking of America," in *A Country I Do Not Recognize: The Legal Assault on American Values,* ed. Robert H. Bork (Stanford, CA: Hoover Institution Press, 2005), 11.

[7] Edwin Meese III, "Interpreting the Constitution," in *Interpreting the Constitution: The Debate over Original Intent,* ed. Jack N. Rakove (Boston: Northeastern University Press, 1990), 13.

conservative judges engage in activism that serves their own partisan ends. What concerns me in this chapter, though, is whether Americans can rule themselves but still permit courts to render legislation unconstitutional in the name of freedom and equality. A society that leaves a number of its most important political questions to the judiciary is a society that would seem to lack confidence in the ability of its other political actors to enact wise or even sensible public laws and policies.

It would be better if Americans did not have to choose between con-stitutionalism and democracy but rather could find a way to eliminate or reduce the tension between them. Constitutional theorists who try to do so have offered a variety of sophisticated theories that attempt to show that judicial review is not so antidemocratic after all. John Hart Ely introduces a theory of representation reinforcement in which judicial review is justified when it enhances the procedural integrity of the political process.[8] Samuel Freeman defends judicial review on the ground that it furthers democratic sovereignty.[9] Michael Perry offers a "functional justification" of judicial review on human rights issues that is supposed to strengthen democratic policy making.[10] Eventually, any plausible defense of judicial review will have to face the charge that judicial review is antidemocratic and explain why a society that relies so heavily on judicial oversight is not a society that is democratic in name only. Typically, such a theory will to try to bring the constitutional and democracy parts of constitutional democracy closer together by redefining democracy or by identifying the empirical flaws of real democracies and showing how judicial review can help to remedy them.

My approach to this question of whether a country can be democratic and at the same time put so much faith in the judiciary is to acknowledge the extent to which judicial review is antidemocratic but argue that that is the price that Americans have to pay if they care about furthering the freedom and equality of all persons under current conditions. What is problematic about the judicial part of judicial review is having judges make important constitutional choices that arguably ought to be made more democratically. A candid defense of judicial review will concede that its exercise is antidemo-cratic in some respects but nevertheless serves other, more important political ends.

In what follows, I will make the case that government for the people need not be a government by the people all of the time, especially when a court

---

[8] John Hart Ely, *Democracy and Distrust: A Theory of Judicial Review* (Cambridge, MA: Harvard University Press, 1980).

[9] Samuel Freeman, "Constitutional Democracy and the Legitimacy of Judicial Review," 9 *Law and Philosophy* (1990–1991), 327.

[10] Michael J. Perry, *The Constitution, the Courts, and Human Rights* (New Haven, CT: Yale University Press, 1982), 91–145.

invalidates a law that infringes on each person's equal right to form, revise, and pursue his or her conception of the good. When legislative majorities do not respect the freedom and equality of everyone, the case for judicial intervention is much stronger, and this position is consistent with the well-known constitutional principle that the Court should look out for discrete and insular legislative minorities that are subject to prejudice. A society that allows legislative majorities to disrespect the freedom and equality of some of its members is a society that fails to comply with the principle of fair treatment that Americans must accept if they are to live together according to mutually acceptable terms. I believe that the strongest justification for judicial review is not that judges are more likely to reach the right results but rather that judges are more capable of publicly justifying their decisions to reasonable dissenters, thereby legitimizing those decisions.

B. A Brief History

A society in which voters already incorporate constitutional considerations into their voting decisions is a society that is beyond judicial review. Judicial oversight would be superfluous if the people themselves or their elected representatives did not propose or enact laws that were clearly or arguably unconstitutional. That would be the most obvious way of connecting the constitutional and democracy parts of constitutional democracy. In the past, though, lawmakers have too often failed to limit themselves to the right kinds of reasons, and at present, there seems to be little reason to believe that this state of affairs will change anytime soon. Thus, with some reservations, most constitutional law scholars have concluded that the judiciary is more institutionally capable of protecting the most important constitutional rights and ensuring the equal treatment of legislative minorities than the other branches of government are.[11]

The controversy over the role that courts should play in the American political system is as old as the country itself.[12] Although most historians believe that the intent of the framers was at least to have the Supreme Court invalidate state laws that conflicted with the Constitution, they did not specify whether the Court could also invalidate federal legislation.[13] In 1803, in *Marbury v. Madison*, Chief Justice John Marshall answered that question in the affirmative by ruling that a part of the Judiciary Act of 1789 was unconstitutional.[14] The Court did not invalidate another federal law until

---

[11] See Paul Brest, "The Misconceived Quest for Original Understanding," 60 *Boston University Law Review* (1988), 238.

[12] See Erwin Chemerinsky, *Interpreting the Constitution* (New York: Praeger Books, 1987), 191.

[13] See, e.g., William E. Nelson, Marbury v. Madison: *The Origins and Legacy of Judicial Review* (Lawrence: University Press of Kansas, 2000), 1–2.

[14] Marbury v. Madison, 5 U.S. (1 Cranch) 137 (1803).

its notorious *Dred Scott* decision in 1857.[15] Unfortunately, American history does not tell us enough about how we should evaluate the institution of judicial review today. Historians do not know whether the founders had a theory of judicial review or if they did have such a theory, whether they expected that the courts alone would exercise it.[16] No official record of what happened at the Constitutional Convention was published.[17] The modern doctrine of judicial review did not exist in the late eighteenth century.[18] As one commentator observes, "[T]heir working understanding of the scope of constitutional activity was sufficiently different from ours."[19] Although we use the same term, that usage should not mislead us into thinking that their idea of judicial review is ours; the founders were not concerned that racial or ethnic minorities would be at the mercy of legislative majorities. Unlike many defenders of judicial review, Chief Justice Marshall did not see judicial review "as a mechanism for protecting minority rights against majoritarian infringement."[20] At the Constitutional Convention, the delegates adopted the proposal for a federal Supreme Court with very little discussion.[21] Whether the Constitution itself authorizes such review of federal legislation is open to dispute, and it is not clear what kind of evidence would settle the issue conclusively.

Some scholars continue to look to historical sources for an answer to the question of the proper scope of judicial review on the assumption that what was originally intended provides some normative support for what should be the case today. It is clear, though, that their world is not ours, and even if the best historical scholarship of the founding period were to indicate that the founders had not wanted federal courts to review the constitutionality of both state and federal laws, Americans still might have independent normative reasons for such review. It is up to us to determine how much weight we decide to give the original intentions of the founders with respect to judicial review; the choice is ours, and we have to take full responsibility for it. A society like our own must have a vision of the polity that it would like to create, and that requires us to assess the strengths and weaknesses of the judiciary. The contemporary division between liberals and conservatives over the results in certain contentious constitutional cases should not distract us from noticing the faith that almost all of us have in the wisdom

---

[15] Dred Scott v. Sanford, 60 U.S. (19 How.) 398 (1857).

[16] See Louis Fisher, *Constitutional Dialogues: Interpretation as Political Process* (Princeton, NJ: Princeton University Press, 1988), 48.

[17] Macedo, *The New Right v. the Constitution*, 13.

[18] Stephen M. Griffin, *American Constitutionalism: From Theory to Politics* (Princeton, NJ: Princeton University Press, 1999), 91.

[19] Nelson, Marbury v. Madison, 82.

[20] Ibid., 83.

[21] Bernard Schwartz, *A History of the Supreme Court* (New York: Oxford University Press, 1993), 12.

of judicial review. Even the most fanatic originalists do not believe that *Marbury v. Madison* should be overturned.[22]

That consensus is real, and Americans are no more likely to abandon judicial review than they are to call for a Jeffersonian constitutional convention every twenty years. The expansive role of the federal judiciary over the course of American history also has contributed to Americans' inability to imagine the review of legislation without judges.[23] As some commentators have noted, the fear of transferring more political power to the electorate reflects skepticism about whether majority rule without judicial oversight can limit the power of the state effectively.[24] The very structure of the federal government is predicated on the assumption that even elite political actors can never be trusted to police themselves.[25] If the wisdom of *The Federalist Papers* can be reduced to a single insight about politics, it is that political power must be dispersed in a balance-of-powers arrangement to ensure that one faction will not grow too powerful and achieve hegemony over its rivals. That future Americans could rely exclusively on nobler motives is off the table.[26] That is not mere cynicism but reflects the fact that those who design governments must make weak assumptions about human behavior. History indicates that it would be foolish to assume that those who have political power will always act in the public interest and not be corrupted by power.

At the same time, constitutional law scholars are less likely to extend this skepticism about human nature to judges. That may be naive or historically unjustified, but it is safe to say that misguided courts, at their worst, can do quite a bit less damage than other political actors, like the president and Congress. Part of the explanation for why courts have assumed such prominence in our political system has to do with political events. The framers did not anticipate the rapid pace of democratization that took place over a relatively short period after the birth of the country and especially during the Jacksonian period. Because of this unexpected democratization, even today one of the most difficult intellectual challenges facing political theorists involves how to induce ordinary citizens to become informed and to think seriously about political issues. The inherent difficulty of reconciling popular

---

[22] Marbury v. Madison, 5 U.S. (1 Cranch) 137 (1803).

[23] On this point, see Griffin, *American Constitutionalism*, 59–87.

[24] See, e.g., Paul Brest, "The Fundamental Rights Controversy: The Essential Contradictions of Normative Constitutional Scholarship," 90 *Yale Law Journal* (1981), 1106.

[25] The Madisonian conception of democracy appears to be premised on this assumption. Madison claims that the latent causes of faction are ingrained in human nature and that the only plausible remedy is controlling their effects. See James Madison, *The Federalist No. 10* (Amherst, NY: Prometheus Books, 2000), 54–7. See also Jeffrey K. Tulis, *The Rhetorical Presidency* (Princeton, NJ: Princeton University Press, 1987), 38–9, 176–7.

[26] As Madison put it, "Enlightened statesmen will not always be at the helm." Madison, *Federalist No. 10*, 57.

participation with public deliberation has generated some doubt in American political thought about the prospects of mass democracy.[27] As a result, those who have sincere democratic sympathies also have been reluctant democrats in the sense that they expect courts to correct the mistakes of legislative majorities. As they see it, judicial review serves as a necessary safeguard against the abuse of political power in a democracy like our own that leaves too little room for serious discourse about the most important political questions.

Whatever the framers may have hoped for, the empirical political science literature on legislative behavior demonstrates that legislators are not more likely to incorporate constitutional considerations into their decision making than judges are.[28] In the current division of labor, courts have the primary responsibility of determining the constitutionality of particular laws, and that knowledge makes it easier for any public official to support legislation that is clearly unconstitutional. If lawmakers exceed their law-making authority, a court can correct their mistake. Today, it would be unrealistic to expect legislators not to vote for a bill on the ground that it was unconstitutional, especially when their constituents or their party wanted them to vote for it. Most legislative behavior is strategic, and that should not surprise us in a political system that, according to most accounts, was set up to provide fair competition for competing interests.

One might conclude that Americans have come to accept judicial review by process of elimination. Whatever the intentions of the founders may have been, on balance, a more active role on the part of courts has strengthened constitutionalism, furthered individual rights, and protected certain groups from unequal treatment. Judicial decisions have helped to adopt the Constitution to changing times. No one could deny the place of the Court in the development of American constitutional meaning, even if the judiciary is not the institution that is primarily responsible for initiating new constitutional understandings. In addition, reliance on courts to correct democratic excess is not entirely out of line with the intent of the framers to empower deliberative majorities at the expense of "uninformed, immoderate, or passionate majorities."[29] If they had been clairvoyant, the framers might have been sympathetic to the idea of having the federal judiciary play a more active part in political decision making at the national level, especially if judicial review could make American politics more deliberative.

---

[27] One of the best articles ever written on the inherent tension between democratic self-rule and philosophical justification is Michael Walzer, "Philosophy and Democracy," 9 *Political Theory* (1981), 379–99.

[28] Today, the "politicians just want to get elected" explanation of legislative behavior is omnipresent in political science literature.

[29] See Joseph Bessette, *The Mild Voice of Reason: Deliberative Democracy and American National Government* (Chicago: University of Chicago Press, 1994), 3.

The problem of democratic government, as Madison characterized it, is "[t]o secure the public good and private rights against the danger of such a [majority] faction, and at the same time preserve the spirit and the form of popular government."[30] According to one scholar, the Madisonian solution was to refine public opinion through informed and dispassionate reasoning about common concerns.[31] The voice of the people must be "pronounced" by their representatives, Madison tells us, so that it will be "more consonant to the public good" than that of "the people themselves, convened for the purpose."[32] The purpose of representation is not to represent interests per se but to mediate, or when necessary, to alter, popular views to maintain a balance of power among the competing factions.

Today, very few Americans would champion the kind of elitism that Madison defends so openly in *The Federalist Papers*. Nor is it evident that an extended republic is any less prone to factions than smaller political units are. Most democratic theorists have welcomed the movement toward mass democracy in the United States as a step toward the actualization of political equality. But they also fear that this movement has rendered election campaigns and ordinary politics less deliberative. One is hard pressed to maintain that American politics today is deliberative or participatory in any meaningful sense, and the conduct of both Republicans and Democrats in the 2008 presidential election campaign is not encouraging. Voters seem to have very little incentive to work through the opposing arguments that underlie important political questions or, even more basically, to gather information concerning them.[33] They seem to be more concerned with appearances, rhetoric, and slogans than with the substance of public policy. Unfortunately, the media has tried to make politics more entertaining to increase viewership. It seems to be inevitable, then, that the advent of mass democracy leads to a trade-off between participation by ordinary people and the quality of deliberation in the public sphere. If the citizenry and legislative bodies cannot

---

[30] Madison, *Federalist No. 10*, 59.

[31] Ibid. Madison writes that the purpose of republican (representative) government is "to refine and enlarge public views by passing them through the medium of a chosen body of citizens, whose wisdom may best discern the true interest of their country, and whose patriotism and love of justice will be least likely to sacrifice it to temporary or partial considerations."

[32] Ibid.

[33] The vast political science literature on voting behavior suggests that voters do not have incentives to digest large amounts of political information, to reach thoughtful decisions, and to consider voting as a public matter. Citizens who do not perceive voting to be a matter of principle or of civic duty have no rational motivation to pay attention to such questions. The result is that the relatively minor inconveniences of gathering information and going to the polls discourage large numbers of citizens from fully participating in political life. Gathering information is costly and often not worth acquiring given the infinitesimally small probability that a single vote can make a difference anyway. The classic account of this view is found in Anthony Downs, *An Economic Theory of Democracy* (New York: Harper and Row, 1957), 36–50, 207–76.

exchange reasons with one another, and a well-ordered democracy requires such exchanges, then courts must fill the void.

C. Judges and Public Reasons

Adherence to an exclusive principle of public reason would require judges to find reasons that others could reasonably be expected to share. In the absence of such reasons, the use of political power with respect to a particular constitutional essential would be illegitimate. Rawls himself later retreated from the position that citizens and public officials had to adhere strictly to an exclusive principle of public reason, offering a proviso where deliberators could rely on comprehensive doctrines or deeper reasons, provided that that they also offered sufficiently public reasons "in due course."[34] Apart from concerns about how and when they would satisfy this proviso, Rawls's retreat from a stricter view of public reason may have resulted from his not wanting to suppress the real reasons that citizens and their elected representatives have for the political positions that they advocate. Lawrence Solum has contended that an ideal of public reason that requires and favors public reasons but allows deliberators to give nonpublic reasons in some situations is more likely to inculcate tolerance.[35] It may be unrealistic, moreover, even under the best of circumstances, to expect ordinary people to exercise the kind of self-restraint that Rawls envisions. The problem is not only that real people are always prone to vote in ways that advance their narrow self-interests. As Kent Greenawalt has pointed out, exercising such self-restraint is likely to be challenging for most ordinary persons when their deepest convictions have political implications.[36]

As a practical matter, ordinary people with the best of intentions may not be able to disentangle public reasons from their deepest convictions to satisfy the minimal requirements of public reasoning, or they simply may care too much about winning. Even citizens who sincerely try to follow norms of public reason probably never can be sure whether their deeper convictions have affected the conclusion that they reach.[37] Nor can they know whether others are also exercising the same self-restraint that they are supposed to be exercising in the name of reciprocity.[38] If ordinary persons cannot play the intellectually demanding role of citizen that Rawls has assigned to them, then it is likely that nonpublic reasons ultimately will determine important

---

[34] John Rawls, *Political Liberalism* (New York: Columbia University Press, 1993), li–lii.

[35] Lawrence Solum, "Constructing an Idea of Public Reason," 30 *San Diego Law Review* (1993), 752.

[36] Kent Greenawalt, *Private Consciences and Public Reasons* (New York: Oxford University Press, 1995), 138.

[37] Kent Greenwalt believes that Rawls expects that those who put forth public arguments will sincerely believe in the soundness of those arguments. Kent Greenawalt, "On Public Reason," 69 *Chicago-Kent Law Review* (1994), 678.

[38] Greenawalt, *Private Consciences and Public Reasons*, 137.

political outcomes. That likelihood cuts in favor of some kind of judicial review in which the responsibility of limiting the reasons that constitute public justification falls on judges who are better institutionally equipped and trained to make these difficult judgments. Without rehearsing any of the familiar arguments about the merits of judicial independence or romanticizing how real judges decide real cases, I am going to assume that courts are more likely, in Rawls's words, to be exemplars of public reason.[39] Reliance on courts to apply a principle of public reason to resolve the most important constitutional controversies not only reflects the preceding practical difficulties associated with expecting such self-restraint from ordinary political actors. In addition, such reliance permits citizens to make whatever arguments that they want to make in the public sphere, including arguments based on their deepest beliefs. As a result, they would not feel that their right to self-expression had been unfairly stifled, that they had been pressured into hiding their real reasons, or that they had been forced to choose between their consciences and their duty of civility to their fellow citizens.

That is not to say that in some important respects it would not be preferable for citizens and legislators to do the job that judges seem to be better intellectually prepared and institutionally situated to do. From a participatory democratic or civic republican standpoint, it is not desirable for judges to be the primary guardians of fundamental rights. As Laurence Tribe puts it, "Constitutional choices must be made; to all of us belongs the challenge of making them wisely."[40] Nevertheless, constitutional law scholars have rarely contested the very concept of judicial review, even in the midst of disagreement over its proper scope and its rationale.[41] Like any other kind of power, judicial power can be abused, but judges are not free to do as they please when they decide cases.[42] Nor could they abuse their power with impunity for very long in a system of checks and balances and free elections. It would not be easy for them to hide their reliance on their undeniably personal convictions in the resolution of constitutional controversies.

The practice of giving reasons is not only integral to legal culture; it is also the defining feature of a society that is committed to public justification. Today, elected officials who take an oath to uphold the Constitution also may restrain themselves from acting on unconstitutional reasons, but this is probably an increasingly rare occurrence as a result of their being used to judicial oversight.[43] Nor do citizens have to put their reasons and arguments

[39] Rawls, *Political Liberalism*, 231–40.
[40] Laurence H. Tribe, *Constitutional Choices* (Cambridge, MA: Harvard University Press, 1985), vii.
[41] One exception is Mark Tushnet, *Taking the Constitution Away from the Courts* (Princeton, NJ: Princeton University Press, 1999).
[42] Kent Greenawalt, *Private Consciences and Public Reasons*, 141.
[43] Abner Mikva, "How Well Does Congress Support and Defend the Constitution?" 61 *North Carolina Law Review* (1983), 587.

in writing so that others can assess them before or after they vote, whereas appellate judges write opinions that are subject to the critical scrutiny of others. That provides the rest of us with an opportunity to confirm that judges are holding lawmakers to an exclusive principle of public reason when they adjudicate constitutional cases.

D. Three Concerns about Judicial Review

In the United States, judicial review is so important because the Court almost always has the final word on the constitutional controversies that it adjudicates. It would not be unexpected, then, for some constitutional scholars to have an ambivalent attitude toward the judiciary and to have proposed different forms of popular constitutionalism.[44] That the vast majority of constitutional law scholars do not support the abolition of judicial review does not mean that they do not have doubts about whether its exercise has produced good consequences. First, it is debatable that the practice of judicial review serves democratic ends or does so often enough to be justified, apart from legitimate worries about separation of powers and federalism. Judges may veto laws that they find to be unconstitutional despite overwhelming popular support for them and in doing so, block progressive legislation, as the Court did in the *Civil Rights Cases* and during the infamous *Lochner* era. From a democratic perspective, when Americans take such questions out of the hands of the electorate, they put considerable faith in judges to make wise decisions for them. At best, such reliance on judicial decision making puts into some doubt the claim that citizens are actually ruling themselves. At worst, such reliance reflects an abdication of the civic responsibility of each citizen to engage in political activity and of the institutional responsibility that elected officials have to uphold the Constitution.

Second, American history reveals not so much that judicial power can easily be abused but that judges who sincerely want to make the right decision make good-faith mistakes, including egregious ones, that can have serious political consequences. For every *Brown* there is a *Plessy*; for every *Griswold* there is a *Lochner*.[45] The recent history of the nomination and confirmation of Supreme Court justices is not promising.[46] More often than not, nominations have had more to do with personal relationships and electoral politics than with merit or judicial experience. President

---

[44] See, e.g., Larry D. Kramer, *The People Themselves: Popular Constitutionalism and Judicial Review* (New York: Oxford University Press, 2004); Cass R. Sunstein, *The Partial Constitution* (Cambridge, MA: Harvard University Press, 1993); Tushnet, *Taking the Constitution Away from the Courts.*

[45] Tushnet, *Taking the Constitution Away from the Courts*, 141.

[46] In 1987, Ronald Reagan's nomination of Robert Bork, the contentious confirmation hearings, and Bork's defeat in the Senate was a watershed. Prior to that event, the judicial ideology of the nominee was not considered very important. Ethan Bronner, *Battle for Justice: How the Bork Nomination Shook America* (New York: Anchor Books, 1989), 123.

Dwight D. Eisenhower chose Earl Warren because he had left him out of his cabinet in 1953 and had promised him the next vacancy on the Supreme Court.[47] A few years later, Eisenhower selected William Brennan on the grounds that he was a state court judge and a Catholic.[48] As it now stands, there is little chance that the best and brightest will be sitting on the federal bench, and it is not obvious how the nomination and confirmation processes can be improved to produce more highly qualified candidates for the federal bench. When the opposition party controls the Senate, there may be more stealth nominees, like David Souter, about which relatively little is known and who can try to be all things to all people. In principle, judicial tyranny is far more serious than that of the other branches of government because federal judges lack direct electoral accountability and are very rarely impeached and removed from office. As Richard Posner puts it, an independent judiciary may replace one set of tyrants with another set.[49]

Third, even at its best, the judiciary falls short of functioning as a Dworkinian forum of principle. As such, a judicial decision is just as likely to exacerbate a pending constitutional crisis as it is to defuse such a crisis. *Dred Scott* suggests that very important political questions are not so easily depoliticized by being turned into legal questions.[50] Today, there is no shortage of commentators who believe that *Brown* is not all that it is cracked up to be. Some political scientists have argued that the decision did little to advance the cause of racial equality.[51] Others have argued that its "most immediate effect in the South was to stymie progressive racial change and to bolster the political standing of racial extremists."[52] Derrick Bell uses *Brown* to exemplify his "interest convergence thesis," in which the Court protects the interests of racial minorities only when those interests converge with those of powerful white elites.[53] Mark Tushnet insists that courts have not done "such as wonderful job as to distinguish them sharply from legislatures."[54] Like conservative critics, Tushnet is fixated on results,

---

[47] Bernard Schwartz, *Super Chief: Earl Warren and His Supreme Court – A Judicial Biography* (New York: New York University Press, 1983), 2.

[48] Kim Isaac Eisler, *The Last Liberal: Justice William J. Brennan Jr. and the Decisions that Transformed America* (Washington, D.C.: Beard Books, 2005), 84, 89.

[49] Richard A. Posner, *The Problems of Jurisprudence* (Cambridge, MA: Harvard University Press, 1990), 6.

[50] Don E. Fehrenbacher, *The Dred Scott Case: Its Significance in American Law and Politics* (New York: Oxford University Press, 1978).

[51] See, e.g., Gerald Rosenberg, *The Hollow Hope: Can Courts Bring About Social Change?* (Chicago: University of Chicago Press, 1991).

[52] See, e.g., Michael J. Klarman, Brown v. Board of Education *and the Civil Rights Movement* (New York: Oxford University Press, 2007), x.

[53] Derrick Bell, "*Brown v. Board of Education* and the Interest-Convergence Dilemma," 93 *Harvard Law Review* (1980), 518.

[54] Tushnet, *Taking the Constitution Away from the Courts*, 129.

but unlike them, he believes that the abolition of judicial review ultimately would serve egalitarian causes.[55]

II. THE DIFFICULTY OF AN EGALITARIAN THEORY OF JUDICIAL REVIEW

A. Popular Constitutionalism

Because of the troubles discussed here, the move away from judicial review would seem to be natural. After all, isn't it possible that democratic majorities might do a better job of producing the right results in constitutional controversies? Larry Kramer has formulated one of the best defenses of "popular constitutionalism" in the past ten years and has challenged the faith that so many Americans have in the judiciary.[56] For that reason alone, the book is worthy of our praise. Kramer also calls attention to the dangers of a Court that embraces a "philosophy of judicial supremacy" and sees itself as the "Constitution's sole authoritative expositor."[57] This kind of critique will always have a place in a country like our own that is prone to relying too heavily of judicial decision making. But Kramer's critique cuts even deeper:

- "Advocates of judicial supremacy ask us nevertheless to turn our disagreements over to judges, arguing that certain characteristics of the judicial process make judges more likely to reach desirable outcomes than politicians or ordinary citizens."[58]
- "The modern Anti-Populist sensibility presumes that ordinary people are emotional, ignorant, fuzzy-headed, and simple-minded, in contrast to a thoughtful, informed, clear-headed elite. Ordinary people tend to be foolish and irresponsible when it comes to politics: self-interested rather than public-spirited, arbitrary rather than principled, impulsive and close-minded rather than deliberate or logical."[59]
- "It comes as no surprise that people who hold these sorts of beliefs would gravitate toward something like judicial supremacy. Seeing democratic politics as scary and threatening, they find it obvious that someone must be found to restrain its mercurial impulses, someone less susceptible to the demagoguery and short-sightedness that afflict common people."[60]

The preceding remarks raise a serious concern about the elitism that may underlie a commitment to judicial review. As Kramer writes, "Supporters

[55] Ibid., 154.
[56] Kramer, *People Themselves*, 228–9.
[57] Ibid., 231.
[58] Ibid., 237.
[59] Ibid., 242.
[60] Ibid.

of judicial supremacy are today's aristocrats."[61] Perhaps a good point can stand to be overstated, but to claim that a particular practice, like judicial review, is elitist or aristocratic is not an argument against such a practice; it is a way of scoring rhetorical points in a democracy. Indeed, our society is laden with all sorts of aristocratic institutions, most of which go unchallenged. As I see it, the main problem with popular constitutionalism does not involve the results that democratic majorities reach but the kinds of reasons that legislative majorities have for imposing their will on legislative minorities.[62] Surely, "the tyranny of the majority" is more than just a slogan, especially to those who have been or are likely to be its victims.[63] Some of us will continue to romanticize direct democracy like Rousseau did, but its operation here in California leaves a lot to be desired. When California voters passed Proposition 8, which used to be called the California Marriage Protection Act, on November 4, 2008, gays and lesbians lost their constitutional right to marry, and it will be little consolation to tell them that they will be denied equal treatment under the law because of the procedural fairness of the initiative process.[64]

No thoughtful person thinks that the Court's decisions are beyond reproach or that just because a majority of the justices believed certain reasons to be sufficiently public they are so. Ideally, other political actors, including the people, would force the Court to be as forthcoming as possible about the reasons that underlie the results that it reaches, and that practice over time would stimulate high-quality constitutional discourse. In the preceding pages, I never meant to intimate that citizens and their elected representatives should be passive. Ideally, they would actively participate in the production of constitutional meaning by offering alternative interpretations of public justification in real cases that would affect not only other Americans but judges as well.

However, Kramer and others who advocate popular constitutionalism have not explained adequately why they believe that ordinary people or their elected representatives will be able to engage in the kind of constitutional argumentation that any serious form of constitutionalism presupposes. Kramer claims that "constitutional law is [not] too complex or difficult for ordinary citizens."[65] But that is simply not true. Almost inevitably, those who favor popular constitutionalism offer toned-down versions in

---

[61] Ibid., 247.

[62] Ibid., 245.

[63] Ibid.

[64] Of course, a number of lawsuits have been filed challenging the validity of Proposition 8 and raising the legal question of whether the same-sex marriages performed in between the California Supreme Court's decision recognizing a constitutional right to same-sex marriage under the California Constitution and the passage of Proposition 8 are still valid. Proposition 8 did not explicitly state that its effect would be retroactive.

[65] Ibid., 248.

which elected representatives end up playing a more prominent role in constitutional decision making. Despite all of his populist rhetoric, Kramer himself is not prepared to turn over constitutional questions to the people themselves, seeking judicial review without judicial supremacy.[66] In California, the initiative process enables voters to overturn a California Supreme Court decision by amending the California Constitution, but no one seems to be eager to repeal Article 5 of the U.S. Constitution to allow Americans to decide constitutional issues in national referenda.

Even though legislative politics is not as unprincipled as cynics would have us believe and judicial practice is not as principled as its most adamant defenders would have us believe, that does not change the basic fact that constitutional law is too complex and difficult for ordinary people.[67] The most honest rationale for the practice of judicial review by judges today is rooted in pessimism about the likelihood that ordinary citizens could ever become literate in constitutional basics. In this sense, many of us are still reluctant democrats who accept a distinction between democracy and constitutionalism and believe that nondemocratic means like judicial review can serve democratic ends or make our society more just. This reluctance probably is a product of the "very real American liberal consensus" that narrows the range of plausible constitutional understandings and practices.[68] Judicial supremacy turns out to be the lesser of two evils; it is a safer bet in an imperfect world where the vast majority of citizens are either incapable of making informed, reflective decisions on basic questions of public morality or unwilling to make the effort to do so.

The reasons that the Court offers on behalf of its decisions are bound to affect whether Americans perceive them as legitimate and whether they are complied with. Without adequate political support, judicial decisions will not be carried out.[69] Yet that should not be the only worry. In the absence of direct democracy in which all competent adults make all of their own collective choices unanimously, it is even more imperative that the reasons that underlie public laws and judicial decisions be as uncontroversial as possible. As I argued in previous chapters, these reasons must be sufficiently public, which means that the Court should ensure that lawmakers have put forth reasons that all reasonable, fair-minded persons should not reject.

For many contemporary democratic theorists, the kind of democracy that exists in contemporary America is not what they have in mind. On the one hand, they acknowledge that our nation has made considerable

---

[66] Ibid., 249–53.

[67] Ibid., 248.

[68] See Rogers M. Smith, *Liberalism and American Constitutional Law* (Cambridge, MA: Harvard University Press, 1985), 4.

[69] Rosenberg, *Hollow Hope*, 15.

progress in expanding the legal and political equality of all of the members of its political community. As Judith Shklar observes, widely accepted rights, such as the right to vote and the right to earn, are powerful symbols of equal recognition.[70] On the other hand, most democratic theorists recognize that democratic practice requires more than formal rights to vote, to run for public office, and to have free elections. Beyond concerns about how economic inequality translates into political inequality, Americans must be prepared to take responsibility for the political power that they exercise collectively or delegate to others to act on their behalf. Their fulfilling of their civic duties means that they ought to be serious, attentive, and open minded when they reflect on public affairs.

At present, to make informed choices when they go to the polls, voters need to be knowledgeable about a wide range of complex subjects like energy policy, international affairs, Social Security, health care, and the environment. However, acquiring such information is time consuming and many Americans may not have been educated well enough in the basics of science, statistics, and history to process that information even if they have the time and are inclined to seek it out. Most political science literature indicates that our campaigns and elections are less about ideas and more about the personality of the candidates.[71] Typically, televised presidential debates are not discursive. Because of the debates' formats, moderators rarely ask follow-up questions, candidates duck questions that they do not want to answer, and they are more concerned with how they appear to undecided voters than they are with the truth of what they claim. Indeed, they are adept at taking what their opponent has done or said in the past out of context to make their positions look more appealing. Their carefully prepared scripts treat important political problems superficially and evade issues or answers that carry electoral risk. My point is not that it would be a good idea for them to be more forthcoming on strategic grounds; obviously, in many instances, doing so would be electoral suicide. The candidate who "wins" the debate is usually the one who scores the most rhetorical points, makes a memorable quip, or is able to impugn the character of his or her opponent without appearing to do so maliciously. Presidential

---

[70] See Judith Shklar, *American Citizenship: The Quest for Inclusion* (Cambridge, MA: Harvard University Press, 1999), 3.

[71] See, generally, Martin P. Wattenberg, *The Rise of Candidate-Centered Politics: Presidential Elections in the 1980s* (Cambridge, MA: Harvard University Press, 1991). There is little doubt that presidential elections in particular have become more personality driven, but political scientists do not agree on the cause of this state of affairs. The cause is probably some combination of the inability of parties to control an expanded media; that such media depends on superficial coverage to maximize audience share; and the shift in issues from economics to culture, making personal attacks more effective at defining the opposition as "un-American" or at least unknown. Younger people are entering politics with less party attachment and issue voting. I owe this commentary to Mike Latner.

debates may do more harm than good to the extent that many citizens are left with the false impression that the debates have helped them to become better informed about the political issues that the country must confront. As one commentator puts it, "What we have ... is a society where public discourse is largely debased by character assassination, fear mongering, and sheer stupidity, and where the corrupting power of money reigns supreme."[72]

Even if that characterization is too harsh, one has to wonder whether our campaigns and elections can be more deliberative. Thoughtful people recognize that this state of affairs is a serious problem, but none of them seems to know what to do about it. The voters are partially to blame, but no candidate for public office will ever say so. Instead, they pander to the electorate and never let viewers forget how smart and knowledgeable Americans like "Joe the Plumber" are. This behavior would be amusing if so much were not at stake. Those who decide to go to the polls often do not evaluate alternative campaign platforms carefully before voting. The citizens who have the most electoral influence – swing voters who must be targeted because their votes are likely to be decisive – are the least politically knowledgeable group of voters.[73] Empirical literature on voting behavior indicates that some voters cannot articulate reasons independent of their party identification for their votes.[74] In addition, citizens often communicate with like-minded people, thus reinforcing their own political opinions and party loyalties.[75] At present, cyberspace does not serve, as Mill might have hoped, as a free marketplace of ideas, because people tend to visit "websites" that confirm their preexisting political convictions.[76] This "enclave deliberation" is hardly what deliberative democrats have in mind when they promote deliberation as the most

[72] Charles Larmore, "Behind the Veil," review of *Lectures on the History of Political Philosophy*, by John Rawls, *New Republic*, February 27, 2008, 47.

[73] In a famous study, Philip Converse found that voters who switch between elections are more likely to be less informed than are those who do not switch. See Philip E. Converse, "Information Flow and the Stability of Partisan Attitudes," *Public Opinion Quarterly* (Winter 1962), 581–2.

[74] The traditional view in political science literature is that voting in presidential elections is primarily determined by party identification. Deviations from this identification (e.g., voting across party lines) that determine outcomes usually result from perceived conditions such as peace and prosperity or from realignment. The classic finding is that ordinary people are poorly informed and cannot articulate the reasons for their vote. See Angus Campbell, Philip E. Converse, Warren E. Miller, and Donald E. Stokes, *The American Voter* (Chicago: University of Chicago Press, 1980), 256–65.

[75] See Bernard R. Berelson, Paul F. Lazarsfeld, and William N. McPhee, *Voting: A Study of Opinion Formation in a Presidential Campaign* (Chicago: University of Chicago Press, 1954).

[76] See Cass. R. Sunstein, *Republic.com* (Princeton, NJ: Princeton University Press, 2001), 58–89.

promising means of enabling citizens to reach mutually acceptable conclusions. As it turns out, the Internet makes it easier for citizens to wall themselves off from views that they oppose. After deliberation with like-minded people, citizens are more likely to move toward a more extreme version of their initial position.[77]

Critiques of voter competence have a long pedigree.[78] If most ordinary citizens are incurably incompetent, then it would be hard to be an enthusiastic supporter of democratic self-rule. As Plato would have put it, the irrational part of the soul should not rule the rational part. Skepticism about the competence of ordinary citizens also motivated Mill's infamous plural-voting scheme, in which better-educated citizens were to be given extra votes to offset the irrational votes of others.[79] Traditionally, those who would prefer the rule of the brightest or most virtuous have produced arguments for restricted access to citizenship rights.[80] As such, many normative political theorists have been reluctant to study the very concept of civic competence.[81] At the very least, true democratic self-rule would seem to require minimal political knowledge and critical-thinking skills on the part of most citizens so that they could make informed political choices.

Shortly after World War I, Walter Lippmann claimed that it was false to believe that voters were "inherently competent" to govern themselves.[82] In the 1930s, researchers found many Americans to be ignorant of basic political facts, inattentive, and uninterested in politics. Citizens often based their votes on uncritical attachments to political parties and very rarely thought critically about the substance of public policy. In 1960, *The American Voter* portrayed a passive citizenry that was unaware and unconcerned about political issues and allowed party allegiance to determine its voting decisions. The vast majority of Americans knew very little about what their government was doing and where the major parties stood on particular issues.[83] Philip Converse claimed that "large portions of an electorate do not have meaningful beliefs, even on issues that have formed the basis for intense controversy

---

[77] Ibid., esp. 51–88.

[78] See, e.g., Walter Lippmann, *Public Opinion* (New York: Harcourt, Brace, 1922); Joseph A. Schumpeter, *Capitalism, Socialism, and Democracy* (New York: Harper and Row, 1942).

[79] John Stuart Mill, *Considerations of Representative Government*, ed. H. B. Acton (London: Dent, 1951), 324.

[80] Karol Edward Soltan, "Introduction: Civic Competence, Democracy, and the Good Society," in *Citizen Competence and Democratic Institutions*, ed. Stephen L. Elkin and Karol Edward Soltan (University Park: Pennsylvania State University Press, 1999), 4.

[81] Ibid., 9.

[82] Lippmann, *Phantom Public*, 20.

[83] Ibid., chap. 8.

among elites for substantial periods of time."[84] On the basis of apparent fluctuations in their public policy preferences, he also concluded that most citizens had no real attitudes, or "non-attitudes."[85] At that time, party identification, as opposed to political issues, was much more likely to predict an individual vote.[86] Even today, most Americans are not knowledgeable about politics.[87] With respect to popular participation, my point is not that most real people are incompetent and uninformed most of the time but that they are too prone to act on reasons that would be unacceptable to an ideal reasonable dissenter. It would be better, of course, if most citizens were more informed, more benevolent, more tolerant, and more civic minded. In the absence of these civic virtues, it would not matter at all what courts did or did not try to do.

When all is said and done, courts cannot save Americans from themselves, but they can help them to understand the implications of a standard of public justification in real constitutional controversies. It would be a mistake to assume that ordinary people are worse than they really are and cannot be trusted to be minimally civic competent or civic minded when they are supposed to be. It would be equally wrong, though, to make unrealistic assumptions about their civic capacities and expect that our democratic politics would magically be rendered more participatory and more deliberative only if our judiciary would stop making many of our most difficult political choices for us. As Frederick Schauer puts it, "We must take the public as it is."[88] We cannot pretend that Americans are political animals by nature any more than we can pretend that ordinary Americans read Supreme Court opinions or would read them and understand them under more ideal circumstances.[89] It is natural to want the best of both worlds, where democratic self-rule does not threaten the fundamental rights of those who lack political clout or have bad luck in the legislative process. For this reason, many political theorists and law professors seek a more democratic liberalism,[90] yet this aim conflicts with just about

---

[84] Philip E. Converse, "The Nature of Belief Systems in Mass Publics," in *Ideology and Discontent*, ed. David Apter (New York: Free Press, 1964), 243–5.

[85] Philip E. Converse, "Attitudes and Non-Attitudes: Continuation of a Dialogue," in *The Quantitative Analysis of Social Problems*, ed. Edward R. Tufte (Reading, MA: Addison-Wesley, 1970), 168–89.

[86] Norman H. Nie, Sidney Verba, and John R. Petrocik, *The Changing American Voter* (Cambridge, MA: Harvard University Press, 1976), 34.

[87] See Michael X. Delli Carpini and Scott Keeter, *What Americans Know about Politics and Why It Matters* (New Haven, CT: Yale University Press, 1996).

[88] Frederick Schauer, *Free Speech: A Philosophical Inquiry* (Cambridge: Cambridge University Press, 1982), 26.

[89] Most Americans do not read U.S. Supreme Court opinions. Jack M. Balkin, "Preface," in *What* Roe v. Wade *Should Have Said* (New York: New York University Press, 2007), xii.

[90] See, e.g., Joshua Cohen, "A More Democratic Liberalism," 92 *Michigan Law Review* (1994), 1503.

everything that we know about voting behavior and how political institutions operate.

In the end, Americans may have to settle for a less democratic liberalism to ensure that the state treats all persons with equal concern and respect. Different people reach different levels of cognitive development, and thus some citizens will be much better equipped to make principled and informed voting decisions. A person who does not realize that reasonable people may disagree on some constitutional essentials is unlikely to be able to deliberate with the sort of minimal sophistication that the practice of principled deliberation in contemporary political life requires. This fact may lead us to conclude that the level of civic competence that public deliberation and voting in a deliberative democracy requires is simply too high for most people.

It is unrealistic, then, to expect ordinary citizens to act as judges in the sense that they interpret the Constitution when they deliberate and vote on the most important political questions, and the prospects for a more deliberative politics have not improved much with the advent of political representation. Typically, legislators face different incentives than judges, and these incentives are bound to affect the extent to which it is institutionally feasible for legislators to engage in principled decision making.[91] As Keith Whittington observes, "The judiciary is largely motivated by a different set of concerns than is the legislature. Although judges might disagree among themselves over matters of political principle just as legislators do, legislators may not bother with such issues at all or give them due regard when they do."[92] There are widely accepted institutional explanations for why legislators are pushed toward risk aversion and blame avoidance in their legislative behavior.[93]

Thus, those who draft statutes often do not give, feel no obligation to give, and in fact may feel obligated not to give reasons on their behalf.[94] We should not compare idealized courts with actual legislatures, but we should also be prepared not to demand too much from actual legislatures in light of their institutional limitations. In our society, the legislative process is pervaded by the existence of special interests, and it is unrealistic to expect legislators to act for the public good as often as they should. Favoritism toward certain special interests in the legislative process comes at the expense of the freedom and equality of others. Normally, law-making bodies are not in a position to make disinterested judgments when such judgments are called

---

[91] See Keith E. Whittington, "In Defense of Legislatures," review, *Law and Disagreement*, by Jeremy Waldron, and *The Dignity of Legislation*, by Jeremy Waldron, 28 *Political Theory* (2000), 696.

[92] Ibid., 699.

[93] Ibid., 697.

[94] Frederick Schauer, "Giving Reasons," 47 *Stanford Law Review* (1995), 636.

for; legislators are not necessarily bad people or worse than the rest of us but are institutionally constrained. It is typical for voters to blame individual politicians for other problems, but a more sophisticated understanding would have to take into account the effects of institutions on legislative behavior.

In short, judicial review is a necessary evil that is premised on the assumption that we are more justified in placing our bets on the judiciary as the branch that can more easily introduce the right kinds of reasons into politics. The freedom and equality of those who are least influential in our society should not be left in the hands of legislators who have too many incentives to ignore these values. Reliance on judicial review is less than ideal from the standpoint of direct democracy, but it has the advantage of not radically departing from the world as it exists today. On the weak assumption that judges are more likely to be impartial, and citizens and their elected representatives are less likely to be fair, a division of labor among the three branches of government is not only practical but also desirable. This may not produce the kind of morally elevated politics that deliberative democrats hope for, but it has the merit of increasing the likelihood that the state will treat politically vulnerable minorities more fairly. In a country where so many of us have so little political influence, people are entitled to know the reasons that lawmakers and judges rely on, especially when inclusion in the decision-making process is out of the question.

III. BACK TO THE COURT

A. Public Justification and Democracy

Because democratic legitimacy in the sense of actual consent on the part of all persons is off the table, Americans must look elsewhere for an institution that is capable of producing reasons that all reasonable persons could be expected to share. The problem is not simply protecting discrete and insular minorities that lack political clout but a much more serious problem of how laws can be legitimate when most people have no direct influence in the legislative process and their pursuit of their respective conceptions of the good may be undermined by laws that are not publicly justified. This fundamental problem of political theory affects what would legitimize a judicial decision. Kermit Roosevelt writes that a legitimate Supreme Court decision is one in which the Court has "taken a reasonable position in terms of deferring and not deferring to the government body whose action it is reviewing."[95] On the surface, this proposition is true, but only because it

---

[95] Kermit Roosevelt, *The Myth of Judicial Activism* (New Haven, CT: Yale University Press, 2008), 3.

is hard to argue against without a more detailed explanation of what a reasonable position consists in. As I have tried to show in the first half of the book, courts should defer only to legislative judgments that are based on sufficiently public reasons; such reasons take the place of actual unanimous consent under conditions where such consent could never be secured.

There is no shortage of critics who will insist that a society that relies so heavily on courts to resolve some of its most important political controversies is a society in which citizens do not rule themselves. This concern is legitimate but should not be overstated. A government for the people need not be a government by the people all of the time, especially when perfect answers – those that will satisfy everyone – do not exist in hard cases. One can concede judicial review is the second-best alternative in a far-from-perfect world. Kramer writes, "Ultimately, we cannot avoid making our best guess about which of our institutions is likely to do the best job in light of what we know about their relative capacities to act responsibly when it comes to the Constitution. It is, however, only a guess."[96] Surely, it is not only a guess, given what historians and political scientists tell us about how our political institutions have operated and continue to operate. The point is not only that we have more reason to put our faith in the judiciary as the branch that has a special ability to infuse principle into politics.[97] Historically, in the United States, legislatures too often have treated minority groups unfairly, and we have little reason to believe that this phenomenon will change for the better anytime soon, as elected representatives have powerful incentives to do what their constituents and parties want them to do.

One of the implications of this book is that Americans, with as much candor as possible, must confront a number of different conflicts: between the popularity of particular reasons in particular cases and their fairness, between democratic self-rule and individual rights, between reasons and results, and between liberalism and democracy. When the state puts forth reasons in a particular constitutional case that turn out to be insufficiently public, and a court rejects these reasons, that exercise of judicial review is justified. After all, those reasons should not have been the basis of a statutory prohibition or classification in the first place. That is probably as close as any constitutional democracy can come to legitimizing its most important constitutional decisions.

B. Reasons and Results

Cass Sunstein is famous for using the institutional imperfections of courts, the cognitive limitations of judges, and the difficulty of predicting

---

[96] Kramer, *Popular Constitutionalism*, 237.
[97] Stephen Macedo, *Liberal Virtues: Citizenship, Virtue, and Community in Liberal Constitutionalism* (New York: Oxford University Press, 1990), 162.

consequences to argue for judicial humility.[98] The risk of judicial error and unintended bad consequences are real, but the flaw of this line of reasoning is that all of that could also be said about legislatures. Even Tushnet concedes that popular constitutionalism cannot ensure that specific results will be produced.[99] Nor has Sunstein shown that the reasons that legislative majorities rely on would be sufficiently publicly justified to reasonable dissenters. As two commentators have pointed out, "Sunstein's model of judicial minimalism comes perilously close to sacrificing such rights for the sake of deliberative processes."[100]

Recently, a number of scholars have attempted to show that judicial decisions, including those of the Court, do not have the significant effects that their proponents have insisted.[101] Sunstein endorses Gerald Rosenberg's position that courts cannot usually bring about social change and believes that this fact supports judicial minimalism.[102] As I see it, though, the hollow-hope argument also cuts in the opposite direction. Interpreted differently, Rosenberg's findings suggest that the Court no longer has to be so concerned with the likely effects of its decisions. In its opinions, the Court gives advice on what the Constitution means, and the American people and their elected representatives can take that advice or reject it. Critics of the judiciary tend to exaggerate its power and potential for abuse. The reality is that the other two branches of government can hold and have held courts accountable in most circumstances and the judiciary can swim against the current of popular opinion for only so long. In addition, these branches can do far more damage than the judiciary ever could, even at its worst.

Judges can try to hold lawmakers to an exclusive principle of public reason and more often than not, my hope is that they will succeed. They are better intellectually equipped and institutionally situated to identify the most important considerations in a constitutional controversy and weigh them appropriately. Historically, of course, the record is mixed. In addition, compared with past practices, the justices are not as actively involved in the production of their opinions from start to finish.[103] All of that said, the case for the judiciary as the best vehicle for public justification turns on what has happened in the past and what is likely to happen in the future. Empirically, there are many variables that make the U.S. Supreme Court a more or less deliberative institution at particular historical moments, but that is not my immediate concern. Rather, the Court has the potential to

---

[98] Sunstein, *One Case at a Time*, 244–58.

[99] Tushnet, *Taking the Constitution Away from the Courts*, 187.

[100] Sotirios A. Barber and James E. Fleming, *Constitutional Interpretation: The Basic Questions* (New York: Oxford University Press, 2007), 148.

[101] See, e.g., Rosenberg, *Hollow Hope*.

[102] Sunstein, *Legal Reasoning and Political Conflict*, 176.

[103] See Kramer, *People Themselves*, 240.

be such a vehicle, despite its institutional imperfections and the fallibilities of its members. Before Americans give up on the Court, those who believe that the judiciary does not really differ from other political institutions must be able to demonstrate that the Court (1) has never functioned as a forum of principle, (2) could never do so even under more ideal conditions, and (3) that other political institutions, such as Congress, could do a better job of publicly justifying constitutional choices.

Those who are skeptical of the thesis the Court has (or could) function as a forum of principle ought to have the burden of proof in showing that, despite glaring institutional differences between courts and legislatures, the latter could take the place of courts. As is stands, they have not shown that any of these three propositions are true, and we simply do not know what legislatures would do if judicial review were abolished.[104] Justified or not, most Americans have faith in the impartiality of the Court.[105] As Jeremy Waldron acknowledges, "[L]egislation and legislatures have a bad name in legal and political philosophy."[106] That bad name, at least in the United States, is more justified than he believes. All things considered, the Court seems to be better equipped to articulate the meaning of freedom and equality and to protect those values from legislative majorities that do not exercise the self-restraint that they are supposed to exercise.

Waldron is probably the best known and most articulate critics of judicial review and observes that "we have a remarkably limited experience of legislative deliberation."[107] He is also right to insist that Americans could learn something from "the great debates in the British Parliament and in legislatures around the world whereby race relations legislation was enacted and abortion and homosexuality decriminalized."[108] At the same time, the American situation is unique. There will always be dissenters to any important constitutional decision, but as I have tried to show, a society that is committed to the freedom and equality of all of its members also has to be committed to judicial review based on public justification. Waldron believes that "there is something to be said" on behalf of a legislative vote – namely that rival views were tallied up fairly – that cannot be said on behalf of a judicial vote.[109] Although there may be something to be said for this view, especially when one, like Waldron, believes that judges base their decisions

---

[104] I borrow the term *forum of principle* from Ronald Dworkin, *A Matter of Principle* (Cambridge, MA: Harvard University Press, 1985), 33.

[105] Kramer, *Popular Constitutionalism*, 232.

[106] Jeremy J. Waldron, *The Dignity of Legislation* (Cambridge: Cambridge University Press, 1999), 1.

[107] Jeremy J. Waldron, "Legislation," in *The Blackwell Guide to the Philosophy of Law and Legal Theory*, ed. Martin P. Golding and William A. Edmundson (Malden, MA: Blackwell Publishing, 2005), 246.

[108] Ibid.

[109] Ibid., 247.

on the opinions that they happen to hold, which presumably are no more justified than those of ordinary people.[110] But is there enough to be said? Waldron may be right about the rest of the democratic world but wrong about the possibility of higher-quality popular and legislative deliberation in the United States. In contemporary America, his use of examples such as racial discrimination, abortion, and same-sex relationships would seem to undercut his claim that Americans should put more faith and power in their law-making bodies.

Legislators often do not give reasons for the laws that they enact and may believe themselves to be justified in not giving any reasons. As Frederick Schauer points out, "The act of giving a reason is the antithesis of authority."[111] That is problematic in a society where dissenters often do not consent to the laws that they are subject to, including those that detract from the quality of their lives. In the end, no one with a democratic sensibility would prefer that courts protect freedom and equality if the people themselves or their elected representatives could perform this function better than courts could. But there is too little reason to take such a chance and emulate a parliamentary system. That may not be music to democratic ears, but judicial review based on public justification has the virtues of not departing too far from American constitutional practice and of not making unrealistic assumptions about the cognitive abilities of ordinary citizens or the institutional abilities of legislators. A society that shares a standard of public justification is a society that tries to avoid imposing laws on dissenters without proper justification. That still leaves plenty of space for Americans not only to dispute judicial decisions but also to challenge the numerous injustices that continue to exist. At the same time, when collective decisions must be made, a judiciary that is committed to public justification is more likely to ensure that the state does not enact laws on the basis of reasons that reasonable people have good grounds for rejecting. As much as possible in an imperfect world, that commitment would protect the freedom and equality of all persons.

---

[110] Ibid.
[111] Frederick Schauer, "Giving Reasons," 47 *Stanford Law Review* (1995), 636–7.

Conclusion

It is central to the liberal tradition that those who exercise political power should respect the consciences of all persons, and the concept of public justification reflects this concern. An exclusive principle of public reason should protect all persons, not only those who happen to constitute a legislative majority in a particular constitutional controversy. In the absence of adequate justification for legal prohibition, people should be allowed to do what they would like to do, and they should not be treated unequally. That is a principle that any society that is committed to respecting the freedom and equality of all of its members must endorse. Otherwise, lawmakers will impose laws on those who do not have adequate reasons to accept them. As much as possible, in developing an ideal approach to constitutional adjudication based on public justification, I have tried to avoid making unrealistic assumptions about human and institutional capabilities. This is a problem that anyone who cares about improving American politics has to face squarely: how stark is the difference between what constitutional democracy is and what it could be under better circumstances? On the one hand, a political or constitutional theorist who believes that America could be more just or more democratic cannot be satisfied with the status quo. In a country that not only has great wealth but also an enviable constitutional tradition, life could be better for many persons in a number of important ways. On the other hand, each theorist will have particular normative aims and will have to prioritize some of them over others. In doing so, theorists cannot be so enamoured of how things could be that they forget how things are and how difficult it is to make dramatic changes even under conditions that are conducive to reform. A responsible constitutional theorist would like to see his or her ideas enacted in some form. Thus, I have tried to work within the limits of what I believe to be possible at this moment in American history by not departing too far from American constitutional theory and practice, but without sacrificing the overarching normative purpose of my theory of constitutional adjudication, which is to ensure that the most important laws are publicly justified. Judicial review can serve that end.

In the preceding pages, I never meant to romanticize judicial review, put judges on a pedestal, glorify the history of American constitutional practice, or suggest that other political actors should be uninvolved in political life. Indeed, numerous empirical studies indicate that the judiciary is not so far removed from politics.[1] My intention has been to show how judicial review could be justified and improved in a democracy such as our own, which is not to say that other political institutions are not equally important. After all, the Court does not declare war or formulate national economic policy. Unlike Rawls and other deliberative democrats, I am not optimistic about the likelihood that most Americans could ever use a principle of public reason to guide their public deliberations and their voting behavior. That is not the kind of skepticism that Plato had in mind when he likened the people to a wild beast, but my hopes for the judiciary, as the institution that can serve as the primary vehicle of public justification in American society, are driven by the belief that no political or constitutional theory should demand too much from the people and their elected representatives. In matters of constitutional essentials, to ask judges to hold lawmakers accountable to a standard of public justification is not to ask the impossible. But to expect the people and their elected representatives to do so is to ignore just about everything we know about American political institutions and voting behavior.

It is hard to miss the chasm between Rawls's vision of a well-ordered society and our political life in its current form, which could be worse but also leaves so much to be desired. One of the assets of my theory of constitutional adjudication is that it does not conflate constitutional and political discourse. Americans are under no self-imposed civic duty to eschew their deepest convictions when exchanging reasons with one another in politics. As a result, my theory leaves plenty of space for them not only to dispute judicial decisions but also to determine whether they are consistent with our ideals of freedom and equality. At the same time, when political choices must be made, a judiciary that is committed to public justification is more likely to ensure that the state does not enact laws on the basis of reasons that reasonable people have good grounds for rejecting. It may turn out that, at times, the existence of such reasons will be disputed and that it will not be clear, to all reasonable people, whether the state has met its burden of proof. That is not an objection to public justification but a reason for putting wise judges on the bench and improving the nomination and confirmation processes.

[1] See, e.g., Lawrence Baum, *The Supreme Court*, 2nd ed. (Washington, D.C.: Congressional Quarterly, 1985), 2.

In a more deliberative democracy than ours, political discourse would be more principled and Americans would be less willing to support legislation that was not publicly justified. In addition, they would take more responsibility for the political choices that public officials make in their name. That Americans tend to turn important political questions into constitutional questions should not serve an excuse for indifference to how courts decide such cases. In the end, through their exercise of judicial review, judges should play the role that dissenters would play in an ideal direct democracy, where collective decisions must be unanimous in the name of avoiding unjustified coercion. This book is premised on the claims that judges can so do competently and can do so better than other political actors, including the people themselves.

Over time, Americans have learned to live in the midst of many antimajoritarian practices and to accept that the constitutional part of constitutional democracy is as important as the democracy part. The tension between them will always exist, but the claim that liberalism is necessarily hostile to democracy, historically speaking, is implausible.[2] Those who are in favor of retaining judicial review are right in believing that antidemocratic means can serve democratic ends but wrong in believing that constitutional adjudication need not be an elitist enterprise. That may not be what democrats want to hear, but it reflects the fact that judges are better equipped to identify public reasons than others are. That will not lead to the ideal society that democrats have envisioned, but it might produce a society that does a better job of justifying its laws to reasonable dissenters, and that would be an improvement that all Americans should embrace.

---

[2] Stephen Holmes, *Passions and Constraint: On the Theory of Liberal Democracy* (Chicago: University of Chicago Press, 1995), 31.

References

Ackerman, Bruce. 1980. *Social Justice in the Liberal State*. New Haven: Yale University Press.

——. 1989. "Why Dialogue?" *The Journal of Philosophy* 86 (1): 5–22.

Alejandro, Roberto. 1993. "Rawls's Communitarianism," *Canadian Journal of Philosophy* 23 (1): 75–99.

Alexander, Larry A. 2005. "Constitutionalism." In *The Blackwell Guide to the Philosophy of Law and Legal Theory*. Martin P. Golding and William A. Edmundson eds. Malden: Blackwell Publishing Ltd., 2005.

Amar, Akhil Reed. 1997. *The Constitution and Criminal Procedure: First Principles*. New Haven: Yale University Press.

Anderson, Terry H. 2004. *The Pursuit of Fairness: A History of Affirmative Action*. (New York: Oxford University Press.)

Aristotle. 1988. *The Nicomachean Ethics*. J.A.K. Thomson trans. London: Penguin Books.

——. 1992. *The Politics*. T.A. Sinclair trans. London: Penguin Books.

Arneson, Richard J. 1990. "Neutrality and Utility." *Canadian Journal of Philosophy* 20 (2) (1990): 215–240.

——. 1997. "The Priority of the Right over the Good Rides Again." *Ethics* 108 (1): 169–196.

——. 2003. "Liberal Neutrality on the Good: An Autopsy." In *Perfectionism and Neutrality: Essays in Liberal Theory*. Steven Wall and George Klosko eds. Lanham: Rowman and Littlefield Publishers Inc.

Audi, Robert. 1989. "The Separation of Church and State and the Obligations of Citizenship." *Philosophy and Public Affairs* 18 (3): 259–296.

——. 2000. *Religious Commitment and Secular Reason*. Cambridge, UK: Cambridge University Press.

The Cambridge Dictionary of Philosophy. 1995. Robert Audi ed. New York: Cambridge University Press.

Balkin, Jack M. 2001. "Preface." In *What* Brown v. Board of Education *Should Have Said: The Nation's Top Legal Experts Rewrite America's Landmark Civil Rights Decision*. Jack M. Balkin ed. New York: New York University Press.

——. 2001. "Introduction," In *What* Brown v. Board of Education *Should Have Said: The Nation's Top Legal Experts Rewrite America's Landmark Civil Rights Decision*. Jack M. Balkin ed. New York: New York University Press.

Barber, Benjamin. 1988. *The Conquest of Politics: Liberal Philosophy in Democratic Times*. Princeton: Princeton University Press.

———. 2007. *Consumed: How Markets Corrupt Children, Infantilize Adults, and Swallow Citizens Whole*. New York: W.W. Norton.

Barber, Sotiros, and James E. Fleming. 2007. *Constitutional Interpretation: The Basic Questions*. New York: Oxford University Press.

Barnett, Randy E. 2004. *Restoring the Lost Constitution: The Presumption of Liberty*. Princeton: Princeton University Press.

Barry, Brian. 1973. *The Liberal Theory of Justice*. Oxford: Clarendon Press.

———. 1995. "John Rawls and the Search for Stability." *Ethics* 105 (4): 874–915.

———. 1995. *Justice as Impartiality*. Oxford: Clarendon Press.

———. 2001. *Culture and Equality: An Egalitarian Critique of Multiculturalism*. Cambridge: Harvard University Press.

Baum, Lawrence. 1985. *The Supreme Court*. 2nd ed. Washington D.C.: Congressional Quarterly Inc.

Beckwith, Francis J. 2007. *Defending Life: A Moral and Legal Case Against Abortion Choice*. New York: Cambridge University Press.

Bedau, Hugo Adam. 1997. "A Reply to Van Den Haag." In *The Death Penalty in America: Current Controversies*. New York: Oxford University Press.

Bedi, Sonu. 2009. *Rejecting Rights: The Turn to Justification*. New York: Cambridge University Press.

Bell, Derrick A. Jr. 1980. "*Brown v. Board of Education* and the Interest-Convergence Dilemma." *Harvard Law Review* 93 (3): 518–533.

Bellamy, Richard. 1999. *Liberalism and Pluralism: Towards a Politics of Compromise*. New York: Routledge.

Benhabib, Seyla. 1989. "Liberal Dialogue Versus a Critical Theory of Discursive Legitimation." In *Liberalism and the Moral Life*. Nancy L. Rosenblum ed. Cambridge: Harvard University Press.

———. 1992. *Situating the Self: Gender, Community and Postmodernism in Contemporary Ethics*. Cambridge: Polity Press.

———. 1996. "The Democratic Moment and the Problem of Difference." In *Democracy and Difference: Contesting the Boundaries of the Political*. Seyla Benhabib ed. Princeton: Princeton University Press.

Bennett, Robert W. 1984. "Objectivity in Constitutional Law." *University of Pennsylvania Law Review* 132 (3): 445–496.

Berelson, Bernard R., Paul F. Lazarsfeld, and William N, McPhee. 1954. *Voting: A Study of Opinion Formation in a Presidential Campaign*. Chicago: University of Chicago Press.

Berger, Raoul. 1977. *Government by Judiciary: The Transformation of the Fourteenth Amendment*. Cambridge: Harvard University Press.

Berkowitz, Peter. 2006. "The Ambiguities of Rawls's Influence." *Perspectives on Politics* 4 (1): 121–133.

Berlin, Isaiah. 1991. "The Pursuit of the Ideal." In *The Crooked Timber of Humanity* New York: Alfred Knopf.

Bertram, Christopher. 1997. "Theories of Public Reason." *Imprints* 2 (1): 72–85.

Bessette, Joseph. 1994. *The Mild Voice of Reason: Deliberative Democracy and American National Government*. Chicago: University of Chicago Press.

Bickel, Alexander. 1962. *The Least Dangerous Branch: The Supreme Court at the Bar of Politics*. 2nd ed. New Haven: Yale University Press.

Bohman, James. 1995. "Public Reason and Cultural Pluralism." *Political Theory* 23 (2): 253–279.

——. 1998. "The Coming of Age of Deliberative Democracy." *Journal of Political Philosophy* 9: 400–425.

Bok, Derek. 2006. *Our Underachieving Colleges: A Candid Look at How Much Students Learn and Why They Should Be Learning More*. Princeton: Princeton University Press.

Bork, Robert H. 1971. "Neutral Principles and Some First Amendment Problems." *Indiana Law Journal* 47 (1): 1–35.

——. 1977. "The Conservative Case for Amending the Constitution." *The Weekly Standard* 2 (24) March 3, 1977.

——. 1990. *The Tempting of America: The Political Seduction of the Law*. New York: Simon and Schuster Inc.

——. 1996. *Slouching Towards Gomorrah: Modern Liberalism and American Decline*. New York: Regan Books.

——. 2003. *Coercing Virtue: The Worldwide Rule of Judges*. Washington D.C.: The AEI Press.

Bowen, William G., and Derek Bok. 2002. "The Meaning of 'Merit'." In *The Affirmative Action Debate*. 2nd ed. Steven M. Cahn ed. New York: Routledge.

Brennan, William J., Jr. 1999. "In Defense of Dissents." *Hastings Law Journal* 50 (1999): 671–682.

Brest, Paul. "The Misconceived Quest for Original Understanding." *Boston University Law Review* 60 (2) (1980), 204–238.

——. 1981. "The Fundamental Rights Controversy: The Essential Contradictions of Normative Constitutional Scholarship." *Yale Law Journal* 90 (5): 1063–1109.

Brettschneider, Corey. 2007. *Democratic Rights: The Substance of Self-Government*. Princeton: Princeton University Press.

Breyer, Stephen. 2005. *Active Liberty: Interpreting Our Democratic Constitution*. New York: Alfred A. Knopf.

Brighouse, Harry. 1998. "Civic Education and Liberal Legitimacy." *Ethics* 108 (4): 719–745.

Bronner, Ethan. 1989. *Battle for Justice: How the Bork Nomination Shook America*. New York: Anchor Books.

Brower, Bruce W. 1994. "The Limits of Public Reason." *Journal of Philosophy* 91 (1): 5–26.

Burton, Steven J. 1992. *Judging in Good Faith*. New York: Cambridge University Press.

Cahn, Steven M. 2002. "Introduction." In *The Affirmative Action Debate*. 2nd ed. Steven M. Cahn ed. New York: Routledge.

Calabresi, Steven G. 2007. "Introduction: A Critical Introduction to the Originalism Debate." In *Originalism: A Quarter-Century of Debate*. Steven G. Calabresi ed. Washington D.C: Regnery Publishing Inc.

Callahan, David. 2004. *The Cheating Culture: Why More Americans are Doing Wrong to get Ahead*. Orlando: Harcourt Inc.

Callahan, Joan C. 2001. "The Fetus and Fundamental Rights." In *The Ethics of Abortion: Pro-Life vs. Pro-Choice*. 3rd ed. Robert M. Baird and Stuart E. Rosenbaum eds. Amherst: Prometheus Books.

Callahan, Sidney. 2001. "Abortion and the Sexual Agenda." In *The Ethics of Abortion: Pro-Life vs. Pro-Choice.* 3rd ed. Robert M. Baird and Stuart E. Rosenbaum eds. Amherst: Prometheus Books.

Campbell, Angus, Philip E. Converse, Warren E. Miller, and Donald E. Stokes. 1980. *The American Voter.* Chicago: University of Chicago Press.

Carpini, Michael X. Delli and Scott Keeter. 1996. *What Americans Know About Politics and Why It Matters.* New Haven: Yale University Press.

Cardozo, Benjamin N. 1949. *The Nature of the Judicial Process.* New Haven: Yale University Press.

Carter, David. 2004. *Stonewall: The Riots that Sparked the Gay Revolution.* New York: St. Martin's Press.

Carter, Stephen L. 1989. "The Religiously Devout Judge." *Notre Dame Law Review* 64: 932–944.

———. 1993. *Culture of Disbelief: How American Law and Politics Trivializes Religious Devotion.* New York: Anchor Books.

Ceaser, James W. 1990. *Liberal Democracy and Political Science.* Baltimore: Johns Hopkins University Press.

Chambers, David. 1996. "What If? The Legal Consequences of Marriage and the Legal Needs of Lesbian and Gay Male Couples." *Michigan Law Review* 95 (2): 447–491.

Chan, Joseph. 2000. "Legitimacy, Unanimity, and Perfectionism." *Philosophy and Public Affairs* 29 (1): 5–42.

Charney, Evan. 1998. "Political Liberalism, Deliberative Democracy, and the Public Sphere." *American Political Science Review* 92 (1): 97–110.

Chemerinsky, Erwin. 1987. *Interpreting the Constitution.* New York: Praeger Books.

Cohen, Joshua. 1989. "The Economic Basis of Deliberative Democracy." *Social Philosophy and Policy* 6 (2): 25–50.

———. 1994. "A More Democratic Liberalism." *Michigan Law Review* 92 (6): 1503–1546.

Converse, Philip E. 1962. "Information Flow and the Stability of Partisan Attitudes." *Public Opinion Quarterly* 26: 578–599.

———. 1964. "The Nature of Belief Systems in Mass Publics." In *Ideology and Discontent.* David Apter ed. New York: Free Press.

———. 1970. "Attitudes and Non-Attitudes: Continuation of a Dialogue," In *The Quantitative Analysis of Social Problems*, Edward R. Tufte ed. Reading: Addison-Wesley.

Craig, Barbara Hinkson, and David M. O'Brien, 1993. *Abortion and American Politics*: Chatham, MA: Chatham House Publishers.

Crossed, Carol. 2006. "Foreword." In Vasu Murti, *The Liberal Case* Against *Abortion.* R.A.G.E. Media.

D'Agostino, Fred. 1996. *Free Public Reason: Making It Up As We Go.* New York: Oxford University Press.

Dahl, Robert A. 1989. *Democracy and Its Critics.* New Haven: Yale University Press.

Devlin, Patrick. 1977. "Morals and the Criminal Law." In *The Philosophy of Law.* Ronald Dworkin ed. New York: Oxford University Press.

Doan, Alesha E. 2007. *Opposition and Intimidation: The Abortion Wars and Strategies of Political Harassment.* Ann Arbor: University of Michigan Press.

Doan, Alesha E., and Jean Calterone Williams. 2008. *The Politics of Virginity: Abstinence in Sex Education.* Westport, CT: Praeger Publishing.

Dawkins, Richard. 2006. *The God Delusion.* New York: Houghton Mifflin Co.

Downing, Lyle A., and Robert B, Thigpen. 1986. "Beyond Shared Understandings." *Political Theory* 14 (3): 451–472.

Downs, Anthony. 1957. *An Economic Theory of Democracy.* New York: Harper and Row Inc.

Dreben, Burton. 2003. "On Rawls and Political Liberalism." In *The Cambridge Companion to Rawls.* Samuel Freeman ed. Cambridge: Cambridge University Press.

Dworkin, Gerald. 1988. *The Theory and Practice of Autonomy.* Cambridge: Cambridge University Press.

Dworkin, Ronald. 1977. *Taking Rights Seriously.* Cambridge: Harvard University Press.

——. 1985. *A Matter of Principle.* Cambridge: Harvard University Press.

——. 1986. *Law's Empire.* Cambridge: The Belknap Press of the Harvard University Press.

——. 1987. "The Bork Nomination." *New York Review of Books*, August 13, 3.

——. 1989. "The Original Position." In *Reading Rawls: Critical Studies on Rawls's 'A Theory of Justice'*, Norman Daniels ed. Stanford: Stanford University Press.

——. 1994. *Life's Dominion: An Argument About Abortion, Euthanasia, and Individual Freedom.* New York: Vintage Books.

——. 1996. *Freedom's Law: The Moral Reading of the American Constitution.* Cambridge: Harvard University Press.

Ronald Dworkin et al., "Assisted Suicide: The Philosophers' Brief." 44 (5) *The New York Review of Books*, March 27, 1997, http://www.nybooks.com/articles/1237 (page 8 of 15).

——. 2006. *Justice in Robes.* Cambridge: The Belknap Press of the Harvard University Press.

——. 1997. "Comment." In *A Matter of Interpretation: Federal Courts and the Law.* Princeton: Princeton University Press.

Eisgruber, Chrsitopher L. 2007. *The Next Justice: Repairing the Supreme Court Appointments Process.* Princeton: Princeton University Press.

Eisler, Kim Isaac. 2005. *The Last Liberal: Justice William J. Brennan Jr. and the Decisions that Transformed America.* Washington D.C.: Beard Books.

Elgin, Catharine Z. 1996. *Considered Judgment.* Princeton: Princeton University Press.

Ely, John Hart. 1973. "The Wages of Crying Wolf: A Comment on Roe v. Wade." *Yale Law Journal* 82 (5): 920–949.

——. 1980. *Democracy and Distrust: A Theory of Judicial Review.* Cambridge: Harvard University Press.

Epstein, Richard A. 1985. *Takings: Private Property and the Power of Eminent Domain* (Cambridge: Harvard University Press).

Eskridge, William N. 1996. *The Case for Same-Sex Marriage.* New York: The Free Press.

——. 2008. *Dishonorable Passions: Sodomy Laws in America 1861–2003.* New York: Viking Books.

Estlund, David. 1998. "The Insularity of the Reasonable: Why Political Liberalism Must Admit the Truth." *Ethics* 108 (2): 252–275.

——. 2003. "The Democracy/Contractualism Analogy." *Philosophy and Public Affairs* 31 (4) (2003): 387–412.

Fehrenbacher, Don E. 1978. *The Dred Scott Case: Its Significance in American Law and Politics*. New York: Oxford University Press.

Feinberg, Joel. 1984. *Harm to Others: The Moral Limits of the Criminal Law*. Vol. 1 New York, Oxford University Press.

Fenno, Richard F. 1978. *Homestyle: House Members on Their Districts*. Glenview: Scott Foresman and Co.

Finnis, John. 1994. "Law, Morality, and Sexual Orientation." *Notre Dame Law Review* 69: 1049–1076.

——. 1996. "Is Natural Law Theory Compatible with Limited Government?" In *Natural Law, Liberalism, and Morality: Contemporary Essays*. Robert P. George ed. Oxford: Clarendon Press.

Fisher, Louis. 1988. *Constitutional Dialogues: Interpretation as Political Process*. Princeton: Princeton University Press.

Fishkin, James S. 1995. *The Voice of the People: Public Opinion and Democracy*. New Haven: Yale University Press.

Fiss, Owen W. "Objectivity and Interpretation." *Stanford Law Review* 34 (4) (1982): 739–773.

Foner, Eric. 1988. *Reconstruction: America's Unfinished Revolution* 1863–1877. New York: Harper Collins Publishers, Inc.

Foucault, Michel. 1979. *Discipline and Punish: The Birth of the Prison*, 2nd ed. Alan Sheridan trans. New York: Vintage Books.

Freeman, Samuel. 1990–1991. "Constitutional Democracy and the Legitimacy of Judicial Review." *Law and Philosophy* 9: 327–370.

——. 2000. "Deliberative Democracy: A Sympathetic Comment." *Philosophy and Public Affairs* 29 (4): 371–418.

——. *Rawls* (New York: Routledge, 2007), 16.

Friedman, Marilyn. 2000. "John Rawls and the Political Coercion of Unreasonable People." In *The Idea of Political Liberalism: Essays on Rawls*. Victoria Davion and Clark Wolf eds. Lanham: Rowman and Littlefield Publishers, Inc.

Friedman, Milton. 1962. *Capitalism and Freedom* (Chicago: University of Chicago Press).

Galston, William. 1982. "Defending Liberalism." *American Political Science Review*. 76 (3): 621–629.

——. 1991. *Liberal Purposes: Goods, Virtues, and Diversity in the Liberal State*. New York: Cambridge University Press.

——. 1993. "What is Living and What is Dead in Kant's Practical Philosophy?" In *Kant and Political Philosophy: The Contemporary Legacy*. Ronald Beiner and William James Booth eds. New Haven: Yale University Press.

——. 2002. *Liberal Pluralism: The Implications of Value Pluralism for Political Theory and Practice*. New York: Cambridge University Press.

Gaus, Gerald F. 1990. *Value and Justification: The Foundations of Liberal Theory*. Cambridge: Cambridge University Press.

——. 1991. "Public Justification and Democratic Adjudication." *Constitutional Political Economy* 2 (3): 251–281.

——. 1996. *Justificatory Liberalism: An Essay on Epistemology and Political Theory*. New York: Oxford University Press.

——. 2003. *Contemporary Theories of Liberalism: Public Reason as a Post-Enlightenment Project*. Thousand Oaks: Sage Publications Inc.

——. 2003. "Liberal Neutrality: A Compelling and Radical Principle," In *Perfection and Neutrality: Essays in Liberal Theory*. Steven Wall and George Klosko eds. Lanham: Rowman and Littlefield Publishers Inc.

Gaus Gerald, and Kevin Vallier, "The Roles of Religious Convictions in a Publicly Justified Polity: The Implications of Convergence, Asymmetry, and Public Institutions," 8, unpublished paper, http://publicreason.net/2008/09/26/ppps-the-roles-of-religious-conviction-in-a-publicly-justified-polity/

Gauthier, David. 1986. *Morals by Agreement*. Oxford: Clarendon Press.

——. "Public Reason." *Social Philosophy and Policy* 12 (1) (1995): 19–42.

Gerhardt, Michael J., Stephen M. Griffin, and Thomas D. Rowe Jr. 2000. *Constitutional Theory: Arguments and Perspectives*, 2nd ed. Lexis Publishing Inc.

Gerstmann, Evan. 2004. *Same-Sex Marriage and the Constitution*. New York: Cambridge University Press.

——. 1997. "Public Reason and Political Conflict: Abortion and Homosexuality." *Yale Law Journal* 106 (8): 2475–2504.

——. 2003. "Neutrality, Equality, and 'Same-Sex Marriage'." In *Marriage and Same-Sex Unions: A Debate*. Lynn D. Wardle ed. Westport, CT: Praeger Publications.

George, Robert P., and Christopher Wolfe. 1997. "'Public Reason' and Reasons for Action by Public Authority: An Exchange of Views: Natural Law and Liberal Public Reason." *American Journal of Jurisprudence* 42 (1997): 31–49.

——. 2000. "Natural Law and Public Reason." In *Natural Law and Public Reason*. Washington D.C: Georgetown University Press.

Ginsburg, Ruth Bader. 1992. "Speaking in a Judicial Voice." *New York University Law Review* 67: 1185–1209.

Graber, Mark. 2007. *Dred Scott and the Problem of Constitutional Evil*. New York: Cambridge University Press.

Graglia, Lino A. 2005. "Constitutional Law Without the Constitution." In *A Country I Do Not Recognize: The Legal Assault on American Values*. Robert H. Bork ed. Stanford: Hoover Institution Press.

Gray, John. 1995. *Enlightenment's Wake: Politics and Culture at the Close of the Modern Age*. London: Routledge Press.

Kent Greenawalt, 1991. *Religious Convictions and Political Choice*. New York: Oxford University Press.

——. 1994. "On Public Reason." *Chicago-Kent Law Review* 69 (3): 669–689.

——. 1995. *Private Consciences and Public Reasons*. New York: Oxford University Press.

——. 1999. "Legitimate Authority and the Duty to Obey." In *The Duty to Obey the Law: Selected Philosophical Readings*. William A. Edmundson ed. Lanham: Rowman and Littlefield Publishers, Inc.

Greenberg, Jan Crawford. 2008. *Supreme Conflict: The Inside Story of the Struggle for Control of the United States Supreme Court*. New York: Penguin Books.

Grey, Thomas. 1975. "Do We Have an Unwritten Constitution?" *Stanford Law Review* 27 (3): 703–718.

Griffin, Leslie. 1997. "Good Catholics Should Be Rawlsian Liberals?" *Southern California Interdisciplinary Law Journal* 5 (3): 297–373.

Griffin, Stephen M. 1994. "Political Philosophy Versus Political Theory." *Chicago-Kent Law Review* 69 (3): 691–707.

——. 1999. *American Constitutionalism: From Theory to Politics*. Princeton: Princeton University Press.

Gunnell, John G. 1986. *Between Philosophy and Politics: The Alienation of Political Theory.* Amherst: University of Massachusetts Press.

Klaus Gunther, Klaus. 1993. *The Sense of Appropriateness: Application Discourses in Morality and Law.* John Farrell trans. Albany: State University of New York Press.

Gutmann, Amy. 1995. "Civic Education and Social Diversity." *Ethics* 105 (3): 557–579.

———. 1980. "Children, Paternalism, and Education: A Liberal Argument." *Philosophy and Public Affairs* 9(4): 338–358.

———. 1987. *Democratic Education.* Princeton: Princeton University Press.

Gutmann, Amy, and Dennis Thompson, 1996. *Democracy and Disagreement: Why Moral Conflict Cannot Be Avoided in Politics and What Should Be Done About It.* Cambridge: The Belknap Press of the Harvard University Press.

Gutmann, Amy. 2003. "Rawls on the Relationship Between Liberalism and Democracy." in *The Cambridge Companion to Rawls.* Samuel Freeman ed. New York: Cambridge University Press.

Habermas, Jurgen. 1990. *Moral Consciousness and Communicative Action.* Christian Lenhardt and Sherry Weber Nicholsen trans. Cambridge: MIT Press.

———. 1995. "Reconciliation Through the Public Use of Reason: Remarks on John Rawls's Political Liberalism." *Journal of Philosophy* 92 (3): 109–131.

Hampton, Jean. 1989. "Should Political Philosophy be Done Without Metaphysics?" *Ethics* 99 (4): 791–814.

Hardin, Russell. 1989. "Political Obligation." In *The Good Polity: Normative Analysis of the State.* eds. Alan Hamlin and Philip Pettit eds. New York: Basil Blackwell Inc.

Hart, H.L.A. 1961. *The Concept of Law.* 2nd ed. New York: Oxford University Press.

Herman, Barbara. 1993. "The Practice of Moral Judgment." In *The Practice of Moral Judgment* (Cambridge: Harvard University Press).

Holmes, Stephen. 1993. *The Anatomy of Antiliberalism.* Cambridge: Harvard University Press.

———. 1995. *Passions and Constraint: On the Theory of Liberal Democracy.* Chicago: University of Chicago Press.

Honig, Bonnie. 1993. *Political Theory and the Displacement of Politics.* Ithaca: Cornell University Press.

Horton, John. 2003. "Rawls, Public Reason and the Limits of Liberal Justification." *Contemporary Political Theory* 2: 5–23.

Hostetler, John A. 1993. *Amish Society.* 4th ed. Baltimore: The Johns Hopkins University Press.

Hunter, James Davison. 1992. *Culture Wars: The Struggle to Control the Family, Arts, Education, Law and Politics in America.* New York: Basic Books.

Hurka, Thomas. 1993. *Perfectionism.* New York: Oxford University Press.

Jaggar, Alison M. 1998. "Regendering the U.S. Abortion Debate." In *Abortion Wars: A Half Century of Struggle 1950–2000.* Rickie Solinger ed. Berkeley: University of California Press.

Jeffries John C., Jr. 2001. *Justice Lewis F. Powell: A Biography.* New York: Fordham University Press.

Kant, Immanuel. [1793] 1994. "Theory and Practice." In *Kant's Political Writings.* Hans Reiss ed. H.B. Nisbet trans. New York: Cambridge University Press.

——. [1781] 1965. *Critique of Pure Reason*. Norman Kemp Smith trans. New York: St. Martin's Press.

——. [1797] 1996. "The Doctrine of Virtue." In *The Metaphysics of Morals*, Mary Gregor ed. and trans. New York: Cambridge University Press.

Katz, Pamela S. 1999. "The Case for Legal Recognition of Same-Sex Marriage." *Journal of Law and Policy* 8: 61–106.

Katznelson, Ira. 2005. *When Affirmative-Action Was White: An Untold History of Racial Inequality in Twentieth Century America*. New York: W.W. Norton.

Kelly, Erin, and Lionel McPherson. 2001. "On Tolerating the Unreasonable." *Journal of Political Philosophy* 9 (1): 38–55.

Kirk, Russell. 1953. *The Conservative Mind: From Burke to Eliot*. 7th ed. Washington D.C: Regnery Publishing Inc.

Klarman, Michael J. 2007. Brown v. Board of Education *and the Civil Rights Movement*. New York: Oxford University Press.

Kleiman, Mark A.R. 1989. *Marijuana: Costs of Abuse, Costs of Control*. New York: Greenwood Press.

Klosko, George. 2000. *Democratic Procedures and Liberal Consensus*. New York: Oxford University Press.

Koppelman, Andrew. 1990. "Forced Labor: A Thirteenth Amendment Defense of Abortion." *Northwestern University Law Review* 84: 480–535.

——. 1994. "Discrimination Against Gays is Sex Discrimination." *New York University Law Review* 69: 197–287.

——. 1997. "Homosexual Conduct: A Reply to the New Natural Law Lawyers." In *Same Sex: Debating the Ethics, Science, and Culture of Homosexuality*. John Corvino ed. Lanham, MD: Rowman and Littlefield Publishers Inc.

Korsgaard, Christine M. 1996. "The Reasons We Share" In *Creating the Kingdom of Ends*. Cambridge: Cambridge University Press.

Kozinski, Alex. 2004. "What I Ate for Breakfast and Other Mysteries of Judicial Decision Making." In *Judges on Judging: Views from the Bench*. 2nd ed. David M. O'Brien ed. Washington, D.C: Congressional Quarterly Press.

Kramer, Larry D. 2004. *The People Themselves: Popular Constitutionalism and Judicial Review*. New York: Oxford University Press.

Kronman, Anthony T. 2007. *Education's End: Why Our Colleges and Universities Have Given Up on the Meaning of Life*. New Haven: Yale University Press.

Kuhn, Deanna. 1991. *The Skills of Argument*. New York: Cambridge University Press.

Kukathas, Chandran, and Philip Pettit, 1990. *Rawls: A Theory of Justice and Its Critics*. Cambridge: Polity Press.

Kymlicka, Will. 1995. *Multicultural Citizenship: A Liberal Theory of Minority Rights*. Oxford: Clarendon Press.

Laird, Bob. 2005. *The Case for Affirmative Action in University Admission*. Berkeley: CA: Bay Tree Publishing.

Larmore, Charles. 1987. *Patterns of Moral Complexity*. New York: Cambridge University Press.

——. 1990. "Political Liberalism." *Political Theory* 18 (3): 339–360.

——. 1999. "The Moral Basis of Political Liberalism." *The Journal of Philosophy* 116 (12): 599–625.

——. 2003. "Public Reason." In *The Cambridge Companion to Rawls*. Samuel Freeman ed. New York: Cambridge University Press.

———. 2008. "Behind the Veil." Book Review of John Rawls, *Lectures on the History of Political Philosophy*. In *The New Republic*. February 27: 47.

Lessig, Lawrence. 1993. "Fidelity in Translation." *Texas Law Review* 71: 1165–1268.

Levi, Edward H. 1949. *An Introduction to Legal Reasoning*. Chicago: University of Chicago Press.

Levin, Mark R. 2005. *Men in Black: How the Supreme Court Is Destroying America*. New York: Regnery Publishing Inc.

Levinson, Sanford. 2006. *Our Undemocratic Constitution: Where the Constitution Goes Wrong (And How We the People Can Correct It)*. New York: Oxford University Press.

Lewis, Anthony. 2007. "The Court: How 'So Few Have So Quickly Changed So Much'." Review of Jeffrey Toobin, *The Nine: Inside the Secret. World of the Supreme Court*. In *The New York Review of Books* 54 (20) December 20: 58.

Lippmann, Walter. 1922. *Public Opinion*. New York: Harcourt, Brace, and Co.

Lister, Andrew. 2005. Review Essay. "How To Defend (Same-Sex) Marriage." *Polity* 00 (0): 1–16.

———. 2008. "Public Reason and Democracy." *Critical Review of International Social and Political Philosophy* 8 (3): 273–289.

———. 2010 "Public Justification and the Limits of State Action." *Politics, Philosophy, and Economics* 9 (3) (forthcoming August 2010).

Lloyd, S.A. 1994. "Relativizing Rawls." 69 *Chicago-Kent Law Review* 69 (3): 709–735.

Low-Beer, F.H. 1995. *Questions of Judgment: Determining What's Right*. New York: Prometheus Books.

Luker, Kristin. 1984. *Abortion and the Politics of Motherhood*. Berkeley: University of California Press.

Macedo, Stephen. 1987. *The New Right v. The Constitution*. Washington, D.C: The Cato Institute.

———. 1990. *Liberal Virtues: Citizenship, Virtue, and Community in Liberal Constitutionalism*. New York: Oxford University Press.

———. 1995. "Liberal Civic Education and Religious Fundamentalism: The Case of God v. John Rawls?" *Ethics* 105 (3): 468–496.

———. 1997. "Sexuality and Liberty: Making Room for Nature and Tradition?" In *Sex, Preference, and the Family: Essays on Law and Nature*. David M. Estlund and Martha C. Nussbaum eds. New York: Oxford University Press.

———. 2000. "In Defense of Liberal Public Reason: Are Slavery and Abortion Hard Cases?" In *Natural Law and Public Reason*. Robert P. George and Christopher Wolfe eds. Washington, D.C: Georgetown University Press.

———. 2000. *Diversity and Distrust: Civic Education in a Multicultural Democracy*. Cambridge: Harvard University Press.

———. 2003. "Homosexuality and the Conservative Mind." In *Marriage and Same-Sex Unions: A Debate*. Lynn D. Wardle ed. Westport, CT: Praeger Publications.

MacIntyre, Alasdair. 1981. *After Virtue*, 2nd ed. Notre Dame: Notre Dame University Press.

MacKinnon, Catharine A. 1987. "Francis Biddle's Sister: Pornography, Civil Rights, and Speech." In *Feminism Unmodified: Discourses on Life and Law*. Cambridge: Harvard University Press.

——. 1993. *Only Words*. Cambridge: Harvard University Press.

Madison, James. 2000. *The Federalist No. 10*. Amherst: Prometheus Books.

Marneffe, Peter de. 1990. "Liberalism, Liberty, and Neutrality." *Philosophy and Public Affairs* 19 (3): 253–274.

——. 1994. "Rawls's Idea of Public Reason." *Pacific Philosophical Quarterly* 75: 232–250.

Marquis, Don. 1989. "Why Abortion is Immoral." *The Journal of Philosophy* 86 (4): 183–202.

Mayhew, David. 1974. *Congress: The Electoral Connection*. New Haven: Yale University Press.

McCarthy, Thomas. 1994. "Kantian Constructivism and Reconstructivism: Rawls and Habermas in Dialogue." *Ethics* 105 (1): 44–63.

McConnell, Michael W. 1988. "On Reading the Constitution." *Cornell Law Review* 73: 359–363.

——. 1995. "Originalism and the Desegregation Decisions." *Virginia Law Review* 81 (4): 947–1140.

——. 2001. "*Roe v. Wade at Twenty-Five: Still Illegitimate.*" In *The Ethics of Abortion: Pro-Life vs. Pro-Choice*. 3rd ed. Robert M. Baird and Stuart E. Rosenbaum eds. Amherst, NY: Prometheus Books.

McPherson, James M. 1988. *Battle Cry of Freedom: The Civil War Era*. New York: Oxford University Press.

McPherson, James M. 1991. *Abraham Lincoln and the Second American Revolution*. New York: Oxford University Press.

Meiklejohn, Alexander. 1948. *Free Speech and Its Relation to Self-Government*. New York: Harper and Brothers.

Meese, Edwin III. 1987. "Law of the Constitution." *Tulane Law Review* 61: 979–990.

——. 1990. "Interpreting the Constitution." In *Interpreting the Constitution: The Debate over Original Intent*. Jack N. Rakove ed. Boston: Northeastern University Press.

Metz, Tamara. 2004. "Why We Should Disestablish Marriage." In *Just Marriage*. Mary Lyndon Shanley, New York: Oxford University Press.

Michelman, Frank I. 1973. "In Pursuit of Constitutional Welfare Rights: One View of Rawls' Theory of Justice." *University of Pennsylvania Law Review* 121 (5): 962–1019.

——. 2003. "Rawls on Constitutionalism and Constitutional Law." In *The Cambridge Companion to Rawls*. Samuel Freeman ed. New York: Cambridge University Press.

Mill, John Stuart. [1859] 1989. *On Liberty and Other Writings*. Stephan Collini ed. Cambridge: Cambridge University Press.

——. [1861] 1951. *Considerations of Representative Government*. H.B. Acton ed. London: Dent.

Miller, Richard B. 1996. *Casuistry and Modern Ethics: A Poetry of Practical Reasoning*. Chicago: University of Chicago Press.

Moon, J. Donald. 1995. "Practical Discourse and Communicative Ethics." In *The Cambridge Companion to Habermas*. Stephen K. White ed. New York: Cambridge University Press.

Moore, Michael. 1985. "A Natural Law Theory of Interpretation." *Southern California Law Review* 58: 277–398.

Murphy, Jeffrie G., and Jules L., Coleman. 1990. *Philosophy of Law: An Introduction to Jurisprudence*. rev ed. New York: Westview Press, Inc.

Nagel, Thomas. 1987. "Moral Conflict and Political Legitimacy." *Philosophy and Public Affairs* 16 (3): 215–240.

——. 1989. "Rawls on Justice." In *Reading Rawls: Critical Studies on Rawls'* A Theory of Justice. Norman Daniels ed. New York: Basic Books.

——. 1991. *Equality and Partiality*. New York: Oxford University Press, 1991.

——. 2003. "Rawls and Liberalism." In *The Cambridge Companion to Rawls*. Samuel Freeman ed. New York: Cambridge University Press.

Neal, Patrick. 2000. "Political Liberalism, Public Reason, and the Citizen of Faith." In *Natural Law and Public Reason*. Robert P. George and Christopher Wolfe eds. Washington D.C: Georgetown University Press, 2000.

——. 2008. "Is Public Reason Innocuous?" *Critical Review of International Social and Political Philosophy* 11 (2): 131–152.

Nelson, William E. 2000. Marbury v. Madison: *The Origins and Legacy of Judicial Review*. Lawrence: University Press of Kansas.

Neuhaus, Richard John, 1994. *The Naked Public Square: Religion and Democracy in America*. 2nd ed. Grand Rapids, Michigan: William B. Eerdsmans Co.

Nie, Norman H., Sidney Verba, and John Petrocik. 1976. *The Changing American Voter*. Cambridge: Harvard University Press.

Nino, Carlos Santiago. 1996. *The Constitution of Deliberative Democracy*. New Haven: Yale University Press.

Nolt, Steven N. 1992. *A History of the Amish*. Intercourse, PA: Good Books.

Noonan, John. 1970. "An Almost Absolute Value in History." In *The Morality of Abortion: Legal and Historical Perspectives*. Cambridge: Harvard University Press.

Nozick, Robert. 1974. *Anarchy, State, and Utopia*. New York: Basic Books Inc.

Nussbaum, Martha. 1986. *The Fragility of Goodness: Luck and Ethics in Greek Tragedy and Philosophy*. Cambridge: Cambridge University Press.

——. 1994. "Skepticism about Practical Reason in Literature and in the Law." *Harvard Law Review* 107 (3): 714–744.

——. 1999. "The Discernment of Perception: An Aristotelian Conception of Private and Public Rationality." In *Aristotle's Ethics: Critical Essays*. Nancy Sherman ed. New York: Rowman and Littlefield Publishers, Inc.

——. 2008. *Liberty of Conscience: In Defense of America's Tradition of Religious Equality*. New York: Basic Books.

O'Brien, David M. 2004. "Preface." In *Judges on Judging: Views from the Bench*. 2nd ed. David M. O'Brien ed. Washington, D.C: Congressional Quarterly Press.

——. 2004. "Judicial Review and American Politics: Historical and Political Perspectives." In *Judges on Judging: Views from the Bench*. 2nd ed. David M. O'Brien ed. Washington D.C: Congressional Quarterly Press.

O'Neill, Johnathan. 2005. *Originalism in American Law and Politics: A Constitutional History*. Baltimore: Johns Hopkins University Press.

O'Neill, Onora. 1989. *Constructions of Reason: Explorations of Kant's Practical Philosophy*. Cambridge: Cambridge University Press.

Oates, Stephen B. 1994. *Abraham Lincoln: The Man Behind the Myths*. New York: Harper Collins.

Okin, Susan Moller. 1999. "Is Multiculturalism Bad for Women?" In *Is Multiculturalism Bad for Women?* Joshua Cohen, Matthew Howard, and Martha C. Nussbaum eds. Princeton: Princeton University Press.

Olafson, Frederick, A. 1990. "Habermas as Philosopher." *Ethics* 100 (3): 641–657.

Paulsen, Michael Stokes. 2005. "Dissenting." In *What* Roe v. Wade *Should Have Said: The Nation's Top Legal Experts Rewrite America's Most Controversial Decision.* Jack M. Balkin ed. New York: New York University Press, 2005.

Perry, Barbara A. 2007. *The Michigan Affirmative Action Cases.* Lawrence: University of Kansas.

Perry, Michael J. 1982. *The Constitution, the Courts, and Human Rights.* New Haven: Yale University Press.

———. 1988. *Morality, Politics, and Law.* New York: Oxford University Press, 1988.

Peters, Shawn Francis. 2003. *The Yoder Case: Religious Freedom, Education, and Parental Rights.* Lawrence: University Press of Kansas.

Pinello, Daniel. 2006. *America's Struggle for Same-Sex Marriage.* New York: Cambridge University Press.

Poole, Keith T., and Howard Rosenthal. 1997. *Congress: A Political-Economic History of Roll Call Voting.* New York: Oxford University Press.

Posner, Richard A. 1990. *The Problems of Jurisprudence.* Cambridge: Harvard University Press.

———. 1997. "Homosexuality: The Policy Questions." In *Same-Sex Marriage: Pro and Con.* Andrew Sullivan ed. New York: Vintage Books.

———. 2001. *Breaking the Deadlock: The 2000 Election, the Constitution, and the Courts.* Princeton: Princeton University Press.

———. 2008. "In Defense of Looseness: The Supreme Court and Gun Control." *The New Republic* 239, August 27: 32–35.

———. 2008. *How Judges Think.* Cambridge: Harvard University Press.

Postema, Gerald J. 2004. "Integrity: Justice in Workclothes." In *Dworkin and His Critics.* Justine Burley ed. Oxford: Blackwell Publishing Ltd.

Putnam, Hilary. 1987. *The Many Faces of Realism.* LaSalle, IL: Open Court Publishing Co.

Quinn, Warren. 1994. "Abortion: Identity and Loss." In *Morality and Action.* New York: Cambridge University Press.

Quong, Jonathan. 2004. "The Scope of Public Reason." *Political Studies* 52: 233–250.

———. 2008. "Three Disputes About Public Justification: Commentary on Gaus and Vallier," p.3, unpublished paper, http://publicreason.net/2008/09/26/ppps-the-roles-of-religious-convictions-in-a-publicly-justified-polity/

Rauch, Jonathan. 2004. *Gay Marriage: Why It Is Good for Gays, Good for Straights, and Good for America.* New York: Henry Holt and Co.

Rawls, John. 1964. "Legal Obligation and the Duty of Fair Play." In *Law and Philosophy.* Sidney Hook ed. New York: New York University Press.

———. 1984. "The Right and the Good Contrasted." In *Liberalism and Its Critics.* Michael J. Sandel ed. New York: New York University Press.

———. [1971] 2003. *A Theory of Justice,* revised ed. Cambridge: The Belknap Press of the Harvard University Press.

———. 2001. *Collected Papers.* Samuel Freeman ed. Cambridge: Harvard University Press.

———. 2001. *Justice as Fairness: A Restatement.* Erin Kelly ed. Cambridge: The Belknap Press of the Harvard University Press.

———. [1993] 1996. *Political Liberalism.* New York: Columbia University Press.

———. 1999. "The Idea of Public Reason Revisited." In *The Law of Peoples.* Cambridge: Harvard University Press.

Raz, Joseph. 1986. *The Morality of Freedom.* Oxford: Oxford University Press.

———. 1990. "Facing Diversity: The Case for Epistemic Abstinence." *Philosophy and Public Affairs* 19 (1): 3–46.

———. 1999. "The Obligation to Obey: Revision and Tradition." In *The Duty to Obey the Law: Selected Philosophical Readings.* William A. Edmundson. Lanham, MD: Rowman and Littlefield Publishers, Inc.

Reagan, Leslie J. 1997. *When Abortion was a Crime: Women, Medicine, and Law in the United States 1867–1973.* Berkeley: University of California Press.

Regan, Tom. 1983. *The Case for Animal Rights.* Berkeley: University of California Press.

Rehg, William. 1990. "Discourse and the Moral Point of View: Deriving a Dialogical Principle of Universalization." *Inquiry* 34: 27–48.

Rehnquist, William H. 1976. "The Notion of a Living Constitution." *Texas Law Review* 54 (4): 693–706.

Reidy, David A. 2000. "Rawls's Wide View of Public Reason: Not Wide Enough." *Res Publica* 6:49–72.

Reiman, Jeffrey. 1990. *Justice and Modern Moral Philosophy.* New Haven: Yale University Press.

Richards, David A.J. 2005. *The Case for Gay Rights: From Bowers and Lawrence and Beyond.* Lawrence: University of Kansas Press.

Ripstein, Arthur. 2007. "Introduction: Anti-Archimedeanism." In *Ronald Dworkin.* Arthur Ripstein ed. New York: Cambridge University Press.

Roosevelt, Kermit III. 2006. *The Myth of Judicial Activism: Making Sense of Supreme Court Decisions.* New Haven: Yale University Press.

Rosen, Jeffrey. 2008. "Justice Delayed: The Case Against California's Gay Marriage Decision." 238 *The New Republic,* June 11: 9–12.

Rosenberg, Gerald N. 1991. *The Hollow Hope: Can Courts Bring About Social Change?* Chicago: University of Chicago Press.

Rossum, Ralph A. 2006. *Antonin Scalia's Jurisprudence: Text and Tradition.* Lawrence: University Press of Kansas.

Rousseau, Jean-Jacques. [1762] 1987. *The Social Contract.* Donald A. Kress ed. and trans. Indianapolis: Hackett Publishing Co.

Sandel, Michael J. 1984. "Justice and the Good." In *Liberalism and Its Critics.* Michael J. Sandel ed. New York: New York University Press.

———. 1994. Book Review, "Political Liberalism." *Harvard Law Review* 107 (7): 1765–1794.

Sander, Richard. 2000. "The Tributaries to the River." *Law and Social Inquiry* 25 (2): 557–563.

Scalia, Antonin. 1989. "Originalism: The Lesser Evil." *Cincinnati Law Review* 57: 849–865.

———. 1994. "The Dissenting Opinion." *Journal of Supreme Court History* Volume: 33–44.

———. 1997. *A Matter of Interpretation: Federal Courts and the Law.* Princeton: Princeton University Press.

Scanlon, T.M. 1984. "Contractualism and Utilitarianism." In *Beyond Utilitarianism*. Amartya Sen and Bernard Williams eds. New York: Cambridge University Press.

———. 1998. *What We Owe to Each Other*. Cambridge: The Belknap Press of the Harvard University Press.

Schauer, Frederick. 1982. "An Essay on Constitutional Language." *UCLA Law Review* 29 (4): 797–832.

———. 1982. *Free Speech: A Philosophical Inquiry*. New York: Cambridge University Press.

———. 1987. "Precedent." *Stanford Law Review* 39 (3): 571–605.

———. 1995. "Giving Reasons." *Stanford Law Review* 47 (4): 633–659.

Schumpeter, Joseph A. 1942. *Capitalism, Socialism, and Democracy*. New York: Harper and Rowe.

Schwartz, Bernard. 1983. *Super Chief: Earl Warren and His Supreme Court –A Judicial Biography*. New York: New York University Press.

———. 1993. *A History of the Supreme Court*. New York: Oxford University Press.

Schwartzman, Micah. 2004. "The Completeness of Public Reason." *Politics, Philosophy and Economics* 3 (3): 191–220.

Shafer-Landau, Russ. 1997. "Moral Rules." *Ethics* 107 (4): 584–611.

Shapiro, Scott J. 2007. "The 'Hart-Dworkin' Debate: A Short Guide for the Perplexed." In *Ronald Dworkin*. Arthur Ripstein ed. New York: Cambridge University Press.

Shenkman, Rick. 2008. *Just How Stupid Are We? Facing the Truth About the American Voter*. New York: Basic Books.

Sher, George. 1997. *Beyond Neutrality*. New York: Cambridge University Press.

———. 2002. "Diversity." In *The Affirmative Action Debate* 2nd ed. Steven M. Cahn ed. New York: Routledge.

Shklar, Judith N. 1991. *American Citizenship: The Quest for Inclusion*: Cambridge: Harvard University Press.

Simmons, A. John. 1979. *Moral Principles and Political Obligations*. Princeton: Princeton University Press.

Singer, Peter. 1975. *Animal Liberation*. New York: Harper Collins Publishers Inc.

Singer, Peter, and Helen Kuhse. 1989. "On Letting Handicapped Infants Die." In *The Right Thing to Do: Basic Readings in Moral Philosophy*. James Rachels ed. New York: Random House.

Smith, Rogers M. 1985. *Liberalism and American Constitutional Law*. Cambridge: Harvard University Press.

———. 1997. *Civic Ideals: Conflicting Visions of Citizenship in U.S. History*. New Haven: Yale University Press.

Soltan, Karol Edward. 1999. "Introduction: Civic Competence, Democracy, and the Good Society." In *Citizen Competence and Democratic Institutions*. Stephen L. Elkin and Karol Edward Soltan eds. University Park, PA: The Pennsylvania State University Press.

Solum, Lawrence B. 1993. "Constructing an Ideal of Public Reason." *San Diego Law Review* 30 (4): 729–762.

———. 1994. "Inclusive Public Reason." *Pacific Philosophical Quarterly* 75: 217–231.

———. 1996. "Novel Public Reasons." *Loyola of Los Angeles Law Review* 29: 1459–1485.

———. 2006. "Pluralism and Public Legal Reason." *William and Mary Bill of Rights Journal* 15: 7–23.

——. 2006. "Public Legal Reason." *Virginia Law Review* 92: 1449–1501.

Sarah Song, 2007. *Justice, Gender, and the Politics of Multiculturalism*. New York: Cambridge University Press.

Solinger, Rickie. 1998. "Introduction: Abortion Politics and History." In *Abortion Wars: A Half Century of Struggle 1950–2000*. Rickie Solinger ed. Berkeley: University of California Press.

Staab, James B. 2006. *The Political Thought of Justice Antonin Scalia: A Hamiltonian on the Supreme Court*. Lanham, MD: Rowman and Littlefield Publishers Inc.

Strasser, Mark. 2003. "The State Interests in Recognizing Same-Sex Marriage." In *Marriage and Same-Sex Unions: A Debate*. Lynn D. Wardle ed. Westport, CT: Praeger Publications.

Sullivan, Andrew. 1997. "The Conservative Case." In *Same-Sex Marriage: Pro and Con*. Andrew Sullivan ed. New York: Vintage Books.

Sunstein, Cass R. 1984. "Naked Preferences and the Constitution." *Columbia Law Review* 84 (7): 1689–1732.

——. 1993. *The Partial Constitution*. Cambridge: Harvard University Press.

——. 1996. *Legal Reasoning and Political Conflict*. New York: Oxford University Press.

——. 1999. *One Case at a Time: Judicial Minimalism on the Supreme Court*. Cambridge: Harvard University Press.

——. 2001. *Republic.com*. Princeton: Princeton University Press.

——. 2003. *Why Societies Need Dissent*. Cambridge: Harvard University Press.

——. 2007. "The Most Mysterious Right." Book Review. *Why the Constitution Can't End the Battle over Guns*. In *The New Republic*. November 19: 46.

Taylor, Charles. 1984. "Foucault on Freedom and Truth." *Political Theory* 12 (2): 152–183.

——. 1989. *Sources of the Self: The Making of Modern Identity*. Cambridge: Harvard University Press.

——. 1994. "The Politics of Recognition." In *Multiculturalism: Examining the Politics of Recognition*. Amy Gutmann ed. Princeton: Princeton University Press.

——. 1995. "Cross-Purposes: The Liberal-Communitarian Debate." In *Philosophical Arguments*. Cambridge: Harvard University Press.

Thayer, James B. 1893. "The Origin and Scope of the American Doctrine of Constitutional Law." *Harvard Law Review* 7: 138–152.

Thernstrom, Stephan, and Abigail Thernstrom. 2002. "Does Your 'Merit' Depend on Your Race: A Rejoinder to Bowen and Bok." In *The Affirmative Action Debate* 2nd ed. Steven M. Cahn ed. New York: Routledge.

Thomson, Judith Jarvis. 1995. "Abortion: Whose Right?" *Boston Review* 20 (3): 11–15.

——. 1971. "A Defense of Abortion." *Philosophy and Public Affairs* 1 (1): 47–66.

Tocqueville, Alexis de. [1835] 2003. *Democracy in America*. Gerald E. Bevan trans. New York: Penguin Books.

Tomasi, John. 2001. *Liberalism Beyond Justice: Citizens, Society, and the Boundaries of Political Theory*. Princeton: Princeton University Press.

Toobin, Jeffrey. 2007. *The Nine*. New York: Doubleday Books.

Tooley, Michael. 1972. "Abortion and Infanticide." *Philosophy and Public Affairs* 2 (1): 37–65.

Tribe, Laurence H. 1985. *Constitutional Choices*. Cambridge: Harvard University Press.

——. 1985. *God Save This Honorable Court: How the Choice of Supreme Court Justices Shapes Our History*. New York: Random House Inc.

——. 1990. *Abortion: The Clash of Absolutes*. New York: W.W. Norton.

——. 2008. *The Invisible Constitution*. New York: Oxford University Press.

Tulis, Jeffrey K. 1987. *The Rhetorical Presidency*. Princeton: Princeton University Press.

Tushnet, Mark. 1999. *Taking the Constitution Away From the Courts*. Princeton: Princeton University Press.

Unger, Roberto. 1975. *Knowledge and Politics*. New York: The Free Press.

Waldron, Jeremy. 1993. "Theoretical Foundations of Liberalism." In *Liberal Rights: Collected Papers: 1981–91*. Cambridge: Cambridge University Press.

——. 1993. "Religious Contributions in Public Deliberation." *San Diego Law Review* 30: 817–848.

——. 1999. *The Dignity of Legislation*. Cambridge: Cambridge University Press.

——. 1999. *Law and Disagreement*. Oxford: Oxford University Press.

——. 1999. "Deliberation, Disagreement, and Voting." In *Deliberative Democracy and Human Rights*. Harold Hongju Koh and Ronald C. Slye eds. New Haven: Yale University Press.

——. 2005. "Legislation." In *The Blackwell Guide to the Philosophy of Law and Legal Theory*. Martin P. Golding and William A. Edmundson eds. Malden, MA: Blackwell Publishing Ltd.

Wall, Steven. 1998. *Liberalism, Perfectionism and Restraint*. Cambridge: Cambridge University Press.

Wall, Steven, and George Klosko, 2003. "Introduction." In *Perfectionism and Neutrality: Essays in Liberal Theory*. Steven Wall and George Klosko eds. Lanham, MD: Rowman and Littlefield Inc.

Walzer, Michael. 1981. "Philosophy and Democracy." *Political Theory* 9 (3): 379–399.

——. 1983. *Spheres of Justice: A Defense of Pluralism and Equality*. New York: Basic Books.

Wardle, Lynn D. 1998. "Legal Claims for Same-Sex Marriage: Efforts to Legitimate a Retreat from Marriage by Redefining Marriage." *South Texas Law Review* 39 (3): 735–768.

Wattenberg, Martin P. 1991. *The Rise of Candidate-Centered Politics: Presidential Elections in the 1980s*. Cambridge: Harvard University Press.

Wenar, Leif. 1995. "Political Liberalism: An Internal Critique." *Ethics* 106 (1): 32–62.

Wechsler, Herbert. 1959. "Toward Neutral Principles of Constitutional Law." *Harvard Law Review* 73 (1): 1–35.

Westmoreland, Robert. 1999. "The Truth about Public Reason." *Law and Philosophy* 18 (3): 271–296.

White, Stephen K. 1998. *The Recent Work of Jurgen Habermas: Reason, Justice and Modernity*. Cambridge: Cambridge University Press.

Whittington, Keith E. 1999. *Constitutional Interpretation: Textual Meaning, Original Intent, and Judicial Review*. Lawrence: University Press of Kansas.

——. 2000. "In Defense of Legislatures." Book Review, Jeremy Waldron, *Law and Disagreement* and Jeremy Waldron, *The Dignity of Legislation*. *Political Theory* 28 (5): 690–702.

———. 2004. "The New Originalism." *The Georgetown Journal of Law and Public Policy* 2: 599–613.

———. 2007. *Political Foundations of Judicial Supremacy: The Presidency, the Supreme Court, and Constitutional Leadership in U.S. History*. Princeton: Princeton University Press.

Williams, Andrew. 2000. "The Alleged Incompleteness of Public Reason." *Res Publica* 6: 199–211.

Williams, Armstrong. 1995. "Two Wrongs Don't Make a Right for Thomas." *Charleston Post and Courier*. August 17: A-13.

Williams, Bernard. 1996. "Toleration: An Impossible Virtue?" In *Toleration: An Elusive Virtue*. David Heyd ed. Princeton: Princeton University Press.

Wolfe, Alan. 1998. *One Nation, After All: What Middle-Class Americans Really Think about God, Country, Family, Racism, Welfare, Immigration, Homosexuality, Work, the Right, the Left, and Each Other*. New York: Viking Books.

———. 2001. *Moral Freedom: The Impossible Idea that Defines the Way We Live Now*. New York: W.W. Norton Co.

Wolff, Jonathan. 1991. *Robert Nozick: Property, Justice, and the Minimal State*. Stanford: Stanford University Press.

Wolff, Robert Paul. 1970. *In Defense of Anarchism*. Berkeley: University of California Press.

Wolgast, Elizabeth. 1994. "The Demands of Public Reason." *Columbia Law Review*. 94: 1936–1949.

Wolin, Sheldon. 1996. Book Review. "The Liberal/Democratic Divide: On Rawls's Political Liberalism." *Political Theory* 24 (1): 97–119.

Wolterstorff, Nicholas. 1997. "Why We Should Reject What Liberalism Tells Us about Speaking and Acting in Public for Religious Reasons." In *Religion and Contemporary Liberalism*. Paul J. Weithman ed. Notre Dame: University of Notre Dame Press.

———. 1997. "The Role of Religion in Political Issues." In *Religion in the Public Square*. Robert Audi and Nicholas Wolterstorff eds. Lanham, MD: Rowman and Littlefield Publishers Inc.

Wood, Gordon S. 1988. "The Fundamentalists and the Constitution." *New York Review of Books*, February, 18: 37–40.

Young, Iris Marion. 1995. "Survey Article: Rawls's *Political Liberalism*." *Journal of Political Philosophy* 3 (3): 181–190.

———. 1997. "Difference as a Resource for Democratic Communication." In *Deliberative Democracy: Essays on Reason and Politics*. James Bohman and William Rehg eds. Cambridge: MIT Press.

Index

abortion rights, 23, 38, 98, 257, 275–290
    in *Casey*, 279
    concept of "personhood" and, 280, 284
    under Equal Protection Clause, 281
    gender equality and, 275–276
    in *Griswold v. Connecticut*, 60–61, 277
    legal history of, 275–276
    in *Meyer v. Nebraska*, 27, 277
    nonpublic reasons for, 281–282
    in *Pierce v. Society of Sisters*, 27, 277
    public reasons for, 282
    reasonable objections to, 289
    Roe v. Wade and, 23, 38, 98, 275
    unreasonableness and, 285
abuses of power, by judges, 278–279,
    300–302
Ackerman, Bruce, 29, 84, 87, 121, 129–130
activist judges, 3
    Bork on, 31
    conservative criticism of, 33
Adarand Construction v. Pena, 266
affirmative action, 94, 263–275
    in *Adarand Construction v. Pena*, 266
    challenges of, 271–275
    Civil Rights Act of 1964 and, 266
    concept of merit and, 273
    consequences of, 271–272
    Equal Protection Clause and, 265
    in *Gratz v. Bollinger*, 268–271
    in *Grutter v. Bollinger*, 93, 266–268
    Harvard Plan and, 266
    legal history of, 263–266
    public justification of judicial decisions on,
        273–274
    public reasons against, 274–275
    racial preferences and, 272
    racial quotas and, 266, 268

    in *Regents of University of California v.
        Bakke*, 264–266
    in *Richmond v. Croson*, 266
Amendment 2, 68, 71–72
The American Voter, 308
Amish sect, 232. *See also Wisconsin v. Yoder*
    children in, 235
    Ordnung in, 232
    state education requirements and, conflicts
        with, 232
animal rights, 174–175
anti-miscegenation statutes, 74
anti-perfectionist liberalism, 121–122,
    225
    public justification of judicial decisions
        and, 121–122
Aristotle, 182, 205
    practical reasoning for, 182
Arneson, Richard, 164–165
Audi, Robert, 121
autonomy
    liberalism and, 234–235
    principle of reciprocity and, 219
    reasoning and, 154, 191
    religious freedom and, 236–237

Bakke, Alan, 264–266, 268
Balkin, Jack, 281
Barnett, Randy, 28–29, 45, 193
Barry, Brian, 106, 154, 203, 224, 242
Baxter, Marvin, 15, 247
Beckwith, Francis, 286
Bellamy, Richard, 212, 220
Bell, Derrick, 302
Benhabib, Seyla, 118, 159, 212
"benign" discrimination, 265
Berkowitz, Peter, 209

Berlin, Isaiah, 222
Bickel, Alexander, 1
Blackmun, Harry, 244–245, 276–277
Bob Jones University v., 181
Bohman, James, 87
Bok, Derek, 272–273
Bork, Robert, 1, 22, 45, 60, 277. *See also*
    originalism, in constitutional
    interpretation
    on judicial activism, 31
    political ideology of, as factor in
        confirmation, 301
Bowen, William, 272–273
Bowers v. Hardwick, 4, 62–64
    Stanley v. Georgia v., 62
Brandenburg v. Ohio, 115
Brennan, William, 47, 302
Brettschneider, Corey, 19, 27
Breyer, Stephen, 292
Brown v. Board of Education, 28, 42,
    72–73, 91
    long-term effects of, 302
Buck v. Bell, 28, 58–59
Burger, Warren, 240
Burke, 44
Bush v. Gore, 24

Calabresi, Steven, 33
California Marriage Protection Act. *See*
    Proposition 8
California Supreme Court, same-sex
    marriage before, 245–246
capital punishment, 149
Carter, Stephen, 4, 216
Casey, 279
Catholic Church, 141, 167, 253
Chan, Joseph, 208
children's rights, 237–238
citizenship, ideals of, 229–230
civic education, purpose of, 235–236
    Amish sect and, conflicts with, 232
    children's rights and, 237–238
civil disobedience, over public justification of
    judicial decisions, 87
Civil Rights Act of 1964, 91
    affirmative action and, 266
Civil Rights Cases, 9, 28, 301
collective decisions, legitimacy of, 179
"comprehensive doctrines," 83
The Concept of Law (Hart), 31
congressional voting behavior, 77
consent
    hypothetical, 196

morality of, 207
    political legitimacy and, 190–191
    in same-sex marriage arguments, 253
    as unanimous, 193–194
constitutional adjudication, 3–5. *See also*
    originalism, in constitutional
    interpretation
    interpretation v. construction in, 32
    "naked preferences" in, 7
    philosophical approaches to, 46–51
    public justification of, 5–7, 10
    reasonable disagreement and, 15–17, 50
    reasonable dissenters and, 10–14
    sufficiently/insufficiently public reasons
        for, 11
    U.S. constitution amended as result of,
        28–29
constitutionalism
    adjudication of, 3–5
    popular, 2, 303–311
constitutional public reason, 139–171
    for economic regulation, 146–147
    empirical claims in, 143–145
    exclusive principle of, 139–145, 156–171
    standards of review for, 146–148
constitutional theory
    deference to legislative majorities in,
        74–80
    equality in, 67–74
    freedom in, 58–67
    indeterminacy and, 30–33
    interpretation v. construction in, 32
    originalism and, 22–23
    public justification and, 51
    unanimous political consent in,
        193–194
    utilitarianism in, 50
"conversational constraints," 87
    in inclusive public reason, 130
Converse, Philip, 307–309
Corrigan, Carol, 15, 247
Craig v. Boren, 265
cruel and unusual punishment, 43
Cruzan v. Missouri Department of Health,
    64

D'Agostino, Fred, 104
Dahl, Robert, 2
Declaration of Independence, 27, 210
defamation, 185
Defense of Marriage Act, 245
deliberative democracy, 87
    ensured participation in, 180

deliberators
  in inclusive public reason, 131–132
  in laissez-faire public reason, 114,
    117–118
  moral judgments for, 156–157
  nonpublic reasons for, 173
  in public deliberation, 178–179
  reasonable disagreement for, 174
De Marneffe, Peter, 130, 208, 218
democracy
  deliberative, 87
  free speech in, 117
  liberalism and, 227
  as political ideal, in public justification of
    judicial reasons, 87, 311–312
  public reason and, 210, 225–227
  unanimous direct, 191
Democratic Rights (Brettschneider), 19
Difference Principle, 80
  as constitutional essential, 147
discourse ethics, 110. See also laissez-faire
    public reason
"discrete and insular minority," 9
discrimination
  racial, 38–39, 55, 265
  reverse, 94, 265–266
  towards sexual orientation, 68, 71–72
District of Columbia v. Heller, 42
Douglas, Stephen, 59–61
Dred Scott v. Sanford, 9, 28, 100, 295, 302
Due Process Clause, 27, 70
Dworkin, Gerald, 191
Dworkin, Ronald, 3, 18, 26, 47, 100, 140,
    201–202, 273
  legal theory of, 49

economic regulation, constitutional public
    reason for, 146–147
Ely, John Hart, 277–279, 293
Employment Division v. Smith, 9, 244–245
"enclave deliberation," 307–308
"endorsement test," 8
"epistemic abstinence," 132–133
  voting and, 133
equality
  in constitutional theory, 67–74
  as political ideal, in public justification of
    judicial reasons, 90–91
Equal Protection Clause, 8–9, 27, 70
  abortions rights under, 281
  affirmative action and, 265
  originalism and, 41
  original public understanding of, 264

racial discrimination under, 38–39
  same-sex marriage under, 14–15,
    248–249
  "separate but equal" under, 28
  Skinner v. Oklahoma and, 59
  welfare rights under, 24
eugenics, 58–59
"exceeding persuasive justification," 67
exclusive constitutional public reason,
    139–145, 156–171
  constitutional judgment in, 156–159
  reasonable disagreement in, 158
  reasonableness in, 161–171
  simplicity of reason as factor in, 160
  skepticism and, 170
exclusive public reason, 110–111, 120–129,
    140–145, 211
  anti-perfectionist liberalism and, 121–122
  constitutional, 139–140, 156–171
  same-sex marriage and, 258–259
  semi-libertarianism and, 121–123
  unreasonableness under, 222–223
"expectations originalism," 40
exploitation, as moral concept, 143
extreme perfectionism, 208

fairness, 221
  in judicial decisions, 89
fallibilism, 215
The Federalist Papers (Madison), 187, 296,
    298
Federal Marriage Amendment, 245
Finnis, John, 62, 168, 252, 254
First Letter Concerning Toleration (Locke),
    44
Fiss, Owen, 30
Florida v. B.J.F., 183
Foucault, Michel, 103
freedom
  in constitutional theory, 58–67
  as political ideal, in public justification of
    judicial decisions, 90–91
"freedom of contract," 28
Free Exercise Clause, 244
Freeman, Samuel, 162, 218, 293
free speech, in democratic theory, 117
fundamentalism, reasonableness and, 167
Future Shock, 33

Galston, William, 213–214, 234
Gaus, Gerald, 90, 107, 110–111, 121, 123,
    147–148. See also exclusive public
    reason

Gauthier, David, 111
gender discrimination, 67–68, 243
    abortion rights and, 275–276
    in *Craig v. Boren*, 265
George, Robert, 168, 252, 288
George, Ronald, 14
Gettysburg Address, 27
Ginsburg, Ruth Bader, 67–68
good, as concept, 88, 203–204, 234
    definition of, 204
    liberalism and, 203
    primary, 208
    unreasonableness and, 220
Graglia, Lino, 1–2
Gratz v. Bollinger, 268–271
Gray, John, 103
Greenawalt, Kent, 13, 124, 129, 173, 176,
        179, 215–216, 220, 282–283, 299
The Greening of America, 33
Gregg v. Georgia, 149
Grey, Thomas, 46
Griswold v. Connecticut, 60–61, 277
Grutter v. Bollinger, 93, 266–268, 270–271
Gutmann, Amy, 87, 227, 233, 236–239

Habermas, Jurgen, 110, 112–120
Habitual Criminal Sterilization Act, 59
Hardwick, Michael, 62
harm, 143
    moral, 252
Hart, H.L.A., 31
Harvard Plan, 266
"heckler's veto," 116
Hialeah, 243
Hobbes, Thomas, 189
    public reason for, 111
Holmes, Stephen, 58–59, 189–190
Horton, John, 212
hypothetical agreement, 113–114
hypothetical consent, 196

"The Idea of Public Reason Revisited"
        (Rawls), 135
impeachment, of judges, 97
inclusive public reason, 110, 129–138
    "conversational constraints" in, 130
    deliberators in, 131–132
    "neutral dialogue" in, 129–130
    pluralism in, 131
    as public principle, 136–137
    for Rawls, 131–138
    rejection of, 133
    scope of, 131–132

self-restraint in, 129
    for voters, 133–134
indeterminacy, in legal rulings, constitutional
        theory and, 30–33
"integrity objection," 216

Jackson, Robert, 27
Jaggar, Alison, 288
Jefferson, Thomas, 27, 210
judges
    abuse of power by, 278–279, 300–302
    constitutionalism adjudication by, 3–5
    impeachment of, 97
    judicial review and, 299–301
    as originalists, 22–23
    political ideology of, 301
    public justification of decisions by, 5–7,
        10
    public overreliance on, 301
    public v. nonpublic reasons for, 145–156,
        175–176, 187–188
    as reasonable dissenters, 12–13
    reasoning based on religious reasons by,
        3–5
judicial activism, 3
    Bork on, 31
    conservative criticism of, 33
    deference to legislative majorities and,
        74–80
    interpretations of, 24
judicial maximalism, 97–98
judicial minimalism, 23, 96–97
judicial reasoning
    deliberations in, 102
    exchange of reasons as part of, 101–102
    persuasion as part of, 102
    populism as approach to, 90
    public justification of, 5–7, 10, 52–54,
        81–108
    public v. nonpublic, 145–156
    Rawls on, 106–107
    reasonable disagreement with, 103–107
    religion as basis for, 3–5
    skepticism and, 103–104
    societal preconditions for, 103
judicial review, 23–30, 291–315
    abuses of power under, 300–302
    criticism of, 303–304
    egalitarian theory of, 303–311
    history of, 294–299
    indeterminacy in, 30–33
    judges and, 299–301
    judicial shortfalls under, 302–303

objective of, 26
originalism and, 34
popular constitutionalism and, 2,
    303–311
public justification of judicial decisions
    and, 311–312
public overreliance on judges and, 301
public reasons in, 299–301
standards of, 53–54, 57
unconstitutionality as part of, 54
Judiciary Act of 1789, 294
justice, as political conception, 161

Kant, Immanuel, 111–112
principle of reciprocity for, 112
Kelly, Erin, 220
Klosko, George, 30
Koppelman, Andrew, 282
Korematsu, 9, 28, 90
public justification of, 148
Kramer, Larry, 2, 303–304
Kuhn, Deanna, 126
Kyllo v. United States, 43

laissez-faire public reason, 109–120, 168,
    211
deliberators in, 114, 117–118
for Habermas, 112–120
in public justification of judicial reasons,
    119
Larmore, Charles, 87, 121, 156, 164,
    169–170
Lawrence v. Texas, 27, 29, 63, 74, 92–93
laws, public justification of, 180–181
Lee v. Weisman, 149–150
legal public reason, 140
legal reasoning, skepticism and, 107–108
legitimacy. *See* collective decisions,
    legitimacy of; political legitimacy
legitimacy of public law, 86
legitimate collective decisions, 179
Leviathan (Hobbes), 44
Levin, Mark, 3
Levinson, Sanford, 19, 25
liberalism, 81–89, 129, 154
anti-perfectionist, 121–122, 225
autonomy and, 234–235
civic education and, 235–236
conception of good and, 203
democracy and, 227
morality and, 224
nonliberal beliefs under, 154–155

perfectionist, 88, 225, 234
political, 156
for Rawls, 224–225
religion under, 219
liberal neutrality, 155
Lincoln, Abraham, 27
Lippmann, Walter, 308
Lister, Andrew, 97
living a good life, 205–206
Lochner v. New York, 28, 79–80
"freedom of contract" in, 28
Locke, John, 44, 189
"logic of persecutors," 78
Loving v. Virginia, 74

Macedo, Stephen, 5, 50, 82–83, 146–147,
    181, 221, 239, 283
MacIntyre, Alasdair, 103
MacKinnon, Catharine, 143
Madisonian democracy, 296
Madison, James, 187, 296, 298
Marbury v. Madison, 294–296
Marquis, Don, 284
marriage rights. *See* right to marriage
marriage, social purposes of, 251
McCarthy, Thomas, 112
McPherson, Lionel, 220
Meese, Edwin, 24
Meiklejohn, Alexander, 117
merit, as concept, 273
Meyer v. Nebraska, 27, 277
Michelman, Frank, 147
Miller, Barbara, 241
Miller, Wallace, 231
Mill, John Stuart, 238
Minersville School District v. Gobitis, 9
Miranda v. Arizona, 57
Moore, Michael, 26
moral harm, 252
morality. *See also* nonpublic reasons
of consent, 207
exploitation and, 143
harm and, 143
liberalism and, as political, 224
reasonableness and, 165–167
stringency of, 185
moral pluralism, reasonable disagreement
    and, 188
Morals by Agreement (Gauthier), 111
"morals legislation," 29

Nagel, Thomas, 87–88, 121, 164, 209
"naked preferences," 7

Neal, Patrick, 135, 217–218
negative rights, 2
Neuhas, Richard John, 216
"neutral dialogue," 129–130
neutrality, 82
    liberal, 155
New York Times, 144
New York Times v. Sullivan, 57, 185
The Nichomachean Ethics (Aristotle), 182,
    205
noncoercive perfectionism, 208
nonoriginalism, in constitutional
    interpretation, 33. *See also* activist
    judges; judicial activism
nonpublic reasons
    for abortion rights, 281–282
    authority of, 201
    for controversial cases, 173
    public deliberation and, 214
    public v., 145–156, 173, 175–176,
        187–188, 201–208
    against same-sex marriage, 258–261
Noonan, John, 280
Nozick, Robert, 83, 189

O'Connor, Sandra Day, 8, 268–270
    "endorsement test" of, 8
Okin, Susan Moller, 243
O'Neill, Onora, 112
Ordnung, for Amish sect, 232
originalism, in constitutional interpretation,
    33–46
    analogical reasoning in, 37–38
    constitutional theory and, 22–23
    critique of, 36–46
    Equal Protection Clause and, 41
    "expectations originalism," 40
    judicial review and, 34
    nonoriginalism v., 33
    "old" v. "new," 46
    public meaning v. author's intentions
        under, 35, 39–40
    Whittington on, 45
Original Position, on public reason, 113
    political legitimacy and, 194–196
    public justification and, 152

Partial-Birth Abortion Ban Act, 150
partisanism, political
    judicial activism and, 3
    on U.S. Supreme Court, 2
Paulsen, Michael Stokes, 277
Perez v. Sharp, 14

perfectionism
    extreme, 208
    noncoercive, 208
    political, 208
perfectionist liberalism, 88, 225, 234
Perry, Michael, 283, 293
personal justification, of judicial decisions,
    public v., 89–90
"personhood," as concept, 280, 284
physician-assisted suicide, 64–67
Pierce v. Society of Sisters, 27, 277
Planned Parenthood v. Casey, 53
Plato, 114
Plessy v. Ferguson, 9, 28, 73, 90
    "separate but equal" in, 28
pluralism
    in inclusive public reason, 131
    moral, 188
    in public reason, 111
    religion and, 215
political legitimacy, 188–199
    consent and, 190–191
    as "good enough," 197–199
    Original Position and, 194–196
    political will and, 192–193
    public justification of judicial decisions
        and, 188–197
political liberalism, 156
Political Liberalism (Rawls), 116, 131, 134,
    147, 188, 218, 226, 228, 257, 281
political partisanism. *See* partisanism,
    political
political perfectionism, 208
political theory, public justification in,
    81–89
political will, political legitimacy and,
    192–193
popular constitutionalism, 2, 303–311. *See
    also* Proposition 8
populism, as approach to judicial reasoning,
    90
pornography, 143
Posner, Richard, 24, 31, 42, 100, 302
Postema, Gerald, 49
Powell, Lewis, 62
practical reasoning, 182
presidential elections, in U.S., 306
    party identification as factor in, 307
primary good, 208
"principled activism," 146
principle of reciprocity, 83
    autonomy and, 219
    for Kant, 112

public justification of judicial decisions and, 150–152
in public reason, 202–203, 215
in reasonableness, 165
religion and, 216
priority of the right, in public reason, 153
privacy rights. *See* rights of privacy
Privilege and Immunities Clause, 264
Roe v. Wade and, 277
Proposition 8, 15, 246, 304
legal challenges to, 304
Proposition 22, 247
public deliberation
nonpublic reasons and, 214
objectives of, 178–179
public reason's influence on, 212–214
public justification, of judicial decisions, 5–7, 10, 52–54, 81–108
on affirmative action, 273–274
for animal rights cases, 174–175
anti-perfectionist liberalism and, 121–122
appeals to truth in, 84
for capital punishment cases, 149
civil disobedience over, 87
as concept, 81–102
consequences of, 96–101
constitutional theory and, 51
deference to legislative majorities and, 74–80
deliberations in, 102
democracy as political ideal in, 87, 311–312
doubt in, 95–96
equality as political ideal in, 90–91
exchange of reasons as part of, 101–102
fairness as factor in, 89
freedom as political ideal in, 90–91
for gender discrimination cases, 67–68
good as concept in, 88
for *Gratz*, 270–271
for *Grutter v. Bollinger*, 270–271
judicial maximalism in, 97–98
judicial minimalism and, 96–97
judicial review and, 311–312
in *Korematsu*, 148
laissez-faire public reason in, 119, 211
laws as result of, 180–181
liberalism and, 154–155
limits of, 172–199
Original Position and, 152
personal v., 89–90
persuasion as part of, 102
for physician-assisted suicide cases, 64–67

political legitimacy and, 188–197
in political theory literature, 81–89
populist approach to, 90
principle of reciprocity and, 150–152
racial discrimination and, 55
for racial segregation cases, 9, 28, 42, 72–73
reasonable disagreement in, 103–104, 107, 173–180
for religious freedom cases, 231–243, 245
for rights of privacy cases, 60–61
for right-to-die cases, 64–67
for same-sex marriage, 97, 99, 245–261
for sexual orientation discrimination cases, 68, 71–72
shared standards in, 94
standards of review for, 53–54, 57, 144–145
states' rights and, 55
as theoretically ambitious, 98
theories for, 77
public reasons, 138
for abortion rights, 282
against affirmative action, 274–275
authority of, 201
constitutional, 139–171
democracy and, 210, 225–227
development of, as societal goal, 229
exclusive, 110–111, 120–129, 211
fallibilism and, 215
Hobbesian, 111
inclusive, 110, 129–138
as indeterminate, 176
in judicial review, 299–301
laissez-faire, 109–120, 168, 211
legal, 140
marginalization within, 221–222
nonpublic v., 145–156, 173, 175–176, 187–188, 201–208
objections to, 200–230
Original Position on, 113
pluralism in, 111
principle of reciprocity in, 202–203, 215
priority of the right in, 153
public deliberation and, restricted by, 212–214
for Rawls, 202
reasonable dissenters and, 186
Reflective Equilibrium on, 113
religion and, 215, 219
respect as part of, 156
as rigged, 209–212
sovereign role in, 111

public reasons (*cont.*)
   standards for, 142
   three conceptions of, 109–111
   as unrealistic, 227–230
   unreasonable people and, 218–225

Quong, Jonathan, 82

racial discrimination, 38–39. *See also*
   affirmative action
   "benign," 265
   public justification of judicial decisions
     and, 55
racial preferences, 272
racial quotas, 266, 268
racial segregation, 9, 28, 42, 72–73
   in *Brown v. Board of Education*, 28,
     72–73
   in *Plessy v. Ferguson*, 28, 73
Rawls, John, 8, 26, 116, 131, 134–135, 147,
   188, 194, 218, 226, 228, 281
   "epistemic abstinence" for, 132–133
   inclusive public reason for, 131–138
   judicial reasoning for, 106–107
   political liberalism for, 224–225
   public reason for, 202
   U.S. Supreme Court for, role of, 6
Raz, Joseph, 132, 154
Reagan, Ronald, 301
reasonable disagreement
   constitutional adjudication and, 15–17,
     50
   for deliberators, 174
   in exclusive constitutional public reason,
     158
   moral pluralism and, 188
   in public justification of judicial decisions,
     103–104, 107, 173–180
   with same-sex marriage, 256–257
reasonable dissenters, 10–14
   definition of, 11
   judges as, 12–13
   public reason and, 186
reasonableness
   abortion rights objections and, 289
   attributes of, 162
   in exclusive constitutional public reason,
     161–171
   fundamentalism and, 167
   personal morality and, 165–167
   principle of reciprocity in, 165
   "reasonable rejectability" as part of, 165
"reasonable rejectability," 10, 165

reasoning. *See also* judicial reasoning; legal
   reasoning, skepticism and
   autonomy and, 154, 191
Reflections on the Revolution in France
   (Burke), 44
Reflective Equilibrium, on public reason, 113
Regents of University of California v. Bakke,
   264–265
   racial quotas in, 266
Rehg, William, 83
Rehnquist, William, 28, 64–67
Reidy, David, 173
religion. *See also* Catholic Church
   Amish sect, 232
   fallibilism and, 215
   judicial reasoning and, as basis for, 3–5
   liberalism and, 219
   pluralism and, 215
   principle of reciprocity and, 216
   public reason and, 215, 219
   same-sex marriage and, 254–255
religious freedom, 9, 231–245
   autonomy and, 236–237
   Free Exercise Clause and, 244
   "representation reinforcement," 292
Republic (Plato), 114
reverse discrimination, 94, 265–266
Richmond v. Croson, 266
"right reason," 169
rights of privacy, 60–61. *See also Bowers v.*
   Hardwick; Florida v. B.J.F.; Griswold v.
   Connecticut; Lawrence v. Texas
   in *Roe v. Wade*, 277–278
   states' rights and, 61
right to bear arms, 42
right-to-die, 64–67
right to marriage, 15. *See also* same-sex
   marriage
Roberts, John, 22
Roe v. Wade, 23, 38, 98, 275
   abuse of judicial power and, 278–279
   constitutional basis for, 276–279
   lack of clarity in, 289
   Privilege and Immunities Clause and,
     277
   reasonable objections of, 289
   rights of privacy in, 277–278
Romer v. Evans, 68, 71–72, 141–142. *See*
   also Amendment 2
Roosevelt, Kermit, 74, 289, 311
Rosenberg, Gerald, 313
Rosen, Jeffrey, 97, 99
Rousseau, Jean-Jacques, 86, 191–193

same-sex marriage, 97, 99, 245–261
  academic arguments against, 249–252
  California Supreme Court on, 245–246
  civil alternatives to, 259
  civil benefits of, 253
  consent in, 253
  Defense of Marriage Act and, 245
  under Equal Protection Clause, 14–15,
    248–249
  exclusive public reason and, 258–259
  legal arguments for, 246
  nonpublic reasons against, 258–261
  opposition to, as unreasonable, 252–261
  Proposition 8 and, 15, 246, 304
  Proposition 22 and, 247
  reasonable disagreement with, 256–257
  religious arguments against, 254–255
Sander, Richard, 271
Scalia, Antonin, 22, 71–72. See also
    originalism, in constitutional
    interpretation
  states' rights for, 38
Scanlon, T.M., 86
Schauer, Frederick, 31–32, 56, 309, 315
Schwartzman, Micah, 175
self-restraint, in inclusive public reason, 129
semi-libertarianism, 121–123
"separate but equal," 28, 70, 97
sexual discrimination, 68, 71–72
sexual orientation, discrimination toward,
    68, 71–72
  in Amendment 2, 68, 71–72
The Shape of the River (Bowen/Bok),
    272–273
Shklar, Judith, 28, 306
"sincerity requirement," 82
skepticism
  exclusive constitutional public reason and,
    170
  judicial reasoning and, 103–104
  legal reasoning and, 107–108
Skinner v. Oklahoma, 59–60
social contract, 191–193
  unanimous direct democracy in, 193
The Social Contract (Rousseau), 86
Solum, Lawrence, 4, 109, 212–213
Souter, David, 302
Stanley v. Georgia, 56
  Bowers v. Hardwick v., 62
states' rights, 38
  public justification of judicial decisions
    and, 55
  rights of privacy and, 61

Sunstein, Cass, 7, 19, 42, 51, 96, 144, 210,
    271, 292, 312–313

Takings Clause, 61
Taylor, Charles, 233–234
A Theory of Justice (Rawls), 131, 188, 194,
    218
Thomas, Clarence, 4, 22
Thompson, Dennis, 87
Thomson, Judith, 286–287
Tooley, Michael, 282
"Toward Neutral Principles of
    Constitutional Law" (Weschler), 72–73
Tribe, Laurence, 29, 91, 282, 300
Tushnet, Mark, 302
Tushnet, Robert, 2

unanimous direct democracy, 191
  in social contract, 193
Unger, Roberto, 155
University of Michigan cases. See Gratz v.
    Bollinger; Grutter v. Bollinger
unreasonableness
  abortion rights and, 285
  concept of good and, 220
  exclusive public reason and, 222–223
  marginalization from, 221–222
  public reason and, 218–225
  same-sex marriage opposition and,
    252–261
  state response towards, 220
U.S. Constitution. See also Equal Protection
    Clause
  constitutional adjudication's influence on,
    28–29
  Due Process Clause in, 27, 70
  Equal Protection Clauses in, 27
  Free Exercise Clause in, 244
  integrity of, 47–48
  as "organic," 47
  Privilege and Immunities Clause in, 264
  restoration of original, 29
  Takings Clause in, 61
  unwritten version of, 70
U.S. Supreme Court
  partisanism on, 2
  Rawls on role of, 6
U.S. v. Virginia, 67–68
utilitarianism, in constitutional theory, 50

value theory of democracy, 27
voters
  behavior of, 298, 307

voters (*cont.*)
  "epistemic abstinence" and, 133
  inclusive public reason for,
    133–134
  legal decisions overturned by, 15
Waldron, Jeremy, 75, 103–104, 150–151,
    157, 213, 314–315
Wallace, George, 100
Wardle, Lynn, 249–252
Warren, Earl, 57, 302
Washington v. Glucksberg, 64–67
welfare rights, under Equal Protection
    Clause, 24
Weschler, Herbert, 72–73

Whittington, Keith, 45, 310
  constitutional interpretation v.
    construction for, 32
Williams, Andrew, 174
Wisconsin v. Yoder, 231–243
  children's rights and, 237–238
  criticism of, 233, 238–239
Wolgast, Elizabeth, 128
Wolin, Sheldon, 226
Wolsteroff, Nicholas, 215

Yoder, Jonas, 231
Yutzy, Adin, 231
Yutzy, Vernon, 241

Printed in Great Britain
by Amazon

36871068R00198